Colossus

The National Capital Region of Delhi is a diverse and unequal space. Its more than 30 million people are sharply differentiated by economic class, religion, caste, education, language, and migration status. Its 45,000 square kilometers is a tapestry of spaces—ghettoes, slums, enclaves, institutional areas, planned and unplanned and authorized and unauthorized colonies, forests, and agricultural fields. In some ways, it is a dynamic society aspiring to global city grandeur; in other ways, it is a bastion of tradition, sectarianism, and hierarchy. *Colossus* details these realities and paradoxes under three themes: social change, community and state, and inequality. From the material condition of the metropolis (its housing, services, crime, and pollution) to its social organization (of who marries whom, who eats with whom, and who votes for whom), this book unpacks the complex reality of a metropolitan region that is emblematic of India's aspirations and contradictions.

Sanjoy Chakravorty is professor of geography and urban studies and the director of global studies at Temple University, Philadelphia. He writes on epistemology, inequality, land, industrialization, and the Indian diaspora in the United States.

Neelanjan Sircar is assistant professor of political science at Ashoka University, Sonepat, and a senior visiting fellow at the Centre for Policy Research, Delhi. He writes on the political economy of India (with a focus on elections), comparative political behavior, and Bayesian methods.

SOUTH ASIA IN THE SOCIAL SCIENCES

South Asia has become a laboratory for devising new institutions and practices of modern social life. Forms of capitalist enterprise, providing welfare and social services, the public role of religion, the management of ethnic conflict, popular culture and mass democracy in the countries of the region have shown a marked divergence from known patterns in other parts of the world. South Asia is now being studied for its relevance to the general theoretical understanding of modernity itself.

South Asia in the Social Sciences will feature books that offer innovative research on contemporary South Asia. It will focus on the place of the region in the various global disciplines of the social sciences and highlight research that uses unconventional sources of information and novel research methods. While recognising that most current research is focused on the larger countries, the series will attempt to showcase research on the smaller countries of the region.

General Editor
Partha Chatterjee
Columbia University

Editorial Board
Pranab Bardhan
University of California at Berkeley

Stuart Corbridge
Durham University

Satish Deshpande
University of Delhi

Christophe Jaffrelot
Centre d'etudes et de recherches internationales, Paris

Nivedita Menon
Jawaharlal Nehru University

Other books in the series:

Government as Practice: Democratic Left in a Transforming India
Dwaipayan Bhattacharyya

Courting the People: Public Interest Litigation in Post-Emergency India
Anuj Bhuwania

Development after Statism: Industrial Firms and the Political Economy of South Asia
Adnan Naseemullah

Politics of the Poor: Negotiating Democracy in Contemporary India
Indrajit Roy

South Asian Governmentalities: Michel Foucault and the Question of Postcolonial Orderings
Stephen Legg and Deana Heath (eds.)

Nationalism, Development and Ethnic Conflict in Sri Lanka
Rajesh Venugopal

Adivasis and the State: Subalternity and Citizenship in India's Bhil Heartland
Alf Gunvald Nilsen

Maoist People's War and the Revolution of Everyday Life in Nepal
Ina Zharkevich

New Perspectives on Pakistan's Political Economy: State, Class and Social Change
Matthew McCartney and S. Akbar Zaidi (eds.)

Crafty Oligarchs, Savvy Voters: Democracy under Inequality in Rural Pakistan
Shandana Khan Mohmand

Dynamics of Caste and Law: Dalits, Oppression and Constitutional Democracy in India
Dag-Erik Berg

Simultaneous Identities: Language, Education and the Nepali Nation
Uma Pradhan

Deceptive Majority: Dalits, Hinduism, and Underground Religion
Joel Lee

Colossus

The Anatomy of Delhi

Edited by

Sanjoy Chakravorty

Neelanjan Sircar

CAMBRIDGE
UNIVERSITY PRESS

CAMBRIDGE
UNIVERSITY PRESS

Shaftesbury Road, Cambridge CB2 8EA, United Kingdom

One Liberty Plaza, 20th Floor, New York, NY 10006, USA

477 Williamstown Road, Port Melbourne, VIC 3207, Australia

314–321, 3rd Floor, Plot 3, Splendor Forum, Jasola District Centre, New Delhi–110025, India

103 Penang Road, #05–06/07, Visioncrest Commercial, Singapore 238467

Cambridge University Press is part of the University of Cambridge.

It furthers the University's mission by disseminating knowledge in the pursuit of education, learning and research at the highest international levels of excellence.

www.cambridge.org
Information on this title: www.cambridge.org/9781108832243

First published 2021
Reprint 2024

Printed in India by Avantika Printers Pvt. Ltd.

A catalogue record for this publication is available from the British Library

Library of Congress Cataloging-in-Publication Data

Names: Chakravorty, Sanjoy, editor. | Sircar, Neelanjan, editor.
Title: Colossus : the anatomy of Delhi / [edited by] Sanjoy Chakravorty and Neelanjan Sircar.
Description: Cambridge, United Kingdom ; New York, NY : Cambridge University Press, 2021. | Series: South Asia in the social sciences | Includes bibliographical references and index.
Identifiers: LCCN 2021005361 (print) | LCCN 2021005362 (ebook) | ISBN 9781108832243 (hardback) | ISBN 9781108935654 (ebook)
Subjects: LCSH: Delhi (India)–Social conditions. | Delhi (India)–Economic conditions. | Delhi (India)–Politics and government. | Delhi (India)–History.
Classification: LCC HN690.D4 C65 2021 (print) | LCC HN690.D4 (ebook) | DDC 306.0954/56–dc23
LC record available at https://lccn.loc.gov/2021005361
LC ebook record available at https://lccn.loc.gov/2021005362

ISBN 978-1-108-83224-3 Hardback

Contents

Figures

Tables

Acknowledgments

More than most books, this one owes its existence to the labor and support of many whose names are never mentioned in these pages. This project simply could not have been undertaken without their expertise, goodwill, and input.

First, we thank the Center for the Advanced Study of India (CASI) at the University of Pennsylvania, Philadelphia. CASI put together the funding for a survey which provided the data that became foundational for this project. It also provided a free-thinking intellectual space in which the ideas and plans for the project blossomed and where a pivotal workshop was held in November, 2017. That workshop was instrumental in generating the first drafts of almost all the chapters here. The Colossus Workshop was designated as one of six in a series of research workshops held in 2016 and 2017 to commemorate CASI's 25th anniversary.

We especially wish to express our gratitude to CASI International Advisory Board members Zia Mody, Parag Saxena, and Marwan Shakarchi for supporting the Colossus project and related workshops, as well as Arjun Raychaudhuri, Munjal and Sejal Jaykrishna, Aditi Kothari, and Devanshi Dalmia. We are also indebted to the CASI staff for their dedicated work on the project. We would like to acknowledge Juliana DiGiustini, CASI's tireless Deputy Director; Mollie S. Laffin-Rose and Georgette Rochlin (both of whom provided invaluable logistical support); and Alan Atchison, Alexandra Sanyal, and Maya Kapur.

Our thanks also go to the Centre for Policy Research (CPR) in Delhi, another fine institution that promotes open and vibrant discourse. Many of the contributors to this volume are or were affiliated with CPR in some capacity during the project. CPR also hosted a workshop in August, 2018, during which several of the key findings and ideas in this book were presented to a large and expert audience. We thank Yamini Aiyar in particular for that. We also thank Priya Rathod, Akashmegh Sharma, Sadhana Senthilkumar (who did much of the back-breaking work to sanitize and organize the survey data so that it could be used and analyzed by researchers), Ilka Vari-Lavoisier (for assistance in piloting and designing the survey), and S. Chandrasekhar at the Indira Gandhi Institute for

Development Research for assistance in thinking through questions of migration and remittances.

Finally, we acknowledge our debt to the India Institute and its leader, Baladevan Rangaraju, for marshalling the resources that actually produced the field survey. Many dedicated individuals worked for months, often in challenging circumstances, to generate the raw material that was processed to culmination in this volume.

Introduction
What Is Delhi?

Sanjoy Chakravorty

Ik roz apni rooh se poocha, ki Dilli kya hai?
Tho yun jawab mein keh gaye: yeh duniya mano jism hai, aur Dilli uski jaan
—Ghalib

One day I asked my soul, what is Dilli?
It replied: Imagine the world is the body, then Dilli is its life force.
—Translation by author

Mirza Ghalib, the eternal poet laureate of Delhi, wrote these words around the time of the Sepoy Rebellion in 1857. The ethos of that time—of *shaiyari* and *ghazal* and *kabootarbaazi*—has been imaginatively explored in popular works such as William Dalrymple's *City of Djinns* and *The Last Mughal*. One hundred and fifty years later, however, Delhi evoked other emotions and names by close observers. In 2000, Denis Vidal, Emma Tarlo, and Veronique DuPont declared Delhi an "unloved city."[1] In 2019, Amita Baviskar named it an "uncivil city."[2] Other contemporary reporters such as Aman Sethi in *A Free Man*, Rana Dasgupta in *Capital*, and Aravind Adiga in *The White Tiger* seem to agree. Sethi writes about the city as a "giant construction site" of perpetual dislocations and hysteria; Adiga and Dasgupta see rampant inequality, corruption, greed, excess, and murderousness spreading from the city to its shiny new borderlands like Gurgaon.

When Ghalib composed his paean of love, there were about 150,000 residents in Delhi, and the city occupied more or less the same area as what is now called Shahjahanabad (Purani Dilli). When Delhi's unlovable new names began to become known in the academic world at the turn of the millennium, the population of the National Capital Territory (NCT), which is now commonly thought of as the city of Delhi, was a little under 14 million. The population of the National Capital Region (NCR), which we can think of as Delhi metropolis, was about 20.5 million. In the next 10 years, by 2011, the city (the NCT) grew by 3 million and the metropolitan region (the NCR) by 6 million. At this moment of writing, the next census of 2021 is still one year away, but estimates suggest that the population of the NCT (Delhi city) is over 20 million and that of the NCR (Delhi metropolis) more than 30 million.

The "unloved and uncivil" city's population *grew* by 20 of Ghalib's beloved Dillis in each of the previous two decades. About 200 Dillis of Ghalib's time now populate the Delhi metropolis. Delhi, rather than Dilli, is now an urban giant—such as Tokyo, Shanghai, Beijing, Jakarta, and Manila—the likes of which the world had scarcely seen before this millennium.

It is time to ask Ghalib's question again: "What is Delhi?" This book is an attempt at an answer. It is the outcome of a large project that began in 2013. At that conceptualization stage, the leaders were the editors of this book and key contributors like Devesh Kapur and Milan Vaishnav. Eventually, over 20 scholars were involved in it at different points, plus a large group that designed a survey and collected data for the project. Despite this considerable effort of thousands of person-hours, the answer provided here is partial. Perhaps, that is inevitable given Delhi's size and complexity; perhaps, all answers to this question are necessarily incomplete. We believe, however, that what is offered here is (at least) original because the angle or perspective from which we look at Delhi is one that has not been used before. This claim is explained in the following paragraphs.

For the prime movers of this project, Ghalib's question was foremost a territorial one. Where does Delhi begin and end? Before making claims about a place, it is necessary to know exactly what is included in its boundaries. By and large, most scholars of Delhi focus on the NCT, which is a union territory with a fixed boundary, or a sub-area inside it. This is the usual view. We took the position that this view is, in several respects, rather limited. City boundaries are notoriously arbitrary. For example, the city of San Francisco in California had about 880,000 people in 2010, whereas the San Francisco Bay Area (technically, the San Jose–San Francisco–Oakland Combined Statistical Area in the US census) was tenfold larger, with 8.8 million residents. People live and work in the San Francisco Bay Area by crossing municipal boundaries every day. Rarely are they aware that they are doing so. These municipal boundaries do not matter much for the economic or social behavior of people or firms in the region.

We take the view that the Delhi metropolitan region is much the same. People crisscross every day between the NCT, Haryana, and Uttar Pradesh—especially Gurgaon, Ghaziabad, Faridabad, and Noida—for work or leisure. They vote in different jurisdictions but live and work in the same region. For practical reasons—because there are now government actions and documents that establish it—we took that larger region to be the NCR.

It is possible that most residents of this region do not know the name "NCR," nor its boundaries, but the same is likely true of all major metropolitan regions in the world—from San Francisco to Jakarta (Jabodetabek is the current official terminology for Greater Jakarta). One cannot fault the residents for not knowing because not only is the NCR a planning region (hence a notional one, that does not collect taxes nor has an elected body) but it also does not have a fixed boundary. After its creation in 1985, new districts were added to the NCR in 2013 and 2015. In this book, we use the 2013 definition of the NCR. This is a contiguous area of about 46,000 square kilometers that had a population of close to 30 million in 2016. It includes the NCT plus 19 districts in Haryana, Uttar Pradesh, and Rajasthan.

Our starting point, therefore, is the most literal answer to the basic question "What is Delhi?" Delhi is India's National Capital Region. We note that this initial answer—that identifies our zone of interest as the metropolitan region—itself separates our approach from the usual analysis of Delhi, which is at the scale of the city or the NCT alone.

Facts

This initial answer may be geographically expansive but it is not poetic. Neither does it say anything about the content—the innards—of this growing body. It is this, the metaphorical anatomy of the organic region called Delhi that interests us. Ghalib's Dilli has been transformed not only in size but also in social composition. To stay with the biological metaphor, what was a simple unicellular organism like paramecium has become a complex organism of many different types of cells that can be distinguished by size and function. We know that it is possible to differentiate social groups in Delhi by economic class, social identity (of religion and caste), education, language, and migration status: Jat and Dalit, Sikh and Muslim, Bengali and Tamil, Haryanvi and Purvanchali, members of resident welfare associations (RWAs) and their security guards and maids, recent migrants who are college students or village brides, and daily wage laborers for Maruti Suzuki and members of parliament. We also know that the metropolis is a tapestry of spaces—neighborhoods, ghettoes, residential enclaves, institutional areas (for example, the Indian Institute of Technology and Jawaharlal Nehru University campuses), planned and unplanned and authorized and unauthorized colonies—and these spaces can be as distinct as separate cities. Therefore, even the most casual observer of Delhi knows that it is an agglomeration of a vast variety of identities and physical spaces.

All this is common, if somewhat unspecific, knowledge. The reason for the lack of specificity is that the state of expert knowledge on Delhi—its facts, patterns, and explanations—is rather limited, and given the size and significance of the metropolis, especially as the capital city of one-sixth of humanity, not a little surprising. The "facts" of Delhi are not nonexistent, but they are thinner than one should expect. The Indian system of data collection— the decennial censuses and many more rounds of sample surveys (72 when this book was written)—does provide basic demographic information, but it is either insufficient in detail or at too aggregate a scale to seriously interrogate our question at hand.

There are three crucial problems with government data on Delhi (which also apply to all of India and all Indian cities). First, there is limited information on social identity (the only identifiers reported in government data are religion and whether an individual belongs to any Scheduled Caste or Scheduled Tribe) and bare-bones information on education, transportation, migration, and so on. Moreover, even this limited information (say, on education or commute to work) has hardly been analyzed for the NCT or the NCR. Second, all the available information is geographically aggregated (to wards in cities); as a result, all urban data are spatially over-bounded to the extent that there is not much that can be investigated at what is typically considered a disaggregate urban scale (say neighborhoods or housing enclaves). Third, there is no statistically valid or reliable information on social attitudes, that is, what the citizens think about important questions on identity, behavior, community, and politics.

We considered it necessary, therefore, to begin our investigations from a stronger foundation of facts that would allow us to make robust statements on the makeup of Delhi. Before we could seek patterns or explanations about its social and physical spaces, before we could provide some summary judgment— that Delhi is like this or Delhi is like that—it was necessary to know what was being summarized. There are two sets of overarching questions.

First, there are questions on subjects on which the Indian government does collect data, but at insufficient detail. There is some information on these questions, but not enough: Who lives where? Where did they come from, and when, and why? What do they do during the day? What do they own? How do they move around? How much education do they have—by age, by gender, by quality? What is the condition of housing? The slums and *jhuggi jhopris*? The authorized and unauthorized settlements? Other physical infrastructure (power, roads, water)? Social infrastructure (education, health care)? Services? Crime? Energy?

Second, there are questions about social and political identities and attitudes that are never asked by the government, nor, as far as we are aware, have they been asked by any nongovernmental organization at the metropolitan scale. What communities do people belong to? Who are their neighbors? How do they get along with other communities (religions, castes)? Whom do they marry? Whom do their children marry? Whom do they eat with? Whom do they not eat with? How has Delhi—and living in an urban milieu—changed them? Men? Women? Religions? Castes? The relations between them? Between generations? Or has Delhi changed them at all? What kinds of problems do people face and how do they solve them? Who are their civic and political representatives, their *neta*s? How are the different social identities of the people (of religion, caste, class, language, migration, education, gender, and age) reflected in party politics?

The Center for the Advanced Study of India–National Capital Region Survey

A very large part of the effort that has gone into this book was in unearthing these facts. It involved the implementation of a large survey to collect information about households in Delhi. To the best of our knowledge, no survey of comparable scale, breadth, and academic rigor has been carried out for Delhi; probably, the only comparable undertaking in India is Janaagraha's survey of Bangalore. As is true of all surveys, it was not possible to ask all the questions that the investigative team wanted, but enough were asked to answer some of the more important questions of fact on the lives and perceptions of the residents of Delhi. The survey was funded by the Center for the Advanced Study of India (CASI) at the University of Pennsylvania, Philadelphia, and was carried out on the ground from late 2015 to early 2016. We call it the CASI–NCR Survey in this book.

The CASI–NCR Survey sample included 5,477 households with 24,693 individual members. Approximately, 61 percent of the sample was from the NCT, 23 percent from Uttar Pradesh, 13 percent from Haryana, and 3 percent from Rajasthan. The bulk of the sample was drawn from the 2014 electoral rolls (with a "random walk" constituting roughly 15 percent of the sample to capture households that may have been missing from the electoral rolls, perhaps because they were very recent migrants). Voting booths served as the primary sampling unit and voter lists as the sample frame (except for the "random walk" element). The data were collected on tablets, concurrent data checks were conducted in real time, and verification/corrections were done using follow-up calls to respondents. The "Statistical Appendix" has some more important details on the design, implementation, coverage, questions, and key methodological features of the CASI–NCR Survey.

Table A.1 in the "Statistical Appendix" shows how the CASI–NCR sample compares with the 2011 Census and National Sample Survey data for the NCT. The closeness of the match suggests that our sample was representative; that conclusions about Delhi can be drawn from it. As discussed later in detail in this chapter, we surely missed some proportion of the population—the well-to-do upper tail of income earners—but that population (whose size we are unable to estimate) is missing from all surveys in India. The CASI–NCR Survey was the mother lode of information that was mined in different ways in 10 of the chapters in this volume. In addition to these data-based analyses, this volume includes four contributions by other established scholars of Delhi who were not associated with the survey. Together, the survey-based and independent analysts have written what we hope are some of the most compelling stories of contemporary Delhi.

Some Missing Pieces

We should note that this is not a comprehensive study. It is limited both by methodology and coverage. Our contributors draw on ideas and methods from several disciplines—from political science, economics, sociology, and geography—on human capital, inequality, demography, migration, marriage, environment, gender, elections, mapping, survey methods, modeling, and so on. But there is the dominance of one method (the CASI–NCR Survey which is attuned to economics and sociology) over others (especially anthropological methods like ethnography and mixed methods like focus groups or interviews). And several important subjects are simply not taken into account.

The survey methodology itself has some inbuilt limitations. Surveys can only provide information on what the respondents know or think, not what is outside these domains, such as expert matters on law or policy, or statistical facts on industry or the economy. Some of these issues—such as laws and policies on housing and infrastructure—are dealt with by this volume's contributors using some (but limited) information from the survey and other sources. Other issues—such as statistics on industry and the economy—are not discussed in this book because our survey did not ask those questions (nor were we able to commission an external expert to carry it out). Therefore, one big gap in our study relates to industry and commerce in Delhi NCR. As a result, the discussions in the following 14 chapters provide some information on the labor market but little on the structure of commerce or industry in the NCR.

The second major subject we did not investigate separately is the land market of Delhi and its land uses. Two of the chapters (Chapters 3 and 11)—on settlements by Heller, Mukhopadhyay, Sheikh, and Banda, and on spatial politics by Srivastava—refer to land issues at some length, but not as central features. We sidestepped the subject of land despite our strong conviction that land use and land markets are essential features of urban form, even perhaps because of it. We argue that to carry out a land-oriented analysis was a different project that required a fundamentally different approach than the one used by us.

The land market in India and Delhi is very important, primarily because land prices in the country are arguably the highest in the world (when we compare similar settings). For example, the peak price of land in Delhi (in its most desirable areas) is twice as high as the peak price in Washington, DC. What is much more remarkable is that the average price of land in the NCT is over 30 times the average price in Washington, DC. These extraordinary prices fundamentally influence land use (that is, who gets to use what land for what purpose), which, in turn, influences access to housing and public goods.

The price of land is, in many ways, the most powerful factor shaping the physical structure of contemporary Delhi and the quality of life for its residents—from the well-to-do, who can and do participate in this market, to the poor, who effectively pay a large tax for sharing the city with an upper-class minority that sets prices that only it can afford. This is true of not only Delhi but almost all Indian cities, especially the large ones. This condition has been exacerbated from about 2000 onward, when the prices began to spike. Before that, prices were what could be called "high" for a low-income nation but not extraordinary as they are now.[3]

Our position, therefore, is not that Delhi's land market is not important; on the contrary, it is, and very much so. In fact, many of the most topical stories about Delhi—such as Gurgaon and Noida, DLF and Unitech, drunken louts in high-class hotels, and *Khosla ka Ghosla*—are indeed about its land market.[4] It may be fair to say that in the social gatherings and watering holes of the city, there is no other subject (other than politics) that occupies more discussion space. But, before we began this project, when we were designing the analytical frame, we agreed that to analyze Delhi from the perspective of its land market would require a different approach than the one we wanted (and different investigators) and would produce a rather different set of findings and book. In addition, because the extraordinariness of the land market is of relatively recent vintage—it is less than two decades old—its effects may not be fully in play yet and may still be dominated by government policies (such as the government's considerable ownership of land in Delhi and its sizable involvement in producing housing stock). Our commitment to the survey method was, at the same time, a turn away from a land-based investigation.

The Structure of the Book

The following 14 chapters in this volume are organized in two parts. Part 1 is the "State of the Metropolis." It has seven chapters on what can be called the material reality of Delhi. Part 2—"Social and Political Change"—has seven chapters on social and political conditions and attitudes, with an emphasis on the transformation (or lack thereof) of social and political behaviors and views.

Part 1 begins with Chapter 1, in which Shrobona Karkun lays out the evolution of the *geography* and *demography* of the city and metropolis using data from the census, satellite images, and historic maps. Neelanjan Sircar studies the ownership of *assets* in Chapter 2; he devises a new index of asset distribution to show the extent of material inequality in the metropolis. In Chapter 3, Patrick Heller, Partha Mukhopadhyay, Shahana Sheikh, and Subhadra Banda, a group that has been working on Indian urban issues at the Centre for Policy Research for several years, provide their insights on Delhi's different forms of *housing* settlements, especially the marginal and unauthorized types. In Chapter 4, Shamindra Nath Roy builds on this to describe and analyze the condition of inequality in key infrastructure *services* (such as access to sewerage, water supply, and roads). In Chapter 5, Khusdeep Malhotra quantifies and analyzes *migration* in the region and shows that it is an exclusionary process that creates a "spatial disadvantage" for recent migrants. Radhika Khosla studies *energy* consumption in Chapter 6, in the context of the specter of rising energy demand in Indian cities. In Chapter 7, Milan Vaishnav and Matthew Lillehaugen analyze *crime* victimization in Delhi in terms of perception, reality, police responses, and consequences.

Part 2 begins with Chapter 8 on *social change* by Sumitra Badrinathan and Devesh Kapur, with a focus on understanding how social groups that are differentiated by religion, caste, and economic class interact with each other through the practice of sharing food (they do not!). Chapter 9, by Megan Reed, continues the examination by looking at *marriage* practices ("arranged," "inter-caste," or "inter-religion") through multiple generations. Chapter 10 is on *education*, in which Deepaboli Chatterjee, Babu Lal, and Rimjhim Saxena present detailed information on educational attainment by age, gender, generation, and labor force participation. In Chapter 11, Sanjay Srivastava examines, at an anthropological scale, how citizenship and *community* are constituted in settings as far apart as demolished slums and high-end RWAs in Gurgaon. Neelanjan Sircar continues that micro-scale approach in his Chapter 12 study of local *neta*s (political intermediaries) and how they solve problems (or not) for a wide range of class constituencies. Adnan Farooqui studies *party politics* at the scale of the NCT in Chapter 13, with an emphasis on the rise of the Aam Aadmi Party (AAP) and the influx of Purvanchali migrants (from Bihar and Uttar Pradesh). In Chapter 14, Awadhendra Sharan brings a long lens and deep knowledge to outline the evolution of the politics and policies on Delhi's air, its one resource that cannot be parceled out by social identity or class or housing type.

Many of the findings and explanations are genuinely new and surprising, even to us, and to many of the Delhi experts before whom we presented some of this material at conferences and workshops. All these contributions—survey-based or not—together create a collection of stories that reflect the richness, diversity, and inequality of material conditions and human experience in Delhi. As a result, our second attempt to answer the question "What is Delhi?" leads to an obvious conclusion: Delhi is not one thing, but many. It is a predictable and banal conclusion, especially for a metropolis as big as Delhi, with as long a history, that is a capital city for arguably the most diverse society in the world, and, as we show later, one that is deeply unequal.

Theories

Our core question—Ghalib's question—seems to demand more. It seems to beg the narration of a meta-story, a story that accounts for all stories. In short, a theory. If we assume that Delhi is not the "life force" of the world (as Mirza Ghalib would have it)—an assumption shared by all our contributors and worldly readers—then is it something else? If it is, what is it? Can we make claims about Delhi that are generalizable? If yes, generalizable to what scale: all cities, all Asian cities, all large cities, capital cities, urban India, or all of India? Is there some international group of cities within which we can place Delhi, is this city merely a large Indian one, or is it unique?

To begin to address these questions, it is necessary to wade into a contentious debate about "urban theory" in international, especially Euro-American, scholarship in urban studies. The core question animating this debate is whether it is possible to have a single approach to understanding cities and urbanization around the world, and if it is possible to do so, what that approach should be. This is the sort of question and issue—global and totalizing—that is important to analysts located in the high citadels of social theory. Let us examine (briefly) how much relevance this has for us.

According to Helga Leitner and Eric Sheppard, leading figures in the movement to "provincialize" urban theory and thereby to decolonize it from Euro-American power over discourse and analysis, "no single theory suffices to account for the variegated nature of urbanization and cities across the world."[5] On the other side are eminent analysts such as Michael Storper and Allen Scott who accuse the post-colonialists of "convoluted philosophical and epistemological abstractions that actually present barriers to any understanding of the urban as a concrete social phenomenon." They argue that despite the obvious dissimilarities between them, "cities are everywhere characterized by agglomeration involving the gravitational pull of people, economic activities … into interlocking, high-density, nodal blocks of land use."[6]

Before we take sides in this debate, it is necessary to ask a basic question: Who is theory for? Who consumes it? In other words, what is the market for "theory"? My assumption here is that the target audience plays a large role in guiding the content of theory. Just as much as Chetan Bhagat writes for a particular readership, and does Arundhati Roy, and, for that matter, do Haruki Murakami and J. K. Rowling, so do urban theorists write for a readership of people like themselves, academics in other Euro-American institutions, who use language and categories that may mean something to each other, but not necessarily to the rest of the world. Theirs is a view from far above. Whether that view yields patterns (as Storper and Scott argue) or not (as Leitner and Sheppard insist), the framework is always global and comparative. In this view, Delhi can often become nothing more than simply another data point whose details of history, society, and politics are not particularly important.

It is surely not unreasonable to suggest that there is some validity in both approaches. All cities are unique, but all cities also have commonalities. All cities have a state that sets the rules of formal behavior and specific codes that shape the built environment. All cities have markets, especially land and labor markets. All cities belong inside nations or cultures that have social norms that influence individual behavior, community interactions, and aesthetics. And certainly, all cities have inequalities of income, wealth, and opportunity. Therefore, one possible approach is an old-fashioned one: to create typologies. Thereby, it may be possible to say that Delhi is like Beijing or Jakarta or Manila (all growing colossal capital cities in Asia) and less like London or Paris or New York (all large cities that grew to prominence before the rise of the Asian giants and have relatively stable populations now).

Though it is possible to agree with many basic tenets of the postcolonial critique (that much urban theory is "neo-orientalist" and that the "Global South" must now lead the way to how cities are understood), it is probably intellectually nihilistic to reach the dead end that, therefore, theorization is impossible. That said, the intellectual utility of an international comparative approach is quite limited, as is the whole hullabaloo over some imagined, comprehensive "urban theory." Even if Delhi is or is not like Beijing or Los Angeles or Jakarta, how does it matter? What difference does either position make to any of these cities, their residents, and policy-makers? None at all.

It may be possible to sidestep this debate over a grand urban theory by narrowing its scope and reorienting its vision. To be clear, the initial questions that interest us and the explanations we seek are those that are relevant to India. If an international approach to urban theory raises the question "how is Delhi like or unlike Beijing?" our initial approach may be simplified as a different question: "how is Delhi like or unlike Mumbai, or Bangalore, or Patna, or Vijaywada?" In this analytical mode, the most intriguing and important questions that arise are the following:

- What are the key features of Delhi's urban condition, that is, the driving forces that have the greatest bearing on the lives of its residents? One way to think of this may be as "a theory of Delhi."
- What can we say about Delhi that can be extrapolated to other Indian cities? Is Delhi a prototype of Indian cities, only larger and more affluent? In other words, we look for signs that a theory of Delhi can lead to "a theory of Indian cities."
- To what extent is Delhi a reflection of Indian society? By this, we mean the social identities, behaviors, inequalities, and competitions that constitute daily existence in the Indian polity. To put it differently: Is Delhi merely a microcosm (albeit a large one) of India?

This approach may lead us toward a theory of Delhi that is also "a theory of India."

We attempt to connect these India-specific and very large questions to three fundamental and very large issues in urban analysis. We consider the following three specific sets:

- social change, focusing on whether urbanization does indeed lead to social change (as it is widely assumed to), especially in how ascribed social identities of religion and caste are understood and embodied in everyday practice,
- community and state, especially the idea that urbanization increases the complexity of both "community" and "state" and the interactions between them, and
- inequality in its multiple forms, with a focus on spatial inequality.

Our goal is to tell a story of Delhi, in and of itself, but also as an Indian city and social space, whose social and political economies are being transformed—rapidly in some ways, less so in others—by the forces of urbanization which are omnipresent not just in India but around the world.

Social Change

One of the stylized facts of urbanization is that it is accompanied by fundamental social change. Not only people do different things (work in factories, offices, and construction sites instead of farms and forests) but they live in different arrangements (in far greater numbers and density), with different neighbors (social groups they may never have encountered in village life), and different types of communities. The biological reproduction patterns of urbanites—such as age of marriage and number of children—are expected to change, as are their social reproduction patterns (on norms, beliefs, faith, self-identity, and rationality). Formal nonreligious (or secular) education is expected to be the key to both reproductive changes—biological and social. More education is expected to produce smaller families and social tolerance. In 1887, in the rising years of European industrialization and urbanization, the German sociologist Ferdinand Tonnies argued that rural life was defined by *gemeinschaft* (community formation through kinship and proximity), whereas urban life was defined by *gesellschaft* (atomized communities characterized by individualism and impersonal interactions). This is generally assumed to be a universal condition.

Urbanization is, therefore, widely considered to be the precondition of modernity. It is the process by which traditional village societies steeped in myth, superstition, illiteracy, and bias become modern, educated societies with a growing scientific temper and acceptance of difference (new concepts and new people). These ideas are so entrenched in the social science discourses on urbanization in Euro-American institutions that they are no longer investigated as open empirical questions. The discussions on urban theory cited earlier do not refer to this form of social change as an issue on which theorization is needed. This, despite the fact that decades of urbanization in Europe and America have failed to eliminate some long-standing biases—the most important of which may be the continuing racial barriers on marriage.

Led by Devesh Kapur, we decided to look at this as an open question, framed in terms of what we called the Ambedkar–Gandhi debate. Mohandas Gandhi had famously remarked that "the soul of India lives in its villages." B. R. Ambedkar, always Gandhi's foil, had urged Dalits to urbanize because "What is a village but a sink of localism, a den of ignorance, narrow mindedness and communalism?" Looked at closely, however, these positions are not different at all; rather, they express the same sentiment from different ideological and normative positions. At the core, both positions are about social identity—fixed and identifiable in villages, and desirably so in Gandhi's view; changing and less identifiable in cities, and desirably so in Ambedkar's view. The assumption that urbanization changes social identity and behavior was, therefore, widely held among the intellectual stalwarts of modern India. What was in question was the desirability of these changes, not their possibility.

But is the assumption that urbanization changes social identity and behavior correct? If yes, to what extent? What aspects of social identity and behavior—if any—have changed in Delhi (and, by extension, urban India)? Our investigators examined this question from multiple angles and the findings are encouraging and dispiriting at the same time. The encouraging news comes from the findings on education reported by Deepaboli Chatterjee, Babu Lal, and Rimjhim Saxena in Chapter 10. They provide strong evidence of convergence between boys and girls in terms of educational attainment, especially among the younger cohorts. Similar trends are seen across India, but in Delhi they are significantly more pronounced. These growing levels of girl education do not, however, seem to be translating into corresponding increases in women's labor force participation. In fact, the most well-to-do households are educating their girl children the longest (as expected), but the indications are that this is for the marriage market rather than the labor market.

This unease turns into dismay when we look at social attitudes. Our survey respondents disapprove of interreligious, intercaste, and even interlanguage and interclass marriages by overwhelming majorities—19 of 20 respondents are against all of these—reports Megan Reed in Chapter 9. Almost all marriages are still arranged by the parents, though in the current generation this tends to happen with the approval or consent of the bride and groom. Not only are marriages communalized, so is food. Sumitra Badrinathan and Devesh Kapur report (in Chapter 8) on the extraordinary level of commensal segregation. They show that close to two-thirds of Muslims and three-quarters of Hindus have *never* had a meal in a nonrelative's home. The lower one's economic standing, the higher the likelihood of commensal segregation. Even among the most well-to-do in our sample, less than half the Hindus would ever think about sharing a meal with Muslims. It is not hard to draw the pessimistic conclusion that social identity and behavior have not changed as much as Ambedkar hoped (and almost every urban scholar assumes is inevitable).

We note that when these findings were presented before expert audiences in India, many individuals reacted with disbelief. They questioned the data and the methods because in their information bubbles this was not the case. We, of course, stand by the rigor and quality of our data and methods. Moreover, given the rising tide of open religious intolerance and violence in the city—most marked in the Hindutva-instigated riots of February 2020 in east Delhi—we suggest that our survey may have captured latent attitudes that are hard to discern through casual observation. Therefore, instead of denying the findings, we seek explanation and understanding.

To begin with, we are not sure of what we would find in village India— whether the Delhi numbers are actually progressive in comparison—because these or similar questions have rarely been asked in Indian villages. One exception is a recent paper by Diane Coffey and her associates, which reports that more than half their rural survey respondents (in Rajasthan and Uttar Pradesh) practice untouchability and are in favor of having laws to ban intercaste marriages.[7] Perhaps, what we found in Delhi is a sign of progress by comparison. But if this is progress, it is excruciatingly slow. The question is why?

One possibility is that recent political discourses—especially the messaging from the hard right, upper-caste Hindutva campaign—have hardened attitudes and boundaries between social groups. India has regressed in social terms, so much so that people feel more emboldened to act discriminatorily and speak about it brazenly to strangers like surveyors. Another possibility is that the dualistic "inner-outer" or "pure-polluted" domain division of Hindu families is a very resilient ideological structure. Several eminent thinkers from Rabindranath Tagore to Partha Chatterjee, and especially Ashis Nandy, have argued that this psychological split enabled Hindu men to deal with deeply injurious structures like colonialism.[8] Control over the inner domain—the family and house—sublimates their lack of control over foreign, secular, modern, and, shall we say, urban forces.

It may be that faced with the plural heterodoxy of urban life, most Indians, especially those with less formal education, dig deeper into their inner cultural resources; they become anti-urban and anti-modern at home, in their private domains. It could also be that the dislocation faced by migrants to the big cities, in addition to the perennial urban problems of inadequate jobs, infrastructure, and services, actually hardens parochial attitudes and solidifies caste and religious identities and networks rather than the opposite. Mike Davis has suggested, "If God died in the cities of the industrial revolution, he has risen again in the postindustrial cities of the developing world."[9] It is possible that god never died in India because the nation never had a secular industrial revolution.

These are mere speculations. We do not have the information needed to investigate this "counterintuitive" finding any further. The fact that we, the analysts, consider this finding counterintuitive rather than natural is a warning to our own analytical frameworks, indeed our own ideology. It is possible that our modern, secular, and urban minds cannot see how our fellow citizens may be just as secure and comfortable in their "pre-modern" ideologies. What is counterintuitive to us is but natural to them. If this is the case, then it is necessary to question, perhaps discard, the "stylized fact" of social change brought about by urbanization. It may happen eventually, and there are small signs of it in our data, but it may take multiple generations for social attitudes and behaviors to change.

Appearances can be deceptive. Despite the visible prosperity of multilane highways and sparkling multistory buildings, inside its residents' houses and minds, Delhi may be much more like village India than one would think. But is this generalizable outside India? Is it possible that urbanization has barely changed social attitudes and behaviors in other countries like Nigeria or Brazil or China? Our position is that generalization may be impossible in this domain because (*a*) societies differ vastly in their ex ante or pre-urban conditions (whereby Brazil and India cannot really be compared) and (*b*) urbanization is not the only force of social change—the state, as in Mao's China, may be the far more compelling power—or cataclysmic events like big wars may influence the speed and direction of social change (for example, in countries like Japan and Vietnam). Fascinating as it is, we do not have the resources to take this conversation much further. We simply submit that the assumption that social change is driven by urbanization everywhere is a Euro-American model that needs to be reexamined from first principles.

Community and State

Urbanization is not only expected to lead to social change and create more atomized and modern (or less-traditional) individuals but is also expected to lead to new forms of community or social groupings. In fact, the decline of traditional forms of community (typically associated with social identity groups) is expected to go hand in hand with the growth of new forms of urban community (groups based on shared interest rather than unalterable identity). A useful way to think about this is in terms of "social capital," especially Robert Putnam's dual conceptualization in his classic *Bowling Alone*. Putnam argued for the existence of both "bonding social capital" (trust and reciprocity *within* groups) and "bridging social capital" (networks of information exchange and collective action *between* groups).[10] This terminology can be used to frame our question at hand: How are "bonding" (in-group solidarity) and "bridging" (between-group cooperation) being impacted by urbanization in general and Delhi in specific? Are caste and other communities based on social identity getting stronger or intercaste and interfaith and other heterogeneous communities based on shared interest or ideology beginning to dominate?

If we merge a hundred years of sociological theory from Ferdinand Tonnies to Robert Putnam, we should expect a declining significance of religious and caste identities and a rising significance of new groupings based on class, location, housing, consumption, politics, education, and so on in Delhi. Examples of the latter would include political parties, RWAs, business collectives, clubs, college alumni networks, arts societies, social media groups, and so on. We have seen previously that some vital forms of social identity—especially religion and caste—remain very strong and are expressed through marriage and eating practices (and, to some extent, through combinations of state of origin, language spoken, and religion that coalesce over festivals such as Durga Puja, Chhaat, Pongal, and Onam). That does not necessarily mean that bonding social capital has grown stronger, but it probably means that it has not grown weaker.

But, at the same time, there is little doubt of the growth of bridging social capital. There are several examples from our authors. In Chapter 11, Sanjay Srivastava discusses the communities of expediency that form around housing: at the upper-class end, there are RWAs that promote the interests of specific housing estates or colonies; in contrast are the groups at the other end of the class spectrum that form to resist eviction, demolition, displacement, and relocation. In Chapter 14, Awadhendra Sharan identifies the long history of citizen involvement and the judiciary's role in policy formation around cleaning Delhi's air and the shifting alliances that form over issues like burning firecrackers during festivals (health and environmental advocates on one side versus religious groups and labor unions on the other). Adnan Farooqui shows in Chapter 13 how the AAP became a major political force by amalgamating new coalitions of recent migrants from Uttar Pradesh and Bihar (Purvanchalis) with well-educated professionals. Patrick Heller, Partha Mukhopadhyay, and the "Cities of Delhi" investigators (in Chapter 3) show how different types of housing communities have formed to interact with the state. We could have added more material on this theme; for example, the activities of business interests (the various chambers of commerce) at one end to protest groups like the Nirbhaya movement, India Against Corruption, and Shaheen Bagh at the other end.

One clear conclusion is that the most important and numerous *new* forms of community arise in order to interact with and influence the state. The "state" in Delhi is unique in India. The NCT is a "Union Territory," which is not quite a "state" such as, say, Haryana or Rajasthan, but has an elected legislature. However, the national government controls the most important domains—police and land. The current state and national governments are at loggerheads. The AAP, which rules in the NCT, is left-oriented, populist, and has migrant and professional class support. The Bharatiya Janata Party (BJP), which runs the national government, is right-wing, espouses Hindutva, and has upper-caste and business-class support. As we know, in addition to Delhi, the NCR includes other large municipal units in other states with their own governments, such as Gurgaon and Faridabad in Haryana and Noida and Ghaziabad in Uttar Pradesh.

In the NCT alone, there are a large number of institutions that undertake planning, create infrastructure, and provide services. Some notable planning institutions include the Delhi Development Authority (of the central government), the Municipal Corporation of Delhi, the New Delhi Municipal Council, the Delhi Cantonment Board, and the Delhi Urban Shelter

Improvement Board (of the state government, which deals with the different forms of legality of settlements). Infrastructure institutions provide power (the Delhi State Electricity Board, NTPC, NHPC, BSES, and Reliance Power), water (the Delhi Jal Board of the state government), and transportation (including public and private bus operators, the metro rail, commuter rail, and, of course, taxis, auto-rickshaws, and ride-hailing apps).

The proliferation of public institutions in a growing and modernizing metropolis like Delhi is to be expected. Modernity goes hand in hand with an expanding state and bureaucracy. In *The Theory of Social and Economic Organization*, Max Weber argued that a bureaucracy is a rational and economizing institutional response to growing state activities. The more a government does, the more arms it needs. More technical experts, more civil servants. This is a widely accepted view, as is the argument that the result is an "iron triangle" of political representatives, bureaucrats, and interest groups.[11] Each unit in this triangle seeks to further its own interests by exerting influence on each other—by using money, votes, protests, and continuous negotiations.

It is inevitable, therefore, that a large and complex metropolis like Delhi will have a correspondingly large and complex bureaucracy and that citizen interest groups will form to interact with and influence it. The NCR not only has India's most complex state and bureaucracy, but Delhi, we need to occasionally remind ourselves, is India's capital. Therefore, it is likely that citizen response in the form of interest group formation is also most intense in the NCR and Delhi—most deal with local issues, but some widely publicized ones do deal with national issues. It appears that some groups have more voice—those with more education, assets, and access—than those groups with greater numbers, that is, the lower-income, less-educated, and marginalized. This is a core problem of inequality, which we discuss further in the following section. But, we are reasonably sure that as far as the growth of new, "bridging" communities is concerned, Delhi is at the forefront of Indian cities.

We expect that this is true in most other countries too (with the possible exception of countries in demographic decline in central and southern Europe and East Asia). Almost everywhere (certainly in the Global South), cities have growing and more diverse populations that coalesce into shifting interest groups and generate new tasks and responsibilities that lead to enlarged bureaucratic states. Capital cities are at the leading edge of these changes (where, for example, new citizen coalitions and bureaucracies are beginning to grapple with climate change) and also host the most significant political events (from protests in Cairo to coups in Moscow). We suggest that this intersection of social and state action is a relatively understudied and under-theorized aspect of urban change that, if pursued further, could yield interesting new ways to think of urban theory.

Inequality

Finally, it is necessary to underline a fundamental feature of cities everywhere and a major focus of the investigations in this volume: inequality. There are good reasons to think that inequality is a defining feature of the Indian society and a driving force of its politics. This is indisputable in the dimension of social inequality—the differences in average life conditions and opportunities for the various social groups, especially between "backward" castes and tribes and "forward" groups such as "high-caste" Hindus, Jains, Sikhs, and others.[12] It is probably fair to say that partisan politics in India is based on these social groupings and inequalities.

But there is little empirical knowledge on the extent of these inequalities and whether they have been growing or narrowing. In general, both the Indian social accounting system of censuses and surveys that collect data and the experts who deal with that data do not have a good sense of the extent of inequality or how it is changing. There are a number of reasons for it—income is never measured, wealth is poorly measured, and the upper tail of the income/wealth distribution in India is always inscrutable. Survey data are useless for information on the well-to-do because surveyors are almost never able to enter the houses and gated apartments in which the upper classes live to ask them about their income or wealth; and even if they could enter, there is no reason to believe that they would be told the truth. The best available evidence suggests that India is a very unequal country, increasingly so. It is possible to argue that inequality in India today—measured for income or wealth—is the highest it has ever been and may be among the highest in the world.[13]

We were, of course, quite narrowly focused on Delhi and acutely aware of the problems of getting good and reliable information on the economic conditions of our respondents. From the very beginning, we had recognized the futility of trying to gather income or wealth data. We knew we would not be able to enter the homes of the rich; no Indian survey has been able to do so and there was no reason to think that ours would be the exception. We also believed that the people who would allow us to enter their homes would likely not be reliable informants on their own economic conditions—either they would not be sure of the specific details (because of the uncertainties of the casual work many of them do) or would not tell us even if they knew. So, we did not ask for income or wealth information (such as ownership of land, housing, stock). Instead, we took a census of what people own—motor vehicles, home electronics, appliances, and so on—that is, their assets. With these data, Neelanjan Sircar created an asset index (in Chapter 2). This is a new and innovative measure that should be useful to scholars in other domains.

This asset index serves three purposes for us. First, it provides a tangible sense of the distribution of material well-being and a comprehensible, if indirect, way to understand inequality. Given the constraints discussed in the previous paragraph, we believe it is not possible—without well-designed government action—to measure the true extent of income or wealth inequality in India. The best that can be done is to get a sense of the extent of material inequality. Second, the asset index can be mapped and thereby provide a visual sense of the geographical differences in well-being. That is, we are able to examine how asset ownership correlates with geographical differences in settlement patterns by social identity (religion, caste, language) and housing type. Third, the asset index serves as a yardstick to compare conditions on other dimensions—such as social groups (Badrinathan and Kapur), services (Roy), education (Chatterjee, Lal, and Saxena), migration (Malhotra), gender (Chatterjee et al.; Reed), marriage (Reed), and political processes (Sircar; Vaishnav and Lillehaugen). Several of our contributors add other measures and aspects of inequality to the asset index in their individual chapters, and the totality provides arguably the most detailed information yet on multidimensional inequality in Delhi and the relationships between the different dimensions.

As a result, we are able to develop insights into *what inequality is* and *what it does* in Delhi. Inequality is the difference in material possessions (for example, car versus two-wheeler versus no motorized vehicle, or air conditioner versus cooler versus fan versus no-cooling device) between social groups and housing types (the fine-grained spectrum between posh and unauthorized, which may be a special feature of Delhi). We see, for example, that marginalized social groups (the Scheduled Castes and Scheduled Tribes) have significantly fewer assets than Sikhs and "upper caste" Hindus and that they live in lower-quality and more crowded housing than the rest of the population. We see clusters of social groups with low assets—Muslims, who are strongly clustered, and the Scheduled Castes, who are also clustered, but less so—and how physically proximate they often are to well-to-do clusters. We also see that asset ownership declines from the core city outward—highest in the center of Delhi, lowest in the outskirts. (As Neelanjan Sircar notes, this is yet another reversal in "urban theory" derived from the US experience of low-income inner cities surrounded by high-income suburbs.) One of the outcomes of this, Malhotra shows, is that recent migrants suffer a "spatial disadvantage" of being forced to locate in settings with inferior housing and services compared to residents of the same economic class who came and settled earlier.

What inequality does is change access to infrastructure services (Roy) and problem-solvers (Sircar), behavior between social groups (Badrinathan and Kapur), and residential location. For example, we see that households with more assets are able to solve their problems related to infrastructure or services considerably more effectively (though, not for crime, which seems to have its own logic). Indeed, the problems themselves differ by class (as Sircar shows), whereby the well-to-do handle day-to-day issues of water supply and sanitation through private means and instead focus on getting more heavy and expensive public infrastructure (such as transportation) shunted in their direction. We see how more educated parents, with higher social capital, are able to provide more years of education for their children. We see that there is a system of "differentiated citizenship" by housing category (Heller et al.) and that the problems related to housing are fundamentally different between classes—from concerns about service quality at the upper end to the reality of negotiating displacement for the weak (Srivastava).

This is how inequality is supposed to work: weaker social groups are expected to have fewer assets, live in worse conditions, and have more problems and fewer resources to solve them. This is the point and purpose of inequality and is surely one of the defining conditions of urban existence. It is also a central question in urban studies everywhere. Marx and Engels had propounded their critique of capitalism inspired primarily by economic inequality and working-class misery in industrializing London and Manchester. Critiques of "late capitalism" in the developed world and globalization continue to focus on urban (or spatial) inequality—expressed through racial and income segregation, concentrated poverty, gentrification, and displacement—in innumerable publications from William Julius Wilson's *The Truly Disadvantaged* to David Harvey's *The Right to the City*.

We suspect, but do not know for sure, that spatial inequality in Delhi is not quite at the level of the paradigmatic cases: industrializing London and Manchester or contemporary Mumbai.[14] We also suspect, but again do not know for sure, that inequality in Delhi is higher than in most Indian cities. Without considerably better data—that only the Indian government can acquire, that too if it is fully committed to the cause—it is not possible to compare inequalities between places in India.[15] We also cannot be sure of whether spatial inequality is increasing or decreasing in Delhi, not merely because we do not have appropriate or longitudinal data but also because we have evidence to conclude that the outcome depends on what is being studied; the stories of income and education, we believe, are not the same, and neither are the trajectories for Hindus and Muslims.

At this point, it is difficult to undertake international comparisons of urban or spatial inequality. One important reason is that the categories or framing devices used for analysis—for example, segregation or deindustrialization—appear to be incompatible at international scale. Economic and social histories may be too diverse in the different regions of the world to use Euro-American categories meaningfully everywhere. If race is the variable of interest (or point of departure) in the United States of America, it is Hukou (the household registration system) in China, tribe and religion in Nigeria, and caste and religion in India. It is possible that the very nature of inequality investigations could be biased if they are framed using categories that were created in different contexts. Nonetheless, there are hopeful signs of the emergence of new investigative approaches, for example, in the segregation research being done in Indian Institute of Management Bangalore.[16] Therefore, despite the considerable challenges of data availability and categorical consistency across the urban world, it is possible that spatial inequality offers the single best approach to the development of global urban theory. The study of cities in the modern period began with the inequalities of space and class; they may converge now on studies of space and social identity. We hope that the findings in this book can contribute to that end.

Some of these findings point to new and urgent questions. We note that the epistemology of urban inequality does not seem to give much attention to the dangers posed by majoritarian politics in polarized societies and cities. The issues—urban inequality and majoritarianism—appear to be separated in two distinct containers of intellectual inquiry, creating two different literatures. We know, however, that the low-income Muslim population of Delhi is also segregated and ghettoized. Our studies (in this book) underline that they are also socially isolated. When majoritarian hatred (in the form of violent and bullying Hindutva) is mobilized into this mix, the outcome is an existential threat for the spatially and socially cornered minorities. The anti-Muslim violence in February 2020 made it abundantly clear to us that standard inequality concepts or statistics are unable to capture the most threatening aspects of isolation and marginalization.[17] We submit that it is necessary to go beyond the usual inequality frameworks to come to grips with the political geography of hate and its mobilization in the information age.

A Partial Answer

At the end, our answer to Ghalib's question—What is Delhi?—is partial and exploratory. Delhi is an urban colossus, for sure, one of the largest metropolitan regions in the world. Our frame of reference to understand Delhi, however, is India rather than the world. And we find Delhi to be, more than anything else, a city that is firmly rooted in Indian society. If there is a dominant story that emerges from this wide-ranging investigation, if there is a metanarrative of Delhi, it may be encapsulated in a single word: *contradiction*. Delhi's residents display the core contradictions of the Indian society. On the one hand, they are more traditional than "expected" from the global literature on urban social change. That is, their social identities of religion and caste do not easily wither away and become replaced by modern, urban identities simply because they live in Delhi. In fact, their social identities can be hardened and mobilized— perhaps more easily than before—against social minorities. On the other hand, Delhi's residents are modern, urban beings in their interactions with the state. They form new communities based on self-interest and negotiate the politics of survival with enthusiasm, even in the face of daunting (and possibly growing) inequalities.

There are many features that make Delhi unusual if not unique. It is a capital city and has been so for three long regimes: the Mughals, the British colonizers, and independent India. Few cities in the world can boast of such a lineage. Delhi's urban design—with a large empty core in Lutyens' imperial city—is most unusual. The multiplicity of the "state," its many state and municipal governments, the abracadabra of service providers, is unmatched in India and may have few parallels in the world. However, if we think of the city not in terms of its inorganic matter (roads, buildings, and so on) but the lives of its people, we see a city that could only be in India. Delhi, for us, represents the pushes and pulls of tradition and modernity in India, its deep, rural well of abundant labor and enduring norms, mistrust and friction between social groups defined by religion and caste, hesitant and slow urbanization, gaping social and economic inequalities, climbing aspirations (especially for the children), and participation in urban politics in all its manifestations.

Notes

1. Denis Vidal, Emma Tarlo, and Veronique DuPont, "The Alchemy of an Unloved City," in *Delhi: Urban Space and Human Destinies,* ed. Veronique Dupont, Emma Tarlo, and Denis Vidal (Delhi: Manohar, 2000), 15–28. The authors were careful to point out that it was not their opinion, but according to others, especially the city's own residents.
2. Amita Baviskar, *Uncivil City: Ecology, Equity and the Commons in Delhi* (New Delhi: Sage Publications/Yoda Press, 2019).
3. For a detailed discussion, see Sanjoy Chakravorty, *The Price of Land: Acquisition, Conflict, Consequence* (New Delhi: Oxford University Press, 2013). See also Sanjoy Chakravorty and Amitendu Palit, "Reframing the Land Debate in India: Bringing the Market Back into a Political Discussion," in *Seeking Middle Ground: Land, Markets, and Public Policy,* ed. Sanjoy Chakravorty and Amitendu Palit (New Delhi: Oxford University Press, 2019), xiii–xxxvii. The data for Washington, DC, are from David Albouy, Minchul Shin, and Gabriel Ehrlich, "Metropolitan Land Values," *Review of Economics and Statistics* 100, no. 3 (2019): 454–466.
4. For a recent stimulating work in this domain, see Veena Talwar Oldenburg, *Gurgaon: From Mythic Village to Millennium City* (New Delhi: Harper Collins, 2018).
5. Helga Leitner and Eric Sheppard, "Provincializing Critical Urban Theory: Extending the Ecosystem of Possibilities," *International Journal of Urban and Regional Research* 40, no. 1 (2015): 228–235. See also Jennifer Robinson, "Comparative Urbanism: New Geographies and Cultures of Theorizing the Urban," *International Journal of Urban and Regional Research* 40 (2016): 187–199.
6. Michael Storper and Allen J. Scott, "Current Debates in Urban Theory: A Critical Assessment," *Urban Studies* 53, no. 6 (2016): 1114–1136.
7. Diane Coffey, Payal Hathi, Nidhi Khurana, and Amit Thorat, "Explicit Prejudice: Evidence from a New Survey," *Economic & Political Weekly* 53, no. 1 (2018): 46–54.
8. See Ashis Nandy, "An Anti-Secularist Manifesto," in "Secularism in Crisis," ed. Geeti Sen, special issue, *India International Centre Quarterly* 22, no. 1 (1995): 35–64.
9. Mike Davis, "Planet of Slums: Urban Involution and the Informal Proletariat," *New Left Review* 26 (2004): 5–34, 30.
10. Robert D. Putnam, *Bowling Alone: The Collapse and Revival of American Community* (New York: Simon & Schuster, 2000). See also James S. Coleman, "Social Capital in the Creation of Human Capital," *American Journal of Sociology* 94 (1998): S95–120.
11. See Fred W. Riggs, "Modernity and Bureaucracy," *Public Administration Review* 57, no. 4 (1997): 347–353. Gordon Adams, *The Iron Triangle: The Politics of Defense Contracting* (New York: Council on Economic Priorities, 1981).

12. We are of the firm view that the "use of the label 'Backward'—which is suggestive of a condition that is ancient and unchangeable—instead of a term like 'Lagging' or 'Marginalized' is especially problematic … one cannot imagine that a marginalized group like African-Americans could officially be called 'Backward'. The use of such language may signal a deeply paternalistic and patronizing attitude among the elite—the government leaders and intellectuals who create categories and labels…." Sanjoy Chakravorty, *The Truth about Us: The Politics of Information from Manu to Modi* (New Delhi: Hachette, 2019), 243–244.

13. Among recent works on the subject, see James Crabtree, *The Billionaire Raj: A Journey Through India's New Gilded Age* (New Delhi: Penguin, 2018). Luke Chancel and Thomas Piketty, "Indian Income Inequality, 1922–2015: From British Raj to Billionaire Raj?" (WID.world Working Paper Series No. 2017/11, 2017), available at https://wid world/document/chancelpiketty2017widworld/, accessed on September 2, 2020; Chakravorty, *The Truth about Us.*

14. Evocative books such as *Maximum City* (by Suketu Mehta) and *Behind the Beautiful Forevers* (by Katherine Boo) show how inequality permeates daily life in Mumbai.

15. Whereas the inequalities of income and wealth cannot be properly estimated in India, it is possible to create an asset index by city or district or state. This index will not have the detail that the CASI–NCR Survey has, but nonetheless will be comparable across jurisdictions. An inter-city comparison was outside our scope, which was Delhi alone, but remains one possible way for other scholars to examine inequality in India.

16. Naveen Bharathi, Deepak Malghan, and Andaleeb Rahman, "Isolated by Caste: Neighbourhood-Scale Residential Segregation in Indian Metros," (IIM Bangalore Research Paper No. 572, 2018), available at https://ssrn.com/abstract=3195672, accessed on July 1, 2020.

17. This is not the first time in recent memory that ethnic violence has flared up in Delhi. In 1984, the Sikhs, an even smaller minority than Muslims, were murdered by the thousands in Delhi (and in smaller numbers in several other cities in India).

PART 1

State of the Metropolis
Overview

The introduction to this book begins with a single question, "What is Delhi?" As we have seen, the answers are not simple. When we embarked on this project, we understood that the intellectual challenge was to deal with Delhi as a whole—at the scale of the entire metropolitan region known now as the National Capital Region (NCR). Today, the administratively defined boundaries of the National Capital Territory of Delhi (that is, the city) only encompass about one-third of the region's population and 50–60 percent of the region's urban population. It turns out that there is a lot more to Delhi than just Delhi, and we know very little about it. Spanning across four states, and including more than 30 million urban residents, varying in caste, religion, economic condition, migration status, among other things, we knew that empirical characterizations of the region would be challenging. It is hardly a surprise that we soon started referring to this project as the "Colossus Project"—which eventually became the title of this volume.

Understanding the National Capital Region at Metropolitan Scale

To begin with, there are existing studies, especially detailed colony-level and neighborhood-level studies in and around Delhi that we cite throughout the book. These have influenced our thinking about these topics. Rather, we wish to emphasize that certain intellectual concepts require an empirical understanding of the metropolitan region as a whole, and the social conditions and differences generated therein. The region functions as an interconnected unit that structures employment, social interactions, and access to public services. Looking at an Indian city at the metropolitan scale allows us to develop new theoretical tools to study urban change and social behavior.

Unfortunately, when we began this project, we did not even have some basic information about the NCR. Where are the urban areas and rural areas in the NCR, and how has the region grown over the past few decades? Where do different caste, religious, and migrant groups live, and what is the welfare/wealth distribution across the region? How do the complex legal frameworks around land tenure and access to public services affect the lives of residents? What is the profile of energy usage and criminal activity in the region?

The first half of this volume is dedicated to provide these basic empirical characterizations of life in the NCR at the scale of the metropolitan region—with a focus on various social and economic inequalities. Certain elements of this characterization are standard for any urban analysis, such as the distribution of built-up area, religion, caste, and wealth. Other features of this characterization are unique to the NCR, such as the types of colonies in which people live, the particulars of migration, and the amount of energy consumption and crime. The latter two subjects, energy consumption and crime, are issues that animate discourse on Delhi within India and internationally, which is popularly seen as an overly polluted city beset with criminal activity. In order to answer these core questions, we developed the Center for the Advanced Study of India–National Capital Region (CASI–NCR) Survey. The data serve as the backbone for Chapters 2–7.

A Spatial Perspective

Although we brought together a diverse set of scholars for this volume, a consensus quickly emerged that any empirical characterization of the region had to explicitly "spatialize" the data—that it would be hard to understand empirical data at the scale of the NCR without seeing how it changed across the spatial expanse of the region. This explicitly spatial lens, which is particularly noticeable in the first five chapters of this volume, provides a natural way of understanding the interconnectedness and inequalities of the whole region and is important to understand the region at the metropolitan scale.

Our chapters focus on describing the complexity of the relationship between space and social phenomena. On the one hand, social phenomena such as economic relations and religious violence shape spatial patterns of residence. On the other hand, the ways in which space is organized—from interaction across communities to access to infrastructure and public services—drive many social and demographic inequalities that we observe. In short, those identity-based and economic inequalities that characterize differences across space may themselves be perpetuated and exacerbated by these very "spatial inequalities." That is, there are "neighborhood effects" that perpetuate vicious or virtuous cycles.

Nowhere is this more obvious than in recent events in Delhi. As we completed this volume, right after the conclusion of the February 2020 election for the Delhi legislature, the city witnessed its worst "communal" (religious) violence in decades—causing 53 official deaths, the vast majority of which were young Muslim men. (The actual death toll is likely significantly higher, as the discovery and documentation of deaths is notoriously difficult in such situations.) The chapters themselves were written before this ugly episode, but the relationship between Hindu–Muslim tensions and spatial and social patterns in the region was a key focus in this part of the volume.

Chapter 1 discusses the historical processes, especially the period around India's Independence (and the Hindu–Muslim violence contained therein), in expanding the borders of modern Delhi. Among other things, Chapter 2 describes how frequent episodes of violence perpetrated against the region's Muslim community have led to their ghettoization. Even more worryingly, our data show that even when Hindus and Muslims live side by side, they very rarely interact with each other—which may actually exacerbate animosity. In an analysis of infrastructure and service inequalities, Chapter 4 describes how Muslims are systematically shunted into colonies with poorer infrastructure and services (holding other socioeconomic factors constant). Indeed, the location of the recent violence in north-east Delhi consistently shows up in our data as a place with large Muslim populations and among the poorest areas in all of the NCR in terms of wealth, infrastructure, and services.

While we may not have seen the exact timing of this violence coming, our data suggest that the NCR is the proverbial powder keg. The social and political structures of the region are systematically arrayed to isolate and intimidate its Muslim population. Given that one of the triggers of the recent violence was a comment made by a politician associated with India's ruling Bharatiya Janata Party, and that Delhi's ruling Aam Aadmi Party has shown reticence in assuaging Hindu–Muslim tensions, we fear that such violence may become more common.

Chapters in Part 1

In Chapter 1, Shrobona Karkun analyzes how the NCR has grown from the end of Mughal rule to date. While the NCR was first administratively imagined in

1985, the serious urban growth in the region has occurred in the last 40 years, as the population has grown exponentially and the administrative boundaries of the region have expanded. In addition to a census-based characterization of the region, Karkun uses modern tools of satellite imaging to spatialize the urban growth of the NCR in terms of green cover, night lights, and transportation networks. One thing becomes clear from this analysis: much of what we consider the NCR today was only created in the recent past. Indeed, many of the insights contained in this volume are new not because previous scholars missed them but because the region has changed so significantly and so quickly. The NCR today is more heterogeneous, and more interconnected, than it has ever been.

This method of understanding the spatial dynamics of residence continues into Chapter 2, where Neelanjan Sircar grapples with the social and economic processes that undergird the spatial location of the NCR's residents at metropolitan scale by attaching social demographics to the patterns of settlement. The focus of this chapter is to detail spatial variation in settlements across the NCR in terms of identity (caste, religion) and asset wealth. Consistent with the discussion in the previous section, he shows significant segregation by caste, and even more so by religion in the NCR. But, unlike Indian villages, the spatial location of residents is based on much more than identity. Sircar argues that dependence of the upper-income groups on poorer, informal labor generates "spatial co-location" of well-to-do and poor, even beyond identity, generating significant heterogeneity in welfare in a small area. The main point here is to move the reader beyond a static conception of space based on the caste and religious identity of inhabitants (which is the way most scholars view Indian villages). Rather, the NCR is highly dynamic, with space constantly being remade by shifting economic relations between the region's inhabitants.

Chapters 3 and 4 focus on understanding the spatial dynamics at play within the administrative boundaries of Delhi. Because Delhi operates as a set of municipal corporations and a union territory at the same time, a focus on Delhi allows us to understand spatial dynamics in an integrated "planned" urban space. Yet, as Patrick Heller, Partha Mukhopadhyay, Shahana Sheikh, and Subhadra Banda show in Chapter 3, the fragmented character of urban governance forces Delhi's residents to fend for themselves, rather than acting as a part of an integrated unit. The ability of Delhi's residents to make demands on the system, in terms of services and infrastructure, is fundamentally a function of the "type" of colony in which they reside. The authors of Chapter 3 modify the analysis of the spatial distribution of assets in Chapter 2 by introducing information about colonies. Planned colonies have legal rights to the government provision of infrastructure and services and have disproportionately wealthy residents, while those living in *jhuggi jhopri* clusters (which look like slums to the untrained eye), with few formal rights for government provision, have disproportionately poor residents. Interestingly, a large swathe of the city lives in "unauthorised colonies"—that have no formal right to services—with a distribution of welfare that largely mirrors that of the city overall. These findings complicate the relationship between the economic standing of a household and its ability to demand services from the government. The authors then use an ethnographic lens to study how different types of colonies negotiate their space in Delhi—what they refer to as "differentiated citizenship"—based on the "Cities of Delhi Project" (carried out at the Center for Policy Research).

Extending the framework described in Chapter 2 and integrating the findings of Chapter 3, distinguishing between identity-based inequality and spatial inequality, in Chapter 4 Shamindra Nath Roy analyzes inequality in access to infrastructure and services across Delhi. In order to conduct this exercise, Roy merges and cross-references between administrative data on Delhi's colonies and household-based measures from the CASI–NCR Survey. The core finding, similar to that of Chapter 2, is that inequality in access to infrastructure and services is more significant in spatial terms than in identity-based terms. Taking Chapters 2–4 together paints a nuanced picture of spatial inequality. On the one hand, a set of social processes (and in the case of religion: confrontations) shapes the spatial distribution of caste, religion, and welfare across the region. On the other hand, the actual colonies in which residents live, and the complex legal and planning frameworks that govern those, have serious implications for the extent to which residents can access infrastructure and services.

With this nuanced understanding of spatial inequality, we explore its implications on matters that are of particular importance to the NCR. Our data show that three out of five households have at least one migrant, and one out of five have a migrant head of household. Indeed, the popular perception of Delhi is as a city of migrants. In Chapter 5, Khushdeep Kaur Malhotra analyzes the lives of Delhi's migrants and how it compares to those who are "native" to the region. Two core findings emerge from this analysis. First, natives of the region have a first-mover advantage whereby migrants who are of similar socioeconomic status are more likely to live in spatially peripheral areas with systematically poorer infrastructure—what is characterized as a "spatial disadvantage" for migrants. Second, the "intersectionality" of migration and gender means that migrant females (who typically come for marriage) are far less likely to be in the labor force, while the interaction between caste and migration shows that Scheduled Castes (SCs) that migrate to the region are far poorer than their native SC counterparts. Malhotra's analysis shows the implication of space as a major factor in inequality. Those that migrate to the city have constrained options for location, which implies that migrant families of similar means as natives must cope with poorer infrastructure and services. Furthermore, the social and spatial dynamics of migration also impact gender and caste outcomes in the region.

Chapters 6 and 7 describe the implications in the lived experience of the region's residents, given the sorts of inequalities we have described in the first five chapters of this volume. In Chapter 6, Radhika Khosla investigates how asset wealth of households in Delhi translates to energy consumption. The core insight of this chapter is that inequalities in wealth also translate to inequalities in energy usage among households. For instance, air conditioners (ACs), by far the most energy consuming of commonly owned household appliances, are owned by about 19 percent of the population of the NCR, while 93 percent of the top 5 percent of wealthiest households in the region own an AC. While energy challenges of Indian cities are well known to all, with frequent power cuts and pollution problems mounting, energy consumption also structures social inequalities in standards of living. As Khosla mentions, the ability to avail of a washing machine or an AC also implies a quality of life upgrade in terms of more free time for other labor or less illness due to heat.

Finally, in Chapter 7, Milan Vaishnav and Matthew Lillehaugen describe the incidence and reporting of crime in Delhi. The key finding is that a significant number of those experiencing crime do actually approach the police and are satisfied with their conduct. But herein lies a significant inequality. Those in lower-caste groups, Other Backward Class (OBC), or SC, are more likely to experience crime. But the more well-off the resident, the more likely he or she is to approach the police—generating a mismatch between who experiences crime and who reports it. Chapter 7 underscores a finding from earlier chapters in the volume that the most negative aspects of city life are likely to be experienced by the most disadvantaged classes in the city. It also points to a phenomenon we explore in more detail in the second part of this volume. Differential willingness or capacity to access state actors, such as the police, engender differences in the ability to cope with the difficulties of living in the city.

CHAPTER 1

Geography and Demography
Mapping the Metropolis

Shrobona Karkun*

Delhi is one of the urban giants of the world. Like Tokyo, Shanghai, Beijing, Seoul, Jakarta, and Manila, Delhi is veritably a colossus of the modern world, a new type of metropolitan being without historic precedent. The urban transformation of this region is increasingly of interest to activists and academics who raise questions about the effects of the rapid recent growth. For example: What are its causes and effects (on issues such as planning, inequality, and social change)?[1] Has the physical transformation into something that could be called a Global City improved the lives of Delhi's inhabitants? While these questions are interesting and important (and are addressed in several chapters in this volume), I offer a spatial perspective on urban transformation in this chapter. The intent is to provide a multi-method narrative of the growth of the National Capital Territory (NCT) and the National Capital Region (NCR). I identify some of the key drivers of urbanization, especially at the regional scale, beyond the confines of the political boundaries of the NCT, and certainly far beyond the Delhi of Mirza Ghalib and William Dalrymple.

There are two reasons for taking this approach. First, it is widely agreed that the extent of urbanization has physically surpassed whatever administrative

* The author thanks the following for their invaluable input in the study: Sanjoy Chakravorty and Neelanjan Sircar for their patience and support in shaping this chapter, Victor H. Gutierrez-Velez for his guidance in remote sensing, Amiya P. Sen and Narayani Gupta provided important direction to understand the complex urban history of the city, Shamindra Nath Roy and Partha Mukhopadhyay, for sharing data and insight on Delhi's census structures. The errors are author's own.

boundaries have been conceptualized over time (such as the NCT now). Second, while the literature on Delhi has largely focused on the NCT (for good reasons), it is necessary now to go beyond it to try to comprehend the NCR as a whole. A series of motifs—such as that of Purani Dilli and Lutyens' Delhi, the milieu of *jhuggi jhopri* clusters and camp slums, the *kothis* of old Delhi, and the gated communities of Gurgaon and Noida—are suggestive of the extent of diversity (and fragmentation) in this large space. Thus, to truly understand the transformation of Delhi into a colossal metropolis, the spatial enquiry needs to take in the entire urban framework of concrete structures, industrial zones, untreated landscapes, planned and unplanned communities, and colonial and postcolonial architectural ambition.

I discuss the geography of space, place, and people of the NCR through a critical examination of archival data, plans, and maps. Mapping offers several advantages for understanding the NCR. First, it allows for a visualization of population and urban development clusters in the entirety of the NCR through a synthesis of census data and historic maps. Second, the analyses can be done at multiple scales—in this case, at the more researched scale of Delhi, the city (or the NCT), and the lesser explored scale of the NCR. Finally, mapping allows a spatial examination and juxtaposition of data from the census, satellite images, and the CASI–NCR Survey. This presents the possibility to uncover many stories of Delhi—from its urban heart to the rural–urban mix at its vast fluid fringes.

The specific techniques of mapping and analysis used here were shaped by the type of data available and included the use of Geographic Information Science tools, satellite images (and their classifications), and manual mapping. The geographic description is at the scale of sub-districts within the NCT and of districts in rest of the NCR. For the sake of continuity of discussion, the specific methods used and their limitations are discussed briefly in the appropriate sections.

The remainder of this chapter is divided into four sections. First is a discussion on the growth of Delhi over time, beginning from descriptions in the historical literature and archival maps. Second is an exploration of the geography of the NCT–NCR continuum using remote-sensing data. Third is an examination of present and historical data in combination with the coverage of the CASI–NCR Survey. The concluding section ties in the themes of space, place, and people in the production of the uneven and heterogeneous urban structures of Delhi.

The Growth of the City and the Region

Delhi's origins go back hundreds of years and the city has often been described as a constellation of cities. Whether they are eight or nine in number[2] and whether one imagines that the mythical Indraprastha of the Mahabharata was located here, the ruins of the early Persian Empires and the Tughlaqs and Lodhis offer relatively little information (by contemporary standards) to understand Delhi's past urban fabric. Rather, it is useful to focus on three more recent political moments that had a long-lasting impact on the city: the Sepoy Rebellion of 1857, the decision to move the capital of British India from Calcutta to Delhi in 1911, and the partition of 1947. Along with the other waves of political events, these three played important roles in the incremental development of Delhi's urban fabric between 1857 and 1956 (Figure 1.1).

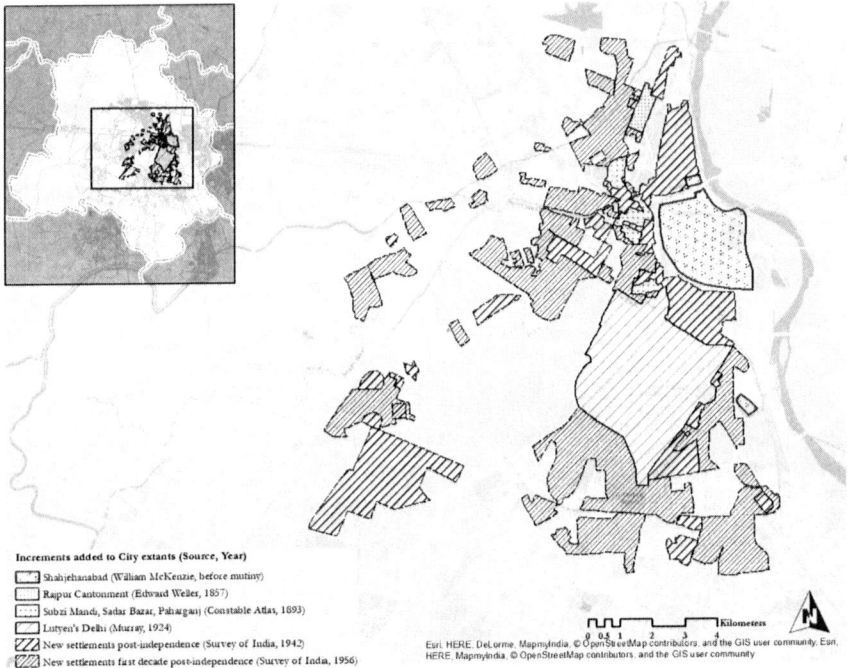

Increments added to City extants (Source, Year)

☐ Shahjehanabad (William McKenzie, before mutiny)
☐ Rajpur Cantonment (Edward Weller, 1857)
☐ Subzi Mandi, Sadar Bazar, Paharganj (Constable Atlas, 1893)
☐ Lutyen's Delhi (Murray, 1924)
▨ New settlements post-independence (Survey of India, 1942)
▨ New settlements first decade post-independence (Survey of India, 1956)

Esri, HERE, DeLorme, Mapmyindia, © OpenStreetMap contributors, and the GIS user community, Esri,
HERE, Mapmyindia, © OpenStreetMap contributors, and the GIS user community

Figure 1.1   Incremental growth over a century

Source: Cartography by author.

Note: The segments show parts of the city developed as an aftermath of (a) the Rebellion of 1857, (b) the development of an imperial capital, and (c) Independence of India and Pakistan.

All along, transportation infrastructure played a critical role. In the mid-1800s and later, the development of railways was of prime importance (detailed in the following sections). After Independence, the gradual yet steady growth of the city was strongly influenced by the development of its road and rail transportation networks. This was influential in generating the sense of an economic region, one different from that bounded by a political demarcation. In the decades after Delhi became the national capital, a series of policies attempted to dissipate congestion, encourage economic development, and provide basic services to high-density areas. This discourse of relieving congestion, "to immediately control and channel the sprawl," also started the conversation about a possible National Capital Region in the *Interim General Plan for Greater Delhi, 1956*.[3] However, the city did not grow across the Yamuna river until the 1970s and the National Capital Region Planning Board did not come into formal existence until 1985. And parts of the NCR which attract global and national investments, such as Gurgaon and Faridabad, did not come

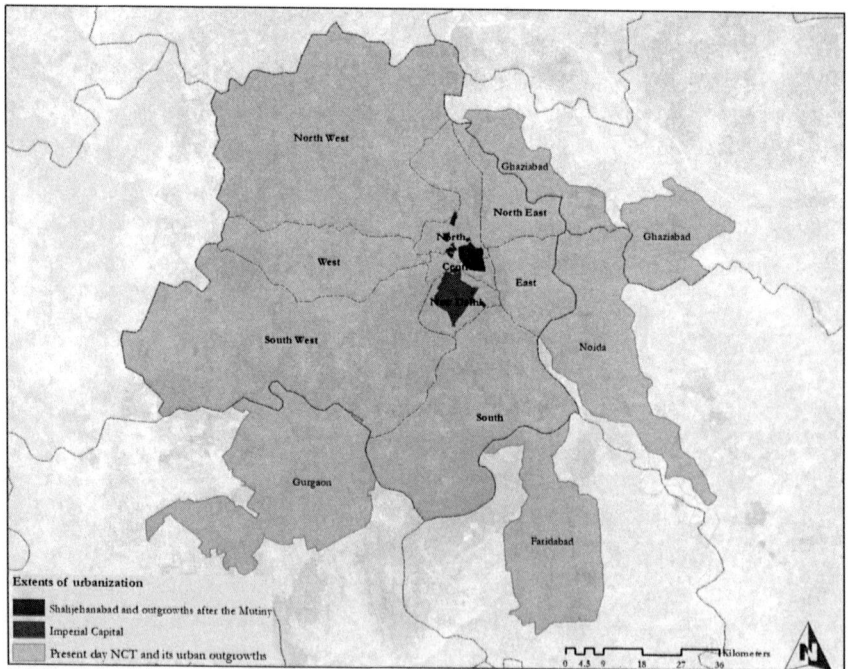

Figure I.2   Comparison of the present extent of the NCT and its neighboring cities (Gurgaon, Faridabad, Noida, and Ghaziabad) with the extents of Dilli/New Delhi before Independence
Source: Cartography by author.
Note: The extent of urbanization in Delhi has been enormous in the last 70 years.

into prominence until the early 2000s. The evolving transportation linkages between Delhi and its outgrowths, hastened with the establishment of the metro rail system—the newest transportation infrastructure to reshape the region—have helped create the idea of the NCR (Figure 1.2).

Before Independence

The origins of the modern urban giant probably begin from Shahjahanabad (what is known today as Old Delhi) immediately after the Sepoy Rebellion of 1857–1858.[4] The city of Shahjahanabad was shaped by achieving a balance of landscaped woodlands and densely populated areas by the Mughals and early British rising power. The site of the city was carefully selected to be placed at the northeastern corner of the Ridge. The Grand Trunk Road was the artery for development of the densely populated, fortified city, and the lush green forests surrounding it—a concept brought together by Mughal design aesthetics.

But, by 1857, the year of the rebellion, the Mughals were rulers in name only, and the fief of the last Emperor Bahadur Shah Zafar was limited to the boundaries of Shahjahanabad. That too disappeared when the British formally deposed and exiled him to Rangoon. The life and times of Delhi immediately before that pivotal period, and since then, have been chronicled in English in the form of colonial atlases, memoirs, travelogues, and literary works.[5] The colonial archive paints an image of pre-1857 Delhi as a place of high culture and great economic wealth (though concentrated in the hands of a few).[6] Percival Spear, Delhi's original biographer, was instrumental in shaping the colonial perception of urban prosperity in *Twilight of the Mughals*. More recently, Narayani Gupta and Robert Frykenberg have further expanded this discussion in the volume *The Delhi Omnibus*. These two volumes provide a rich narrative of the various eras of Delhi and pay special attention to its urban history, culture, and society.[7]

In the British colonial atlas from the 1870s, *The British Empire*, Delhi and the nearest town of colonial significance, Meerut, are described thus

> Delhi, a celebrated city on the Jumna. Pop. 150,000. The city, seven miles in circumference, is entered by eleven gates. The Mogul's palace is a magnificent building, and the principal mosque, which cost £100,000, has been restored by the British Government. It has a college for English, Arabic, Persian and Sanscrit, and a large observatory.... Meerut is a capital of a district. Pop. 30,000. Two miles north of the town is a military cantonment, headquarters for the Bengal artillery, with a military prison.[8]

Apart from signature Mughal landmarks, Delhi presented other locational advantages and potential to be further developed. Gupta notes that Delhi's location and regional geography played an important role in its urbanization in this time period. By the 1860s, the construction of the railways was beginning to transform Delhi into a major trading center. The location of Delhi between the *doab* of Punjab and Rajasthan made it an important distribution center for the whole of north India. Delhi *tehsil* (sub-district) covered an area of 683.97 square kilometers in 1880, including the hinterlands, described by Gupta as a 7-kilometer radius around Shahjahanabad, which was defined by the Yamuna, Upper Yamuna Canal, and Delhi Ridge.[9] The hinterland covered a heterogeneous landscape of at least four types of soils which determined the land use.

The Rebellion of 1857–1858 not only transferred power but also transformed the lives of the people of Dilli in the next decade. Narayani Gupta notes in *Portrait of the City* that the transformation was marked by mass displacement and demolition in the walled city, followed by half a century of increase in trade, construction, and population. The railway project, which has its own complicated story of origin,[10] became an important factor to boost Delhi's economic growth. The development of the railways led to the demolition of the fort walls and displacement of workers. Shopkeepers and farmers, who operated out of the bazaar next to the fort walls, were displaced to Kishanganj to make space for the railway station. After 1857, conscious efforts were made to boost trade.[11] Gupta notes that "by 1877, Delhi was drawing away trade from Amritsar."[12] The chief imports were rice, sugar, iron, brass, and copper, and the exports were raw cotton from the hinterlands and leather goods produced locally. Increase in trade aided the transformation of the city into a mercantile center to go along with its administrative past.

Increasing manufacturing and production activities from the start of the 1860s to the 1890s led to an increased migration of workers and shopkeepers to the city—a majority of whom were male and tended to settle in the hinterlands. The distribution of workers by occupation varied in the city and the suburban hinterlands. Where at least half of the male population in the suburbs were engaged in manual labor, only a third of the male population in city were manual laborers, which suggests that the city had a substantially higher proportion of professional workers than the suburbs. In the Census of 1901, the population had reached 405,000. Hindus were the more prosperous majority group while Muslims were an enfeebled minority after the annihilation and exile of the erstwhile ruling class. Gupta also notes that the leading castes of the region had embraced trades and crafts that had traditionally been associated with Muslims.

With the growth of the population, there was an expected increase in the volume of housing and building activity. The center of commerce remained in the congested Chandni Chowk area. Building activity heightened in the 1880s and 1890s, but the pattern of settlements in the hinterlands and the poorer parts of the city was haphazard. A majority of construction involved encroachment of neighboring plots or roads and purchase of suburban plots to add more rooms per family.

Fifty years after the Rebellion of 1857, a plan for an imperial capital was proposed by Edward Lutyens, and in the decade of the 1920s, Lutyens' plan for the colonial capital was actualized. His vision of the city was based on a nodal network (similar to Paris and Washington, DC), with a central avenue connecting the parliament and the house of the viceroy. According to Menon, "Lutyen's baroque city plan and the setting of capital complex on Raisina Hill invested the project with qualities of landscaped order and monumentality which were to become established as the hallmarks of the urban environment of Delhi ... and this is largely why Delhi 'looks different'."[13]

The green and forested areas of Delhi were also historically created and governed by the choices of the urban elite. The colonial culture of the state initially influenced the treatment of the space beyond human settlements in ways that were aligned with colonial sensibilities. Mann and Sehrawat write that between 1883 and 1913, Delhi Ridge was developed to address the deforestation, which had occurred in the years of construction after the rebellion, for example, for shooting ranges for the Raj. After several proposals, the site for the proposed forest was selected at the north end of the ridge.[14] The end result was a city with striking monuments in a modern setting surrounded by indigenous and marginalized rural communities.[15]

Independence and Delhi in the Next 70 Years

The Independence and partition of India influenced the next phase of the urban growth and architecture of Delhi. The large-scale population redistribution and refugee crisis from the partition brought in the Punjabi community, and over time, their experiences and cultural preferences began to influence the aesthetics of the city. At the same time, the newly independent Indian State began to create architectural landmarks that further developed the baroque style of planning initiated during the colonial rule, while inserting architectural elements of a Hindu revivalist ideology.[16] This shaped the urban fabric of New Delhi and south Delhi in a number of ways. New Delhi grew as an extension of the imperial plan, extending to the south of the city and giving birth to neighborhoods such as Lajpat Nagar and South Extension. The influx of a large refugee population and the development of the capital led to congestion in the city again. Bopegamage notes that "almost overnight, the city's population increased by 103.4 percent. The sudden influx of immigrants brought pressure on the living space of the city proper. Some took accommodation in the abandoned houses, some settled down in the suburbs and some in the satellite towns."[17]

It was soon apparent that the population had surpassed what the previous plans had accounted for and a planning intervention was needed. Amrit Kaur spells out this urgency in the Interim General Plan (IGP) 1956:

> Delhi also suffers from the unplanned sprawl of all metropolitan areas, a sprawl made possible by the radius of reach of the motor car which in turn, has its revenge in cluttering up the roads. Green spaces and open recreation areas recede further and further. Unplanned growth in Delhi has caused population to run ahead of water supply and sewerage capacity.[18]

The primary recommendation of IGP 1956 was to decentralize in order to relieve congestion. However, these efforts were not completely successful. Menon attributes this failure to the "presence of and power of bureaucracy in a strongly state-controlled economy."[19] The absence of cohesive master plans between the 1960s and 1980s has been attributed by Gautam Bhan to a "failure of planning."

From the perspective of architecture and housing development, Menon attributes the changes in the next two decades to utilitarianism and catalytic policies of the state along with the perpetual search for "Indianness." Housing in the city was by and large developed under the influence of local politicians and supervised by young architects who learnt the trade on the go. Early Delhi Development Authority (DDA) housing was based on austere socialist values, which did not allow for extravagances in construction. Thus, the housing was characteristically bland, with steep stairs, flat roofs, and plastered or lime-washed walls, punctuated by functional sunshades. On the other hand, the elite in the city designed against this austerity with the construction of versions of "Spanish villas with icing-like decorations" giving birth to the gaudy style of *kothi* housing and residential enclaves. This style of architecture further spread across middle-class neighborhoods in the 1980s and 1990s.[20]

In the 1980s, two new forms of housing rapidly grew across the city: "developer" housing, which replaced some of the older housing stock, and "group housing" projects in the periphery of the city. This phase of development was largely influenced by the monopoly of the DDA in land ownership and thereby its control of land values in the NCT. Along with private group housing, a new form of elite urban space began taking shape on Mehrauli Road in the form of farmhouses. In the 1962 plan, these spaces were proposed as part of a green belt where urban agriculture could be practiced. In reality, these lands are used—then, as now—as marriage gardens, weekend getaways, and other recreational activities. Anita Soni describes the increase in the number of farmhouses in Mehrauli as one of the many ways by which asymmetric access to political power not only determined access to land but also predetermined the deterioration of agricultural land and Delhi's urban environment.[21] This infill development began to strengthen Delhi's linkage with Gurgaon (now Gurugram) that in the 2000s became Veena Oldenburg's "Millennium City."[22]

Before the economic reforms of 1991, Delhi had become a strong regional magnet for economic and industrial development, an identity that has only become stronger since then. According to Phillipe Cadène, Delhi is now part of larger industrial chains along which a number of industries and industrial nodes are located. Ludhiana and Delhi form two pivotal points of this space. The construction industry is largely concentrated around Delhi. The metallurgical industries stretch from east Delhi to Haryana and Rajasthan. In essence, Delhi and its outgrowths exert control over the entire industrial space, especially through the number of corporate headquarters located in the NCR. Delhi's political centrality plays an important role in exerting control over the industrial corridor.[23]

Seeing from the Sky: The National Capital Region from above

In 2017, Delhi NCR was an urban agglomeration of nearly 30 million people. McKinsey's 2010 report on Indian cities argued that it was poised to grow even more as an urban region in the coming decades.[24] The NCR today contains 30 districts, 21 of which are outside the NCT boundaries. The NCR is spread across four states (plus the NCT) and covers an area of over 55,000 square kilometers (or 13.6 million acres). The region, as seen in Figure 1.3, includes places as far-flung as Muzaffarnagar and Kurukshetra, Alwar and Bharatpur, Mathura and Aligarh, and Bulandshahar and Hapur.

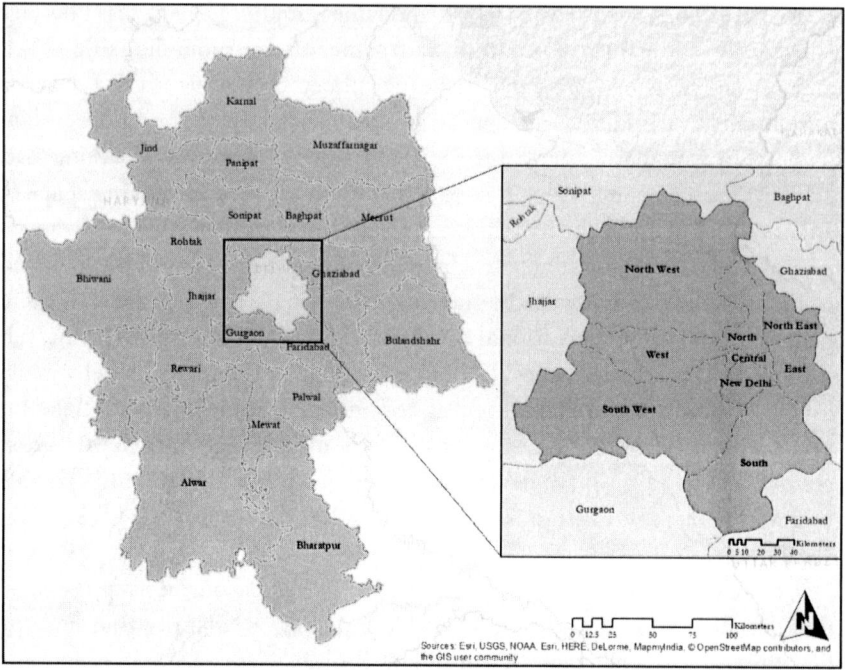

Figure 1.3   Districts of Delhi NCR

Source: National Capital Region Planning Board, see http://ncrpb.nic.in/.

Note: Along with 9 districts in Delhi (inset), the region is composed of 2 districts within Rajasthan, 13 districts in Haryana, and 6 districts in Uttar Pradesh.

The space of the NCR is a diverse landscape and varied topography of plains, hills, and a portion of the Thar Desert. The Earth Observation Programme and other satellite products are helpful in identifying the variation in the landscape and its physical transformation in recent decades. Along with the visible spectrum of light, satellite images also capture various wavelengths of infrared radiations reflected from the surface of Earth that enable researchers to understand the physical form of land covers and water from the neighborhood to the planetary scale.

In this section, I explore the extent of the urbanized landscape in the NCR and reflect on its ecological impacts. I have utilized remote sensing (or, the Earth Observation) technique of supervised classification for this purpose. Multispectral satellite images from Landsat missions, captured in 2011 and 2016, point to a complex relationship between natural–human environments in the region. In terms of urban structures, the region exhibits a network of dense urbanized centers, with cities and towns connected by major roadways.[25] In contrast, the landscape around these centers exhibits a great variance including large forest canopies, the northern end of the Aravallis at the southwestern side of the NCT, and a flat agricultural land use at the east.

A preliminary study of the land cover changes in the NCT in Figure 1.4 shows an increase in urban land cover. While urban forms can be heterogeneous (in density and age), the process of recognizing these categories requires a

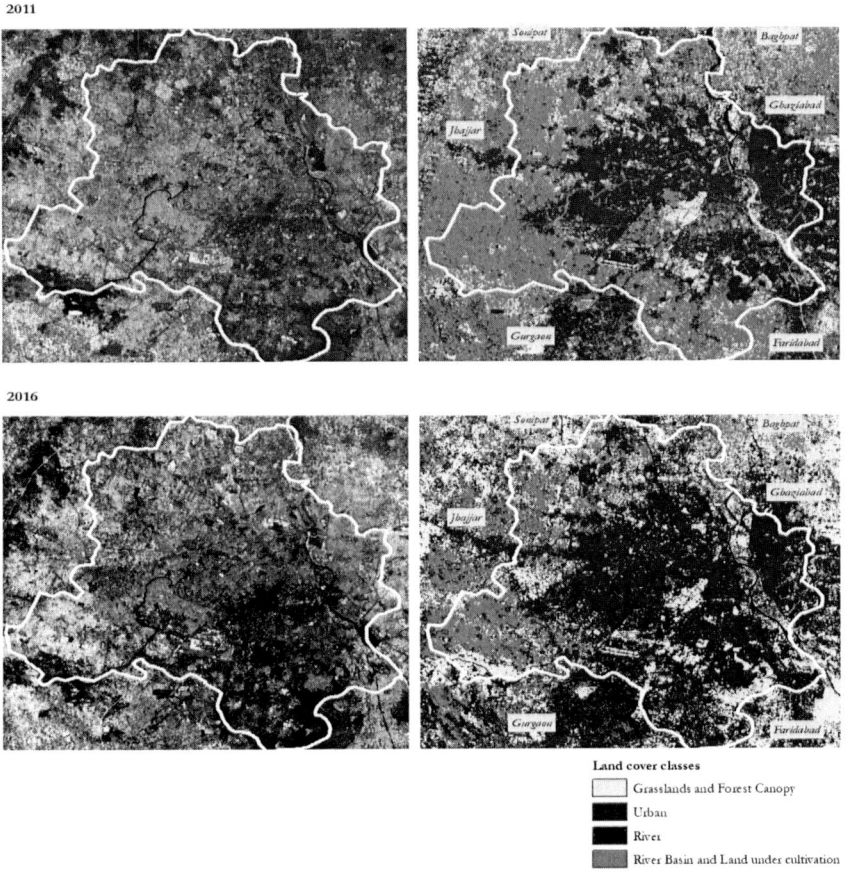

Figure 1.4 Mapping extents of urbanization with the Earth Observation Programme between 2011 and 2016

Sources: Satellite images for 2011 and 2016 captured by Landsat 5 MSS (multispectral scanner) and Landsat 8 satellites, respectively, published by United States Geological Survey. Analysis by author.

Notes: A composite satellite view of the NCT and its immediate vicinity (*left*). The urban footprint derived from supervised classification processes (*right*) shows expansion at the edges.

sophisticated analytical model (with some uncertainty because the classification of remotely sensed images involves some assumptions which may not accurately reflect reality). The categories of urban, water, and other uses are the more familiar classes used in urban remote sensing. In this context, the term "urban" refers to land cover where some built structure has been detected during the process of supervised classification.

Similarly, mapping the concentration of night-lights based on the "Earth at night" maps released by the National Oceanic and Atmospheric Administration (NOAA)–National Aeronautics and Space Administration (NASA) Suomi National Polar-Orbiting Partnership (NPP) program gives an approximation of urbanized areas in the NCR. In dense urban areas, the concentration of night-lights is increasingly being used to examine the extent of urban development (and development in general).[26] Here, we have also captured night-lights to understand the extent of urban infrastructure at the scale of the NCR.

The images on the left in Figure 1.5 show the quantity of light reflectance, whereas the images on the right map areas of high concentration of night-lights within the region. A comparison of false color "heat maps" reveals a steady growth of the brightest portions of the region between 2012 and 2016. The largest bright node in the region originates from Delhi NCT and includes the nearby urban centers of Gurgaon, Noida, and Faridabad. The concentration of bright pixels also increased along the highways and transportation corridors. Along with the expansion of existing bright clusters, new hotspots of brightness also appear in Muzaffarnagar district. The relative difference of hotspots in the 2016 image in northwestern NCR (especially in Jind) can perhaps be explained by seasonal electricity outages and crop burning. Studies have also noted a low-intensity haze around these bright spots, which could be an artifact of how these images were processed.

In both the analyses, it is difficult to conclude whether such urbanization has left us with a better (or worse) environment. An examination of vegetation indices for the NCT has shown an overall decrease in healthy green vegetation and an increase of land covers which are not vegetated. The classification results indicate a shift in how green spaces are conceived and utilized, seen in Figure 1.4. The intensity of built-up areas and a disproportional gap with green spaces has increased over time. Our finding is consistent with a study from Morya and Punia, who find a similar trend of increased built-up area and decline in agricultural land. This decrease also contributes to the overall decline in total ecosystem services in the NCT and eventually "lead to the lesser access of services at higher cost, especially to the poor."[27]

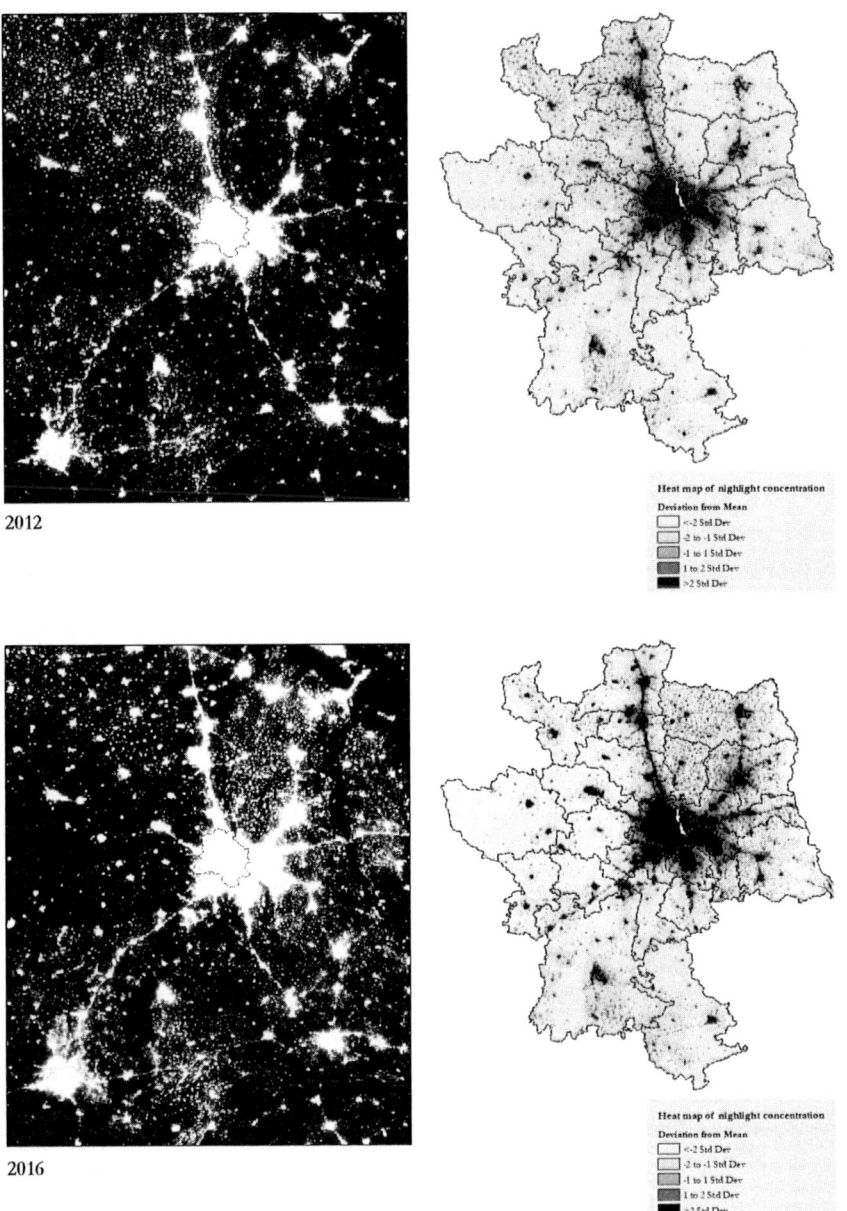

2012

2016

Figure 1.5   Analysis of night-time lights in the NCR

Sources: NASA–NOAA Suomi-NPP satellite, released by NASA Earth Observatory. Analysis by author.

Note: The NCR in "Earth at night" maps released in 2012 and 2016 (left). Heat map of the bright spots in the region (right). Brightest spots in the images appear in darkest gray.

The large change in the urban footprint over the 2010s explored in this section suggests that the scale of urbanization was possible by defying the principles of site selection and landscape design at a regional scale. The inferior "Othering" of green spaces to the built environment, similar to Sharan's account of air quality in this volume, has played a significant role. However, such development comes at the cost of an irreversible impact on the ecology of the region.[28]

Seeing Like a State: The National Capital Region and Political Boundaries

The National Capital Region Planning Board, a regional development body, defines the NCR in terms of districts within its five regions, a definition that has seen some changes since the publication of the last regional plan in 2005. The initial plan consisted of the districts of Meerut, Baghpat, Ghaziabad, Gautam Buddh Nagar, and Bulandshahar from Uttar Pradesh (UP) and Faridabad, Gurgaon, Palwal, Mewat, Rewari, Panipat, Sonipat, Rohtak, and Jhajjar in Haryana. Only certain *tehsils* (sub-districts) of Alwar in Rajasthan were included. In 2013, Bhiwani, Mahendragarh, and Jind districts in Haryana and Bharatpur district in Rajasthan were included in the NCR through the National Capital Region Planning Board Act, 1985; in 2015, Muzaffarnagar district in UP was made part of the NCR as well (Figure 1.6). Understanding this administrative organization of spaces and the distribution of people is essential to fully grasp the social realities of the region, especially since the NCR is the only metropolitan region in India which is governed by four state jurisdictions and their inevitable political contentions.

To understand the extent of urbanization in the NCR, let us begin with the definition of "urban" in India. In its current form, the Registrar General and Census Commissioner of India defines urban in the following two ways:

1. all places with a municipality, corporation, cantonment board, notified town area committee, and so on; and
2. all other places which satisfy the following criteria:
   i. a minimum population of 5,000,
   ii. at least 75 percent of the male main working population engaged in nonagricultural pursuits, and
   iii. a density of at least 400 persons per square kilometer.

Figure 1.6   Making of the NCR boundaries—regions included in 2013 and 2015 are represented with hatched overlays

Source: National Capital Region Planning Board, see http://ncrpb.nic.in/.

Urban agglomerations (UA) are defined separately for amalgamated urban units, which have a clearly defined core and outgrowths and a population of over a million. In the 2011 Census, the NCR included nine UAs (Table 1.1).

Table I.I   Urban agglomerations (UA) within Delhi NCR in 2011 Census

UA name	State	Municipal corporations, census towns, and outgrowths
Delhi	the NCT	26
Gurgaon	Haryana	2
Karnal	Haryana	2
Bahadurgarh, Rohtak	Haryana	2
Alwar	Rajasthan	2
Bharatpur	Rajasthan	4
Muzaffarnagar	Uttar Pradesh (UP)	2
Meerut	UP	2
Ghaziabad	UP	2

Source: Author.

Population growth is an important measure of urbanization. Figure 1.7 shows the total population of Delhi and its leading urban outgrowths (Gurgaon, Faridabad, Gautam Buddh Nagar [that used to be known as Noida], and Ghaziabad) for the last 11 censuses. The population of this urban unit was reported to be over 1.4 million in the 1901 Census and the share of the NCT was about 405,000. In the next decade, the region saw a population decline due to plague, malaria, and other epidemics, especially in Gurgaon, whereas the NCT's population increased by 8,000. With the development of Lutyens' Delhi, the NCT's population in the 1921 Census increased by 74,000. From this point onward, we not only see an increasing rate of population growth in

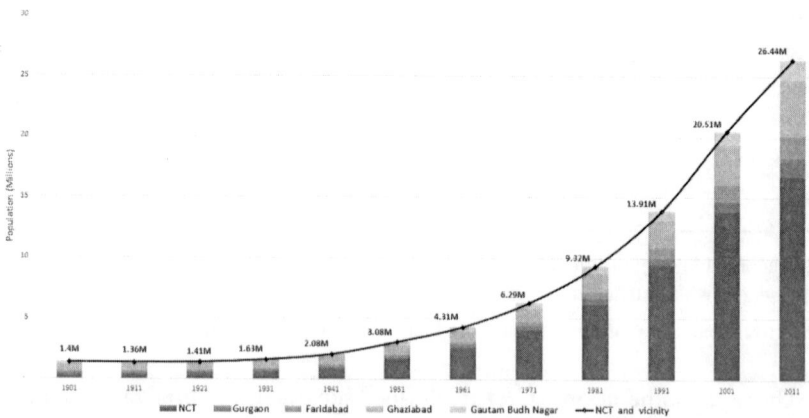

Figure I.7   Change in population of the NCT and its nearby districts
Source: Series A2 tables—Decadal variation in population since 1901, Census of India.

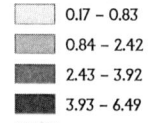

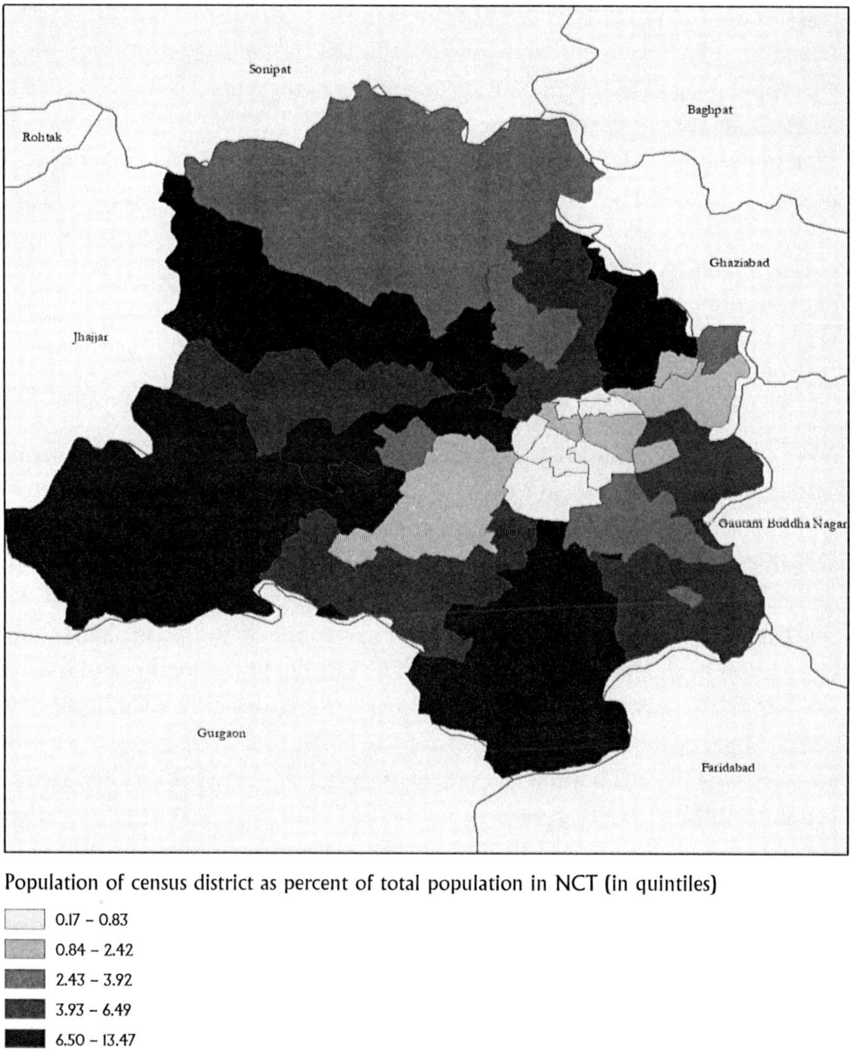

Population of census district as percent of total population in NCT (in quintiles)

- 0.17 – 0.83
- 0.84 – 2.42
- 2.43 – 3.92
- 3.93 – 6.49
- 6.50 – 13.47

Figure 1.8   District-wise population distribution in the NCT (as percent of total)
Source: Author's calculations from the Census of India, 2011.

the region but also see a rapid increase in the population share of the NCT in comparison to its outgrowths. Over a century, the population of the NCT rose from less than half a million to over 16 million in the 2011 Census.

Next to the NCT, Ghaziabad has the second largest population share. Even though its population increase has not been as rapid as the NCT, it has increased from 495,000 to 4.8 million over a century. In 1901, Gurgaon and Faridabad were rural entities and Gautam Buddh Nagar (Noida) did not exist. Thus, we see a relatively low growth in population in these units. The rapid growth in Gurgaon was not seen in earnest until the 1991 Census, whereas industrial development in Faridabad reflected a steady increase in total population from the 1981 Census. Since the state boundary of the NCT has remained stable since its conception in 1956, we can also infer an increase in population density over time. Between the 1991 and 2011 Censuses, the mean population density of the NCT increased from 1,170 to 1,812 persons per square kilometer.

Current Outlook from the 2011 Census

Mapping the data from the 2011 Census down the census hierarchy—states, districts, sub-districts, and wards—reveals interesting demographic and spatial patterns. In this section, the demographic data of the NCR is examined at a district level (see Figure 1.9). However, for the NCT, the largest and densest part, the analysis was conducted at the sub-district level. Although the Registrar General and Census Commissioner of India considers some population in the NCT to be rural, I have considered the total population of the NCT to be urban since the NCT lacks rural governance structures.

In the 2011 Census, the districts of the NCR have seen a steady decadal growth. The overall population increased by 21.2 percent in the NCT, 23.5 percent in Haryana, 25.2 percent in UP, and 22.1 percent in the Rajasthan sub-regions. At the level of districts, these rates differ significantly, with central Delhi and New Delhi showing a negative growth from the previous census; that is, population declines. In absolute values, the population of the NCT grew by 2.9 million, while rest of the NCR saw a population growth of 7.7 million (3.6 million in UP, 1.1 million in Rajasthan, and 3.0 million in Haryana).

The NCT is home to a population of 16.78 million people, ranging from 28,000 residing within the sub-district of Connaught Place to over 2.2 million people in Saraswati Vihar. In terms of population share, the highest quintile resides in Najafgarh, Patel Nagar, and Hauz Khas, whereas the lowest quintile of population is observed in Lutyens' Delhi and its vicinity. Outside of the NCT, the population of the NCR districts ranges from 900,000 to 4,680,000. The highest quintile of population (8.33–11.31 percent in the distribution) resides in Ghaziabad, Alwar, Muzaffarnagar, and Bulandshahar districts, whereas Rohtak, Jhajjar, Rewari, Palwal, and Mahendragarh report

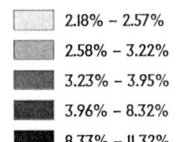

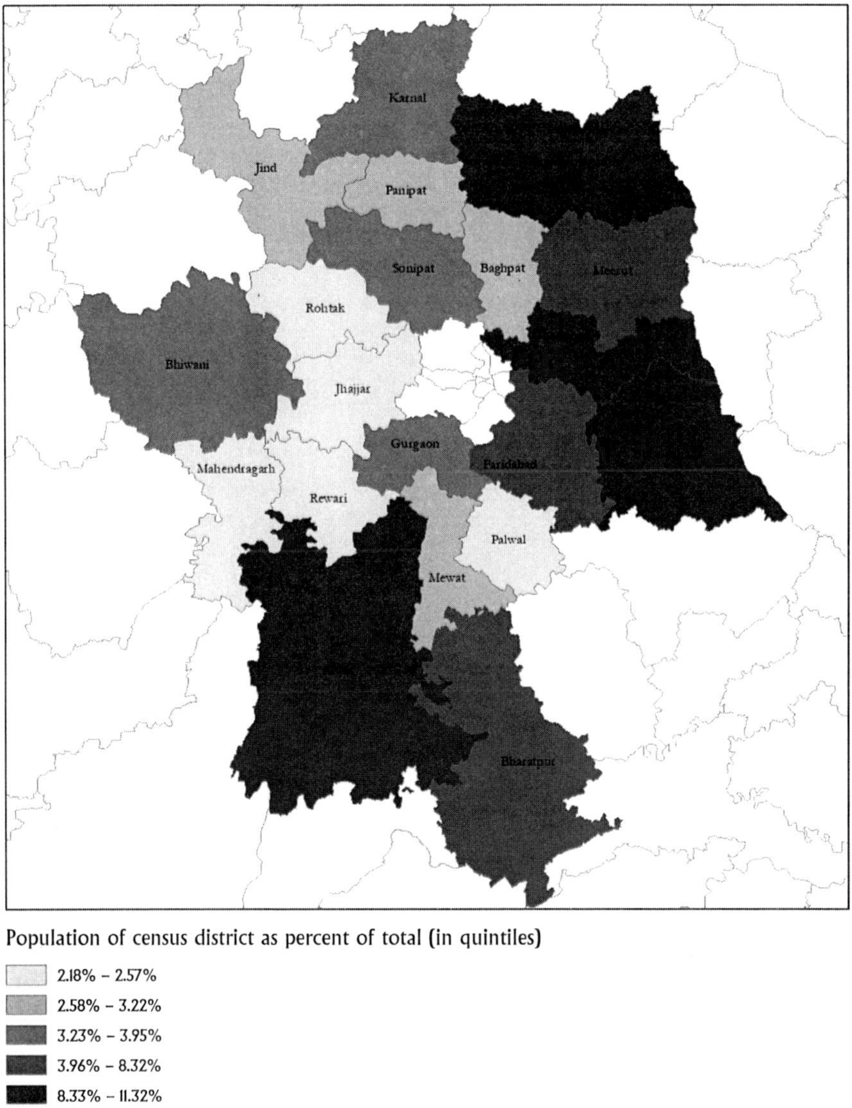

Population of census district as percent of total (in quintiles)

- 2.18% – 2.57%
- 2.58% – 3.22%
- 3.23% – 3.95%
- 3.96% – 8.32%
- 8.33% – 11.32%

Figure 1.9   District population in the NCR (as percent of total)
Source: Author's calculations from the Census of India, 2011.

the lowest proportion of the NCR population (2.17–2.56 percent), as seen in Figure 1.10.

Population density in the NCR also showed a variation of density clusters. Within rural areas, the population density ranged from 284.1 to 773.3

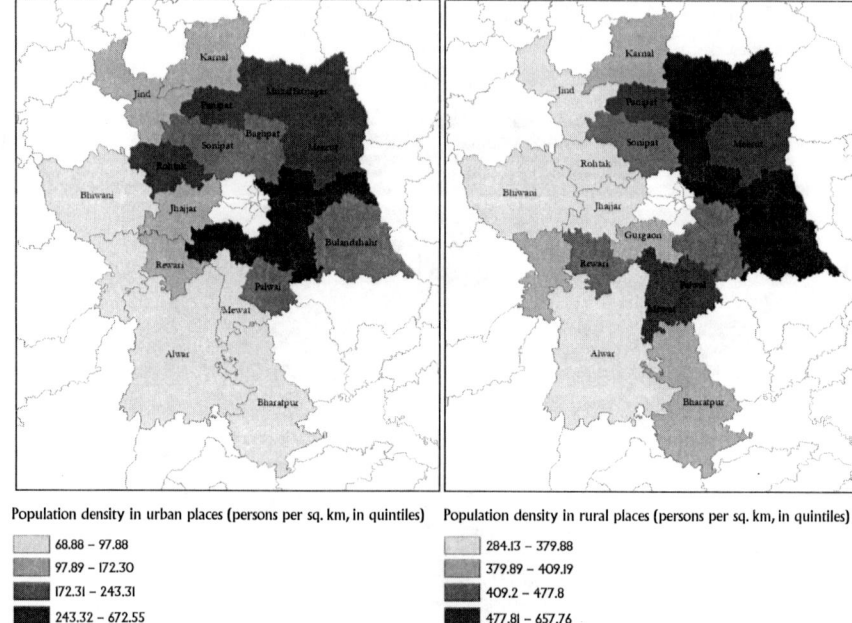

Population density in urban places (persons per sq. km, in quintiles)

	68.88 – 97.88
	97.89 – 172.30
	172.31 – 243.31
	243.32 – 672.55
	672.56 – 1710.06

Population density in rural places (persons per sq. km, in quintiles)

	284.13 – 379.88
	379.89 – 409.19
	409.2 – 477.8
	477.81 – 657.76
	657.77 – 773.3

Figure 1.10   Density of urban and rural population in the NCR
Source: Author's calculations from the Census of India, 2011.

persons per square kilometer. Urban areas indicate greater spatial variation of population density—the lowest quintile of population density is 68–156 persons per square kilometer and the highest quintile of population density is 842–1,710 persons per square kilometer. The NCR districts in UP are consistently part of high-quintile classes of urban and rural population densities. On the opposite side, Alwar's population falls under the lowest quintile of population density in both urban and rural areas, as mapped in Figure 1.10.

Similarly, the sociocultural tables released by the census (C-Series) reveal clusters of high- and low-population groups sorted by social identity and socioeconomic conditions, which include religion and caste information among others.

Outside the NCT, a large majority of the NCR is made of a population that identifies as Hindu. The percentage of such population varies in the range of 57–90 percent by district, except for Mewat, Haryana, where Hindus make up 20 percent of the population. Islam is the next dominant religion in the NCR. The Muslim population is relatively evenly distributed in UP, while Rohtak, Rewari, and Mahendragarh show consistently low proportions of

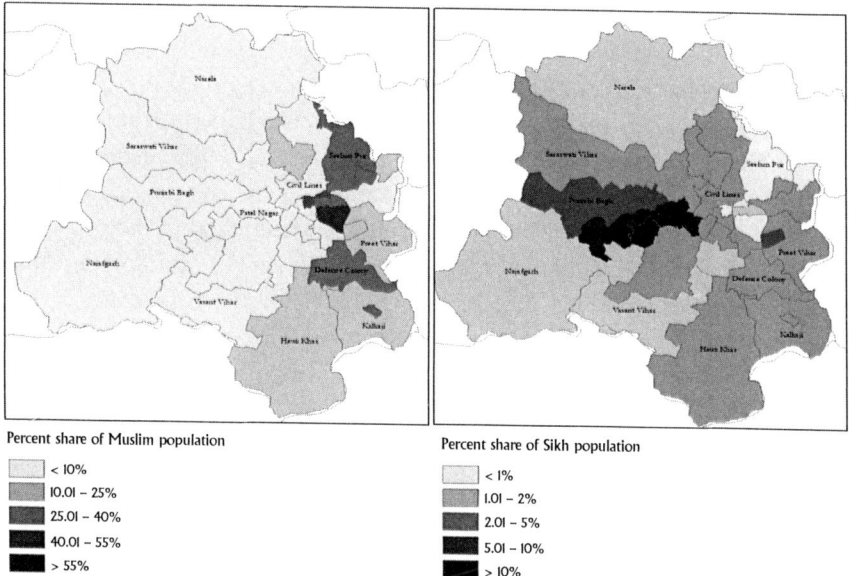

Percent share of Muslim population

	< 10%
	10.01 – 25%
	25.01 – 40%
	40.01 – 55%
	> 55%

Percent share of Sikh population

	< 1%
	1.01 – 2%
	2.01 – 5%
	5.01 – 10%
	> 10%

Figure 1.11   Distribution of Muslims (*left*) and Sikhs (*right*) in the NCT sub-districts
Source: Author's calculations from census data.

Muslims (<1 percent of the district population). Inside the NCT, Sikhs and Muslims have dominant localities, a vestige from its past. Within the NCT, the Muslim population is more concentrated in east Delhi. In sub-districts of Seelampur and Kotwali, 25–50 percent of the population identify themselves as Muslims. These figures go beyond 50 percent in Daryaganj. The Sikh population is concentrated around Punjabi Bagh, Patel Nagar, Rajouri Garden, and Karol Bagh (Figure 1.11).

The Centrality of Transportation

I end this chapter with a few words about transportation, which, as noted earlier, has been instrumental in the growth of the NCT and the NCR. In the precolonial era, waterways and roads played an important role in providing access to the Mughal capital and provided strategic routes for travelers in the East–West Corridor. The development of the railways during colonial rule solidified Delhi's locational importance as an important node on both the east–west and north–south routes. In the contemporary period, the locational importance of Delhi as a transportation hub cannot be emphasized enough. Transportation feeds the industrial corridors emanating from Delhi;

supports the production centers of the region; provides access to national and international markets; and has helped the growth of tourism, export industries, and higher education in Delhi.

In the last several decades, perhaps most conspicuously from the 1982 Asian Games held in the city, massive investments have been made in roads, rail, and most recently, metro rail infrastructure. These have provided support for regional economic development and been instrumental in increasing the physical spread of the region, perhaps hastening the need to think of the NCR as a planning entity.[29] The Gurgaon and Ghaziabad UAs are increasingly well-connected with central Delhi. These connections have become even stronger with the development of the Delhi Metro Rail Corporation (DMRC) and its extensions: Rapid Metro, Noida Metro, and Metro-Link to Bahadurgarh (Figure 1.12). Delhi Metro is viewed as a major success story, at least in terms

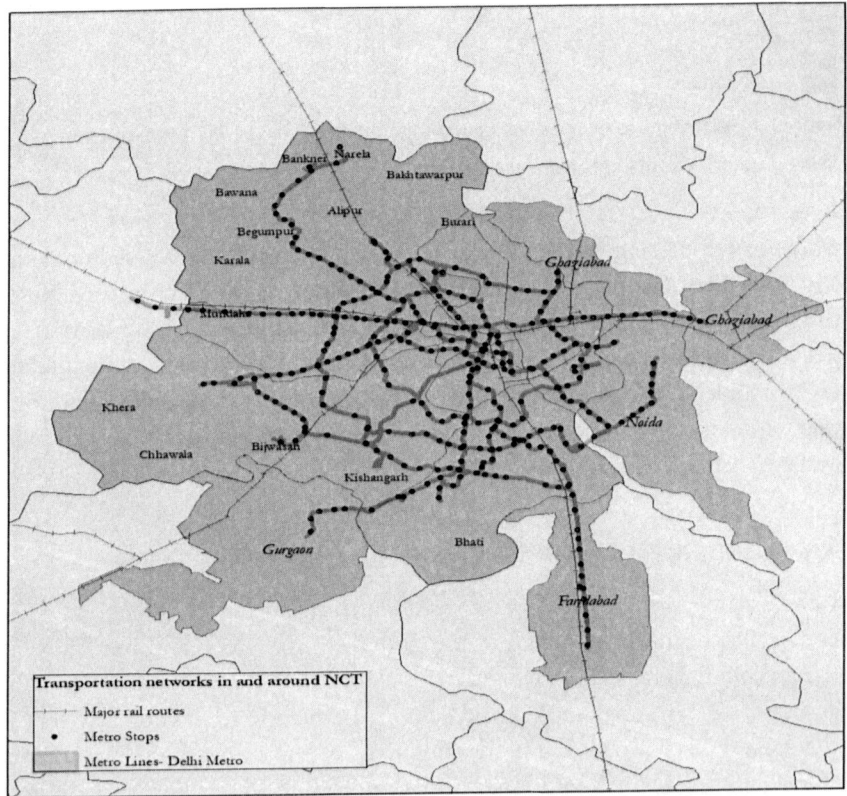

Figure 1.12   Transportation network in the NCR, including major roads (in gray) and metro stops (in black)

Source: Author.

of project implementation, with 285 fully functional stations and another 195 under development.[30] The Rapid Metro network of Gurgaon with 11 stations and the Noida Aqua Line with 21 stations are built to connect commuters to the DMRC network. Since its inception in 2000, the Delhi Metro has enlarged the possibility of rapid commuting in the region and created new multi-modal transportation options for daily commuters.

The story of Delhi is one of complex and heterogeneous growth—over time and space. The narrative of urban transformation from Shahjahanabad to Delhi, to the NCT, and to the NCR has been sometimes erratic, sometimes continuous, and, in recent decades, explosive. The words of Percival Spear still resonate: "After the people, came the city."

In IGP 1956, Amrit Kaur posed an important question—for an uncontrolled multi-jurisdictional space such as Delhi, how do we begin to define the region? Sixty-three years later, now that Delhi NCR is a vaster, even more complicated, heterogeneous space, we are yet to find a satisfactory answer. The heterogeneity explored in this chapter through multidisciplinary perspectives of history, Earth Observation, and demographic mapping points to a vast space that faces serious challenges brought on by extraordinary population growth and an uneven urban fabric. The remaining chapters in this volume take on some of these challenges.

Notes

1. See Gautam Bhan, "In the Public's Interest: Evictions, Citizenship and Inequality in Contemporary Delhi," (ProQuest Dissertations and Theses Global).
2. William Dalrymple, *City of Djinns: A Year in Delhi* (London: Harper Collins, 2011), Kindle edition, 85. In the book, Dalrymple identifies seven dead cities and the eighth city as the Delhi of today. Gordon Cullen's 1960 plan for the Ford Foundation Team and the Town Planning Organization was aptly named *The Ninth Delhi*.
3. Town Planning Organization, *Interim General Plan for Greater Delhi, 1956* (New Delhi: Ministry of Health and Family Welfare, 1956), i–v, available at http://ncrpb.nic.in/pdf_files/Interim%20General%20Plan%20for%20Greater%20Delhi.PDF, accessed on January 24, 2019.
4. The ruins of earlier capitals are now conserved in parts of Delhi around Jahanpanah City Forest.
5. In Delhi's urban history, this era is also referred to as the Twilight period.

6. Denis Vidal, Emma Tarlo, and Veronique Dupont, "The Alchemy of an Unloved City," in *Delhi: Urban Space and Human Destinies*, ed. Veronique Dupont, Emma Tarlo, and Denis Vidal (Delhi: Manohar, 2000), 15–28.

7. Thomas George Percival Spear, Narayani Gupta, and Robert Eric Frykenberg, *The Delhi Omnibus* (New Delhi: Oxford University Press, 2002).

8. Keith Johnston, *Keith Johnston's British Empire* (Edinburgh: W. E. A. K Johnston, n.d.).

9. Narayani Gupta, "Delhi and Its Hinterlands: The Nineteenth and Early Twentieth Centuries," in *Delhi through the Ages*, ed. R. E. Frykenberg (New Delhi: Oxford University Press, 1986), 139. In the next 100 years, the area would increase to 573 square miles to the present extent of the NCT.

10. Stephen Legg, "Governmentality, Congestion and Calculation in Colonial Delhi," *Social & Cultural Geography* 7, no. 5 (2006): 709–729, available at doi: 10.1080/13698240600974721. Legg argues that the construction of the railways was a way of deploying "governmentality" and strategically reducing the odds of another recurrence of the Sepoy Rebellion, whereas Narayani Gupta suggests that the project was part of famine relief efforts.

11. Narayani Gupta, "Delhi between Two Empires, 1803–1931: Society, Government and Urban Growth," in *The Delhi Omnibus*, ed. Thomas George Percival Spear, Narayani Gupta, and Robert Eric Frykenberg (New Delhi: Oxford University Press, 2002), 43.

12. Ibid., 43.

13. A. G. Krishna Menon, "The Contemporary Architecture of Delhi: The Role of the State as Middleman," in *Delhi: Urban Space and Human Destinies*, ed. Veronique Dupont, Emma Tarlo, and Denis Vidal (Delhi: Manohar, 2000), 147.

14. Northern Delhi was site to some of the famous Mughal gardens under Shahjehan's rule. Dalrymple recounts the story of the deterioration and disrepair of these gardens in *City of Djinns*, 197–200. See also Awadhendra Sharan's essay in this volume, *Vitiated Airs*.

15. Michael Mann and Samiksha Sehrawat, "A City with a View: The Afforestation of the Delhi Ridge, 1883–1913," *Modern Asian Studies* 43, no. 2 (2009): 543–570, available at doi:10.1017/S0026749X07002867. See also Narayani Gupta, "Introduction," in *The Delhi Omnibus*, ed. Thomas George Percival Spear, Narayani Gupta, and Robert Eric Frykenberg (New Delhi: Oxford University Press, 2002), xiv–xv.

16. Menon, "The Contemporary Architecture of Delhi," 148.

17. A. Bopegamage, *Delhi: A Study in Urban Sociology* (Bombay: University of Bombay, 1956), 51, available at https://archive.org/details/in.gov.ignca.15045/page/n19, accessed on January 25, 2019. Bopegamage also notes that the

population density of Old Delhi Municipality was 132,555 persons per square mile (approximately 51,182 persons per square kilometer) in the 1951 Census. The total population in Mehrauli, Narela, and Najafgarh (then satellite townships) remained under 10,000.

18. Town Planning Organization, *Interim General Plan for Greater Delhi*, iii.

19. Menon, "The Contemporary Architecture of Delhi," 149–150.

20. Ibid., 151–153.

21. Anita Soni, "Urban Conquest of Outer Delhi: Beneficiaries, Intermediaries and Victims: The Case of Mehrauli Countryside," in *Delhi: Urban Space and Human Destinies*, ed. Veronique Dupont, Emma Tarlo, and Denis Vidal (Delhi: Manohar, 2000).

22. Veena Talwar Oldenburg, *Gurgaon: From Mythic Village to Millennium City* (Harper Collins, 2018), Kindle edition.

23. Philippe Cadène, "Delhi's Place in India's Urban Structure," in *Delhi: Urban Space and Human Destinies*, ed. Veronique Dupont, Emma Tarlo, and Denis Vidal (Delhi: Manohar, 2000), 241–244.

24. McKinsey Global Institute, *India's Urban Awakening: Building Inclusive Cities Sustaining Economic Growth* (McKinsey & Co, 2010), 16, available at https://www.mckinsey.com/~/media/mckinsey/featured%20insights/urbanization/urban%20awakening%20in%20india/mgi_indias_urban_awakening_full_report.ashx, accessed on September 10, 2020.

25. Ankita Choudhary and Milap Punia, "Urban Form and Regional Development of National Capital Region," in *Marginalization in Globalizing Delhi: Issues of Land, Livelihoods and Health*, ed. Sanghmitra Acharya, Sucharita Sen, Milap Punia, and Sunita Reddy (New Delhi: Springer, 2017), 43–66. Choudhary and Punia conclude, "The cities with good connectivity and as part of NCT's contiguous spread have higher degree of complexity in the shape. These towns experienced greater expansion because of urban growth and benefits out of urban agglomeration economics."

26. X. Li, C. Elvidge, Y. Y. Zhou, C. Y. Cao, and T. Warner, "Remote Sensing of Night-Time Light," *International Journal of Remote Sensing* 38, no. 21 (2017): 5855–5859, available at https://doi.org/10.1080/01431161.2017.1351784.

27. Chandra Prakash Morya and Milap Punia, "Ecosystem Services in NCT Delhi," in *Marginalization in Globalizing Delhi: Issues of Land, Livelihoods and Health*, ed. Sanghmitra Acharya, Sucharita Sen, Milap Punia, and Sunita Reddy (New Delhi: Springer, 2017), 81–96.

28. Janhvi Pahnanchikal, "Why the Aravalli Forest Range is the Most Degraded Zone in India," *Outdoor Journal*, September 20, 2018, available at https://www.outdoorjournal.com/uncategorized/aravalli-forest-range-degraded-zone-india/, accessed on May 20, 2020.

29. Matti Siemiatycki, "Message in a Metro: Building Urban Rail Infrastructure and Image in Delhi, India," *International Journal of Urban and Regional Research* 30, no. 2 (2006): 277–292.
30. M. Ramachandran, *Metro Rail Projects in India: A Study in Project Planning* (New Delhi: Oxford University Press, 2011).

CHAPTER 2

Assets and Spatial Inequality

Neelanjan Sircar

Introduction

India is now the fastest urbanizing country in the world, and such urbanization is typically associated with opportunities for greater income, education, and social mobility.[1] But the city is far from a monolithic whole; it encompasses makeshift slums to wealthy gated neighborhoods and everything in between. It is becoming increasingly clear that simply "growing up in a city" has little meaning—*where* you grow up in the city matters a lot for a bevy of social and economic outcomes.[2] At the same time, global capital is engendering unprecedented inequalities in economic well-being,[3] and rising land prices in many cities are pushing disadvantaged populations to the fringes of urban areas.[4]

If the disadvantaged are systematically pushed to the urban periphery, they are likely to be "peripheral" to the social gains from urban growth, a phenomenon that has already been observed in many Western cities and urban agglomerations.[5] Under these circumstances, disadvantaged populations benefit little from investment in the urban core and remain segregated from wealthier residents and their tools of wealth generation; there is a genuine fear that urbanization does little for the social mobility of the disadvantaged in such a scenario. The National Capital Region (NCR) has seen soaring land prices and incomes since the 1990s along with very high rates of in-migration, exactly the conditions under which one might expect increasing peripheralization of disadvantaged populations. For these reasons, understanding the spatial distribution of marginalized caste/religious groups and economic well-being at the scale of the entire NCR is of critical importance.[6]

There are, however, good reasons to believe that the described model of "spatial inequality" and peripheralization in the previous paragraph does not translate well to the NCR or many urban contexts in the Global South. Classic models of urban spatial inequality have largely been developed in the West and are typically imbued with a very particular understanding of racial and immigrant relations. The experience of India's marginalized urban communities, namely Scheduled Castes (SCs) and Muslims, (while deeply problematic) cannot be easily compared to the black experience in America or the immigrant experience in Europe.[7] Furthermore, much of the Western urban experience is drawn from contexts with a largely formal labor market, with workers that had explicit contractual relationships with factories, a far cry from the present Indian context where more than 90 percent of the labor force is in the informal sector.[8] Indeed, a great many scholars have noticed that cities of the Global South "look different" from their Western counterparts—often with permanent, wealthy colonies located adjacent to makeshift, poorer colonies—but much of this literature is focused on the aesthetic quality of cities. For instance, the study of "informal urbanism" analyzes the urbanization process as it operates outside of formal rules and regulations. Here, the word "informal" is neither a description of social nor labor relations in contrast to formal, contractual relationships.[9] While the "urban turn" in Indian sociology has yielded many insights on Indian urbanization,[10] there remains much to do in order to broaden our understanding of the complex patterns of spatial inequalities in Indian cities and the social relations and conflicts that undergird them.

The core aim of this chapter is to move beyond descriptive differences in the patterns of urbanization in Indian cities as compared to many Western cities, that is, those in North America or Europe, and to provide a hypothesis as to why these differences are observed. I argue that the structure of economic transactions between wealthy and poor citizens in Indian cities generate incentives for *spatial co-location* between wealthy and poor citizens. In simple terms, spatial proximity between the provider of labor and the consumer of labor acts as an enforcement mechanism in a universe of largely informal contracts, causing the poor to settle near the wealthy in Indian cities (often in the core of the city).

This is not to deny that spatial inequalities in Indian cities are also shaped by pre-modern pasts and caste and religious conflict, but these are issues that strongly shape spatial inequalities in rural India as well—and generate a baseline level of inequality in Indian cities. A focus on the structure of economic relations, and how these relations have changed over the last two decades, sheds light on the *dynamics* of spatial inequality in urban India. This is of particular importance in a "city-state" such as Delhi where 2011 Indian Census estimates that more than a third of its residents are born elsewhere. A place such as the NCR, with large migrant inflows, is experiencing perpetual demographic transformations of its neighborhoods.

The challenge in providing an empirical characterization of spatial inequality at the level of an urban agglomeration stems from a lack of fine-grained data that allow for nuanced claims over as large and complex a spatial terrain as the NCR. Unlike many Western countries, which can provide census or survey data on income at a very local scale, no such data source exists in India. The Indian census does not provide economic wealth data, and household asset data from the census cannot be disaggregated beyond the municipal ward (with widely varying population size and an average population of over 60,000 per ward in Delhi in 2011). The National Sample Survey (NSS) provides detailed economic data, but the sample size is neither large enough in the NCR nor is the data geo-coded,[11] so estimations of spatial inequality are difficult. The CASI–NCR Survey provides asset data on a representative sample of nearly 5,500 households in the NCR, the vast majority of which are geo-coded. This provides sufficient data, in tandem with appropriate statistical models, to provide the first known measurement of spatial inequalities in caste, religion, and economic well-being at the scale of the NCR.

This chapter describes how Indian villages, in which spatial location is almost completely a function of caste and religion, differ from spatial location in Indian cities, where a potential for conflict undergirds urban spatial location of caste and religious groups. But urban Indian space is not as segregated by caste and religion as the Indian village and it is not the fundamental basis upon which neighborhoods are organized; spatial location in the city is fundamentally transformed by informal, trust-based social and economic interactions between poor and wealthy citizens. Thus, the Indian urban population is likely to sort in a way that keeps the wealthy and poor in close spatial proximity.

This empirical argument proceeds in three steps. First, I look at spatial segregation by caste and religion in the NCR using data from the CASI–NCR Survey. Then, I characterize wealth inequality by caste and religion. Finally, I show that the levels of wealth inequality due to spatial co-location are greater than what can be explained by caste and religion—suggesting a further economic dimension to spatial location of the NCR's residents beyond the role of identity. More precisely, while there is significant ghettoization of the SC and Muslim communities (with far greater ghettoization of the Muslim community), the scale of inequality across rich and poor residential clusters in spatial proximity is greater than inequality purely due to religion and caste. This suggests that, unlike Indian villages, the clustering of poverty and wealth in the NCR is not simply an identity-based phenomenon but one that is rooted in the nature of economic exchange between citizens.

The Study of Urban Spatial Inequality

The modern empirical study of urban space can be traced to the University of Chicago in the early 20th century (the "Chicago School"), which used the US city of Chicago as a laboratory to understand processes of urbanization. At the time, the Chicago and New York City metropolitan areas were undergoing significant expansion through migration and urban planning. Parallels to the current growth of urban studies in India, and the present study of the NCR, should be noted.

The Chicago School focused on characterizing the impact of social and spatial structures on human behavior—in contrast to the prevailing orthodoxy at the time which viewed social behavior as primarily being driven by individual-level biological, demographic, or psychological factors. The explicit spatialization of social behavior from an empirical perspective is evident in the views of Chicago School stalwart Robert E. Park:

> It is because social relations are so frequently and so inevitably correlated with spatial relations; because physical distances so frequently are, or seem to be, the indexes of social distances, that statistics have any significance whatever for sociology.[12]

This theoretical orientation led to a research agenda at multiple spatial scales, from the neighborhood to the overall organization of urban space across neighborhoods. Ernest Burgess, in laying out the macro-spatial vision of the Chicago School, envisioned cities as naturally tending toward a series of concentric circles emanating from a core business district. Surrounding the core business district would be an area of deprivation followed by an area of industrial workers. The periphery of the city would consist of high-end residential homes and suburban commuters. Cities would tend to this core-periphery equilibrium through the transformative power of real estate and land prices:

> Our investigations so far seem to indicate that variations in land values, especially where correlated with differences in rents, offer perhaps the best single measure of mobility, and so of all the changes taking place in the expansion and growth of the city.[13]

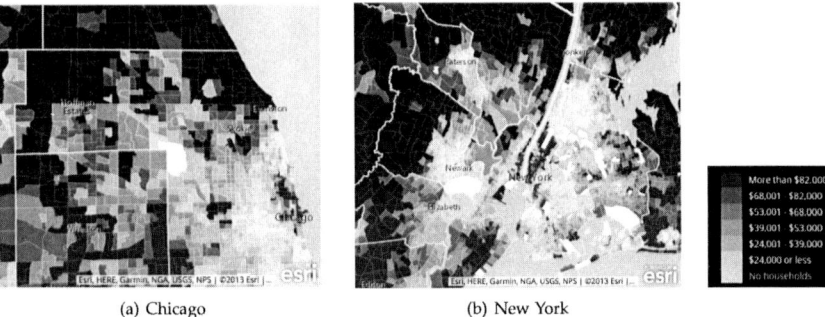

(a) Chicago   (b) New York

Figure 2.1 Spatial inequality in Chicago and New York City in 2013

Source: ESRI project located at: https://www.arcgis.com/home/item.html?id=3fb082c63cl9 4b34893lelbbe2a94c65.

Notes: The maps (a, b) display spatial inequality provided by the Esri SmartMaps project of urban census tracts in the USA. The darker the shade, the wealthier the tract. Both cities show a concentric circle pattern with a wealthy core.

A century after their investigations into urban life, the observations of the Chicago School on core–periphery settlement patterns and the power of land prices are deeply influential.[14] Figure 2.1 displays spatial inequalities in Chicago and New York, from Esri's SmartMaps project, over US census tracts. Each of these cities displays a wealthy core ("The Loop" in Chicago and Manhattan in New York City), followed by a ring of poverty, extending out to a wealthier outer ring of suburbs. These patterns are broadly consistent with concentric circles of poverty and wealth, as hypothesized by the Chicago School.

Insights from the Chicago School have been important for theorists of urban gentrification. In his influential essay "The Right to the City," David Harvey details the process of extending the wealthy core and pushing the poor to the periphery in New York City "through fiscal disciplining of democratic urban governments, land markets, property speculation and the sorting of land to those uses that generated the highest possible financial rate of return under the land's 'highest and best use'."[15] Indeed, as Harvey evocatively describes, this is a process that has taken place in most Western cities.

But this core–periphery conception of urban space, and the mechanisms associated with it, does not fit Indian urban realities very well. Harvey makes scant mention of Indian cities in his piece, only describing the impending demolition of Dharavi, one of Asia's largest slums, due to the value of the land upon which it sits in Mumbai's urban core. (Dharavi is still very much standing.) Urban land and real estate prices are also growing rapidly in India,[16] but the spatial organization of most Indian cities does not seem to respond in the same manner, with a hodgepodge of wealthy and poor neighborhoods usually located side by side. These sorts of observations have led some theorists to call for the development of new urban theory for the Global South.[17] If land prices and incomes in the NCR are soaring, and a large number of migrants are being drawn to the area, what prevents the NCR from following the pattern of Chicago or New York City?

Spatial Organization of Caste and Religion in the National Capital Region

While the Chicago School is often credited with the first rigorous studies of the social construction of race and assimilation (discarding the explicitly racist theories that were prevalent at the time), the core–periphery theory of spatial settlement is striking in the absence of race in many of its conceptualizations. The USA's experience with identity politics has largely been a function of the extraordinary institutionalized racism perpetrated against its black population, and today, it is well-understood that the spatial patterns observed in American cities have much to do with the relations between white and black populations. In particular, the so-called "white flight" describes a large-scale migration of urban white populations in the post–World War II period to the "suburbs," leaving a ring of poor black neighborhoods in the city.[18] To be sure, core–periphery patterns are also observed in cities in European nation-states without these racial dynamics, but even then, many of these core–periphery phenomena seem to be driven by a contentious politics against immigrants.[19] Yet, the American experience with race—as opposed to immigration—is in principle a better comparison for India's identity politics because, like the black community, India's SCs and Muslims are not "outsiders."[20] At the same time, India's experience with identity politics is fundamentally different than that of America.

To grapple with the role of identity in the spatial organization of any Indian city/urban agglomeration, one should begin by contrasting Indian urban space with the Indian village. Indian villages are traditionally divided into caste-specific neighborhoods (often referred to as a *tola* or *para*). When a particular caste group (*jati*) is sufficiently numerous, this form of spatial clustering leads to a neighborhood being perfectly identified with the caste group.[21] For instance, local villagers will simply use the name Yadav Tola to denote the neighborhood inhabited by the Yadav caste. Even when a caste group is not sufficiently numerous, it will typically locate in a neighborhood with other caste groups of similar social status. Thus, in Indian villages, the basis for spatial location is explicitly caste (and sometimes religious) identity. Settlement patterns in Indian cities, and thus urban space, are quite different. To be sure, history, status hierarchies, and caste networks may lead to significant identity-based clustering in cities, but identity need not be the explicit basis for spatial location in most urban areas. For instance, the Delhi neighborhood of Malviya Nagar is not explicitly intended to be dedicated to a single caste or religious group, even if particular groups might be more numerous. More to the point, whatever Malviya Nagar's demographic composition may have been when it was founded in the 1950s (by refugees from Pakistan), its population has changed significantly as Delhi has continued to grow.

How do the identities of caste and religion manifest themselves in the city and structure spatial location? In a recent study on the spatial location of Muslims in Delhi, Gayer argues that Delhi's Muslim community often practices "self-segregation" for greater security under the threat of communal (religious) violence. The author quotes a journalist who sums up the principle succinctly:

My brother ... lived in a Hindu *mohalla*. Madan Lal Khurana, who would later become Chief Minister of Delhi, led Hindu mobs which threatened Zakir Bagh. My brother and his family decided to move to Noop Nagar [a Muslim dominated locality of Jamia Nagar].... Now, nobody feels threatened any longer.[22]

While caste discrimination is still practiced in urban areas, there is significantly less threat of such large-scale urban violence along caste lines. The reasons for this disjuncture between religious and caste violence are not easy to discern. It may, however, be stated, as a matter of fact, that anti-Muslim violence has been a common tool for urban political mobilization, particularly in north India, whereas the same cannot be said of anti-SC violence (this is not to deny the scale of anti-Dalit violence in India or previous caste riots across India).[23] Thus, while SC neighborhoods in *bastis* (slums) are still prevalent, one does not expect the same level of ghettoization of the SC population as for the Muslim population due to this form of violence in a place like the NCR.

And yet while Muslim ghettos are prominent in many Indian cities, such ghettos often neither constitute the "inner city" nor the "periphery" as they do in so many American cities—indeed many Muslim ghettos are located very close to wealthy, Hindu areas, and studies of caste/religious segregation in

India have not found the level of segregation faced by the black community in America.[24] As Frey describes, the spatial separation between blacks and whites was aided in large part by discriminatory institutions and housing policies in the suburbs.[25] If, in urban India, groups that display animosity toward each other, and have very different economic profiles, continue to live in close proximity to each other, it is important to understand the social processes that lead to such a spatial organization of the population.

Socioeconomic Sorting and Heterogeneity in the National Capital Region

In one of the earliest empirical analyses of urban space, Berry and Spodek find that socioeconomic status is the chief determinant of spatial location in a detailed study of six Indian cities.[26] For instance, conducting a temporal analysis of urban space, they argue that even though religion was the basis of spatial location in the Indian city of Pune in 1822, by 1937 socioeconomic status was the chief determinant in sorting populations. Working in Trilokpuri–Mayur Vihar in eastern Delhi, Veronique Dupont reports a "segregated mixture" of different socioeconomic classes due to an economic strategy of underprivileged groups to locate close to a wealthy population to take advantage of the latter's dependence on labor. This work represents the most careful empirical work to date on urban space within the NCR, noting residential segregation on a fine scale with "wide socio-economic variety of settlements and residents at the level of a zone."[27] At the same time, due to data constraints in economic data and geo-location, these observations cannot map the socioeconomic mixture at the macro-spatial scale of an urban agglomeration—making the explicit comparison between Indian urban space and traditional core–periphery models challenging. That is, even if zones are internally differentiated, the spatial organization of the urban agglomeration may still tend toward a core–periphery dynamic based on the relative proportion of socioeconomic classes in each zone.

The underlying assumption in the Chicago School framework, as discussed earlier, is the power of real estate and land prices to structure residence in the city. The space and distance play a role in spatial location for residents insofar as it structures the physical and opportunity costs of travel to work. This means the poor are often willing to move to a cheaper, more peripheral location if the increased costs related to travel are not too onerous. The phenomenon of "pricing out" the poor is a remarkably efficient way of creating a core–periphery settlement pattern.

But unlike the context studied by the Chicago School, and other theorists of urban space in the West, the relationship between citizens, labor, and services in India is largely in the informal sector. This means that bonds between employer and employee are often shaped by trust and regular interaction, rather than a formal contractual relationship. To the extent that these bonds of trust and interaction are shaped by physical distance, the spatially proximate location of rich and poor, employer and employee, can be sustained and population sorting purely based on land prices can be mitigated.

A simple example will help clarify the principle. Until recently, if one wished to return home late at night from many of Delhi's wealthy "colonies," he or she would have to rely on the local taxi stand. These taxi stands were located near the colony and could be trusted to regularly ferry people in and out of the colony safely at all hours of the day. As "aggregator services" such as Uber and Ola have gained in popularity, taxi drivers have shifted to driving for these services and taxi stands are disappearing around Delhi. The aggregator services match a potential passenger with a driver based on a contractual relationship operating on mobile phones and backed by the code of conduct of the company (although safety concerns persist). The co-location (or previous interaction) of driver and passenger is no longer needed as it was before. While the taxi industry may be changing, informal bonds of trust are still largely required for domestic help, house repairs, and many commercial transactions, from those who live nearby. Many important interactions between citizens in the NCR are based on these informal bonds of trust, from whom to invite for dinner in the home to whom to approach to solve a neighborhood-level grievance. Much of this volume is dedicated to empirically characterizing these trust-based interactions.

From the previous discussion, one can cull two basic conditions under which a more spatially heterogeneous pattern than core–periphery settlement will be observed. First, there must be an explicit incentive for labor, service, or otherwise economically/socially dependent classes to locate near a population with high economic consumption (net of costs of living and transportation)— even if they are from caste and religious groups that display animosity toward each other. Second, those with high economic consumption must display a preference to use labor or service that is spatially proximate. Under these conditions, the basis for residential clustering is forthrightly socioeconomic and not based on identity. Importantly, even if the wealthy do not desire to live near poorer settlements such as *basti*s, as is typically the case, the very structure of socioeconomic dependence guarantees a spatially heterogeneous pattern of settlement.

Hypotheses

In sum, two concrete hypotheses may be discerned from this explanation of spatial inequalities in the NCR:

H1. *Socioeconomic spatial clustering*: If socioeconomic status, and not identity (caste or religion), is the basis for the relative location of urban residential clusters, then identity-based economic inequality should be less pronounced than spatial inequalities.

H2. *Informal bonds of trust*: If economic and social dependencies are driven by informal bonds of trust, then there should be spatially proximate location of rich and poor residential clusters and less of a pronounced core–periphery residential pattern.

Economic Well-Being in the National Capital Region

This section describes the approach to the measurement of economic well-being that will be used throughout the volume. At the outset, it should be noted that measuring income, consumption, expenditure, assets, or any other correlate of economic well-being from household surveys is known to be difficult, especially in developing countries such as India. According to the International Labour Organisation, more than 90 percent of India's workforce is engaged in informal labor, yielding intermittent and unstable income from many sources. In such contexts, households typically "smooth" their expenditure and consumption over the year, so measures of regular consumption are thought to be more closely related to economic well-being.[28] Even then, consumption patterns are likely to be highly uneven throughout the year, so the reporting can be noisy or flawed. More problematically, much of this income may come from legally dubious transactions or remain undeclared for taxation purposes, so households have little incentive to truthfully report their incomes or expenditures. For this reason, the core measure of economic well-being used throughout this volume is an index constructed from household assets, many of which are directly observable to the surveyor. Furthermore, the set of assets at a household's regular disposal is arguably a more meaningful measure of well-being than more volatile income/expenditure flows.

Figure 2.2 displays the percentage of households in the NCR owning selected assets, alongside a comparison with data collected from the urban sample of the 66th round (2010–2011) of the NSS. The NSS was chosen for the comparison because it is a recent large-scale, high-quality survey that collects

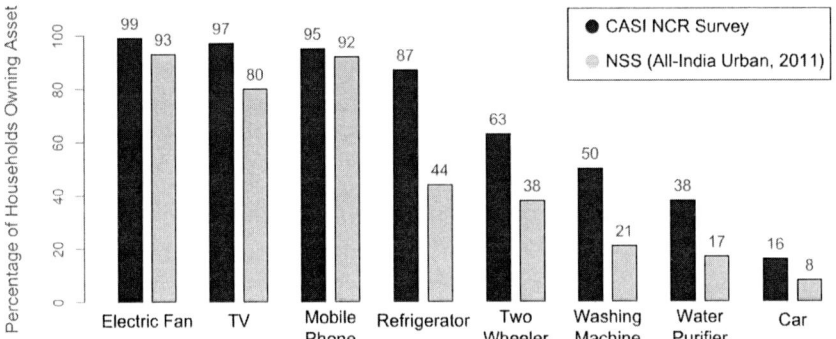

Figure 2.2   Selected household assets in the NCR versus urban India

Source: Author's calculations from the CASI–NCR Survey data.

Note: The graph displays the percentage of households owning specified assets and compares these values to those obtained for urban India in the 66th round (2010–2011) of the NSS. The NCR displays greater levels of wealth, with much higher ownership of rarely owned assets.

data on the specified assets (unlike the Indian census). It is worth noting that there is little agreement between the census and various nationwide sample surveys on asset ownership. Furthermore, because the NSS estimates are from several years ago, one should expect a higher rate of present asset ownership than reported in the NSS data. Nonetheless, even accounting for a reasonable rate of growth in asset ownership in recent years, the NCR is likely far wealthier than the rest of urban India.

In the NCR sample, there is a near full penetration of electric fans, televisions, and mobile phones. Across more rarely owned assets, the NCR sample registers almost double the ownership rates of the NSS urban sample in 2011. Such assets not only point to a higher standard of living but also may have wealth-generating effects. Significantly greater ownership of refrigerators and water purifiers likely yields health benefits and may register an economic impact by reducing health costs and days of work lost. In the NCR, where wages are among the highest in India, the opportunity cost of time away from work is particularly high. Ownership of two wheelers (motorcycles or scooters), cars, and washing machines allows one to spend less time on travel and household work. On the whole, a large share of households in the NCR now demonstrate a pattern of asset ownership consistent with a robust middle class. For instance, the washing machine has been singled out as an object of middle-class aspiration;[29] today, the median household in the NCR owns one.

Constructing the Asset Index

The CASI–NCR Survey collected information on a large number of assets and it can be difficult to summarize the level of economic well-being from these assets in a parsimonious manner. It is, thus, preferable to construct a single index of economic well-being from the assets and to do so in a manner that minimizes researcher discretion. In order to construct the index, a two-parameter item response model is estimated from the data. The item response approach described here provides an intuitive, statistically robust method of calculating indices of economic well-being. Although the model is equivalent to a specific parameterization of confirmatory factor analysis,[30] in practice much of the factor analysis used is not statistically equivalent to the two-parameter item response model.[31] Factor analysis focuses on modeling the correlation structure between variables in an index, but the actual protocol in constructing indices, the so-called "factor scores," can be unclear. By contrast, the item response approach is focused on estimating the index directly. The remainder of this section is devoted to providing some intuition for how the model works and the economic well-being index outputted from it.

The model estimates three kinds of *parameters*: asset parameters, discrimination parameters, and the asset index for each household. The first step in the model is to determine how much information owning a particular asset gives about wealth within the sample. Looking at Figure 2.2, almost 9 in 10 households own a refrigerator, so owning this asset says little about wealth. On the other hand, only 4 in 10 households own a water purifier, so owning a water purifier may say more about wealth. Notice, the relationship between wealth and the asset has nothing to do with the relative price or cost of the asset (a refrigerator may very well cost more than a water purifier) but rather the relative likelihood of ownership. Figure 2.3 provides a visualization of the two-parameter item response model. A single dimension, poor to rich (left to right) is envisioned. The asset parameters denote the relative contribution of the asset to wealth. Because refrigerators are widely owned, the refrigerator parameter is placed far to the left, while the water purifier parameter (more rarely owned) is placed further to the right. Intuitively, a household that has exactly the same asset index score as the asset parameter has a 50 percent of owning the asset, for example, a household with an asset index score at the "water purifier point" would have a 50 percent chance of owning a water purifier. Naturally, a household that has an even chance of owning a water purifier is likely wealthier than a household with an even chance of owning

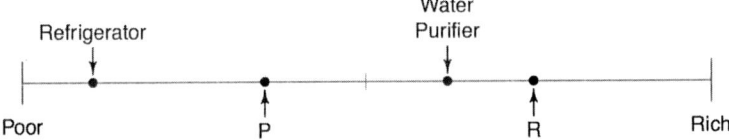

Figure 2.3 The two-parameter item response model
Source: Author.

a refrigerator, explaining the relative location of the refrigerator and water purifier asset parameters.

After plotting each of the asset parameters on the poor–rich dimension, the asset index score for each household is estimated from the pattern of assets owned by the household. Consider two households, P and R. The pattern of ownership indicates that P is likely to own a refrigerator but unlikely to own a water purifier. Then, the asset index score for P will be between the asset parameters for the refrigerator and the water purifier as P has more than a 50 percent chance of owning a refrigerator and less than a 50 percent chance of owning a water purifier. If the pattern of ownership indicates that R is likely to own both a refrigerator and a water purifier, then the asset index score for R will be placed to the right of both of the asset parameters for the refrigerator and the water purifier. This example is depicted in Figure 2.3.

Finally, the model estimates discrimination parameters, which denote the weight of the asset in the estimated asset index. Intuitively, the presence of certain assets will indicate a wealthier household, even if many wealthy households choose to forego owning the asset. For instance, the landline phone is associated with wealth but many wealthy households may have chosen to cut their landline connections due to mobile phones. In such a case, while the asset parameter for the landline may be placed toward the right of the dimension (only 7 percent of households in the sample have a landline), a low discrimination parameter for the landline would make sure it has little impact on the estimated asset index for households. The inclusion of a discrimination parameter means that the model is less sensitive to which assets are included (and the discretion of the researcher) for index creation, as the model will automatically decide what is and what is not important for the index.

Intuition about the Asset Index

Because the index is constructed through a statistical model, it can be difficult to develop an intuitive feel for the asset index. It should be noted that even the measures of income and expenditure do not have any meaning in and of themselves for measuring inequality without proper adjustment for costs of living and relative wages. The remainder of this section provides some intuition for the constructed index.

For this volume, an asset index was created from whether the household owned the following 15 assets: air conditioner, desktop computer, laptop computer, tablet, Wi-Fi internet connection, dongle (a computer attachment for internet access), landline phone, two wheeler (motorcycle/scooter), water purifier, microwave oven, DVD player, smartphone (that is, phone with internet), car, refrigerator, and washing machine. Other assets such as electric coolers, televisions, and electric fans were not included because of high levels of ownership across the sample that did not differentiate well between households. Nonetheless, the estimates for the asset index did not seem particularly sensitive to alternate baskets of assets. All item response models were estimated in Bayesian framework through the program JAGS, called through the statistical framework R.

Figure 2.4a depicts the estimated distribution of the asset index over the sample using a kernel density plot. The distribution displays a central tendency around zero, with some small deviations from a true normal distribution, as it is somewhat skewed to the right with slight non-monotonicity at values less than zero. The standard deviation of the distribution is approximately 0.875. Because the raw index values have little meaning, it is often easiest to report changes in this assets measure as differences in percentiles (as done in this chapter) or in the number of standard deviations of the underlying index distribution.

Figure 2.4b depicts the relationship, estimated from a bivariate binary logistic regression, with 95 percent predictive intervals of the index to three selected assets: refrigerator, washing machine, and car. The bounds on the horizontal axis correspond to the 5th and 95th percentiles of the asset index. Graphs such as this are useful tools to move back and forth between the index and a profile of assets. For instance, in this index a value of 0.5 is associated with a probability of ownership of 0.995, 0.781, and 0.153 for refrigerators, washing machines, and cars, respectively. This sort of calculation can be made for each asset in the asset index at every value in the index. This also demonstrates the essence of index creation in this setting. There is a positive association between the ownership of assets, that is, a higher probability of owning a washing machine is associated with a higher probability of owning a car, albeit with very different probabilities. The item response model extracts this common association between the ownership of various assets, while accounting for differences in the relative likelihood of owning each asset.

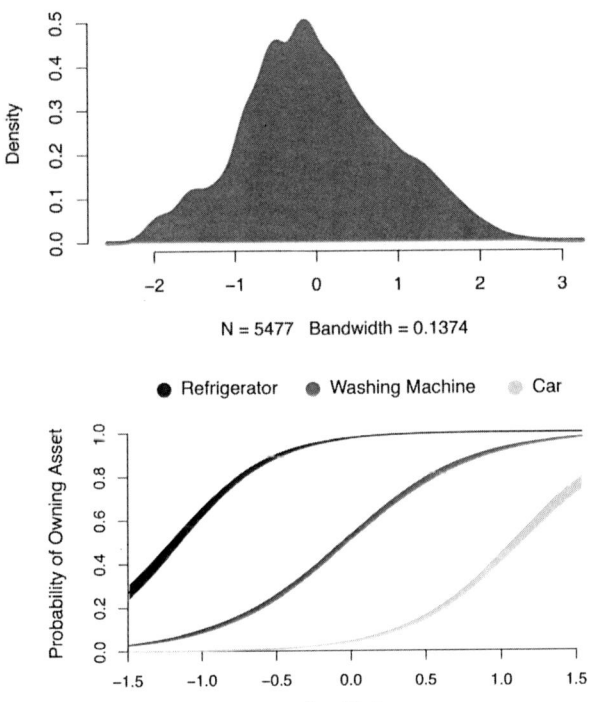

Figure 2.4 Understanding the asset index

Source: Author's calculations from the CASI–NCR Survey data.

Notes: (a) The graph in the top panel displays a kernel density plot of the asset index, showing a distribution of values with a central tendency. (b) The graph in the bottom panel displays the relationship, estimated from a bivariate binary logistic regression, with 95 percent predictive intervals of the index to three selected assets: refrigerator, washing machine, and car. In all cases, there is a positive relationship to the index, although with very different estimated probabilities of ownership.

Identity-Based Inequality and Ghettoization

This section looks at the role of identity, that is, caste and religion, in the NCR. Of particular interest is the spatial distribution and economic wealth/poverty of disadvantaged communities, namely the SC and Muslim communities. Indeed, if certain communities are highly spatially "clustered," one would say that the community is ghettoized. The spatial distribution of identity matters because the opportunity to interact across different caste or religious groups is likely to attenuate group inequality and biases.[32] Furthermore, the distribution of economic wealth by identity group allows one to determine the extent to which inequalities persist across identity groups.

The sample includes 5,449 households that provided usable religion information of which 86.2 percent are Hindus, 10.9 percent are Muslims, and 2.1 percent are Sikhs (based on the religion of the head of the household). There is significantly more nonresponse on caste identity, as it can be a sensitive issue, with 4,763 households providing usable caste information. Of these households, again based on the caste of the head of the household, 37.0 percent are General Caste, 41.0 percent are intermediate/Other Backward Class (OBC), 15.8 percent are SCs, and 6.2 percent are Scheduled Tribes (STs).[33]

Spatial Distribution of Caste and Religion

To gather some sense of how the process of urbanization has impacted caste and religious identities, it is useful to understand the extent to which populations of the same caste/religion are clustered together. As discussed earlier, in the traditional organization of the Indian village, neighborhoods are almost completely inhabited by a single caste/religious community. How much do things change when one moves to the city? Of particular interest is the urban spatial distribution of disadvantaged communities in the sample, SCs and Muslims. As described in previous data work on identity-based segregation, this sort of comparison between SCs and Muslims is not feasible using Indian census data.[34] The maps in Figure 2.5 compare the population density of SCs and Muslims in the sample with the overall population density of the sample.

Figure 2.5a displays the spatial density of the overall population, with darker areas describing areas of higher density. When compared with the spatial density of SCs in Figure 2.5b, some clustering of the SC population can be observed in pockets of the northeast edge of Delhi and south Delhi. Of note is the absence of density in the SC population from southeast and northwest Delhi, two areas that show a reasonably dense population in the overall map (Figure 2.5a). This provides evidence that there is some amount of identity-based spatial clustering for the SC population. The spatial density of the Muslim population in Figure 2.5c shows far more dense clustering of the Muslim population in the NCR (with much more population in and around Delhi and very dense clusters in north and south Delhi). This suggests that the Muslim population in the NCR is far more clustered, or ghettoized, than the SC population in the NCR.

The observations from the spatial density maps are borne out in simple data summaries. One way to understand spatial ghettoization for a community is to characterize how much more frequently a household from the community

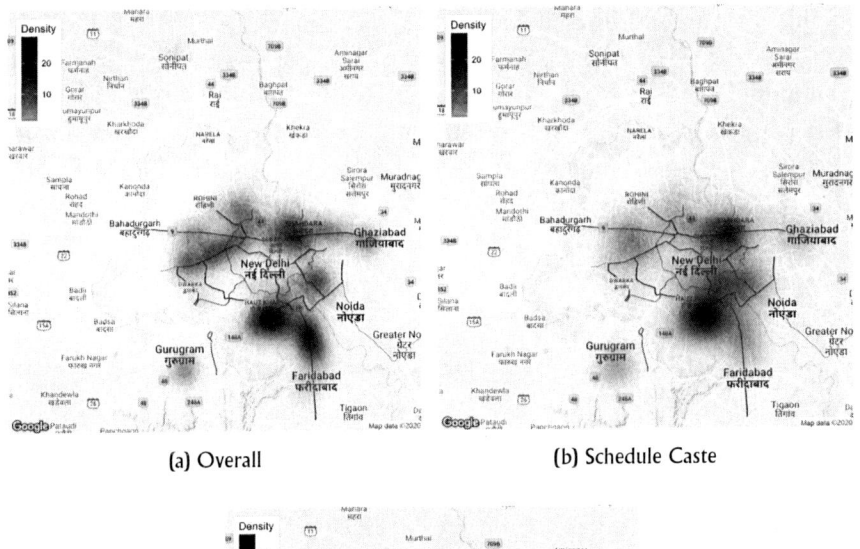

(a) Overall   (b) Schedule Caste

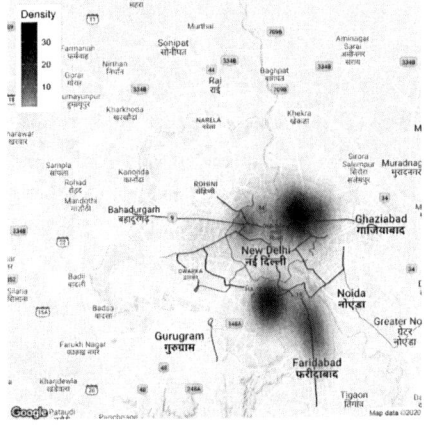

(c) Muslim

Figure 2.5   Spatial distributions of overall, SC, and Muslim populations

Source: Author's calculations from the CASI–NCR Survey data.

Notes: This figure (a, b, and c) displays the spatial density using kernel density estimation implemented in the ggmap package in the R statistical framework. Not all households had retrievable geographic information. (a) It displays the spatial density for the overall population (for the 4,380 households that had usable geographic information). (b) It displays the spatial density for Scheduled Caste households (for the 611 households that had usable geographic information). (c) It displays the spatial density for Muslim households (for the 517 households that had usable geographic information). The Muslim population is noticeably more spatially clustered than the overall and Scheduled Caste populations.

would meet another household from the same community within 1 kilometer of its home. Given that 15.8 percent of the population is from the SC community, if SCs were perfectly integrated (uniformly distributed) across the population, one would expect that approximately 15.8 percent of the households within 1 kilometer of an SC household's home would also be from the SC community. In the NCR, however, 31.1 percent of households within 1 kilometer of an SC household's home are also from the SC community, suggesting significant spatial ghettoization of the SC population. Similarly, if the Muslim community were fully integrated, Muslim households would only make up approximately 10.9 percent of the households within 1 kilometer of a Muslim household's home. In the NCR, however, 39.9 percent of households within 1 kilometer of a Muslim household's home are also from the Muslim community. This demonstrates that the Muslim community is far more ghettoized than the SC community; despite being a smaller percentage of the population, Muslims are much more likely to live within 1 kilometer of each other as compared to SCs.

There are natural criticisms of characterizing integration/ghettoization by a 1 kilometer "buffer" or zone around each household. First, identity-based clusters may actually be smaller than a 1 kilometer buffer, so the level of clustering is artificially reduced in the above metrics. Second, and more important, spatial integration/ghettoization does not say anything about the level of interaction with one's neighbors. In order to address this issue, survey respondents were asked to characterize their interactions with the adjacent residence/neighbor. The differences between SCs and Muslims are starker in this data. If a household from SC community interacted with its neighbors, the neighboring household was also from the SC community 44.2 percent of the time. If a household from the Muslim community interacted with its neighbors, the neighboring household was also from the Muslim community 80.6 percent of the time.

These data suggest that, in terms of interaction (arguably the most important metric), there has been significantly more spatial integration for the SC community than for the Muslim community in the NCR. Differences in the rates of neighbor interaction and spatial clustering (especially for the Muslim community) suggest that identity-based polarization may be occurring even among spatially proximate populations.[35] Given the caste/religious organization of Indian villages, almost all of India's rural residents have neighbors from the same caste/religious community. Therefore, as compared to their rural lives, the SC community in the NCR interacts in spaces with greater caste diversity, whereas the NCR does not offer the Muslim community a significantly more diverse space of interaction than the Indian village. In short, even in the NCR, the Muslim community remains a population that faces high levels of ghettoization.

Economic Inequalities by Caste and Religion

A natural measure of well-being for a category is the relative wealth of the median person in the category. Because the raw asset index values are not easily interpretable, the data are transformed into percentile values assuming a normal distribution. The Bayesian framework in which the model is estimated permits direct measurement of the uncertainty in the wealth of the median individual in each category (based off 3,750 simulations of the posterior distribution).

Figure 2.6a displays the wealth of the median person in selected religious communities in percentile terms with 95 percent predictive intervals of the median. Similarly, Figure 2.6b measures the median wealth of the four major caste groupings in percentile terms with 95 percent predictive intervals. In terms of religion, the Sikh community is much wealthier than other religious communities, with the median household in the Sikh community predicted to be at the 81st percentile of the asset index. The median household in the Hindu community (51st percentile) is right around the median of the entire population, which is not surprising given the percentage of Hindus in the sample, and the Muslim community is significantly poorer than the other communities with the median household at the 39th percentile of the asset index. With respect

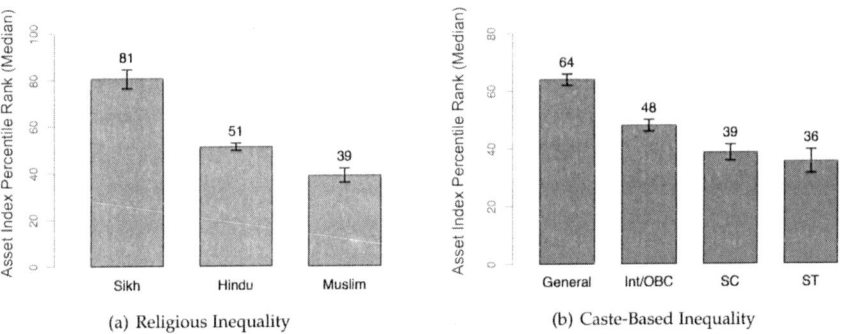

(a) Religious Inequality   (b) Caste-Based Inequality

Figure 2.6   Identity-based inequality in the NCR
Source: Author's calculations from the CASI–NCR Survey data.

to caste status, General Caste households are significantly wealthier than the median household in the population, with a median household at the 63rd percentile of the asset index, while the median intermediate/OBC household (48th percentile) is near the median of the entire sample. SCs and STs are significantly poorer, with a median household predicted to be at the 39th and 36th percentile, respectively.

The data show that, at least in terms of the asset index, the Muslim and SC communities are relatively similar in levels of wealth. Yet, as discussed earlier, the pattern of social interactions differs markedly between SCs and Muslims. If SCs interact with a larger number of people outside of their own community, it at least provides opportunities for greater social integration of the SC community than the Muslim community—something that needs to be considered when analyzing the larger principle of social inequality.

Economic Well-Being across the National Capital Region

To get a broad sense of the economic well-being across the NCR, it is useful to analyze the asset index across different zones of the NCR. For this analysis, the region is split into three zones: Delhi, suburbs, and outskirts. Since the entire region has been built around Delhi, it is in a genuine sense the core of the city. Next, the suburban zone contains many households that either commute into Delhi for work or are employed in the rapidly increasing corporate sector. These areas' surrounding areas are well-known to citizens of the NCR as being integrated with Delhi through, among other things, the metro. The suburban zone is defined as the cities of Faridabad, Ghaziabad, Gurugram (Gurgaon), and Noida. Finally, the outskirts contain urban settlements that are often too far from Delhi for daily commuting or have recently been included in an ever-expanding NCR, and include households that often do not see themselves as connected to Delhi. The outskirts contain cities such as Alwar, Meerut, and Panipat. All told, Delhi, the suburbs, and the outskirts include 3,352, 712, and 1,413 sample households, respectively.

Figure 2.7 shows the distributions of raw asset scores of Delhi, the suburbs, and the outskirts in what is known as a "violin plot." The violin plot displays the distribution of the raw asset score by zone using a kernel density–type algorithm—where the shape is wider, there are more households. The white dots correspond to the median and the gray box displays a traditional "box plot" of the distribution. As one might guess, as one moves from Delhi to the suburbs to the outskirts, the median asset score drops; therefore, in macro-

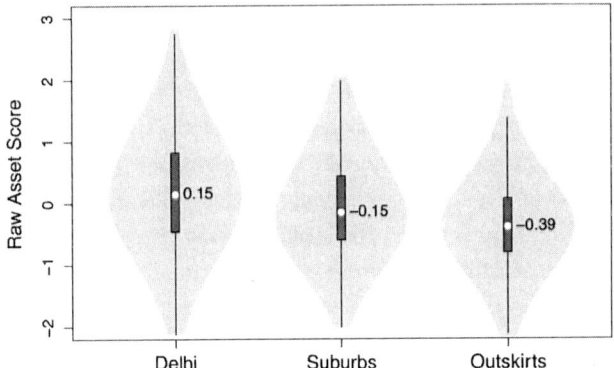

Figure 2.7 Violin plots of raw asset wealth score over core–periphery categorizations in the NCR

Source: Author's calculations from the CASI–NCR Survey data.

spatial terms, there is some evidence for a wealthier core and a poorer periphery. At the same time, Figure 2.7 shows that there is very wide variance in asset scores *within* each zone, suggesting that macro-spatial categorizations such as zones miss a lot of the internal variation in wealth.

Spatial Inequality

In order to provide a more nuanced picture of the spatial distribution of wealth, it is useful to explicitly generate a map of the asset index across the NCR. There are 4,380 usable geo-coded households in the data set and every cluster which was sampled in the survey has some geo-coded households, yielding good geographic coverage of the usable data. The challenge in mapping the spatial distribution of the asset index is to take the observed asset index values (at 4,380 dispersed points over the NCR) and to draw a meaningful "surface" over the map to observe the spatial distribution. In order to do this, radial smoothing of the asset index through a spatial spline with 100 knots was employed, following Crainiceanu et al.[36]

The challenge of characterizing spatial distributions of economic wealth merits a brief discussion. At a "microscopic" lens, one will always observe some measure of wealthy and poor living near each other in a major city, whether one is measuring New York City or Delhi. But just because there are some poor people in a neighborhood, or one city block, does not mean that the neighborhood on the whole is poor (or rich). To address this natural economic heterogeneity, it is desirable to provide a "smoothed" measure of the predicted mean or median wealth across the space, as it allows the analyst to understand the relative variation in wealth across larger scales, such as the urban agglomeration. A second potential problem is when there is a lack of data to generate enough variation in these smoothed estimates. If the data are too sparse over the scale that is being studied, then the method will show little variation in wealth across the space. Taking these ideas together, when one observes significant variation in wealth across the space after smoothing methods, it implies there is sufficient data to pick up this variation and that it is not due to microscopic phenomena.

Figure 2.8 displays the estimated spatial distribution of the asset index over percentile values, as before. Broadly, the blackish areas are in the bottom quartile of economic well-being, the whitish areas are in the top quartile of economic well-being, with various shades of gray in between. In order to present meaningful predictions, where there is sufficient data, the map displays predictions only for households for which there were at least five other spatially proximate (within 1 kilometer) households measured in the data.

Figure 2.8a displays the spatial inequality at the scale of the urban portions of the NCR, although some of the outer edges of the NCR, such as Panipat, Alwar, and Bharatpur, are omitted from this map for the sake of presentation. Figure 2.8b zooms in on central Delhi and surrounding areas to get a sense of spatial inequality at a smaller scale. The estimates are finer in this region due to population density and thus a larger sample size. Both maps demonstrate a highly heterogeneous spatial residential pattern across the NCR. Figure 2.8a does show that outer regions of the NCR are somewhat poorer, but the pattern of residential clusters of economic well-being is far from the concentric circle pattern observed in cities such as Chicago and New York City, with disconnected clusters of wealth in the northwest, central, and southern portions of Delhi. Of particular note is the great variation in the economic well-being observed in the larger suburbs of Delhi, Faridabad, Ghaziabad, Gurugram, and Noida, quite different than the economic homogeneity that is usually ascribed to suburbs in the West. Figure 2.8b demonstrates the extraordinary economic heterogeneity in residential clusters, even at a smaller scale, with very poor residents in the eastern and northern flanks of the city and parts of Old Delhi surrounded by wealthy clusters in Civil Lines and Mayur Vihar. This is consistent with the economic heterogeneity observed in Delhi by Dupont.[37]

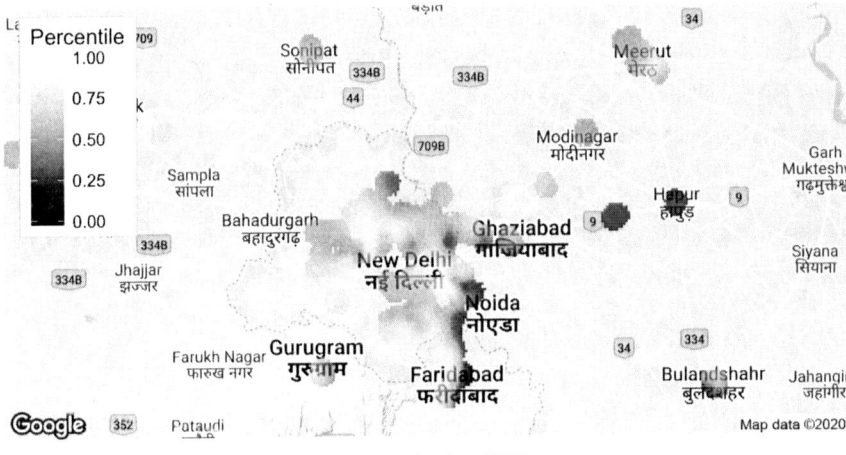

(a) Scale of urban NCR

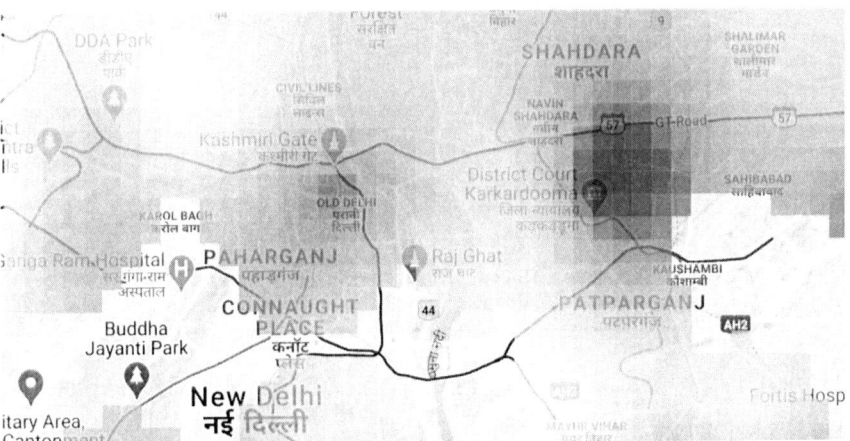

(b) Close-up of central Delhi and surrounding areas

Figure 2.8   Spatial inequality in the NCR

Source: Author's calculations from the CASI–NCR Survey data.

Discussion of Hypotheses

The first hypothesis pertains to the differences between spatial inequality and identity-based inequality, namely that differences in the asset index purely based on identity will be less pronounced than differences between residential clusters in the asset index. For the poorest communities in the sample, a median household has a percentile rank between 35 and 40, and, other than the Sikh community, median households for each community are well below the top quartile. However, Figure 2.8 displays many residential clusters with median asset index values in the top or bottom quartile, sometimes in close physical proximity, suggesting spatial factors beyond identity associating wealth to residence. Thus, there is strong empirical evidence for the first hypothesis. This is not to deny the important role of identity in shaping economic inequalities. Indeed, Figure 2.8b displays a cluster of poverty in Old Delhi, a heavily Muslim area. However, unlike villages in India, residential clusters in urban NCR are not completely determined by identity, accounting for the observed differences. This result is seemingly the opposite of earlier work looking at differences between economic and caste segregation in cities.[38] While those studies provide detailed analysis of urban segregation, particularly in identity terms, they must operate within the data constraints of the Indian census—so segregation is characterized as differences in populations in municipal wards (which are quite large), as opposed to the more fine-grained residential clusters that can be picked up in spatial analysis. Furthermore, because the census does not collect income or consumption data, these analyses use male literacy rate as a proxy for economic well-being, but the strictures of the urban labor market often demand certain levels of education, thereby dampening inequality purely in terms of literacy.[39]

The second hypothesis pertains to the spatial distribution of economic well-being in the NCR, namely that the spatial distribution of the asset index should not follow a concentric circle core–periphery pattern such as that of Chicago or New York City. Figure 2.8a provides very strong evidence that a concentric circle core–periphery pattern is not observed in the NCR, with very poor and very wealthy residential clusters located in close physical proximity to each other. While the edges of the NCR do seem poorer than the core (most of the whitish surface corresponding to the top quartile in the asset index is located within the boundaries of Delhi), concentric circles of wealth/ poverty cannot be discerned. A closer look at residential clusters in Figure 2.8b further demonstrates the extraordinary spatial heterogeneity in wealth within a small area, a pattern that is rarely observed in Western cities. This provides strong evidence for the second hypothesis. Furthermore, prevailing theories of peripheralization do not envision strong economic heterogeneity in residential clusters in the suburbs and outskirts of cities, while Figure 2.7 shows a significant variation in wealth in these areas. Indeed, a median person in the suburbs is wealthier than more than one-third of Delhi, and the median person in the outskirts is wealthier than more than one-quarter of Delhi. This lends credence to the argument that the pattern of residential location in the NCR is driven more by social and economic dependence, yielding great economic heterogeneity locally.

Conclusion

The dominant paradigms in understanding spatial inequalities in urban areas were developed in the West. These paradigms have limited relevance for many developing world contexts, where identity-based conflict has different characteristics and histories and where a substantial proportion of labor and service is in the informal sector. This generates incentives for poorer residential clusters, as the source of labor and service, to locate in close physical proximity to wealthy residential clusters, the consumers of such labor and service—even when these clusters contain caste or religious groups that have engaged in social conflict. Two major lessons can be drawn from this insight. First, the core–periphery model of spatial inequality, and the role of real estate prices in guaranteeing this spatial distribution, is compromised in such a setting, generating far more economic heterogeneity in residential clusters across urban space than seen in the West. Second, the logic of urban location in the NCR is rooted in economic and social dependence, which moves beyond religion or caste. This implies that urban space affords the opportunity to unsettle traditional hierarchies that are more present in rural areas.

Unlike the aggressive process of gentrification, peripheralization of the poor, and increasing ethnic and economic segregation now being observed in Western cities, the current spatial patterns of settlement in the NCR provide some hope for mitigating social division. One noticeable feature of the social process that undergirds spatial location in the West is the role of "exit" by high-status populations, whether it be the aforementioned white flight from black communities in Detroit or "native" relocation from immigrant communities in Stockholm. This does not seem to be as important a feature of spatial location in Indian cities, perhaps due to the economic dependence between high-status populations and marginalized communities.

Will the economic basis for residential location lead to greater caste and religious integration? Significant challenges remain to make Indian cities a site of social integration. First, a fair amount of social segregation is still present in the NCR, as shown in this chapter, with Figure 2.5c and a number of statistics suggesting a number of separated "Muslim neighborhoods" in particular. Institutions will need to be built that guarantee the safety of *each* community in the city to further spatial and social integration. Second, while the city may unsettle explicit identity-based residential location, it also engenders economic competition between different communities, potentially leading to greater social strife. Third, and most important, interaction between castes and religions in India is governed by a set of highly pervasive "purity rules" that prevent regular interaction between different communities, even if they live in close proximity to each other. Without a concurrent diminution of these norms, the scope for social integration is limited.

Nonetheless, the economic heterogeneity of residential clusters at all scales may provide significant opportunities for economic and social mobility. For a child growing up in a poor residential cluster that is physically close to residential settlements of all economic classes, what are his or her chances for social mobility? How does this compare to similarly poor children growing up in villages or far from other economic classes? Economic and social mobility in India is known to be low compared to a number of Western countries.[40] This is due in significant part to poor investment in human capital and other public goods. For poorer children, the scope for an education with sufficient quality to learn in-demand skills is low. There are potential reasons to be more optimistic in an urban setting with a spatial pattern of settlement such as the NCR. First, many children will likely have access to a marginally better education in the city, due to, among other things, better tutors, less teacher absenteeism, and greater choice of schools.[41] Second, even investment in wealthier areas will likely have positive spillovers to surrounding areas, from local public goods to benefits from increased commercial activity. Finally, the "weak social ties" that form regular interaction with other social classes may yield greater economic opportunities in the future.[42]

As this chapter has shown, *space* is now the most powerful predictor of economic well-being in urban areas, more than traditional measures of identity. Ultimately, urban areas are fundamentally differentiated by their spatial pattern of residential settlement; identity-based tensions, restrictive social norms, and even non-farm and highly specialized labor exist to a significant extent in rural areas as well. As geo-coded data sets with large sample sizes at the level of an urban agglomeration slowly become available, the empirical study of urban space has a bright future and the capacity to address many unanswered questions in the study of urban India. As India undergoes a process of rapid urbanization, and citizens negotiate their positions in urban space, this research agenda will yield deep insights into the great social transformation taking place in India.

Notes

1. Devesh Kapur, "How Will India's Urban Future Affect Social Identities?" *Urbanisation* 2, no. 1 (2017): 1–8.

2. Raj Chetty and Nathaniel Hendren, *The Impacts of Neighborhoods on Intergenerational Mobility II: County-Level Estimates* (NBER Working Paper, 2015), available at https://scholar.harvard.edu/files/hendren/files/nbhds_paper.pdf, accessed on October 1, 2020.

3. Thomas Picketty, *Capital in the 21st Century* (Cambridge: Belknap Press, 2014).

4. Sharon Zukin, *Naked City: The Death and Life of Authentic Urban Places* (New York: Oxford University Press, 2009).

5. David Harvey, "The Right to the City," *The New Left Review* 53 (2008): 23–40.

6. Sanjoy Chakravorty and Somik V. Lall, *Made in India: The Economic Geography and Political Economy of Industrialization* (New York: Oxford University Press, 2007). It is important to note that there have been studies at the level of regional spatial inequality across India.

7. Oliver C. Cox, "Race and Caste: A Distinction," *American Journal of Sociology* 50, no. 5 (1945): 360–368.

8. Santosh Mehrhotra, "Informal Employment Trends in the Indian Economy: Persistent Informality, but Growing Positive Development" (Working Paper No. 254, International Labour Organisation, Geneva).

9. Ananya Roy, "Slumdog Cities: Rethinking Subaltern Urbanism," *International Journal of Urban and Regional Research* 35, no. 2 (2011): 223–238. This work discusses an older understanding of "informal" in urban studies that is used to describe a "deproletarianized" class of labor that is poor and marginalized. But none of the standard uses of "informal" in urban studies are relational (for example, describing modes of economic exchange or agreements).

10. Gyan Prakash, "The Urban Turn," in *Sarai Reader 02: The Cities of Everyday Life*, ed. Ravi S. Vasudevan, Jeebesh Bagchi, Ravi Sundaram, Monica Narula, Geert Lovink, and Shuddhabrata Sengupta (Sarai: New Delhi, 2000), 2–7.

11. When data are "geo-coded," one can discern the exact geographic location at which the data were collected. This is usually done by providing the global position system (GPS) coordinates of the location at which the survey or census for the household was conducted.

12. Robert E. Park, "The Concept of Position in Sociology," *Papers and Proceedings of the American Sociological Society* 20 (1926): 14.

13. Ernest W. Burgess, "The Growth of the City: An Introduction to a Research Project," in *The City*, ed. Robert E. Park, Ernest W. Burgess, and Roderick D. McKenzie (Chicago, IL: University of Chicago Press, 1925), 62.

14. Michael Dear and Steven Flusty, "Postmodern Urbanism," *Annals of the Association of American Geographers* 88, no. 1 (1998): 50–72. This is not to say

there has not been criticism of the framework. Certain US cities such as Detroit and Los Angeles have a poor core and a wealthier outer ring—although this is still a core–periphery, concentric circle-type pattern, as in the Los Angeles School of Urban Theory.

15. Harvey, "The Right to the City," 34.

16. Sanjoy Chakravorty, *The Price of Land: Acquisition, Conflict, Consequence* (New Delhi: Oxford University Press, 2013).

17. Dear and Flusty, "Postmodern Urbanism," 50–72.

18. William H. Frey, "Central City White Flight: Racial and Nonracial Causes," *American Sociological Review* 44, no. 3 (1979): 425–448.

19. Roger Andersson, "Socio-spatial Dynamics: Ethnic Divisions of Mobility and Housing in Post-Palme Sweden," *Urban Studies* 35, no. 3 (1998): 397–428.

20. This is not to deny that the politics of Hindutva (Hindu nationalism) is engaged in a project of "othering" the Muslim community. For instance, the recent drafting of the Citizen Amendment Act (CAA) has explicitly attempted to call into question the citizenship status of a portion of India's Muslim population. But unlike "immigrant populations," India's Muslim population would not, by and large, identify itself as being from elsewhere.

21. Amita Sinha, "Social and Spatial Order in Villages in India," *Landscape Research* 15, no. 3 (1990): 12–19.

22. Laurent Gayer, "Safe and Sound: Search for a 'Good Environment' in Abul Fazl Enclave, Delhi," in *Muslims in Indian Cities: Trajectories of Marginalisation*, ed. Laurent Gayer and Christophe Jaffrelot (New Delhi: HarperCollins, 2013), 232.

23. Paul Brass, *The Production of Hindu–Muslim Violence in Contemporary India* (Seattle, WA: University of Washington Press, 2003). Paul Brass notes this phenomenon as well. He describes how despite intercaste competition in the Hindu community and inter-*baradari* competition among the Muslim community, in Aligarh, periods of religious polarization yield the election of militant Hindu representatives and generate Muslim unity.

24. Surinder K. Mehta, "Patterns of Residence in Poona, India, by Caste and Religion: 1822–1965," *Demography* 6, no. 4 (1969): 473–491.

25. Frey, "Central City White Flight: Racial and Nonracial Causes," 425–448.

26. Brian J. L. Berry and Howard Spodek, "Comparative Ecologies of Large Indian Cities," *Economic Geography* 47 (1971): 266–285.

27. Veronique Dupont, "Socio-spatial Differentiation and Residential Segregation in Delhi: A Question of Scale?" *Geo-forum* 35, no. 2 (2004): 157–175.

28. Angus Deaton, "Measuring Poverty in a Growing World (or Measuring Growth in a Poor World)," *Review of Economics and Statistics* 87, no. 1 (2005): 1–19.

29. Leela Fernandes, "Nationalizing 'the Global': Media Images, Cultural Politics and the Middle Class in India," *Media, Culture & Society* 22 (2000): 611–628.

30. Yoshio Takane and Jan de Leeuw, "On the Relationship between Item Response Theory and Factor Analysis of Discretized Variables," *Psychometrika* 52, no. 3 (1987): 393–408.

31. Steven P. Reise et al., "Confirmatory Factor Analysis and Item Response Theory: Two Approaches for Exploring Measurement Invariance," *Psychological Bulletin* 114, no. 3 (1993): 552–566.

32. Gordon W. Allport, *The Nature of Prejudice* (Cambridge, MA: Perseus Books, 1954).

33. The Jat population is coded as an "intermediate" caste due to a popular demand for backward caste status. Although Delhi and Haryana do not officially recognize the Scheduled Tribes (ST), the survey still allows respondents to identify in this category.

34. Trina Vithayathil and Gayatri Singh, "Spaces of Discrimination: Residential Segregation in Indian Cities," *Economic and Political Weekly* 47, no. 37 (2012): 60–66; Pranav Sidhwani, "Spatial Inequalities in Big Indian Cities," *Economic and Political Weekly* 15, no. 22 (2015): 55–62.

35. Raphael Susewind, "Muslims in Indian Cities: Degrees of Segregation and the Elusive Ghetto," *Environment and Planning A* 49, no. 6 (2017): 1286–1307. The author argues that the Muslim community can face high levels of ghettoization even in mixed areas due to the "mental maps" of citizens.

36. Ciprian M. Crainiceanu et al., "Spatially Adaptive Bayesian Penalized Splines with Heteroscedastic Errors," *Journal of Computational and Graphical Statistics* 16, no. 2 (2007): 265–288.

37. Dupont, "Socio-spatial Differentiation and Residential Segregation in Delhi," 157–175.

38. Vithayathil and Singh, "Spaces of Discrimination," 60–66; Sidhwani, "Spatial Inequalities in Big Indian Cities," 55–62.

39. According to the 2011 Indian Census, the literacy rate of males above the age of 6 in Delhi is 91 percent and 82 percent across India, so one does not expect a very large variation of well-being measured purely in literacy terms.

40. Sam Asher, Paul Novosad, and Charlie Rafkin, "Estimating Intergenerational Mobility with Coarse Data: New Methods and Estimates Across Time, Space, and Communities" (2020), available at https://www.dartmouth.edu/~novosad/anr-india-mobility.pdf, accessed on September 20, 2020.

41. In Delhi, according to many measures, government schools are outperforming private schools. For instance, 96 percent of those graduating from a government school in Delhi passed their school-leaving exams compared to 93 percent from private schools. Furthermore, greater investment in education (and health) for the masses in Delhi is likely to have some impact. See, for instance, https://www.bbc.com/news/world-asia-india-51353525, accessed on February 5, 2020.

42. Mark Granovetter, "The Strength of Weak Ties," *American Journal of Sociology* 78, no. 6 (1973): 1360–1380.

CHAPTER 3

Housing and Settlements
Invisible Planning, Visible Exclusions

Patrick Heller, Partha Mukhopadhyay,
Shahana Sheikh, and Subhadra Banda

Introduction

Delhi is India's richest city, and as the capital of the nation, it has long enjoyed a favorable treatment from the center. As the home to the country's national bureaucracies, it also benefits from a large base of secure, well-paid, government jobs. Over the last decade, the city has grown at an average real rate of 10 percent and has benefitted from a dramatic increase in large-scale infrastructure development. Yet, despite these advantages, Delhi is a deeply divided city marked by layers of social exclusion.

In the modern imaginary, the city represents the promise of freedom and opportunity. It marks a social space that is less constrained by traditional identities and one in which greater social interaction and density support economic dynamism. If development must, as Amartya Sen has so influentially argued, be based on strengthening basic capabilities, then the city can surely be a privileged site of capability enhancement. Indeed, the migrants who flood the city often come in search of better livelihoods, education, health, and basic services. But as any resident of Delhi knows, the quality of such services varies dramatically across neighborhoods, and the part of the city one lives in significantly impacts one's ability to take full advantage of what the city has to offer. This chapter summarizes findings from the Cities of Delhi (CoD) (citiesofdelhi.cprindia.org) project based on fieldwork from the end of 2012 to the middle of 2015.[1] We document the extent to which India's capital is marked by different settlement types, defined by diverse degrees of formality, legality, and tenure, which taken together produce a highly differentiated pattern of access to basic services.[2]

This chapter has three objectives. The first is to document as carefully as possible the quality and scope of access to basic services in the less privileged areas of the city. We focus on basic services such as electricity, water, sanitation, and solid-waste removal because these are clearly constitutive of core capabilities, relatively easy to measure (as compared to health or educational services), and well within the reach of a city such as Delhi under current levels of economic development, with a per capita gross state domestic product of more than USD 8,000 in purchasing power parity terms. Our second objective is to map the distribution of these services and, in particular, to understand how they are unevenly spread across different settlement types. Of course, inequality of access to basic services is to some degree a result of income differences (class) and social status (community and caste). But we specifically want to focus on inequalities that are tied to legal and spatial categories, both because these have generally been less studied in the literature on urban inequality in India, but also because these drivers of inequality are much more amenable to policy interventions than class or status differentials. The third objective is to identify the mechanisms through which inequality across settlement types actually works. This meant trying to understand the histories, the legal frameworks, and the institutional and "political arrangements" that have produced and reproduced highly unequal settlement types.

The chapter draws on 10 cases studies from CoD (Table 3.1). The criteria of selection and research methods are fully detailed in the project overview report.[3] We focus on three types of "unplanned" settlement: the *jhuggi jhopri* clusters (JJCs), the unauthorized colony (UAC), and the resettlement colony (RC). At a very broad level of generalization,

- JJCs are settlements where tenure is most tenuous,
- UACs are settlements in which claim to land may be less tenuous, where residents have often purchased land from a third party, but which are built without planning permissions, and
- RCs are planned and legal developments to which some residents from JJCs are relocated, usually after the JJCs' demolition. Here, the tenure is granted by the state, but with a very impaired ability to transact. Despite being planned, RCs are often without basic services.

Collectively, we refer to these as "excluded settlements." As we explain in detail in the next section, all three are to varying degrees excluded by law and/

Table 3.1 Cities of Delhi, case sites

Settlement type	Settlement name	Most recent official size estimate	Estimated population	Year of foundation	Location (region of Delhi)	Location
JJC	Anantram Dairy Harijan Basti	311 *jhuggis*	1,750–2,000	1972	south Delhi	Core
	F Block Punjabi Basti	455 *jhuggis*	5,000	1975–1985	west Delhi	Core
	Indira Kalyan Vihar	2,315 *jhuggis*	25,000–30,000	1978	south Delhi	Semi-core/semi-periphery
	Kusumpur Pahari	4,909 *jhuggis*	50,000	1974	south Delhi	Semi-core/ semi- periphery
	Sanjay Camp	4,250 *jhuggis*	25,000–30,000	Late 1970s	south Delhi	Core
	Jai Hind Camp	1,000 *jhuggis*	5,000–6,000	~ 2000	south Delhi	Semi-core/ semi- periphery
RC	Savda Ghevra	8,686 plots	50,000	2006	northwest Delhi	Periphery
	Mangolpuri	28,478 plots	300,000–350,000	1975	northwest Delhi	Semi-core/ semi-periphery
	Madanpur Khader	10,484 plots	150,000	2000	south Delhi	Semi-core/ semi- periphery
UAC	Sangam Vihar (agglomeration of UACs)	No official estimate	1,000,000	1979	south Delhi	Periphery

Source and notes: The "estimated population" is based on an average household size of five. The size estimates for the JJCs are taken from Delhi Urban Shelter Improvement Board's (DUSIB) list of JJCs for 2014. The sources and years for the size estimates of the resettlement colonies vary: the size estimate for Savda Ghevra is for 2013 and is based on an interview with a DUSIB official on June 11, 2013, that for Mangolpuri is for 2006 and is based on Delhi's City Development Plan (IL&FS Ecosmart Limited, "City Development Plan: Delhi," chapter on urban poor and slum (New Delhi: Department of Urban Development, Government of National Capital Territory of Delhi, 2006), and that for Madanpur Khader is for 2001 and is based on DDA's data (see http://www.dda.org.in/planning/slums_jj_rehabilitate.htm, accessed on March 13, 2015). The "location" classification is based on distance from Connaught Place (CP), which can be considered the default center of Delhi. Distance between 0 and 10 kilometers from CP = core, between 10 and 20 kilometers from CP = semi-core/semi-periphery, and between 20 and 30 kilometers from CP = periphery.

or practice from full inclusion in the city's infrastructure and service delivery functions.

Settlement Types and Differentiated Citizenship

The government of Delhi's own estimates place only 23.7 percent of the city's population in what are designated as "planned colonies."[4] The balance of Delhi's population resides in what are either entirely "illegal" settlements or areas that were never authorized for development and, as such, never properly planned.[5] The absence of planning means not only that the physical space of the settlement was not laid out in accordance with basic building codes or public space requirements (including road and access grids) but that the settlement is not integrated into the city's bulk infrastructure delivery system.

Table 3.2 summarizes the eight types of settlements found in Delhi, categories differentiated by the degree to which they are legal and planned. The resulting classification represents a grid of differentiated citizenship. The first three columns provide a listing of settlement types and their populations as defined and enumerated by the state of Delhi. The third column is a categorization, drawing from Gautam Bhan, of the legality of each settlement type and the degree to which it is planned.[6] The fourth column, based on work by Augustin Maria, summarizes how each category translates into access to a key service, water.[7]

There is a clear pattern of differentiation: the scope and quality of service delivery is both legally, and in terms of official policy, directly mapped onto these grid-differentiated categories based on tenurial status. The numbered list of settlement types in Table 3.2 runs from the most illegal (JJCs) to the most legal (planned colonies). Planned colonies (23.7 percent) are legal and planned and generally have access to a full set of services (reliable electricity supply, piped water, sewage, paved roads, solid-waste collection). These are zones of what might be called full citizenship and accommodate Delhi's wealthier classes and public employees in government provided accommodation. This is, in other words, the "inclusive city" of Delhi, to use the term now favored in policy circles. Two other settlement types, the "urban village" and the "rural village," are oddities; these are areas that have been grandfathered, partially exempted from standard planning requirements and somewhat legal.

"Unauthorized-regularized colonies" (URCs, 12.7 percent) started illegally as "unauthorized colonies" but have been subsequently legalized (if not fully planned). Despite their legal incorporation into the city, URCs have poor

Table 3.2 Types of settlement and population in New Delhi

Type of settlement	Estimated population for 2000 (million)[a]	Share of total Delhi population[b]	Legality[c]	Individual water supply[d]
JJCs	2.07	14.80%	Illegal and unplanned	No right
SDAs	2.66	19.10%	Legal but unplanned	Right, but restricted for technical reasons
UACs	0.74	5.30%	Illegal, unplanned but secure	No right
RCs	1.78	12.72%	Legal, planned, and informalized	Right, but not delivered
Rural villages	0.74	5.30%	Zone of exception	Exempt
Regularized—UACs	1.78	12.72%	Legal but unplanned	Good
Urban villages	0.89	6.35%	Zone of exception	Good
Planned colonies	3.31	23.70%	Legal and Planned	Good
Total population	13.96	100%		

Sources: a and b are sourced from Government of National Capital Territory of Delhi, Economic Survey of Delhi 2008–09 (New Delhi: Government of National Capital Territory of Delhi, 2009); c is adapted from Gautam Bhan, "Planned Illegalities: Housing and the 'Failure' of Planning in Delhi; 1957–2010," Economic and Political Weekly 48, no. 24 (2013): 58–70, and d is adapted from Augustin Maria, "Urban Water Crisis in Delhi: Stakeholders Responses and Potential Scenarios of Evolution," IDD–RI Idee Pour le Debat 6 (2008).

service levels.[8] Slum-designated areas (SDAs) are the officially recognized "slums" of Delhi, formally notified under the Slum Areas (Improvement and Clearance) Act 1956. The entire area of the walled city and its extension have been notified as SDAs. Once notified, an SDA has improved access to basic services and due procedure prior to an eviction must be followed.

The next three categories—the focus of this chapter, and what we collectively label "excluded settlements"—exist at the margins of citizenship. In JJCs (14.8 percent), RCs (12.7 percent), and UACs (5.3 percent), residents have at best highly discretionary rights to basic services.

Unauthorized colonies are illegal, built outside of development plans and in contravention of zoning regulations. In most cases, UACs emerged when private developers illegally developed land demarcated for agricultural use for residential purposes and sold off individual plots. Because the land has been developed illegally and outside the master plan (it is "unauthorized"), residents have no formal "right" to services, but because individual households have bought their plots, they have a claim to tenure and are generally secure from eviction. Periodic waves of regularization by the city have given this tacit claim to tenure legitimacy, though no UAC was regularized between 1984 and 2012.[9] Perhaps due to this de facto security of tenure, many residents have invested in their properties, and UACs are considerably built-up and multistoried buildings are common.

Jhuggi jhopri clsuters are like squatter settlements. The term "squatter"— often used by courts and government agencies—emphatically marks these populations in the eyes of the state as temporary sojourners. The category encompasses everything from the shacks of migrant on-site construction workers who stayed back even after a project ended in built-up settlements that are often more than four decades old. Thus, even in the cases we document where JJC households had paid for their plots, the state confers no de facto recognition of property. Indeed, the state has clearly chosen to simply ignore this population, and it was not until the passage of the Delhi Urban Shelter Improvement Board (DUSIB) Act 2010 that an estimated 1.5 million JJC residents received legislative recognition.

Finally, RCs mark the ultimate paradox of the state's power to classify its citizens. These colonies are legal and planned, the result of entirely state-driven action, and specifically the sites to which evicted JJC households are relocated. Yet, as we shall see, nowhere is the gap between legal designation and policy practice more pronounced and more emblematic of planned state failure. Despite being "planned," most RCs are actually deprived of basic services.[10]

If Table 3.2 represents the state's classification of citizenship and, as we document in this chapter, does lead to highly varied levels of basic services, it is important to note that the figures reported in this table are clearly inaccurate. The population shares in Table 3.2 are routinely reproduced in Delhi government reports, commission documents, and academic publications. However, no one has ever remarked that the data for two of the settlement types are identical to that of two other settlement types: "unauthorized colonies" and "rural villages" each are estimated to have a population of 740,000, and "resettlement colonies" and "regularized-unauthorized colonies" 1.78 million each. Moreover, the population for "unauthorized colonies" is clearly far off the mark. The Government of National Capital Territory of Delhi's (GNCTD) Unauthorized Colonies Cell puts the figure at 4 million, about a quarter of Delhi's 2011 Census population. Based on 2012 electoral data, Joshi, Pradhan, and Sidhwani calculate that settlements with the municipal tax classification that includes UACs account for 37 percent of voters in Delhi.[11] Similarly, the figure for JJCs is at best a guess. In 2014, the agency responsible for JJCs, the DUSIB, estimates the JJC population of Delhi at 304,188 *jhuggi*s and, for nearly a year, it has continued to state that data on which this is based is "tentative and is in the process of being verified." The linked data set, when compared with the previous data set of 2011 (as part of which DUSIB estimated that there were 418,282 *jhuggi*s in Delhi) reveals large changes in the numbers of *jhuggi*s in various JJCs, and in their areas; though minor changes are expected and understandable, large variations are difficult to make sense of.

This differentiation is also visible in the results of the survey that form the basis for this volume. The polling stations that formed the survey units were post-coded to settlement types based on their location.[12] An asset index was constructed for each household in the survey,[13] which represents the economic condition of the household.

Figure 3.1 shows the share of population in three settlement types, namely planned colonies, JJCs, and UACs, that comes from different deciles of the asset index. That is, if a settlement type had exactly the same distribution as the National Capital Region (NCR) as a whole, it would be flat, that is, 10 percent for all deciles. So, deciles more than 10 percent are over represented in the settlement and vice versa. For example, only 2.4 percent of the population in the planned colonies come from the second decile (that is, the bottom 10–20 percent of households as measured by the asset index) and 22.3 percent from the top decile, while 25.3 percent of the JJC households come from the bottom 10 percent of households and 0.6 percent are from the top 10 percent. In the UACs, 7 percent of the households are from the bottom 10 percent, while 13.6

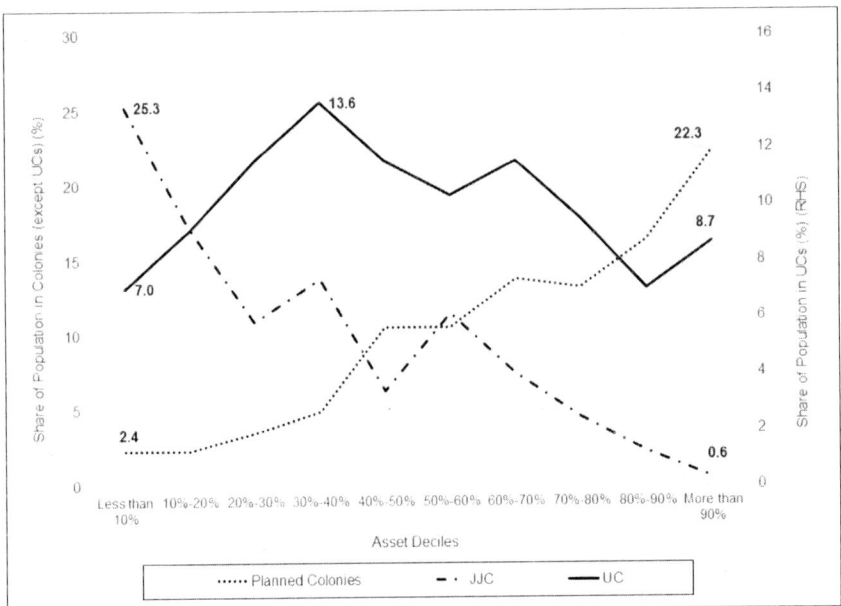

Figure 3.1 Distribution of households by asset index in different settlement types
Source: Authors' calculations from the CASI–NCR Survey data.

percent of households are from the fourth decile, that is, households drawn from 30 to 40 percent of the asset index and 8.7 percent from the top decile. Thus, the households in the UACs are relatively reflective of the population, with little more in the middle but not too much off at either end.

Figure 3.2 shows the share of households within a polling station that have some kind of household water-treatment device (the survey did not have a question about the source of water supply, so this is more a private good than a measure of access to water). Note that basic filter or a sophisticated reverse osmosis system would both qualify (the devices themselves could range in cost from about USD 20 (approximately INR 1,500) for basic filters to expensive varieties that costs 20 times as much) and so the measure is a little coarse. Even so, the distribution shows that fewer households in the JJCs have such devices, with the modal value being around 30 percent, that is, the share of households having such a device that shows up most frequently for polling booths post-coded as JJCs is about a third. For UACs, this modal value is about 60 percent and it is about 90 percent in planned colonies.

Apart from reinforcing the results in Figure 3.1, it additionally shows the failure of the state to provide basic services such as safe drinking water to homes even in planned areas. The scale and sophistication of the investment in

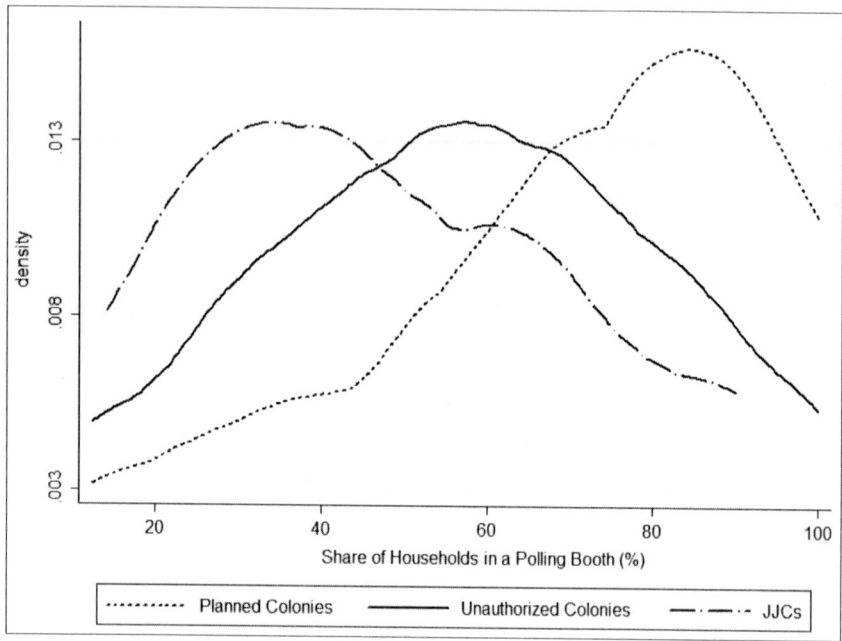

Figure 3.2   Share of households using devices to treat water by type of settlement
Source: Authors' calculations from the CASI–NCR Survey data.

supplementary treatment to cope with this state failure may vary by the wealth of the household but even the most privileged cannot get the state to deliver— they can at most insulate themselves from the consequences of state failure.

These patterns also presage another aspect of Delhi, the multiplicity of "political arrangements," discussed later in this chapter in the section on negotiated citizenship. This is visible from the wide variation within each type of settlement and the degree of overlap between the "worst" type, JJCs, and the "best" type, planned colonies seen in Figures 3.1 and 3.2, indicating the extent to which these elements are negotiable.

Another example of the ambiguity of state's classification exercise is the conflicting estimates of Delhi's slum population. The 2011 Census counts 14.6 percent of the city's households in slums. Yet the categories of JJC and designated slum in Table 3.2 alone show slums housing 34 percent of the population, and that does not even include RCs and the significant portion of UACs that clearly meet the definition of slums. This problem of basic enumeration underscores two governance issues that we highlight throughout the chapter. First, the relative illiteracy of the state applies more to unplanned than planned areas of the city and suggests that the state is generally more indifferent to the condition of unplanned settlements. Second, various reform efforts such as the regularization of UACs and rehabilitation of JJCs (discussed later) have been undermined by the state's poor level of information about these settlements, a problem that itself stems from the degree to which exercises in classification have become highly politicized.

This parenthetical point about the state's lack of will and capacity should not, however, detract from the fact that this classification grid is in effect a map of highly differentiated social citizenship. To move from Category 1 (JJCs) to Category 8 (planned colonies) is to move up the scale of citizenship from the slum resident evicted from his home, with no rights to the city's services—the resettlement of whom one judge of the Supreme Court of India equated to rewarding a "pickpocket"[14]—to a full and proper citizen who secures services as a matter of rights. In the next section, we document the level of services in unplanned colonies. Before doing so, we briefly examine the historical roots of the governance patterns that have produced this classification grid.

As Gautam Bhan has carefully shown, spatial exclusion in Delhi is not a product of failed planning, but of planning itself.[15] The practice begins at the highest level of state development and is driven by the city's most powerful agency, the Delhi Development Authority (DDA). Created in 1957, the DDA is a central government agency (not reporting to the GNCTD) that has full responsibility for land management and development, including public housing. The DDA is also responsible for providing land for resettlement, and thus they determine the location of RCs. It is by far the most powerful agency in the city and has exclusive jurisdiction over the land it owns in the NCTD.

Successive master plans for Delhi (issued in 1962, 1990, and 2007), prepared by the DDA, have both systematically undersupplied the amount of land notified for urban development and undersupplied the estimated required stock of low-cost public housing.[16] Despite a consistently high rate of population growth of over 4.2 percent between 1951 and 2001 (it since decreased to 1.9 percent between 2001 and 2011), the city has opened up new land for housing development only in small and irregular increments and at a pace that has lagged behind population growth. By the end of the 1970s, the DDA had developed only 13,412 acres of the 30,000 acres it had planned to develop for residential use,[17] and the 1980s saw no new land notified for development even as the city's population grew by 3.2 million.[18] Compounding this problem has been the slow and highly skewed pace of housing construction. An analysis of annual DDA reports reveals that not only has the agency consistently fallen behind in delivering the number of planned housing units but that the stock of built housing has skewed dramatically in favor of higher-income groups. This trend has persisted over decades. During the 1960s, the "high-income group" secured 50 percent of the new stock while the percentage going to the "low-income group" fell from 5.5 to 1.9 percent of the total stock.[19] In the most recent decade, of the 33,052 houses completed between 2004 and 2013 (a paltry number in itself), fewer than 10 percent were designated for the "economically weaker sections." We calculate that, of the 979,073 houses built between 2003 and 2010, fewer than 23,000 (2.3 percent) were built by the DDA.

The DDA's failure to develop land and housing has been met by the massive construction of "unauthorized" settlements outside the limits of the plans and occupation of undeveloped land within the city. Bhan provides a graphic proof of these historical patterns of spatial exclusion by mapping the location of UACs and shows that they have mushroomed in neat concentric patterns, always on the edge of the outer limits of the planned city.[20]

Various government documents[21] fully acknowledge that much of the city has gone unplanned but the link with policy is rarely acknowledged. More often than not, the problem is seen as one of growth and migration simply outstripping the capacities of the local state. Three observations belie this view. First, as we have seen, the housing that the DDA has provided has a clear class bias to it. While the DDA has been proactive in providing housing to the higher income groups, it has systematically failed to provide for the poorer sections of society. Second, the language of the DDA itself is one of closure and privilege. In various annual reports, the authority has addressed the problem of the illegalities of its own making in language that fully justifies exclusion. The 1980–1981 report, for example, speaks of its efforts to "protect" the city from unplanned settlements through a "vigorous program … to fence the vacant pockets so that the lands are saved from encroachments."[22] In its 2003–2004 annual report, the DDA reports that the "Land Management Department carried out some major demolition operation during the year which has drawn praise from all sections of society as well as press except the land mafia."[23] The DDA sees itself as ensuring "organized and structured development of haphazard growth" and celebrates its role in building parks, maintaining sports facilities and golf courses, and preserving the city's cultural heritage, even going so far as to dub itself, in reference to the eight historical empires that claimed Delhi as a capital, "as the 9th builder of the grand city of Delhi."[24] Third, the overall pattern of investment in the city, especially in the past two decades, has clearly favored upper-middle class infrastructure over land development and housing for the poor.[25] In recent decades, the DDA has become far more committed to valorizing returns on land than planning for an inclusive city. Thus, even as the agency has systematically failed to develop enough land and housing to accommodate the city's growing population, it has generated vast surpluses from its land dealings, a process that might be summarized as accumulation without development.[26] In 2013–2014, the DDA had INR 202.71 billion in investments in three accounts (Nazul II, GDA, and earmarked funds) and a further INR 55.7 billion set aside for pensions, gratuities, provident funds, and so on.[27]

Differentiated Citizenship

This section provides an overview of the mechanisms and effects of differentiated citizenship by summarizing findings of the CoD case studies. Because of the pervasive social cleavages that characterize Indian society, one might be tempted to see highly unequal levels of service delivery in the city as little more than extensions of social inequality. Our research shows that, independently of these social criteria (class, caste, community), settlement types also impact levels of service delivery. Who you are may matter but where you live clearly matters as well, and probably more.

First, in our own fieldwork we found little evidence of overt caste discrimination.[28] In most of the JJCs, there are large concentration of Dalits (the proportion of Scheduled Castes in slums is 27 percent versus 15.6 percent in the nonslum population), but even across JJCs with similar proportions of Dalits, levels of services vary dramatically. In contrast to the vast literature on the US ghetto that points to specific state policies that have produced a unique, racially defined and spatially concentrated category of "urban outcasts,"[29] we found little evidence that state policies or interventions specifically discriminated against lower castes. Similarly, while settlement types correspond to class almost by definition, many settlements are home to various classes, and most notably, being middle class in Delhi does not in any way guarantee access to decent services, as witnessed in UACs. Instead, our 10 field cases provide clear and decisive evidence that settlement type is the basis for policies and practices that produce highly differentiated levels of service delivery. In Delhi, access to basic services—most notably water, sanitation, and solid-waste removal—is a function of the intertwining of space and legality.

Because JJCs and UACs are illegal, the state is not required to provide them basic services. In fact, the courts have ruled that agencies in charge of service delivery are under no obligation to provide services to JJCs and UACs, and in one instance, they explicitly barred service providers from delivering piped water to JJCs. In contrast, RCs are legal and in principle planned (that is, developed within a properly authorized area and in accordance with planning guidelines) but, as we shall see, are denied to full services in practice. Having said this, in all these excluded settlements, through a highly complex mix of political patronage, department pragmatism, and myriad community and private solutions, some basic services are delivered, however poor and intermittent. We begin by briefly describing the quality and nature of the water and sanitation they receive.

Across the board, the most incessant complaints and demands in excluded settlements are water related. With the exception of the older, settled Mangolpuri RC, none of the 10 excluded settlements has piped water that comes from the city's bulk water system. The excluded settlements all instead depend on a mix of tanker trucks, borewells (powered by either electric or hand pumps that tap groundwater directly), and water purchased in individual containers or from kiosks. Water delivery is, as a result, very uneven, and subject to highly discretionary arrangements and steep price differentials. For potable water (*meetha pani*), settlements rely heavily on tanker trucks operated also by private enterprise but mostly by the Delhi Jal Board (DJB), which are a ubiquitous sight in these settlements and a source of widespread anger and frustration.

In Kusumpur Pahari JCC, tankers arrive routinely and on time and are carefully directed by an "elected" *pradhan* to selected points throughout the settlement. We witnessed long lines to collect water, but the process was generally orderly and it was clear that residents knew when and where to queue for water. The *pradhan* kept a register of tanker truck delivery and communicated regularly with the DJB to solve problems. This arrangement conforms to the system of scheduled and routine delivery that the DJB claims to be implementing as a matter of policy. But this is actually the exception. In all our other field sites, tanker water delivery is unpredictable and the object of chaotic scrambles as households (often, women and girls who have stayed home from work and school, respectively) rush to fill plastic containers. Most of these tankers are dispatched by the DJB, but we also recorded many cases of private tankers, part of what the media has reported as a growing "tanker mafia." But even DJB tankers are subject to discretionary arrangements. For example, in Baljeet Nagar-F Block JJC, the arrangement reported by our respondents consisted of a complicated process in which a group of 8 to 10 households get a tanker "passed" by making payments of up to INR 4,000–5,000 (USD 55–70) to DJB officials, in return for which "contributing" households are guaranteed 200 liters per week. "Non-members" are left to pay INR 15 per 40 liters on delivery. In both cases, it should be emphasized that residents are paying for what is supposed to be a free public service.

In no settlement is tanker truck water sufficient, and communities also rely heavily on borewells (also known as tube wells). The groundwater in Delhi is often salty or contaminated by chemicals or leakage of sewage, so this groundwater is used only for cleaning and washing and referred to by residents as *khara pani* (salty water). Borewells are set up by households, private entrepreneurs, or government agencies. When a government agency provides a borewell, it is often through the work and to the credit of the local member of legislative assembly (MLA) (of Delhi), and the borewell often carries an inscription to that effect. But water from public borewells is spotty at best. In our site visits, we found as many dried-up government borewells as functioning ones, and most of our respondents report using private borewells. The DJB claims to have installed 4,128 borewells[30] in the city, but with a population now exceeding 18 million, this is clearly insufficient and has been dwarfed by private installations, which one media report in July 2014 put at 465,000.[31] Private borewells are expensive, however, with residents paying INR 1,000–1,500 per month to private operators, whereas they pay only INR 100 per month to access DJB wells. Private borewells are regulated in principle, but it is widely acknowledged that few have the requisite authorizations.

The situation for toilets is just as stark. Even in the limited situations where sanitation facilities are available, the disposal of fecal matter presents a massive health challenge in densely populated slums. More than anything else, the marker of the excluded settlements is the complete absence of sewerage systems. With the exception of one of the RCs (Mangolpuri), none of the settlements we studied are linked to bulk sewerage lines. These communities are left with four options for disposing of human waste: building in-house toilets that are not connected to the sewage system but to tanks (these are often not septic tanks, but simply storage tanks which are periodically emptied by private suction trucks) and often to stormwater drains (where they exist), using ill-maintained community toilet complexes (CTCs), defecating into plastic bags, or defecating in the open.

The nature of houses in JJCs, especially characterized by high density and in many cases a few built-up stories, does not generally allow for indoor toilets. Unauthorized colonies and RC residents are far more likely to have more permanent forms of housing and often have the space for an indoor toilet. But in sanitation terms, these facilities remain deeply problematic. Indoor toilets are either flushed to outside drains or routinely vacuumed out by privately contracted "bowsers." In the first case, sewage flows into streets, open canals, or drainage pipes, which are otherwise meant for "storm water." In both cases, the "sanitation service delivery chain" breaks down, meaning that there is no proper control over how waste is transported, treated, and disposed. Open raw sewage is a common sight (and complaint) in these communities. In Savda Ghevra RC, we found open spaces planned as playgrounds that were submerged by raw sewage and fecal sludge. There and in Indira Kalyan Vihar JJC, we also found that residents had built pit latrines with tarpaulin walls for privacy. In all the settlements we researched, we heard the complaint that during the monsoon, sewage spills out into the open, sometimes flooding homes.

Community toilet complexes are common in JJCs and RCs (but not UACs) and are prone to the same problems. First, the sanitary quality of CTCs depends on good maintenance and a reliable source of water. We only found one instance of a well-managed and well-maintained CTC. All the others were beset by operational problems often tied to inadequate maintenance by the agency that constructed the CTC. A common story is that shortly before elections, a local politician gets a CTC built but no one assumes responsibility for maintenance including day-to-day cleaning and periodic cleaning of the linked septic tank. In one JJC, three different CTCs had been provided by three different agencies, but none had running water. Complaints from women that they are harassed when they use the complexes are widespread, and most women avoid CTCs altogether at night. Most CTCs charge INR 1 per visit, a barrier just high enough that most children forgo CTCs. Further, there appears to be confusion over who owns which CTC.

From our 10 case studies, we can draw the following conclusions about basic service delivery in Delhi. First, and as summarized in Table 3.3, access to water and sanitation in excluded settlements is very poor. As one might anticipate, the problem is most acute in JJCs. Sangam Vihar, despite being the largest agglomeration of UACs in the city and having two MLAs, is very poorly serviced. Most surprising, though, was the finding that of the three RCs we studied, two (Savda Ghevra and Madanpur Khader) had neither piped water nor sewage systems. Despite the fact that both these colonies were planned, and that site visits confirmed that layouts were designed to accommodate bulk infrastructure, the residents of these colonies must make do without these basic public services. Second, our findings leave little doubt that independently

Table 3.3 Basic services in cities of Delhi, case site services, based on fieldwork in 2012–2015

Settlement type	Settlement name	Water	Sewerage and toilets	Drains	Solid waste	Electricity
JJC	Anantram Dairy Harijan Basti	NDMC pipeline with six taps in the *basti*, taps at the CTC, and an NDMC water tank	No individual toilets; all depend on a well-managed CTC	Underground drainage system	One *dhalao* about 50 meters away, with regular collection	NDMC provided but with *kachha* (temporary) bills
JJC	F Block Punjabi Basti	DJB tankers, tube wells, and households located in neighboring colonies	One CTC that is poorly managed, individual toilets with storage pit built in half the houses	No drainage system	No *dhalao* nearby; an Municipal Corporation of Delhi (MCD) truck passes by and garbage can be thrown in it if it stops	Legal metered connections (BSES Rajdhani), informal electricity supply, sharing electricity with neighbors
JJC	Indira Kalyan Vihar	Piped-water supply (same pipes providing drinking and non-drinking water), tube wells, tapping of main water lines, and water tankers	Four currently functional CTCs, private toilets with outlets into large drain	Narrow stormwater drains	One *dhalao* at a corner of the settlement; collection of garbage does happen but overflow of garbage in areas surrounding the *dhalao* is a common sight	Legal metered connections (BSES Rajdhani)
JJC	Kusumpur Pahari	Majority depend on DJB tankers, private tube wells within the JJC	Dysfunctional CTCs, many go for open defecation; a very few have built individual toilets	Narrow stormwater drains	One *dhalao* in the middle of the settlement along the main road that runs through the settlement	Legal metered connections (Reliance-BSES); there are families that still do not have electricity as they cannot afford to pay the bill

Contd

Table 3.3 contd

Settlement type	Settlement name	Water	Sewerage and toilets	Drains	Solid waste	Electricity
JJC	Sanjay Camp	One hand pump, public tube well, public taps in neighboring market areas, water taps, water tanker	One CTC which is inadequate, many go for open defecation	Only one part of the *basti* has drains	No *dhalao*, instead seven garbage dumpsters placed at different points in and around, garbage also thrown in the open near the railway line	Informal electricity supply
JJC	Jai Hind Camp	Only tankers: some are of DJB, others are paid for; private water tankers for nondrinking water	Open defecation; common constructed toilets and bathrooms for a minority part of the JJC	No drainage system	No *dhalao* in walking distance, private collection of garbage for minority part of JJC	Informal electricity supply
RC	Savda Ghevra	DJB water tankers for drinking water and private tube wells for nondrinking water	No sewer lines; one CTC per block but inadequate and poorly maintained in most cases; individual private toilets built by residents with "septic tanks"; open defecation by poorer households	Stormwater drains constructed but poorly maintained	NGO-based door-to-door collection of garbage for many blocks; *dhalao* for disposal; garbage also thrown in the open, uninhabited spaces	Received legal metered connections (TPDDL [Tata Power Delhi Distribution Limited]) a few months after resettlement
RC	Mangolpuri	Piped-water supply since about 20–25 years	Sewer lines approximately laid down 10–15 years ago; most households have toilets connected to the sewage system; CTC users are mostly tenants and JJC dwellers within the colony	Underground drainage system; it also has open stormdrains	MCD garbage van comes regularly; households have privately appointed cleaners in the inner lanes; there are also a few *dhalaos* within the colony	Received legal metered connections in the early 1980s

Contd

Table 3.3 contd

Settlement type	Settlement name	Water	Sewerage and toilets	Drains	Solid waste	Electricity
RC	Madanpur Khader	Privately installed hand pumps for nondrinking purposes; DJB tankers and privately purchased water jars for drinking purposes	No sewer lines; CTCs that rely on "septic tanks"; some CTCs are dysfunctional, and residents usually defecate in the open at night; some households have built private toilets with "septic tanks"	Drains constructed but poorly maintained	MCD designated *dhalaos* (several of which are being renovated); households have privately appointed cleaners in the inner lanes; NGOs also collect garbage from households for a fee	Legal metered connections (BSES Rajdhani)
UAC	Sangam Vihar (agglomeration of UACs)	Majority depend on government and private tube wells, a few residents procure water from DJB and private water tankers	No sewer lines; individual toilets that empty into "septic tanks" which are often simple cesspools with no protection against seepage; open defecation by poorer households	Stormwater drains running along the *pucca* roads but poorly maintained	Private contractor for door-to-door collection in a few blocks; MCD "tipper" vehicles pass through the main roads and garbage can be thrown in them directly	Formal electric supply has happened in stages: 1988 (electric substation for electricity provision for area inhabited prior to 1981), 1999 (single point delivery system); the late 2000s [legal metered connections from BSES Rajdhani]

Source: Authors.

of their class or status, the level at which citizens in Delhi access services is clearly tied to the type of settlement they live in, a finding supported by two important quantitative studies.[32] Three, though the legal status of settlements explains part of the exclusion, it does not explain the dramatic difference within settlements types. All JJCs are illegal and not entitled to services; yet, across JJCs, the level of actual servicing as provided through second-best solutions (tankers trucks and CTCs) does vary significantly.

In the absence of reliable public provisioning for water and sanitation, communities have little choice but to resort to various market solutions. These market solutions are not, however, those of well-functioning, competitive markets, but rather markets that are based on a range of artificial scarcities that generate high rents captured by strategically positioned elites. Communities thus pay a high premium to secure these basic services, a premium from which the planned settlements of the city are exempt. But the direct financial costs that are imposed on the urban poor almost pale in comparison to the high social and political costs they endure to access the most basic services. Securing water and finding a way to go to the bathroom in excluded settlements is time-consuming, unpredictable, and often humiliating and imposes a particularly high burden on women.

Negotiating Citizenship

If citizenship in the city is extremely differentiated, it is also highly negotiated. The citizens of excluded settlements do not have legal rights to services, but they do, as we have seen, secure some public services through second-best solutions. But within the legal and policy parameters that are defined by settlement types—the state's classification system for service delivery—there are a whole range of political intermediations, legal ambiguities, regulatory gaps, and local practices that give shape to the final set of arrangements. We specifically label these "political arrangements" to emphasize two points. First, they are indeed political in the sense that the outcome reflects the relative capacity of a community to engage with the state through representatives and negotiate for particular forms of provisioning. Second, we call these "arrangements" rather than settlements to underscore how tenuous and fragile they are. Unlike a right, a given community's capacity to organize and negotiate with the state represents a delicate equilibrium built on ever-shifting political and institutional alignments. In the following paragraphs, we present evidence from selected cases that illustrate the range and multiple logics of such political arrangements.

F Block of Punjabi Basti (different from the UAC called F Block Punjabi Basti and also known as Gayatri Colony) is a long established but highly vulnerable JJC. First settled 50 years ago on the site of a stone mine, the settlement has continued to grow despite repeated evictions, most recently in 2011. At that time, a large number of *jhuggi*s were bulldozed, but the eviction drew the attention of Delhi's legal rights NGOs who generated some media publicity and secured a court stay. The settlement was quickly rebuilt but continues to be deprived of services. There is no sewerage system and most residents defecate in the open or operate the most basic dry latrines. The water situation, described earlier, is among the most precarious we documented.

Yet, because of the experience of eviction, the community is well organized, has ties to NGOs, and boasts an energetic *pradhan* who appears to enjoy widespread community support. In 2008, as part of cultivating political ties to the then MLA, respondents report that the settlement even raised INR 50,000 to fund a *jagran* (all-night Hindu ritual) in his honor. Despite these displays of loyalty, many residents have had a largely adversarial relationship to their MLA and, in particular, accuse him of having misled them when they were evicted in 2011. Some claim he was complicit in the eviction, working with an erstwhile central government minister to free the land for developers. The community has nonetheless continued to engage with local authorities, routinely sending petitions and delegations to state agencies and strategically shifting their electoral support to another party in the assembly elections of 2013. But this degree of engagement has had little effect, especially in curtailing the predations of state agencies. In addition to having to pay for public tanker trucks, residents report paying DDA "officials" for constructing new *jhuggi*s (INR 10,000–20,000) as well as for making any improvements to existing *jhuggi*s. We collected similar reports from many other JJCs, but in F Block the practice seems to be especially pernicious and organized. Residents describe a finely tuned system of surveillance in which informants (some of whom are referred to as DDA "guards") report to the police, who in turn report to the DDA. One resident summarized the inexorable logic of the arrangement: "If you add two rows of bricks to increase the height of your jhuggi and don't pay, four rows of bricks will be demolished."

The residents of F Block do not approach the state as citizens or even as clients of a patronage regime in which votes are exchanged for benefits. Instead, they approach the state as supplicants in a highly unbalanced and insecure arrangement where their only point of leverage seems to be their refusal to disappear and their ability to pay fees. The vulnerability of this community is underscored by the state's apparent ability to simply make them invisible. Though the community has been surveyed on numerous occasions and appeared on the DUSIB list of JJCs in 2011 with an estimated 455 *jhuggis*, the houses at F Block disappeared in a 2014 data set released by the DUSIB, with a "no *jhuggis*?" label attached to its location on the accompanying map. In a revised data set released the same year, the number reappeared on the data set, but the map continued to say "no *jhuggies* found."

The highly insecure position of F Block's residents can be contrasted with the Anantram Dairy Harijan Basti, a JJC located in the core of the city. As its name implies, Anantram has a large population of Dalits, yet boasts a clean and well-serviced complex of community toilets and showers, open but well-maintained drainage systems, and a predictable supply of clean water. Most of the 300+ *jhuggis* are built of brick, some have a second floor, and the vast majority have stone-slab roofing. Residents report that they do not fear eviction and this is reflected in the reported price of *jhuggis*, which can reach as high as INR 1 million (or 10 lakhs), by far the highest we recorded in the six JJCs we studied. We found that the community enjoyed more or less consistent delivery of all basic services and could engage directly with state agencies to address problems. For example, when the local community water tank is close to empty, a simple call to the local New Delhi Municipal Council (NDMC,[33] the government agency in charge of that part of Delhi) office brings a tanker to refill the tank. In addition, there are also community standposts.

The location of this community in the jurisdiction of the NDMC—the heart of the city's political and social elite—might provide an obvious answer to why it is better serviced. But this interpretation is contradicted by the extremely poor and highly vulnerable status of two other JJCs we studied in the area, Sanjay Camp and Sonia Gandhi Camp. We found that both were at the lowest end of service delivery (similar to F Block), and a part of Sonia Gandhi Camp was actually demolished during the course of our fieldwork. If Anantram stands out, it is because it has benefitted from a political arrangement that takes the form of community-based clientelism.

For 15 of the past 20 years, this JJC was represented by an MLA who was highly organized and proactive in delivering services for the community. The MLA not only visited on a regular basis but was also an active ex officio member of the local neighborhood committee and presided over a local association of Dalit laborers (the Harijan Mazdoor Sudhaar Sabha, or Dalit Labour Improvement Society). Residents praise him widely for his work in the community and he is always invited to weddings and other social events.

In many respects, Anantram represents a classic case of successful political leveraging, precisely the kind that, Chatterjee has influentially argued, represents the only means by which the poor in urban India can successfully press claims on the state.[34] The success with which this community has brokered its relationship to the local state by leveraging representation must, however, be carefully qualified. First, the brokerage capacity of this MLA is unusual. In most areas of the city, political representation is divided between municipal councillors and an MLA. But the NDMC area where Anantram sits does not have a municipal councillor. The MLA as such not only wields monopoly representation but also has much more leverage over the local bureaucracy than is the norm for most MLAs. Second, as is the case with all patron–client arrangements, the services that the patron provides, however substantial, come at the expense of citizenship. Thus, on the one hand, the MLA proudly told us that he has the power to protect the community from eviction. On the other hand, the electricity bills that the community receives provide an unambiguous reminder of their client status. The top of the bill begins with a clear disclaimer (in English): "Purely temporary arrangement without confirming any legal right." Third, the coherent organization of the community and its overall political efficacy masks an underlying power structure marked by caste dominance. Though the community is predominantly Dalit, it is dominated by the Gujjar community. The *pradhan* is a Gujjar, and the Gujjars exercise control over all construction in the community. Several Dalit respondents also reported that the police work with the Gujjars in exacting illegal payments for changes to *jhuggis*. Most telling though is the system for water distribution. During our first field visits, we were impressed by the calm and orderly fashion in which residents line up to collect water from the taps installed by the NDMC. It was only later that we discovered that the "lines" are in fact caste hierarchical, with Gujjars having the right to queue up first and to collect as much water as they like while other castes are limited to only four buckets.

The four other JJCs in our sample all fell somewhere along the spectrum of the acute vulnerability seen in F Block to the organized clientelism of Anantram. But two generalizations about JJCs can be made. First, though most have been around for more than three decades, with the exception of Anantram, none has experienced significant improvements in water delivery or sanitation. Second, all display some degree of internal organization in the form of local associations, but in almost every case, local self-organization is tied to dependence on an elected representative. F Block is an exception here.

The local *pradhan* has independent local support and the community has strategically shifted its electoral support. But this relative capacity for self-assertion is itself tied to the fact that F Block is politically excluded with little effective representation. In all the other cases, the local *pradhan* (or *pradhan*s) and existing community associations are all closely tied to an elected politician and have little independent engagement with the state. Interestingly, in at least two of the settlements in our sample, residents (excluding community representatives) had little direct interaction with the state, interacting instead via brokers, or *dalaal*s, who are typically residents of the settlement and know "how to get work done."

The "work" often does not involve delivery of community-level basic services, but instead meeting individual requirements such as a voter ID card. There is, of course, a payment for this, but residents differentiate between this—a payment for a service efficiently rendered—and a bribe.

It would of course be perfectly reasonable to tie both of these conditions—material exclusion and political dependency—to the highly insecure tenure status of the JJC. Undoubtedly, the threat of eviction looms large over the lives of those who live in *jhuggi*s and provides elected representatives with significant leverage. However, in examining our next two excluded settlement categories—UACs and RCs—it becomes clear that this precariousness is hardly limited to JJCs.

Unauthorized colonies are also extremely heterogeneous, but in general, because residents actually have some degree of a proprietary claim to tenure, even if the settlement as a whole is unauthorized, they are not as vulnerable as residents of JJCs. In contrast to JJC residents, none of our UAC respondents ever expressed concern about eviction, and residents have clearly invested in their homes. Three- to four-storied structures are common sights in UACs, as are extensive privately installed and controlled borewells and water-distribution systems. Nonetheless, according to legal and policy instruments, including the master plan, UACs are not entitled to services, and a history of regularizing UACs (which produces the mouthful oxymoron "regularized-unauthorized colonies") keeps them in a legal and political limbo. Before each election, governments make promises about regularization, and in 2008 when there was a call for applications from UACs, 1,639 of them applied. As documented in a CoD report, the process of regularization is itself fraught with bureaucratic hurdles, legal gymnastics, and political manipulation, and the outcome is always highly uncertain.[35] Recently, in December 2019, the parliament enacted the National Capital Territory of Delhi (Recognition of Property Rights of

Residents in Unauthorized Colonies) Act,[36] which recognizes the property rights of residents in UACs by securing the rights of ownership or transfer or mortgage in favor of the residents of such colonies who are possessing properties on the basis of power of attorney, agreement to sale, will, possession letter, or any other documents including documents evidencing payment of consideration. This law confusingly appears to confer property rights on residents of UACs without explicit provisions on regularization of such colonies.

Since regularization and elevation to full citizenship remains elusive, UACs must also negotiate for services. The cases we selected were all located in Sangam Vihar, a city within the city that residents proudly report is the largest UAC in Asia. The settlement has a grid-like structure, but the lanes are so narrow and choked that no public buses can enter. Sangam Vihar is partitioned into blocks, and service delivery arrangements vary dramatically across blocks. Most residents rely on private pipes that deliver water to select households from large borewells.[37] Some of the borewells are public but most are private, and the system of pipes is entirely private, with two or three sets of pipes a common sight in many streets. Households negotiate supply and prices individually with "operators," who are widely reported to work with elected representatives. The resulting rents appear to be significant, as revealed by a natural experiment. In early 2014, when for a brief moment the water system was brought under community control, monthly prices fell from INR 1,500 to INR 100. The service is expensive and unreliable. Water is only delivered at certain hours, and most residents collect water in plastic buckets. The system is also clearly unsustainable. The electric borewells now in operation replaced hand pumps that went dry in the 1980s when the water table dropped. Although the water table continues to drop, we saw no evidence that the government is taking action. Despite the fact that there is a main trunk water line that links Sangam Vihar to a nearby water treatment plant, as of 2013 there were no plans to link the community through network pipes.[38]

So, what explains this perniciously low level of services? The answer is clearly not poverty or market forces. The rates that residents pay for water are well above rates in planned colonies. Moreover, countless residents we interviewed insisted that they wanted to be "regularized" so that they can pay taxes and access proper services. The low-level service equilibrium instead results from a complex web of power relations between residents, elected officials, local entrepreneurs, and state agencies. Residents report that municipal agents, with the help of the police, collect thousands of rupees from residents undertaking new construction, and that they get information about new projects from builders, contractors, and building-supply shopkeepers. This predation is so routinized that residents do not speak of corruption, or theft, or violation of the law, but rather of something that the state just does. Respondents reported this activity by saying that the "the police ask for INR 10,000–20,000," or "[one] has to give Rs 20,000—Rs 30,000 to the police." A senior local political representative explained the power equation in simple terms: "If I am strict and I tell the police and MCD not to collect money, they will not allow any construction at all."[39] With respect to the water-distribution system and the private operators who are protected by politicians, one respondent descried the logic of the protection rackets: "Mafia log hain; dabang log hain woh aur apnee hee chalwate hain" (They are mafia people, they are powerful people and what they want happens). In other words, all the key actors benefit from the current equilibrium, except of course, the residents.

But these are hardly passive citizens. In contrast to many JJCs, Sangam Vihar has strong associational structures that exist independently of political parties. The primary impetus for organization has been the hope of regularization. Going as far back as the mid-1980s, a local welfare association was formed to petition the government for regularization. The association lobbied its representative who wrote to the relevant minister at the time. Claiming a population of 100,000, the representative noted that "without regularization the Colony is lacking in basic amenities like water, electricity, post office, bus service etc.… I shall be grateful if you kindly get the matter looked into for necessary action."[40] Having secured no gains by the mid-1990s, residents started forming resident welfare associations (RWAs) on a block level and again started organizing for regularization. RWA representatives showed us thick sheaves of paperwork they had submitted to various government agencies over the years. At the time of our fieldwork, nearly 30 blocks in Sangam Vihar had formed RWAs. Some RWAs had formal structures, with regular elections supervised by government officials residing in the colony, while others were basically run by those who volunteered. In response to a call by the government in 2008 for regularization applications, the block-level RWAs formed a colony-wide association, the Mahasangh. The hope was not only that the *Mahasangh* would give them more clout as a community but that some of the more experienced and capable blocks could help others with the complex application process. Eventually, most of these blocks of Sangam Vihar submitted applications, which in most cases ran into hundreds of pages complete with block layouts. As of 2013, only five blocks had been officially "regularized" (although two of these, which we studied in detail, were yet to receive better services), and most of the RWA officials we interviewed were despondent about the prospects for regularization. Most in fact dismissed the process as a little more than an election stunt, trotted out before each Delhi assembly election, and pointed out that the "regularized" blocks were well connected to the ruling party at the time of regularization.

The low-level service equilibrium is sustained by the fact that settlements such as Sangam Vihar—despite being home to as many as a million people and an estimated 190,000 voters, despite being fairly well-off compared to JJCs, and despite being relatively well organized—are, at the end of the day, "unauthorized." These settlements are, in other words, caught in a legal-political netherworld that fundamentally compromises their citizenship. The MLA captured this democratic paradox of citizens without a city when he noted that by law he was not able to spend special development funds that each MLA receives on Sangam Vihar. As he explained to the Delhi State Assembly, "Though my voters are authorized, I am an unauthorized MLA because I speak for an unauthorized community."[41]

We now describe some of our key findings on RCs.[42] First, these settlements are almost invariably located on the outer edge of the city and generally only accessible by a single access road. This limits access to the public transportation grid (which is poor to begin with) and exacerbates the overall spatial dislocation of housing from work. Second, though RCs are planned to accommodate basic services and located in low-density areas where the costs of laying basic infrastructure are low, basic water and sanitation have not been delivered. The Master Plan of Delhi 2021 claims that "sewage facilities have been provided in all the Resettlement Colonies,"[43] but in two of the three large RCs (Savda Ghevra and Madanpur Khader), where we conducted fieldwork, there was no sewerage or piped water for populations of approximately 50,000 and 150,000, respectively.[44] Residents in both settlements depended either on private borewells or tanker trucks for water. In the absence of sewage facilities, spaces that had been planned for public facilities are filled with pools of raw sewage or piles of garbage. Third, residents stay on allocated plots (now apartments), but plot sizes have shrunk from 17.5–66.9 square meters[45] (or 21–80 square yards) in the 1960s and 1970s to 12.5–18 square meters in the current period. Moreover, construction is entirely private and not subject to any enforced regulations. Multitiered brick homes are built with inadequate frame support and are subject to collapse. Internal latrines are not designed to manage sewage effectively. Informal businesses that produce solid waste and air pollution proliferate in open spaces.[46] Fourth, though the developmental state has absconded from its service delivery commitments, the predatory state is in full view. As is the case for all our excluded settlements, RCs are subject to the full range of "payments" for construction.

Governance in Delhi

Differentiated citizenship in Delhi is not the result of governance failures—as the good governance literature would insist—but rather a result of how the city is governed. Many of these governance problems can be attributed to democratic deficits.

The first and the most glaring is the disempowerment of elected representatives, a key obstacle to vibrant democracy. Across all the cases we studied, we found that municipal councillors have a very limited role to play largely because all of the key governance and delivery functions are located at the state or center. Indeed, among the basic services that this project surveyed, solid-waste disposal is the only service that sits under the jurisdiction of these councillors. MLAs play a much more important role. But here again, institutional constraints produce perverse incentives. The average MLA in Delhi represents over 200,000 people, a good-sized city in most countries and a level of aggregation that does not allow for working closely with communities. They also do not make policy. The state assembly meets only rarely and most policy is made either within powerful bureaucracies or at higher levels of political power, such as the union government, which controls land and the police in the state. In securing their electoral position, MLAs are thus limited to distributing patronage. In other words, rather than promoting the delivery of public goods such as piped water, they have a stake in preserving the delivery of discrete goods such as tanker trucks.

The second democratic deficit consists of the weakness of effective citizenship. As we have seen, in practice the residents of excluded settlements cannot make demands for services based on their rights. Instead, they are limited to negotiating unstable and suboptimal arrangements for service delivery that are expensive and often socially debilitating. Urban reformers have recognized this problem in India and elsewhere, and this has given rise to calls for strengthening democratic participation. In virtually all official policy documents on urban governance, there is a recognition that the complex processes of urban transformation cannot be achieved in a sustainable manner without community participation. Our findings, however, suggest that these exhortations to work with citizens have not been supported with new practices and institutional designs. For example, the process of regularization of UACs, which in principle affects 4 million people, has been opaque and highly bureaucratic, and at no point has involved any kind of community participation. The complete disengagement of government institutions from communities is also manifest in the area of service delivery. In the excluded settlements where we conducted fieldwork, we were often struck by the total absence of the service-delivery state. In sharp contrast to the presence of the predatory elements of the state, none of the service-delivery agencies had offices in any of our sites and we rarely encountered officials from these agencies in our visits.

The eight settlement categories into which the city is divided represent, in effect, a form of differentiated citizenship. In law and in practice, each settlement type receives a different level of service delivery. Planned colonies represent about a quarter of the city and enjoy a full array of services. In the rest of the city, service levels are highly uneven. Electricity is the only exception: it is now widely available across all settlement categories. Where a citizen lives in Delhi determines the level of basic services to which he or she is entitled. These services are essential to supporting basic core capabilities such as health, education, and economic opportunity. Differentiated citizenship, as such, sustains and amplifies inequality by excluding residents from basic services. What is more, the extent of this exclusion seems to be growing.

Conclusion

Will this change? In February 2015, a newly formed political entity, the Aam Aadmi Party (AAP, the name in Hindi translates as the common man's party), swept the elections to the NCTD legislative assembly, winning 67 of 70 seats, riding on a wave of anti-corruption sentiment from the middle class[47] and a base of political support in the informal settlements. Since then, until recently, the AAP has been in the news more for a volatile political engagement with the union government. That culminated in a court battle with the lieutenant governor over the exercise of powers and for its differences with the municipal corporations that were governed by a different political party, the Bharatiya Janata Party (BJP), which was and is also the party currently running the federal government. In part, as a result of this perception, the AAP was unable to reproduce its electoral performance in the local elections held in April 2017 and was unable to come to power in any of the municipal corporations, which, thus, continue to be under the control of the BJP. Later, in 2019, the BJP won all seven parliamentary constituencies with a majority of the popular vote in a three-cornered contest. Since then, AAP's communication has changed to emphasize changes it has made on the ground in Delhi, especially in the delivery of public education and health services and in advocating for regularization of UACs. Recently, at the time of writing, the federal BJP government (which regulates issues of land in Delhi) has enacted legislation, making it possible for residents of UACs to acquire full property rights, but the details remain unclear even as the city moves to its next legislative assembly election. The AAP campaigned on a platform of less differentiated citizenship and equitable service provision for the Delhi Assembly elections held in February 2020. The party won a massive victory (discussed in Chapter 13 in this volume), but it was not clear whether this was the issue on which the voter made their choice, or whether they chose on polarizing identity issues (specifically Hindutva). Now that the AAP has a mandate, the question to ask in a few years is whether citizenship in Delhi remains as differentiated and negotiated as it is today. Until then, citizenship in Delhi is likely to remain differentiated and negotiated.

Notes

1. We gratefully acknowledge the research and support of Ben Mandelkern, Bijendra Jha, Ram Pravesh Shahi, and Sonal Sharma, as well as useful comments and feedback from other colleagues at Centre for Policy Research, Brown University, and participants at the workshop on Delhi and the NCR held in November 2017 at Center for Advanced Study of India (CASI), University of Pennsylvania.

2. The Government of National Capital Territory of Delhi (GNCTD) defines eight types of settlements in the city, including "planned colonies." The other seven settlement types in Delhi, as defined by GNCTD, are: slum-designated areas, *jhuggi jhopri* clusters, unauthorized colonies, regularized unauthorized colonies, resettlement colonies (RCs), urban villages, and rural villages.

3. Patrick Heller, Partha Mukhopadhyay, Shahana Sheikh, and Subhadra Banda, *Exclusion, Informality and Predation in the Citi pes of Delhi: An Overview of the Cities of Delhi Project* (New Delhi: Centre for Policy Research, 2015).

4. Ministry of Environment and Forests, Government of India, and Planning Department, Government of National Capital Territory of Delhi, *Delhi Urban Environment and Infrastructure Improvement Project (DUEIIP) Status Report for Delhi 21* (New Delhi: Government of India and Government of National Capital Territory of Delhi, 2001).

5. Cities of Delhi, *Categorisation of Settlement in Delhi*, policy brief (New Delhi: Centre for Policy Research, 2015).

6. Gautam Bhan, "Planned Illegalities: Housing and the 'Failure' of Planning in Delhi; 1957–2010," *Economic and Political Weekly* 48, no. 24 (2013): 58–70.

7. Augustin Maria, "Urban Water Crisis in Delhi. Stakeholders Responses and Potential Scenarios of Evolution," *IDD-RI Idee Pour le Debat* 6 (2008), available at https://www.iddri.org/sites/default/files/import/publications/id_0806_maria_urban-crisis-water-delhi.pdf.

8. Anna Zimmer, "Enumerating the Semi-visible: The Politics of Regularising Delhi's Unauthorised Colonies," *Economic and Political Weekly* 47, no. 30 (2012): 89–97; Bhan, "Planned Illegalities," 58–70.

9. *Common Cause v. Union of India*, CWP No. 4771/1993.

10. Usha Ramanathan, "Illegality and the Urban Poor," *Economic and Political Weekly* 41, no. 29 (2006): 3193–3197.

11. Bhanu Joshi, Kanhu Charan Pradhan, and Pranav Sidhwani, "Urban Voting and Party Choices in Delhi," *Economic and Political Weekly* 51, no. 5 (2016): 64–72.

12. The authors thank Shamindra Nath Roy (see Chapter 4 in this volume) for help with the post-coding and analysis.

13. For details, see Chapter 3.

14. *Almitra Patel v. Union of India*, 2 SCC 679 (2002).

15. Bhan, "Planned Illegalities."

16. Ranjana Sengupta, *Delhi Metropolitan: The Making of an Unlikely City* (New Delhi: Penguin Books India, 2007); Bhan, "Planned Illegalities," 58–70.

17. Abhijit Datta and Gangadhar Jha, "Delhi: Two Decades of Plan Implementation," *Habitat International* 7, nos. 1–2 (1983): 37–45.

18. Bhan, "Planned Illegalities," 60.

19. Datta and Jha, "Delhi," 42.

20. Bhan, "Planned Illegalities," 61–62.

21. For instance, several economic surveys of the GNCTD as well as the Master Plan of Delhi 2021; Delhi Development Authority, *Master Plan for Delhi: 2021* (New Delhi: Delhi Development Authority, 2007;—repr., 2010).

22. Delhi Development Authority, *Annual Report 1980–81* (New Delhi: Delhi Development Authority, 1981).

23. Delhi Development Authority, *Annual Report 2003–04* (New Delhi: Delhi Development Authority, 2004), 50.

24. Delhi Development Authority, *Annual Report 2011–12* (New Delhi: Delhi Development Authority, 2012), 1.

25. Patrick Heller and Partha Mukhopadhyay, "State-Produced Inequality in an Indian City," *Seminar* 672 (2015): 51–55.

26. Shahana Sheikh and Ben Mandelkern, "The Delhi Development Authority: Accumulation without Development," a report of the Cities of Delhi project (New Delhi: Centre for Policy Research, 2014).

27. Delhi Development Authority, *Annual Report 2013–14* (New Delhi: Delhi Development Authority, 2014), 50.

28. Though the existing quantitative data on caste segregation is in its infancy in India, three existing studies do support this claim. Vithayathil and Singh, as well as Sidhwani, find that at the ward level, there is evidence of spatial segregation of Dalits. But the reported levels, as measured by the index of dissimilarity, are very modest when compared to levels in the United States of America and South Africa (Schensul and Heller). Singh also finds that migrant status and neighborhood, but not caste, explain marked differentials in access to water and sanitation. See Trina Vithayathil and Gayatri Singh, "Spaces of Discrimination: Residential Discrimination in Indian Cities," *Economic and Political Weekly* 47, no. 37 (2012): 60–66; Pranav Sidhwani, "Spatial Inequality in Big Indian Cities," *Economic and Political Weekly* 50, no. 20 (2015): 55–62; Daniel Schensul and Patrick Heller, "Legacies, Change and Transformation in the Post-Apartheid City: Towards an Urban Sociological Cartography," *International Journal of Urban and Regional Research* 35, no. 1 (2011): 78–109; Gayatri Singh, "Freedom to Move, Barriers to Stay: An Examination of Rural Migrants' Urban Transition in Contemporary India" (PhD diss., Brown University, Rhode Island, 2014).

29. Loic Wacquant, *Urban Outcasts: A Comparative Sociology of Advanced Marginality* (Cambridge: Polity Press, 2008).

30. Delhi Jal Board, "District Wise Ground Water Data with respect to Borewells and Tubewells of Delhi," January 28, 2014, available at http://delhijalboard. nic.in/sites/default/files/District_wise_data.pdf, accessed January 15, 2020.

31. Mail Today Bureau, Borewells Suck Delhi Future Dry, *India Today*, July 8, 2014, available at https://www.indiatoday.in/india/story/borewells-suck-delhi-future-dry-199618-2014-07-08, accessed January 15, 2020.

32. Sidhwani finds that there is much more spatial segregation by level of services (access to water and sanitation) than by caste or class (as measured by both assets and education) provides quantitative support for our finding; Sidhwani, "Spatial Inequality in Big Indian Cities." For another spatial study which finds that with similar findings (location matters more than individual status), see Singh, "Freedom to Move, Barriers to Stay."

33. The New Delhi Municipal Council (NDMC) governs about 3 percent of Delhi's land area, located in the center of the city and dominated by planned housing for members of India's parliament and officers of the executive and the judiciary, including the prime minister, president, chief justice, and officers of the judiciary, civil services, and so on.

34. Partha Chatterjee, *The Politics of the Governed: Reflections on Popular Politics in Most of the World* (New York: Columbia University Press, 2004).

35. Shahana Sheikh and Subhadra Banda, "The Thin Line between Legitimate and Illegal: Regularising Unauthorised Colonies in Delhi," a report of the Cities of Delhi project (New Delhi: Centre for Policy Research, 2014).

36. Ministry of Law and Justice (Legislative Department), "The National Capital Territory of Delhi (Recognition of Property Rights of Residents of Unauthorized Colonies) Act 2019" (New Delhi: Government of India, 2019).

37. See also Suneetha Dasappa Kacker and Anuradha Joshi, "Pipe dreams? The Governance of Urban Water Supply in Informal Settlements, New Delhi," *IDS Bulletin* 43, no. 2 (2012): 27–36.

38. This may have changed since the time of our fieldwork. The Aam Aadmi Party government (see the concluding section of this chapter) of the GNCTD claims that 1,669 kilometers of new water pipelines have been added in its tenure. Paras Singh, "Water No Longer a Pipe Dream for Them," *Times of India*, June 23, 2019, available at https://timesofindia.indiatimes.com/city/delhi/water-no-longer-a-pipe-dream-for-them/articleshow/69919608.cms, accessed on January 15, 2020.

39. Interview on May 10, 2013.

40. Kishan Chand Bainiwal, member of the standing committee, Municipal Corporation of Delhi, "Letter to Dalbir Singh, Minister of State for Urban development, Nirman Bhavan, New Delhi," January 30, 1987.

41. Interview with the member of legislative assembly of Sangam Vihar Assembly Constituency, May 10, 2013.

42. Due to space limitations, we are unable to present more details about RCs here. For further details, see Heller et al., *Exclusion, Informality and Predation in the Cities of Delhi.*

43. Delhi Development Authority, *Master Plan for Delhi*, 238.

44. Population estimates for the newer RCs are not available in official documents, and these estimates were provided to us by residents living in these areas. The exception was Mangolpuri which over the past decade has received sewage and piped water. Mangolpuri is from the first wave of RCs and was founded over 40 years ago.

45. IL&FS Ecosmart Limited, "City Development Plan: Delhi," chapter on urban poor and slum (New Delhi: Department of Urban Development, GNCTD, 2006).

46. In Madanpur Khader, which is located in the vicinity of a large hospital, an open space has been converted into a business that recycles medical waste. Barefoot children wade through heaps of refuse picking out recyclables. Nearby households complain that the wastes collect in their drainage pipes.

47. Poulomi Chakrabarti, "Urban Middle Class Politics: India's Third Democratic Upsurge," India in Transition, Center for Advanced Study of India, University of Pennsylvania, September 26, 2016, available at https://casi.sas.upenn.edu/iit/poulomichakrabarti, accessed on October 3, 2020.

CHAPTER 4

Services

Spatial Inequality of Basic Infrastructure

Shamindra Nath Roy[*]

Introduction

One of the most visible facets of urbanization in India is that it cannot be associated always with a rising standard of living or equal opportunity in terms of the generation of economic and social capital. While there are substantial ambitions of upward mobility among the rural people when they move to cities,[1] their urban destinations remain more unequal than their village homes, and this inequality has been continuously rising since the early 1990s.[2, 3] There is also an increasingly large aspirational push in rural spaces to acquire urban characteristics, which is evident in the gradual convergence in consumption behavior,[4] or increasing investment in education, especially in places such as census towns which are rapidly morphing from rural to urban.[5] However, this drive toward being urban leads to a more complex set of social, political, and institutional processes of city building, which is often coupled with the fuzzy coalitions between the "business class" and the "political class"[6] and is responsible for a divisive landscape marked by not only a visible inequality of income but also inequality in housing, security of land and tenure, basic infrastructure, and access to social safety nets.

While it is widely understood that urban inequality is multidimensional,[7] the vectors of it are also diverse, ranging from social, economic, political, and more importantly, spatial. While dealing with public goods such as basic infrastructure, the question of spatial inequality, or "spaces *where* people live" becomes more important, primarily due to two reasons. The first is related to

---

[*] The author gratefully acknowledges the help of Nooren Fatima for this chapter.

the continuously dynamic and haphazard nature of urban growth, which is an offshoot of a much "informalized planning regime,"[8] where planning not only regulates but also "determines and limits" the spaces for urban inhabitance[9] across social and economic lines. This often results in informalities in terms of inhabitation and production of city space, and the supply of basic services gets constrained due to the violation of planning regulations. It is worth noting that such spatial informalities are diverse and access to services varies by the different ways these spaces are settled, ranging from squatting on public land to building structures on land not earmarked for residential housing. The second factor that makes spatial inequality interesting relates to the wider question of citizenship and variation of micro-political orders in differentiated city spaces. The diverse ways through which the local societal actors in different kinds of urban spaces negotiate with the state for services control how the inequalities in basic infrastructure mutate over space and time.[10]

This chapter deals with spatial inequality in terms of the provision of basic services in Delhi, using a previously unexploited quantitative framework. In order to do so, it draws inferences from the wide range of in-depth studies that deals with the taxonomy of settlements in Delhi and the variation of basic infrastructure across them. The objective of this chapter is to quantitatively check whether the broad patterns of such inequality, as described in the qualitative and policy literature,[11] hold true if the spatial classifications of the settlements are mapped with large-scale survey data.

Spatial Segregation in Delhi: Insights from Previous Research

The drive to build Delhi as one of the engines for growth has not been fully fulfilled, as the city is mainly "dependent on public resources and never built a comparative advantage in any particular economic sector."[12] However, the push certainly entailed the rise of consumerism and middle-class ideologies[13] which resulted wide socio-spatial polarization, channelized by a pool of legal, paralegal, and extralegal set of operations. Like any other big Indian city, Delhi is segregated by caste and occupation. While these traditional forms of inequalities persist, they are relegated to much lower spatial scale, in neighborhoods often called as "mohallas" or "colonies."[14] The postcolonial urban growth pattern is marked by more severe spatial inequalities than social inequalities,[15] where very different economic groups live much closer to each other while economic inequality across identity lines is less prominent.[16] This chapter investigates whether similar spatial discontinuities persist in terms of basic infrastructure such as access to metered water connections or properly paved roads. Though most of this basic infrastructure is generally not private but public, the focus here is on spatial inequality and the variation across socioreligious groups and migrants—by considering the spatial concentration of particular groups in specific areas of the city[17] and their correlation with inferior quality of services.[18]

Database and Methodology

Delhi is a complex mosaic of more than 2,000 unique colonies[19] or local neighborhoods[20] and numerous sub-colonies, which are distributed across both urban and rural spaces.[21] These colonies have very different social and economic profiles while their spatial footprint seems to be very mixed, an offshoot of a carefully instrumented exclusionary planning process[22] where semiformal or informal settlements pertaining to very different legalities are encouraged to grow around formal or planned settlements. The formal or planned colonies, which are constructed under master plans and enjoy the best of trunk infrastructure provided by the state, accommodate only one-fourth of the city's population.[23] The rest of the population resides in seven other kinds of informal colonies,[24] which are quite different in terms of security of land and tenure and provision of basic infrastructure—where services are often self-provided by the inhabitants or almost nonexistent. However, most of the studies dealing with this kind of spatial inequality are either qualitative or limited at the municipal ward level,[25] as the published government data do not provide enough spatial granularity to study the complex urban space of Delhi.[26] The Center for the Advanced Study of India–National Capital Region (CASI–NCR) Survey provides a representative sample of 3,349 households in the National Capital Territory (NCT), Delhi, which have randomly been chosen from 311 geo-located polling booths (PBs)[27] in the city. Each PB covers a set of specific localities in which the sample households are distributed. Mapping these PB localities with the eight specific settlement types of Delhi provides a unique opportunity to uncover the micro-spatial inequality in such a complex urban space. The total number of localities/colonies[28] covered by the PBs considered under the CASI–NCR Survey is 858, which is roughly 34 percent of all the colonies in Delhi.[29]

Since the CASI–NCR data did not collect the colony-type information during the survey, there are multiple steps through which such matching has been accomplished. The primary sample unit of the survey was PBs, which are matched to the colonies using the electoral rolls.[30] This information was then matched with the colony-type database,[31] where each colony covered by the survey was classified into eight broad groups.[32] The third step involved labeling the 311 PBs as per the composition of all the 858 colonies falling into them. There are two main problems that have appeared while matching and aggregating the colony-type to PBs:

1. One PB usually had multiple localities mapped to it, and each PB needed to be assigned a particular colony category depending upon the colonies contained therein. While 256 out of 311 PBs (82 percent) only have one of the eight unique kinds of colonies, the rest (18 percent) are very mixed in composition with up to three different types of colonies in one PB. The number of colonies within a PB also varies a lot and can go up to 17 colonies in a PB. All the 311 PBs and the 3,349 households falling in them are, therefore, divided across two main categories, either a "unique PB" or a "mixed PB." The unique PB households are further categorized into eight different types of colonies, thereby taking the total colony category to nine, together with the mixed colony PBs.

2. For some of the PBs, it was not possible to neatly categorize some of the colonies as they were not found in the colony-type database or some of them are divided into different types of sub-colonies.[33] While some of these could be identified using Google Earth imagery, the colonies which could not be categorized are labeled as "uncategorized" or "mixed colonies."

The distribution of colonies by the CASI–NCR Survey fits well with the government estimate of most type of colonies (Government of National Capital Territory of Delhi [GNCTD], 2008–2009), except the *jhuggi jhopri* clusters (JJCs), slum-designated areas (SDAs), regularized-unauthorized colonies (RUCs), and somewhat in the case of planned colonies (Table 4.1). While the surveyed colonies are evenly distributed across Delhi (Figure 4.1) other than the southern fringes,[34] the differences in estimates can be mostly due to classifying some PBs as mixed, where a neat categorization could not be made. However, the higher share of RUCs may also be attributed to the fact that this study categorized a lot of settlements which were regularized as early as the 1960s but now look like planned colonies despite remaining RUCs. These kinds of discrepancies could only be addressed through field visits, which was outside the scope of this study.

Table 4.1   Comparison of settlement typologies in Delhi

Type of colonies	Share (%) to total population (GNCTD)	Share (%) to total population (CASI–NCR Survey)	Share (%) to total households (CASI–NCR Survey)
JJCs	14.8	5.4 (8.8)	5.2 (8.6)
Slum-designated areas	19.1	1.7	1.7
Unauthorized colonies	5.3	6.9	7.2
Jhuggi jhopri (JJ) resettlement colonies	12.7	14.1	13.9
Rural villages	5.3	5.1	4.9
Regularized unauthorized colonies	12.7	32.2	31.6
Urban villages	6.4	6.8	7.1
Planned colonies	23.7	9.5 (13.2)	10.2 (14.0)

Sources: Economic Survey of Delhi, 2008–2009, and author's calculations from the CASI–NCR Survey data.

Notes: The figures in parentheses are the shares of colony if the broader definition is considered. By broader definition, it refers to the household/population of a colony if it is uniquely situated in a PB as well as in a mixed PB.

Delhi as a Mixed Space

Spatial heterogeneity in the urban space of Delhi is evident in the literature.[35] The modified CASI–NCR Survey data, now blended with the colony information, facilitates characterizing the contours of such mixed space across geographical, social, and economic lines. Figure 4.2a shows that the core and eastern fringes of the city are much more populated by mixed colonies, where

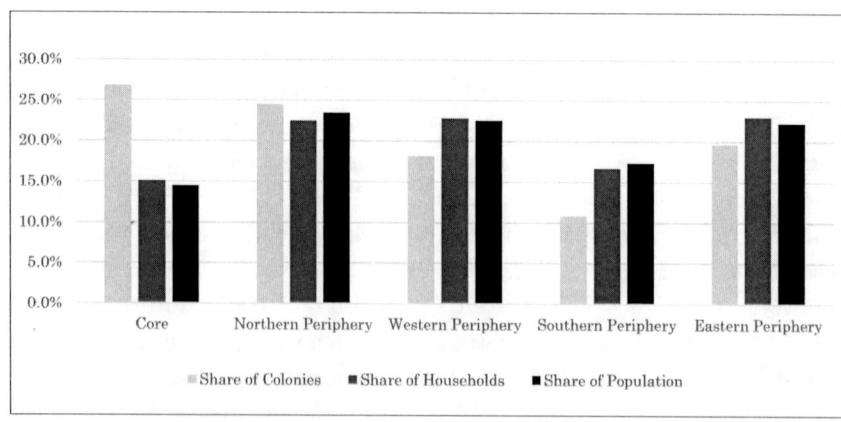

Figure 4.1   Distribution of colonies in the NCR

Source: Author's calculations from the CASI–NCR Survey data.

there are numerous sub-colonies, which are subject to very different legalities, planning, and service regulations. These areas, along with some parts of the inner northern periphery, are also the spaces where each PB often comprises multiple colonies (Figure 4.2b).

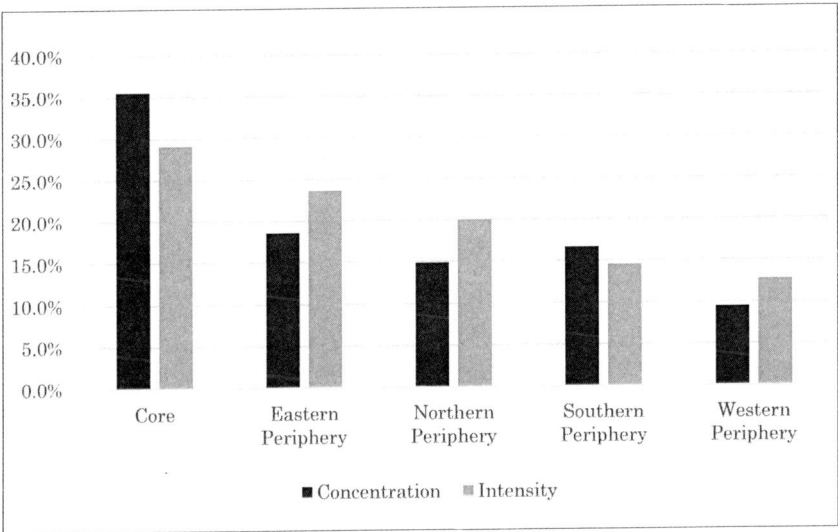

(a) Distribution of mixed colonies

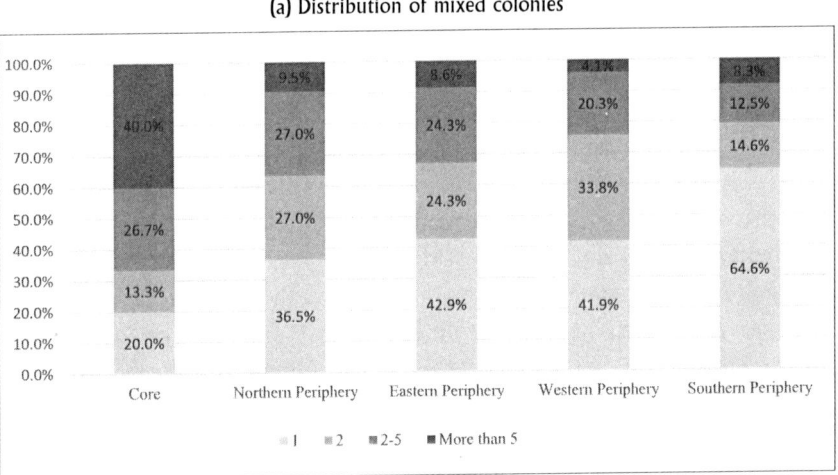

(b) Number of colonies by PBs

Figure 4.2   Distribution of mixed colonies

Source: Author's calculations from the CASI–NCR Survey data.

Note: "Concentration" refers to share of mixed colony PBs to total PBs in a particular space while "Intensity" refers to share of mixed colony PBs in a particular area to all mixed colony PBs.

About 26 percent of the PBs in core districts and more than 15 percent in the eastern periphery consist of two or more different kinds of colonies nested within each other. The average distance of the two nearest but unique PBs containing different kinds of colonies is a little less than 1 kilometer throughout the city; while in 60 percent of cases, a planned colony is encircled by some form of informal colony within a radius of 1 kilometer. Such mixed spatiality is more prevalent in the areas just falling at the boundary of core growth areas of the city (Figure 4.3a), which have grown significantly over the period 1975–1990, and where large and dense colonies built by private developers were common.

These areas mainly remained as unauthorized colonies (UCs) (Figure 4.3b), as they were built outside the development area of the master plan, a process infamously marked as "planned illegalities."[36] Eventually, some of these colonies were regularized by the government across different periods, and thus transformed to very mixed neighborhoods over time (Figure 4.3c).

The diversity in the settlement type and built form is also associated with the social mosaic of the city. This is due to the fact that social and economic segregation in Delhi is driven by the spatial organization of the capital and the consequent processes of land development.[37] The CASI–NCR Survey data also reflects this, where the share of salaried government employees or people engaged in other high-end jobs, such as finance, real estate, or business activities, is substantially high in planned colonies. The JJCs show variations in industries and nature of work, but the type of occupations is quite different from the affluent neighborhoods. The RUCs, resettlement colonies, or urban villages have a more mixed profile (Table 4.2). This diversity is because of the fact that a lot of the older resettlement colonies, RUCs, and urban villages are located as enclaves across and near the city core, and provide low-cost rental housing to the migrant population around workplaces and a diverse range of accommodation quality. As per the CASI–NCR Survey, around 77 percent of the renter population and 65 percent of the migrant workforce[38] of the city reside in these three kinds of colonies.

This picture of occupational diversity is also reflected in the wealth profile of the colonies, where the median household in a planned colony ranks at the 72nd percentile of the asset index[39] despite constituting only 10 percent of the city's population (Table 4.1). On the other hand, the percentile rank for median households in RUCs stands at 53 and 28 for JJCs, signifying very different kinds of wealth distribution across settlements.

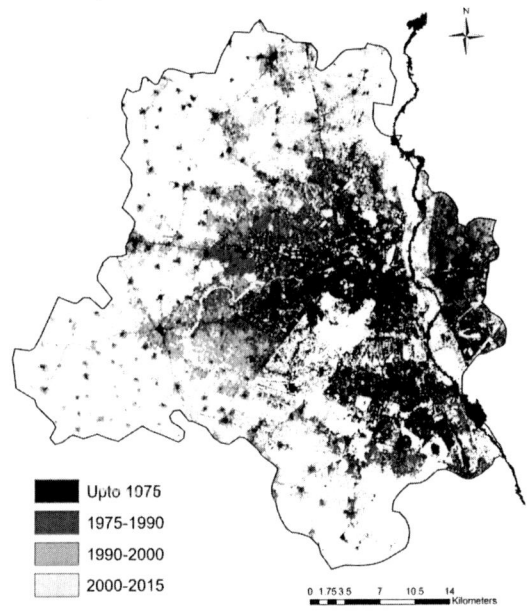

(a) Built-up growth of Delhi

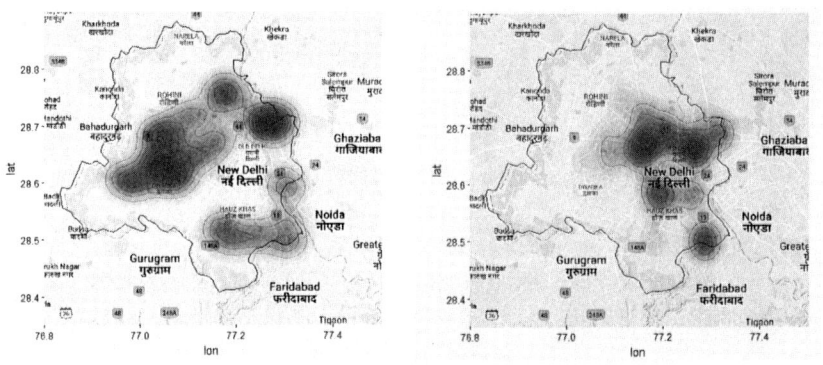

(b) Distribution of RUCs and UCs   (c) Distribution of mixed colonies

Figure 4.3   Spatial distribution by colony type

Sources: Global Human Settlement Layer built-up grids and author's calculations from the CASI–NCR Survey data.

Notes: (a) It shows the growth trajectories of Delhi. It is evident that most of the unauthorized colonies (UCs) and regularized unauthorized colonies (RUCs) are situated at the growth area of 1975–1990. Also, the growth of built-up areas is actually limited around the core and inner peripheries and are not much increased since the 1990s, thereby contributing to high densities in the existing clusters. (b, c) These images show the density of households in UCs, RUCs, and mixed colonies (the darker the distribution, higher the density of households).

Table 4.2 Distribution of occupations across settlements

Colony types	Skilled	Semi–skilled	Unskilled: casual laborers	Unskilled: others	Total persons
Planned colonies	61.9%	16.7%	8.7%	12.7%	252
Urban/Rural villages	49.0%	27.9%	19.9%	3.2%	977
RUCs/UCs	42.1%	39.1%	16.4%	2.3%	299
Resettlement colonies	45.6%	32.4%	17.1%	4.9%	386
JJCs/T-huts/SDAs	20.0%	35.3%	42.7%	2.0%	150
Total	47.6%	29.6%	18.4%	4.5%	2064

Source: Author's calculations from the CASI–NCR Survey data.

Notes: Skilled: legislators, senior officials and managers, professionals, technicians, and associate professionals; semi-skilled: clerks, service workers, and shop and market sales workers; unskilled: craft and related trades workers, plant and machine operators and assemblers, and elementary occupations. The shares are calculated only for those workers for whom a job classification could be attained. The cells add up to 100 percent row wise.

The social cleavages of the city become more discernible across settlements than the ward level.[40] Other work using the CASI–NCR Survey data[41] shows that identity-based segregation is evident among spatially proximate populations, and such ghettoization is very common among the Muslims of the NCR.

This analysis finds that Muslims not only tend to spatially concentrate in certain parts of the city[42] but also overwhelmingly cluster in slums (JJCs and SDAs) as compared to any other settlements.[43] About 60 percent of the SC households are found to be concentrated in resettlement colonies, RUCs, JJCs, and SDAs. The upper-caste households, on the other hand, are mainly distributed across the planned colonies (Figure 4.4). This level of segregation across settlements suggests that the internal spatial structures of the city indeed fortify and influence the progression of social structures. However, given the variegated spatial nature of the city, it can be understood that very different social groups often live in closer spatial proximity, a fact determined by the economic relationships between various segments of the urban population. This is a very common occurrence across SCs but not so much across the Muslims, as one-fourth of the SC population resides in mixed colonies with both planned and unplanned built forms, while the share of Muslims staying in such colonies is less than 10 percent.[44] This confirms basic intuitions about the heavier spatial clustering of Muslims as compared to SCs.[45]

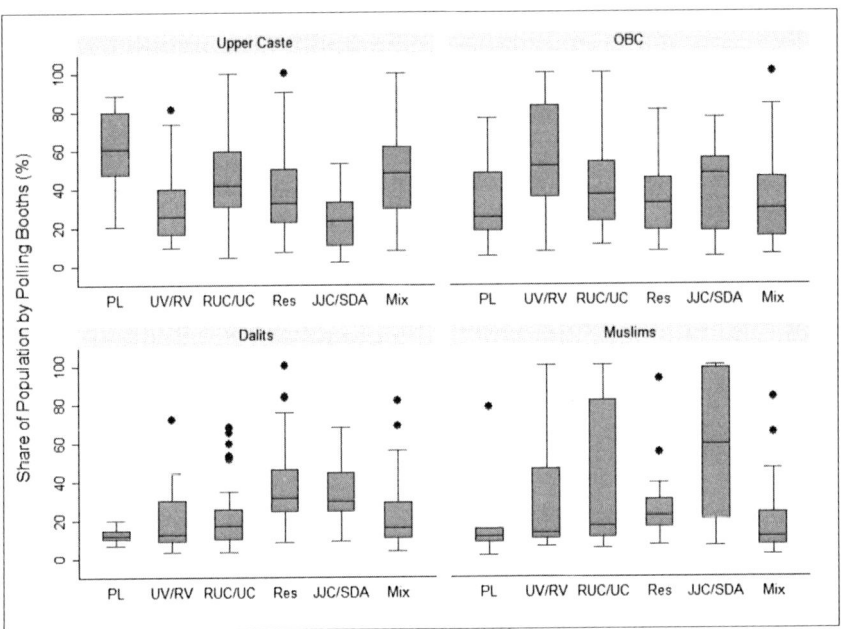

Figure 4.4   Distribution of social group by settlement type

Source: Author's calculation from the CASI–NCR Survey data.

Notes: PL, UV/RV, RUC/UC, Res., JJC/SDA, and Mix stand for planned colonies, urban villages/rural villages, regularized unauthorized colonies/unauthorized colonies, resettlement colonies, *jhuggi jhopri* clusters/slum-designated areas, and mixed colonies, respectively.

Spatial Differentiation in Basic Infrastructure

Spatial inequality in access to basic services in Delhi is evident in the literature and has been studied at multiple levels and scales, starting from Delhi's versatile urban mosaic which incorporates villages, towns, and transitional areas such as census towns (CTs) to municipal wards and census enumeration blocks.[46] Out of the many vectors of urban spatial inequality—the legality of tenure, location, and age of the settlements—there are three main factors that create "precarity" in access to basic infrastructure in Delhi. While access to certain facilities, such as electricity, is almost universal across settlement types, there are differences in access to piped-water supply and sanitation.[47] This section analyzes the spatial differentiation in the NCT, and broadly in the NCR, based upon the three facets of inequality mentioned earlier, and for certain key infrastructures such as sewerage, water supply, and access to road facilities.

Segregation, albeit Co-location?

The co-location of a very different quality of infrastructure in closer proximity is not uncommon in a mixed space such as Delhi. Figure 4.5a shows evidence of this phenomenon, as the access to motorable *pucca* (paved) approach roads to houses varies drastically in proximate neighborhoods.[48] The share of households with motorable *pucca* approach road around 1 kilometer of a household, which does not have one, is 72 percent. Such differentiations are largely a product of the legality and densification of settlement types, with planned colonies having almost 100 percent motorable *pucca* road access, followed by 60 percent in UCs and only 38 percent in JJCs (Figure 4.5b). These sorts of patterns describe a segregated pattern of basic infrastructure, which is very much spatially discontinuous in nature. Lots of these patterns are evident in the northern, western, and eastern peripheries, where mixed neighborhoods are common. Similar patterns can be observed for other infrastructures too, such as access to a piped-water connection[49] or underground sewerage network. The share of households with a piped-water connection is 73 percent in planned colonies, which is 55 percent in RUCs and resettlement colonies but only 26 percent in JJCs which have the minimal security of tenure. The share of piped water in 1 kilometer neighborhood of a planned colony in a mixed area such as east Delhi is only 52 percent. In central Delhi's Inder Lok area, the share of piped-water supply in the planned DDA flats is 100 percent, while in the nearby JJCs of Shahzada Bagh, it drops to 33 percent. Such factors are important because it shows that the spatial inequality in access to infrastructure across the variegated urban spaces of Delhi is not necessarily a failure of planning, but an offshoot of failures created by selective planning.

Core–Periphery Differentials

The differentiation by location in terms of basic services is evident in the spatial distribution of the underground sewerage network (Figure 4.6a). The share of households which have access to sewer networks is higher in the core districts of the NCT (60 percent) and the more prosperous southern periphery (70 percent) than in the northern (19 percent) or western periphery (39 percent). This core–periphery link, however, seems to be discontinuous in nature in the NCR, where the NCT neighborhoods have much less coverage of underground sewerage than the PBs falling at the outskirts of the NCR[50] (Figure 4.6b). In the case of water, the differences between core and periphery are not as high

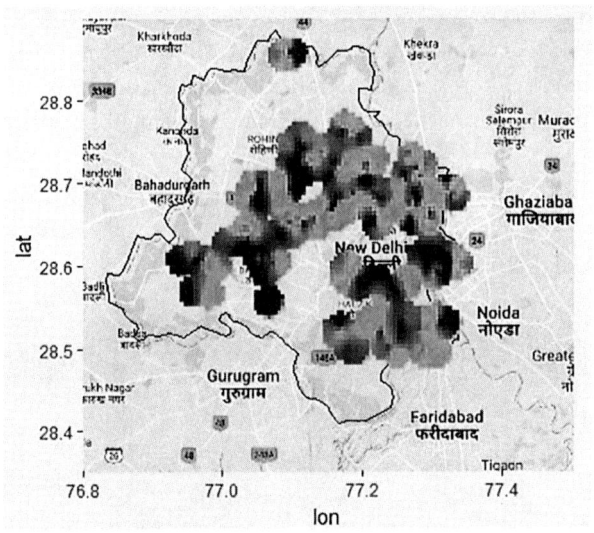

(a) Spatial distribution of motorable *pucca* roads across PBs

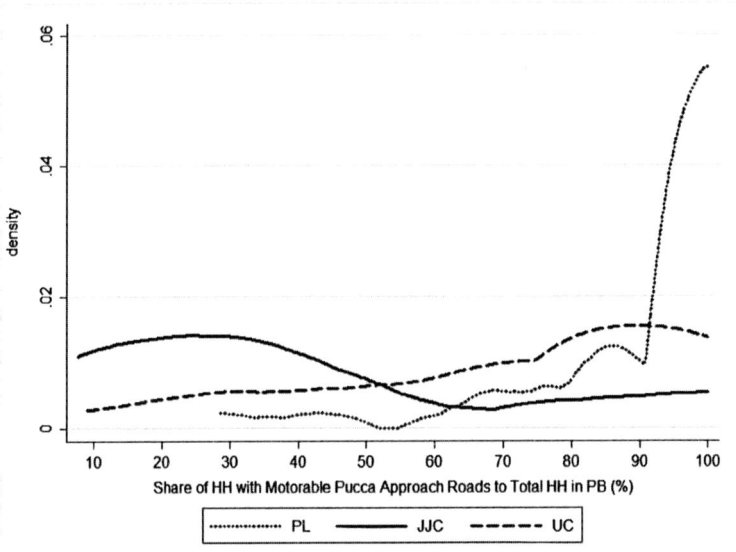

(b) Distribution of motorable *pucca* roads across different settlements

Figure 4.5   Spatial distribution of motorable *pucca* roads

Source: Author's calculations from the CASI–NCR Survey data.

Notes: Percentage share refers to percentage of households with motorable *pucca* approach roads to total households in a PB. The darker the shade, more households have access to roads. PL, JJC, and UC stand for planned colonies, *jhuggi jhopri* clusters, and unauthorized colonies.

as sewerage, though only 50 percent of households report to have piped water in the northern periphery, in comparison to 70 percent in the south.

The differences across core–periphery geographies also seem to transcend across the typology of settlements and their entitlement to different services in

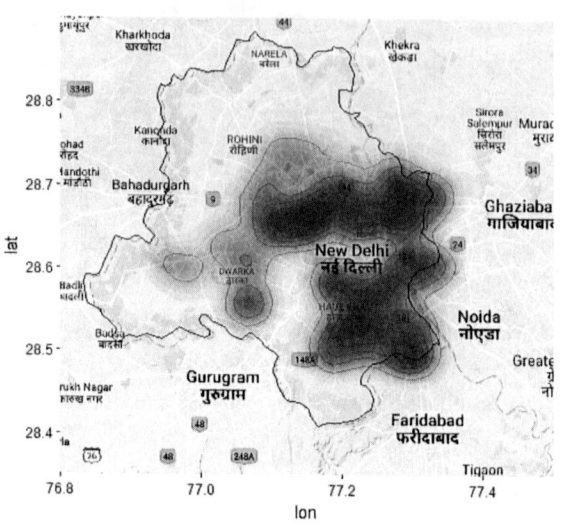

(a) Spatial distribution of underground drainage in the NCT

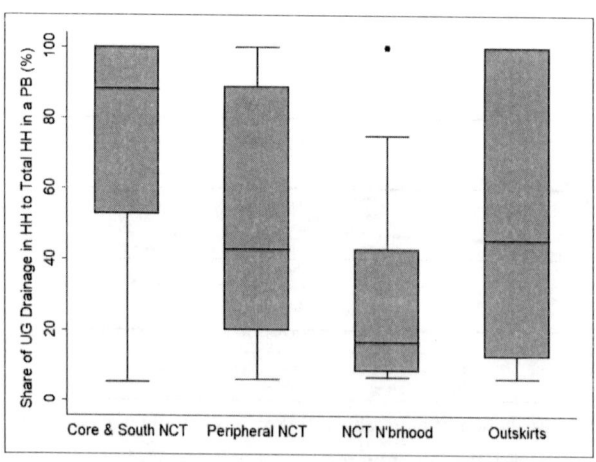

(b) Core–periphery distribution of underground drainage in the NCR

Figure 4.6   Spatial distribution of underground drainage

Source: Author's calculations from the CASI-NCR Survey data.

Note: It shows the density of households with underground drainage across Delhi (the darker the distribution, higher the density of households).

Delhi. Urban villages which are closer to the core have piped-water supply in 82 percent households, while it is 60 percent for rural villages in the peripheries. Most of the new resettlement colonies, which came up mainly during the last decade, are located in the periphery. The share of households with underground sewerage in these settlements is only 14 percent, in comparison to 47 percent in the JJCs, which are mainly located in the city core. The share of households with piped-water supply is 35 percent in these newer resettlement colonies, which is slightly higher than JJCs (26 percent). Such differentiation is interesting as households from the JJCs are relocated to these colonies, and the relocation sites are supposed to have planned basic services.[51] In addition to the economic costs borne by slum dwellers when they move from core to periphery, there are significant disadvantages incurred from unavailability of basic services, which result in low occupancy of flats or plots allotted in these settlements.[52, 53] On the other hand, JJCs show significant investment in housing despite their insecurity of tenure and low-quality services, where 67 percent of the houses are well-built *pucca* houses.

Differences over Time

The differential legalities of settlements in Delhi is also a transformative process and the legal status of settlements along with the service provision they are entitled to changes over time. The UCs and their process of regularization is an example of one such temporal process. Though various policy documents of GNCTD indicate that "provision of service and infrastructure does not correlate with whether or not a UC has been regularized,"[54] the government usually does not provide basic infrastructure until these spaces are regularized. Since the UCs in Delhi have gone through several waves of regularization since 1962, there are considerable differences between the infrastructure of older RUCs that were regularized up to 1980s and the 895 UCs that got regularized in 2012.[55] Many of the older RUCs such as Ramesh Nagar or Tilak Nagar in west Delhi also transformed into spaces where a lot of planned private development came after they were regularized, with associated development in basic infrastructure. Since RUCs are also a peripheral development, the newer RUCs are subjected to core–periphery differentials in infrastructure as well. The CASI–NCR Survey data shows that 46 percent of the households in older RUCs have access to underground drainage, while the share for newer RUCs[56] is only 28 percent. The share of households with piped-water supply in the older RUCs is 66 percent, while it is 58 percent for the newer

RUCs. About 47 percent of the newer RUCs have access to treated water,[57] in comparison to 72 percent of households in older RUCs. The resettlement colonies are another kind of settlement that came up sequentially over time as a result of successive slum-relocation drives. The CASI–NCR Survey covers 100 households from nine different resettlement colonies that came up after the 1990s, which show very different levels of access to basic services than the 365 households in the older 40 resettlement colonies. The share of underground drainage for households is 14 percent in the newer resettlement colonies and 49 percent in the older resettlement colonies. There are differences in piped-water supply as well, which is 35 percent for newer colonies and 63 percent for older resettlement colonies. Other than the JJCs, the share of other sources such as borewells and tankers is significantly greater among the newer resettlement colonies (65 percent) and new RUCs (42 percent) than any other colonies because residents are captive consumers to the informal providers with limited ability to control either service quality or price.[58]

Spatial inequality in basic infrastructure in Delhi is a multifaceted issue, and its manifestation changes over time. Processes such as the relocation of JJCs or regularization of colonies create a lot of differentiation across and within settlements, not only in terms of access to basic infrastructure but also to other welfare mechanisms. For example, access to ration cards, which is a very important proof of residential identity and one of the main instruments of food security entitlements, is available to 72 percent of households in JJCs, which reduces to 58 percent households in resettlement colonies. Hence, relocating to new locations is not necessarily accompanied by a renewal of identity, which further problematizes the concept of planning as a tool to promote social equity in cities.

Spatial versus Social Inequality

A lot of the discussions in the previous sections imply that there is a link between the social identities of the population in Delhi and the spaces in which they reside, where specific social groups tend to concentrate in certain kinds of settlements (Figure 4.7). Naturally, one should check whether spatial inequality in access to basic services is simply an extension of social inequality. However, settlements such as UCs and urban villages are heterogeneous in terms of their socioeconomic characteristics, and there are differences across social groups within a particular settlement category in terms of incomes and private assets, if not across public services.[59] The present study attempts to explore both inter- and intra-settlement differentiation in relation to access to basic amenities across social groups. While there are variations across different amenities such as underground drainage or piped-water supply in households, this section focuses more on the overall housing conditions, which include the type of housing (*kuchha*, semi-*pucca*, or *pucca*) [makeshift, semi-permanent, permanent structure], availability of toilet in the house, availability of piped water in the house, and the congestion factor of the house represented by the number of persons per room living at the house. Households that have access to the first three facilities, that is, if it has a *pucca* house,[60] a functional toilet, and a piped-water connection have been grouped as "houses with basic amenities." The share of households with such houses, along with congested houses across socioreligious groups and spatial divisions, has been described in Figures 4.7a and 4.7b. It can be observed that while there are differences across socioreligious groups in terms of housing qualities, it is not as much as the spatial categories, for example, where 70 percent of the houses in planned colonies have all the three facilities, compared to 20 percent in JJCs or SDAs. Similar facts apply to the congestion factor of houses, where half of the households in JJCs or SDAs stay in houses where more than two people have to share one room. RUCs, UCs, and resettlement colonies show mixed results and it is worthwhile to take a closer look at the distribution of social groups and their access to quality housing in these colonies, given the mixed nature of social composition in these places.

The share of households living in houses with the selected basic amenities across PBs/localities does not show any strong correlation with the PB-wise share of two most segregated socioreligious groups: the SCs and the Muslims, although the associations are negative and statistically significant.[61] Since each PB constitutes one unique kind of locality, other than the mixed PBs, it can be inferred that the abundance of SCs and Muslims in settlements do exhibit lower housing quality than settlements where their share is lower, but the gap is not as significant as one might think. The share of households living in houses with basic amenities is 43 percent in those PBs which are comprised of at least 75 percent SC and Muslim populations, which is slightly lower (54 percent) than the other PBs. There are also wide variations in basic services in settlements located in different geographies but with similar shares of marginalized groups. Around 54 percent of the population in the JJCs of the core area of the city is composed of SCs and Muslims, which is 50 percent in the JJCs of eastern peripheries. But the share of households with piped water in the JJCs of the core is 26 percent, while it is only 3 percent in the JJCs of

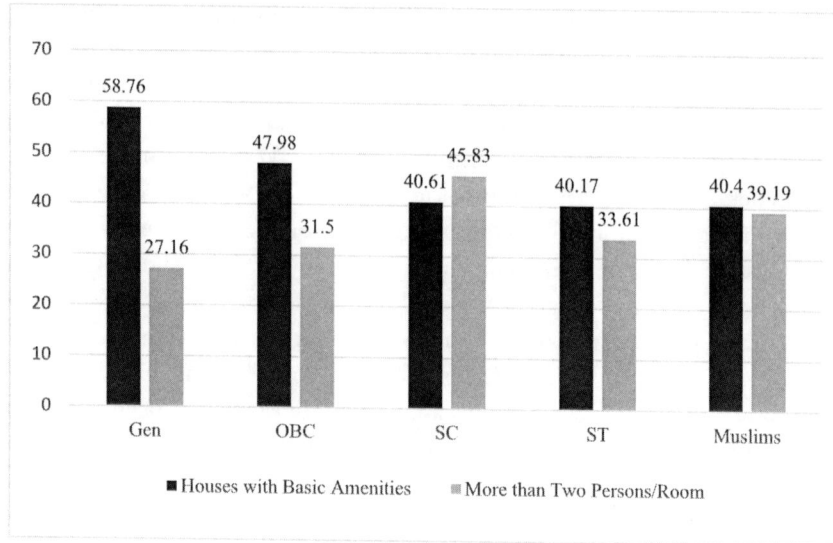

(a) Social divisions in housing quality

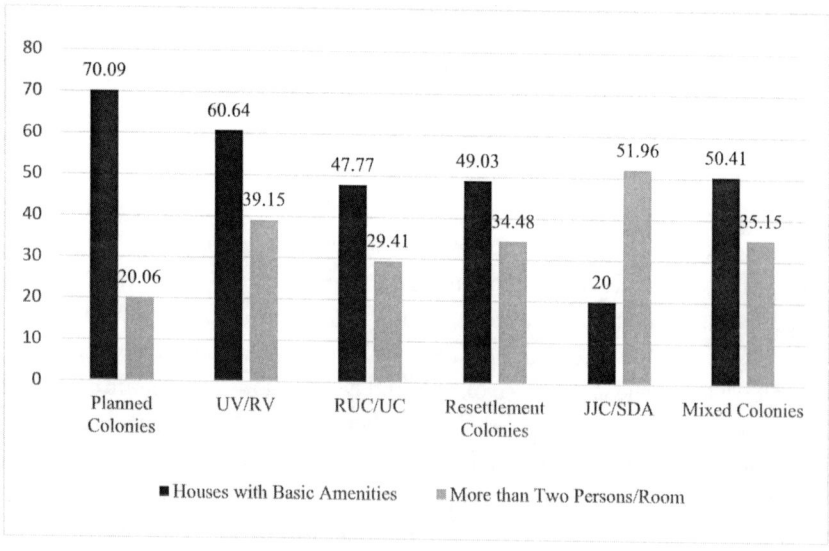

(b) Spatial divisions in housing quality

Figure 4.7   Distribution of basic amenities and congestion by social group and settlement type

Source: Author's calculations from the CASI–NCR Survey data.

Note: PL, UV/RV, RUC/UC, Res., JJC/SDA, and Mix stand for planned colonies, urban villages/rural villages, regularized unauthorized colonies/unauthorized colonies, resettlement colonies, jhuggi jhopri clusters/slum-designated areas, and mixed colonies, respectively.

Table 4.3   Probability of living in a house with basic amenities

Type of settlements	SCs and Muslims	Upper caste Hindus and OBCs	Lowest quartile of asset	Top quartile of asset
Urban/rural villages	56.2% (0.056)	65.1% (0.029)	52% (0.027)	72.4% (0.022)
RUCs/UCs	42.4% (0.031)	46.7% (0.017)	35.1% (0.015)	56.9% (0.016)
Resettlement colonies	52.4% (0.043)	46.8% (0.030)	37.6% (0.025)	59.4% (0.025)
JJCs/SDAs	19.1% (0.042)	30.1% (0.048)	19.5% (0.029)	36.9% (0.044)
Mixed colonies	40% (0.044)	52.3% (0.026)	38.4% (0.022)	60.1% (0.022)

Source: Author's calculations from the CASI–NCR Survey data.

Note: Probabilities shown as percentages; standard errors are in parentheses.

the eastern periphery. Hence, there is not much evidence that the state policies discriminate more along social than spatial lines in terms of basic services.

The intra-settlement diversity in certain colonies such as urban villages or RUCs is noticeable, so it is worthwhile to look whether services vary across social divisions within these colonies. A binary logistic regression with the quality of good housing (measured by the three parameters discussed earlier) as a dependent variable has been computed, where the socioreligious identities and the types of settlements have been taken as the predictors. The asset index and the location of the settlements, that is, whether they are located at the core or any of the peripheries, are controlled for in the regressions. The CASI–NCR Survey sample is not large enough to calculate the differentials across each socioreligious group within colonies. Hence, the sample has been divided into two groups: households belonging to the SCs and Muslims and other households, which includes Hindu upper castes and Other Backward Classes (OBCs).[62] The total households analyzed for the sample are 2,895, of which 27 percent are SC and Muslim households.

Predicted probabilities calculated from the model[63] have been shown in Table 4.3, which shows that while upper castes and OBCs have higher probability of living in a house with basic amenities except in the resettlement colonies, their gap with the SCs and Muslims is not that large, especially as compared to the case of the two asset categories. Resettlement colonies, where plots or flats have been assigned to relocated households from JJCs, show a higher proportion of SCs and Muslims, which further highlight the fact that the discrimination on social factors while allotting houses is not common. On the other hand, RUCs or UCs, being placed in the top 25 percent of the income quartile, do not guarantee decent-quality housing. The distributions

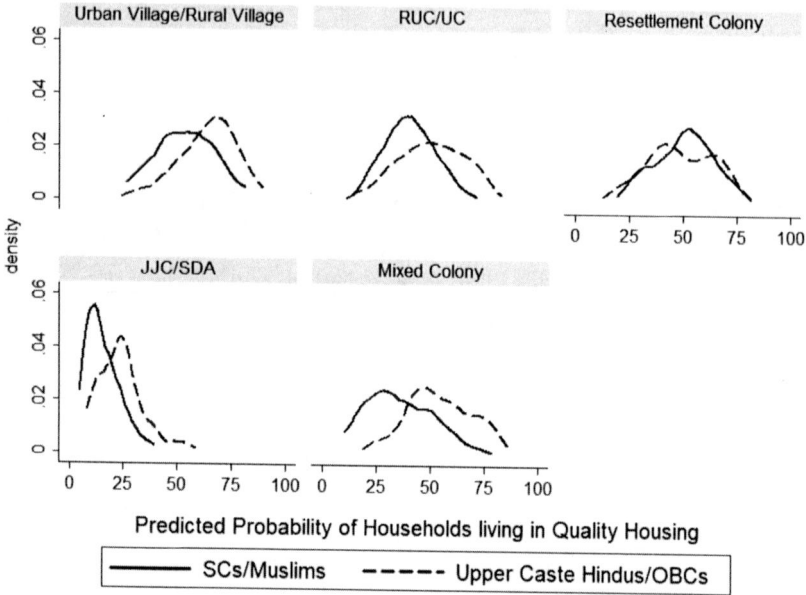

Figure 4.8 Predicted probabilities of decent housing across social group and colony type
Source: Author's calculations from the CASI–NCR Survey data.

of probabilities, generated for each household based on the model, have been shown in Figure 4.8. The within-colony variations, even in JJCs, do not show a big gap between two different social groups, but the difference is evident if compared to other informal colonies.

Conclusion

This chapter attempts to decode the spatial inequality in basic services in Delhi NCR using a previously unexploited quantitative framework. The availability of geo-coded data on household amenities, attached with the categorization of settlements, help to understand how factors such as spatial illegality can be used as instruments of selective exclusion for public services. Despite certain limitations on the availability of suitable indicators, the study findings corroborate broadly with the qualitative literature, which shows that differentiations of basic services across spatial lines are very significant in Delhi, much more than can be simply explained by social differences. This chapter also finds that in Delhi, the spatial inequality in services relates to visible core–periphery differentials and the supply of basic services becomes more even across settlements over time. The level of spatial inequality in services is so sharp that it also dominates over economic inequality, that is, being middle class does not guarantee access to decent water supply or sewerage systems in the city. The link between prosperity and spatiality needs to be investigated in greater detail, in order to check why intra-settlement variations arise, and if increased economic potential of a settlement growing over time has anything to do with these outcomes. For example, it is important to see whether the differentiation that is evident between older and newer RUCs grows sharper if looked across RUCs of different property tax categories. The study shows that there is ample scope to study spatial disparities and diversities in the urban spectrum of Delhi if future survey instruments take care of the differential spatial and legal mosaic of the city.

While the chapter analyzes the picture of spatial inequality in detail, it does not look at how people negotiate for basic infrastructure in different kinds of settlements and the social and economic dimensions of it. While the qualitative accounts for these processes are available, similar kinds of quantitative exercises can be executed with the CASI–NCR Survey data. A detailed analysis of these matters will be useful to check how the local political and bureaucratic machineries work to interact with this spatial inequality and how the manifestations of such negotiations differ in varied contexts of inequality.

Appendix

Table 4A.1 Summary of binary logistic regression (odds ratios)

Variables	Model 1	Model 2
Social group (ref.: privileged groups: upper castes and OBCs)		
Marginalized groups: SCs and Muslims	0.799** (0.0754)	
Settlement type (ref.: urban/rural villages)		
RUCs/UCs	0.491*** (0.0621)	
Resettlement colonies	0.559*** (0.0841)	
JJCs/SDAs	0.202*** (0.0426)	
Mixed colonies	0.569*** (0.0822)	
Asset index	2.044*** (0.0992)	2.050*** (0.0998)
Geography (ref.: core)		

Contd

Table 4A.1 Contd

Variables	Model 1	Model 2
Northern periphery	0.756* [0.1128]	0.762* [0.1142]
Western periphery	1.104 [0.1628]	1.092 [0.1617]
Southern periphery	1.224 [0.1849]	1.226 [0.1871]
Eastern periphery	0.977 [0.1408]	0.946 [0.1379]
Social group settlement type (ref.: upper castes and OBCs in urban/rural villages)*		
UC/OBC* RUC/UC		0.472*** [0.0683]
UC/OBC* resettlement colonies		0.470*** [0.0828]
UC/OBC* JJCs/SDAs		0.230*** [0.0602]
UC/OBC* mixed colonies		0.589*** [0.0976]
SCs/Muslims* urban/rural villages		0.689 [0.1794]
SCs/Muslims* RUCs/UCs		0.395*** [0.0717]
SCs/Muslims* resettlement colonies		0.591** [0.1311]
SCs/Muslims* JJC/SDAs		0.126*** [0.0388]
SCs/Muslims* mixed colonies		0.358*** [0.0807]
Constant	1.673*** [0.2637]	1.737*** [0.2907]
Log likelihood	−1812.71	−1808.84
χ^2	383.17***	390.92***
N		2,895

Source: Author's calculation from the CASI–NCR Survey data.

Notes: Dependent variable: 0 = not a decent house, 1 = decent house.
Standard errors in parentheses: * $p < 0.1$, ** $p < 0.01$, *** $p < 0.001$.

Notes

1. Arup Mitra, "Social Capital, Livelihood and Upward Mobility," *Habitat International* 32, no. 2 (2008): 261–269.
2. Himanshu, "Recent Trends in Poverty and Inequality: Some Preliminary Results," *Economic and Political Weekly* 42, no. 6 (2007): 497–508, available at https://www.jstor.org/stable/4419235; Vamsi Vakulabharanam and Sripad Motiram, "Understanding Poverty and Inequality in Urban India since Reforms: Bringing Quantitative and Qualitative Approaches Together," *Economic and Political Weekly* 47, nos. 47–48 (2012): 44–52, available at https://www.jstor.org/stable/41720409.
3. The urban Gini index referring to consumption inequality has increased from 0.32 in 1993–1994 to 0.38 in 2011–2012, while rural Gini has marginally increased from 0.26 to 0.29 during the same time period (National Sample Survey Office [NSSO], 49th and 68th rounds).

4. Shuchi Bansal, "Blurring the Line between Rural and Urban Markets," *Livemint*, March 3, 2014, available at https://www.livemint.com/Opinion/qaqfntfBTFjFQVzNovQX0M/Blurring-the-line-between-rural-and-urban-markets.html, accessed on May 23, 2018; "India and Bharat are the Same, Says IMRB Study," *Livemint*, December 12, 2014.

5. Surinder Singh Jodhka and Partha Mukhopadhyay, "Social and Economic Transformations in Small Towns of India," *Thoughtspace Episode 20*, Centre for Policy Research, January 24, 2018.

6. Patrick Heller, Partha Mukhopadhyay, and Michael Walton, "Cabal City: Regime Theory and Indian Urbanization," (working paper, Centre for Policy Research, New Delhi, 2016), available at http://cprindia.org/research/papers/cabal-city-regime-theory-and-indian-urbanization, accessed on November 1, 2020.

7. S. Chandrasekhar and Abhiroop Mukhopadhyay, *Multidimensions of Urban Poverty: Evidence from India* (Mumbai: Indira Gandhi Institute of Development Research, 2007), available at http://www.igidr.ac.in/pdf/publication/WP-2007-008.pdf, accessed on November 1, 2020.

8. Ananya Roy, "Why India Cannot Plan Its Cities: Informality, Insurgence and the Idiom of Urbanization," *Planning Theory* 8, no. 1 (2009): 76–87.

9. Gautam Bhan, "Planned Illegalities," *Economic and Political Weekly* 48, no. 24 (2013): 59–70.

10. The process through which local actors bargain with the state and through which the state visualizes and institutionalizes its local connections is kind of symbiotic and is bound by a range of informal set of rules, networks, and ties. This relationship is termed by various scholars as "embeddedness" of the local state. Peter Evans and Patrick Heller, "Human Development, State Transformation and the Politics of the Developmental State," in *The Oxford Handbook of Transformations of the State*, ed. Stephan Leibfried, Evelyne Huber, Matthew Lange, Jonah D. Levy, and John D. Stephens (New York: Oxford University Press, 2015), 691–713.

11. Patrick Heller, Partha Mukhopadhyay, Subhadra Banda, and Shahana Sheikh, "Exclusion, Informality, and Predation in the Cities of Delhi," a report of the Cities of Delhi project (New Delhi: Centre for Policy Research, 2015), available at http://citiesofdelhi.cprindia.org/wp-content/uploads/2015/12/Cities_of_Delhi-Overview.pdf, accessed on November 1, 2020.

12. Ibid.

13. Véronique Dupont, "The Dream of Delhi as a Global City," *International Journal of Urban and Regional Research* 35, no. 3 (2011): 533–554.

14. Veronique Dupont, "Socio-spatial Differentiation and Residential Segregation in Delhi: A Question of Scale?" *Geoforum* 35, no. 2 (2004): 157–175.

15. Pranav Sidhwani, "Spatial Inequalities in Big Indian Cities," *Economic and Political Weekly* 50, no. 22 (2015): 55–62.

16. See Chapter 2 of this volume.

17. Ghazala Jamil, *Accumulation by Segregation: Muslim Localities in Delhi* (New Delhi: Oxford University Press, 2017); see Chapter 2 of this volume.

18. Ibid.

19. There are three databases that provide a list of colonies spread across the National Capital Territory (NCT)-Delhi. These are the databases provided by the municipal valuation committee (MVC), the property tax department of the Municipal Corporation of Delhi (MCD), and the MapmyIndia geographic information system (GIS) application of the MCD. The number of unique colonies across these three sources differs substantially. In a cumbersome exercise in their paper, Joshi and others found that the number of unique colonies in the MVC database is 2,450, while for the property tax list, it is 2,309 and 2,498 in the MCD GIS. Bhanu Joshi, Kanhu Charan Pradhan, and Pranav Sidhwani, "Urban Voting and Party Choices in Delhi," *Economic and Political Weekly* 51, no. 5 (2016): 65, available at https://www.epw.in/journal/2016/5/review-urban-affairs/urban-voting-and-party-choices-delhi.html.

20. Ibid.

21. About 67.5 percent of the NCT-Delhi lives in statutory towns, while 30 percent resides in census towns, and 2.5 percent lives in villages. Delhi has a Panchayat Act (1954) but the state government has not accepted elected representatives from them since 1989 while getting councillors elected for MCD from the same area. Hence, it is one particular kind of space where rural is defined only by spatial plan and not by governance and villages are served by an urban local body.

22. Patrick Heller and Partha Mukhopadhyay, "State-Produced Inequality in an Indian City," *Seminar*, no. 672 (2015): 51–55.

23. GNCTD, Economic Survey of Delhi, Statement No. 14.4. 2008–2009.

24. The different types of informal settlements, as identified by the GNCTD, are: (*a*) JJCs or " *jhuggi jhopri* clusters" which are basically identified but nonnotified slum clusters, (*b*) slum-designated areas (SDAs) which are slum-like areas notified by the "Slum areas improvement and clearance act, 1956," (*c*) resettlement colonies where the people from evicted JJCs are relocated in planned plots or flats, (*d*) unauthorized colonies (UCs) which are residential colonies built on agricultural land, (*e*) regularized unauthorized colonies (RUCs), (*f*) rural villages which are also known as "Lal Dora," and identified as rural residential land under the master plan, and (*g*) urban villages which are a section of rural villages notified as urban as they got shifted to the urbanized locations of the city over time. While JJCs and UCs are regarded as a direct violation to the master plan, the other kinds of informal settlements are subjected to a variety of tenure and building regulations. The access to services in these settlements also vary a lot. For details, see the reports from

"Cities of Delhi" project (http://www.cprindia.org/sites/default/files/policy-briefs/Categorisation-of-Settlement-in-Delhi.pdf).

25. Trina Vithayathil and Gayatri Singh, "Spaces of Discrimination: Residential Segregation in Indian Cities," *Economic and Political Weekly* 47, no. 37 (2012): 60–66.

26. Delhi is divided into five urban local bodies: the three MCDs of north, south, and east; New Delhi Municipal Council; and Delhi Cantonment Board. The MCD area is divided into 272 wards which are the lowest unit at which urban basic infrastructure data is available. However, each ward on an average has a population of 60,000 (Census of India, 2011), with substantial variation. The number of colonies in each ward varies from 8 to 10 on average (as per the MCD property tax list and the MCD GIS list) and can go up to more than 50 in some peripheral wards of the city.

27. While geo-coding a polling booth (PB), the midpoint of all the colonies it covers has been considered. The average number of households in a PB is 15, and mean number of individuals residing in a PB is 75.

28. The terms PBs, settlements, localities, and colonies have used in this chapter interchangeably.

29. If the MCD-GIS colony numbers are considered.

30. There were three sets of data to start with: The first one was the colony-type data, extracted from the electoral rolls, where the number of colonies falling within a PB boundary was enlisted. The second one was a combined database of colonies in Delhi, for which a neat categorization was available. The third one was the database of 3,349 households mapped with 311 PBs. During the matching exercise, the first data set was matched with the second one, and the combined data was again matched with the third data set to get a final account of households with geo-coded PBs and type of colonies falling into it.

31. This is a database collated from various government and public policy documents or academic materials aggregated by the Cities of Delhi project by Centre for Policy Research.

32. As described in note 5 in this chapter, in addition to the planned or formal colonies.

33. Ganesh Pura, a neighborhood of the Tri Nagar assembly constituency of New Delhi, is a good example of this. This was originally a UAC, parts of which have been regularized by two different regularization drives, one in the early 1960s, while another within 1978–1982. During the course of time, a lot of housing and commercial development in and around this place took shape of the privately planned colony, and the built form was mixed as well. Hence, it was not possible to label it as one particular type of colony.

34. The "core" or central part of the city refers to colonies falling in central Delhi and New Delhi districts. The northern periphery constitutes colonies falling

in north Delhi and north-west Delhi districts, the western fringes refer to west Delhi and south-west Delhi districts, the southern periphery refers to south Delhi and south-east Delhi districts, and the eastern periphery refers to east Delhi, Shahdara, and north-east Delhi districts.

35. Gautam Bhan and Arindam Jana, "Reading Spatial Inequality in Urban India," *Economic and Political Weekly* 50, no. 22 (2015): 49.

36. Ibid.

37. J. Brush, "Recent Changes in Ecological Patterns of Metropolitan Bombay and Delhi," in *Indian Cities: Ecological Perspectives*, ed. Vinod K. Tewari, Jay A. Weinstein, and V. L. S. Prakash Rao (New Delhi: Concept, 1986), 121–149; Veronique Dupont and Arup Mitra, "Population Distribution Growth and Socio-economic Spatial Patterns in Delhi: Findings from the 1991 Census Data," *Demography India* 24, no. 1 (1995): 101–132.

38. The Center for the Advanced Study of India–National Capital Region (CASI-NCR) Survey used two ways to capture a migrant: one is the "narrower" place of birth definition, where an individual is considered as a migrant if his/her place of birth differs from the current place of residence, which is Delhi in this case. Since the areal limits of Delhi are not clear to all people, a "broader" definition of migrants is used to capture more people, which includes his/her reason for movement into Delhi and their year of arrival into the city, in addition to the place-of-birth response. Any analysis involving migrants in this chapter used this broader definition.

39. For details of the asset index, see Chapter 2 of this volume.

40. Refer to the previous note.

41. Refer to note 40 of this chapter.

42. Half of the Muslim population resides in 18 out of the 311 PBs of the city.

43. This corroborates with the pattern derived from a much larger survey on slums. Abhijit Banerjee, Anjali Bharadwaj, Rohini Pande, and Michael Walton, *Delhi's Slum-Dwellers: Deprivation, Preferences and Political Engagement among the Urban Poor* (International Growth Centre, 2011), available at https://www.theigc.org/wp-content/uploads/2014/10/Banerjee-et-al-2011-Policy-Brief.pdf, accessed on November 1, 2020.

44. The value of dissimilarity index is 0.50 in case of Scheduled Castes (SCs) if calculated across different settlements/PBs. This index goes down to 0.32 while calculated across municipal wards, see Vithayathil and Singh, "Spaces of Discrimination". Considering the temporal difference in the two data sets, this means while 31 percent of the SC population needs to be shifted across wards to attain an equitable distribution between SCs and non-SCs, 50 percent of SCs require to be shifted for equal share across settlements/PBs. For Muslims and non-Muslims, the value of the index is much higher than SCs (0.62).

45. Ibid.

46. Sohail Ahmad and Mack Joong Choi, "Identifying and Measuring Dimensions of Urban Deprivation in Delhi: A Town Level Analysis" (Third International Conference on Infrastructure Systems and Services: Next Generation Infrastructure Systems for Eco-cities [INFRA], IEEE, 2010), 1–5, available at https://ieeexplore.ieee.org/abstract/document/5679210/; I. S. A. Baud, Namperumal Sridharan, and Karin Pfeffer, "Mapping Urban Poverty for Local Governance in an Indian Mega-City: The Case of Delhi," *Urban Studies* 45, no. 7 (2008): 1385–1412; Naveen Bharathi, Deepak Malghan, and Andaleeb Rahman, "Isolated by Caste: Neighbourhood-Scale Residential Segregation in Indian Metros," *SocArXiv* June 9 (2018), available at https://www.iimb.ac.in/sites/default/files/2018-06/WP%20No.%20572.pdf. All pieces were accessed on November 1, 2020.

47. Ibid.

48. The prediction surface of motorable *pucca* road density is created by fitting a spatial spline of 2-kilometer buffer around each of the 311 PBs.

49. The CASI–NCR Survey does not ask any direct questions on the availability of piped water in the household. Instead, it asks how the household pays the water bill. This study assumes if a household pays a bill for water, it has a piped-water connection. This obviously underestimates some of the households connected to piped water, as water supply up to 20,000 liters per month to households is free in Delhi since March, 2015.

50. The core–periphery distribution of amenities, especially out of the NCT, can also be influenced by the spatial nature of the survey data, as cities in the NCR are not often covered by sewerage facilities where most of the population is concentrated or vice versa. This can be checked by plotting the ward-level population density from census with the amenities information from the survey data. Unfortunately, the ward identifier was not available for cities outside the NCT, where the survey households were located to check this issue.

51. Cities of Delhi, "Rehabilitation of JJCs in Delhi," Centre for Policy Research, May 2014, available at http://citiesofdelhi.cprindia.org/wp-content/uploads/2015/09/Rehabilitation-of-JJCs-in-Delhi.pdf, accessed on November 1, 2020.

52. Shinjini Ghosh, "Lack of Basic Amenities Pinches DDA Flat Residents," *The Hindu*, August 20, 2017, available at https://www.thehindu.com/news/cities/Delhi/lack-of-basic-amenities-pinches-dda-flat-residents/article19528254.ece, accessed on May 27, 2018.

53. The 2010 guidelines of GNCTD recommend allotment of Economically Weaker Section (EWS) flats to the relocated households from JJCs, instead of undeveloped plots that used to be allotted earlier. Findings from the CASI–NCR Survey data shows that flats in RCs have a piped-water supply of 67 percent, which is not much higher than houses (58 percent) that are built on plots.

54. Shahana Sheikh and Subhadra Banda, "Regularizing Delhi's Unauthorized Colonies: The Thin Line between Legitimate and Illegal," Centre for Policy Research, 2014, available at http://citiesofdelhi.cprindia.org/wp-content/uploads/2015/09/Regularising-Delhis-UACs.pdf, accessed on November 1, 2020.

55. For a detailed account on Delhi's regularization drive, see Bhan, "Planned Illegalities," 59–70 or Sheikh and Banda, "Regularizing Delhi's Unauthorized Colonies."

56. Newer RUC refers to any of the surveyed RUCs that regularized in 2012, while all the others are older RUCs. The CASI–NCR Survey covers 83 newer RUC PBs and 14 older RUC PBs. The total number of households surveyed in newer RUCs are 921, while it is 137 for older RUCs.

57. The CASI–NCR Survey does not ask any direct questions on treated-water supply. However, it includes the ownership of water purifiers/RO (reverse osmosis) as one of the asset questions. This study considers that a household has access to treated water if it has access to a water-purifying instrument.

58. Suneetha Dasappa Kacker and Anuradha Joshi, "Pipe dreams? The Governance of Urban Water Supply in Informal Settlements, New Delhi," *IDS Bulletin* 43, no. 2 (2012): 27–36.

59. Abhijit Banerjee, Rohini Pande, Yashas Vaidya, Michael Walton, and Jeff Weaver, "Delhi's Slum-Dwellers: Deprivation, Preferences and Political Engagement among the Urban Poor," (proceeding, International Growth Centre Conference [Growth Week 2011], 2011), available at https://www.theigc.org/publication/delhis-slum-dwellers-deprivation-preferences-and-political-engagement-among-the-urban-poor-working-paper/, accessed on November 1, 2020.

60. *Pucca* refers to stone walls with a concrete ceiling.

61. The Pearson's correlation coefficient between the two indicators is −0.189, significant at the 1 percent level. The Moran's I coefficient, which measures the association of the concentration of SCs and Muslims in a PB and the share of quality housing in a cluster of five neighboring PBs, also shows a negative but statistically significant value (−0.287), which means that while PBs with higher SCs and Muslims show low-quality housing, they are surrounded by houses with good-quality housing and basic amenities. This indicates to the spatially discontinuous pattern of infrastructure distribution, as discussed in previous sections.

62. Scheduled Tribes (STs) have been dropped from the analysis as their numbers are very small in planned and resettlement colonies. Also, planned colonies have been dropped as the sample of SCs/Muslims are negligible in them.

63. Detailed output from the model is available in Table 4A.1 in "Statistical Appendix."

CHAPTER 5

Migration

Persisting Inequalities and Spatial Disadvantage

Khushdeep Kaur Malhotra*

Introduction

Humans have always moved. Yet in our chronically mobile society, migration continues to be perceived as a pathology which has incited frequent violence globally, as seen in the resurgence of right-wing nationalism in the 2000s, and invited political backlash. India is no exception to this. Be it the "Bangladeshi" migrant in Assam, the "Rohingya" in Jammu, or the "Bihari" in Delhi, the figure of the migrant has become highly villainized in the current urban discourse.

Although it is international refugee migration that dominates the news cycle routinely, the numbers of people migrating internally, that is within national borders, far outstrip international migration. In India, the 2011 Census classified 454 million Indians (37 percent of the total population) as internal migrants.[1] Much like international migrants, internal migrants, in particular those who come from rural areas and for whom migration is often

* The author wishes to thank Sanjoy Chakravorty and Neelanjan Sircar for their continuous support through the conception, data analysis, and writing of this chapter. Thanks are also due to Bàladevan Rangaraju, Shrobona Karkun, Shamindra Nath Roy, Kanhu Charan Pradhan, and Matthew Lillehaugen for their help with the geographic information system data and other aspects of analysis, as well as to the Center for the Advanced Study of India at University of Pennsylvania in Philadelphia and the Centre for Policy Research in New Delhi for generously extending their resources while this chapter was being written.

a livelihood strategy,[2] encounter a lesser citizenship than their nonmigrant counterparts.[3] Held responsible in large part for India's rapidly burgeoning urbanization crisis, migrants are often accepted economically while being rejected socially.[4] That is, while they are essential for the provision of cheap labor and day-to-day services, they are also blamed for the poor livability of Indian cities.

Sadly, despite the United Nations' Millennium Development Goals (MDGs) advocating the inclusion of migrants in the overall development of cities, the policy response to internal migration in India has largely mirrored the public sentiment against migration. Short of implementing direct controls on population movement, welfare policies link the provision of subsidized food, education, and healthcare to those who are "Below the Poverty Line (BPL)"[5] to the permanent place of residence and ensure that these benefits cannot be claimed elsewhere. The latest in this line of policies, the Smart Cities initiative, which promises to "solve" the many problems of Indian cities in an inclusive way, has already been criticized as having left behind the most vulnerable and poor urban Indian citizens, owing to its onus on "exclusionary urbanization."[6] The effect of such an urbanization process is the reinforcement of the very identity-based inequalities that migrants, especially from rural settings, are often hoping to escape.

The Unequal Geography of Migration in Indian Cities

Viewed as the panacea for overcoming the rigid sociopolitical structures dominant in rural India, such as caste, class, and religion, cities continue to be an aspirational mecca for India's most marginalized citizens. Urban sociologists argue that the cultural and economic environment, and heterogeneity, that urbanization brings to cities erodes the rigid sociopolitical structures dominant in rural India, such as caste, class, and religion[7] and creates opportunities for social mobility.[8] Yet the trajectory of exclusive urbanization has seen inequalities deepen in the urban scape of Indian cities and threaten the gains which come with both migration and urbanization.[9]

Among the earliest scholars of spatial segregation, Mehta analyzed longitudinal data from Pune to find the greatest levels of segregation by caste and class, for both the lowest and the highest classes in the city.[10] Although Desai and Dubey find that caste inequalities are less pronounced in bigger cities compared to their smaller counterparts and developed villages,[11] another study of spatial inequalities across 10 Indian cities finds that urbanization does not reduce spatial segregation based on caste and religion.[12] Miklian and Sahoo's survey of the urbanization patterns of three Indian cities finds that four groups, namely Dalits, Adivasis, Muslims, and migrants, are overwhelmingly concentrated among the poorest neighborhoods in these cities.[13] The survey also concludes that a neighborhood's location determines the level of services it receives. The authors report that informal settlements located on city peripheries are "planning black holes," that is, these areas are largely ignored in the urban planning schemes and lack access to basic services such as sanitation, health, and drinking water. The same study also finds that recent migrants experience the highest levels of exclusion, regardless of their socioreligious identities.

The Urban Transformation of Delhi

Among the top recipients of migrants in India, Delhi–National Capital Region's (NCR) development has been driven by a quest to create a world-class city that catalyzes economic growth, leading to drastic consequences for the reorganization of its urban space.[14] Under the guise of urbanization, the Delhi Development Authority's (DDA) Master Plan for Delhi 2021 (after DDA's third revision proposal of the master plan in 2007), for example, has set forth a legal precedent which explicitly promotes the building of infrastructure that is "planned" and legitimizes the routine clearance of informal settlements in the name of "sanitizing spaces of the global city."[15] Characterized as a "patchwork of deeply segregated localities,"[16] in recent years Delhi has also witnessed the creation of exclusionary spaces through gated enclaves and restricted entry malls and green spaces.[17] During the Commonwealth Games, Delhi's urban transformation depended on migrant labor, yet also informal settlements were demolished on which migrants depended, leaving 3 million people homeless and 100,000 families displaced.[18]

Dupont's study of Mayur Vihar in Delhi too provides further evidence of how space is selectively transformed in the locality.[19] She concludes that segregation in Delhi is not merely the effect of income differentials but also results from a process of social selection by both institutions and private individuals, based on caste, religion, professional status, and geographic origin. Applying Lefebvre's theory of the production of space, Kudva illustrates how such spatial rearrangements in the urban space of Delhi generate spaces of informality in the periphery of the city and argues that they work to restrict mobility "by tightly circumscribing urban spaces which are available to informals, thus limiting their ability to generate knowledge on the city and to occupy it."[20] Beyond the physical transformation of spaces, Gooptu argues that the mobilization of the urban poor also leads to their political exclusion, because of the capture of urban spaces by the middle classes.[21]

Lefebvre wrote of space as a reservoir of resources, a medium which instead of being a neutral entity, is instead active both as an "instrument and goal, as means and as end."[22] That is, space is deeply implicated in social processes and "social relations are so frequently and so inevitably correlated with spatial relations."[23] Consequently, exclusionary spatial arrangements can and do reflect the hierarchies of advantage available to members of a society, and as Dupont and Morgan show, can translate to stratification which continues through generations.[24, 25]

It follows then that it is not simply moving to an urban area but where one lives in an urban setting that shapes migrants' social interactions and networks, health outcomes, and sense of self and community. In Delhi, evidence from the National Sample Survey Office (NSSO) suggests that migrants are among its poorest citizens. The NSSO reports that approximately 20 percent of the migrants who moved to Delhi in 2008–2009 lived on a weekly wage less than INR 1,500.[26] Migrants also overwhelmingly live in informal settlements such as *jhuggi jhopris*, lack access to basic infrastructure,[27] and pay an "urban health penalty."[28] Parts of Haryana, Rajasthan, and Uttar Pradesh (UP) that comprise the NCR, which has recently seen an increasing influx of migrants, too continue to suffer from the "metropolis development syndrome," with effects of development still remaining disparate between the core metropolitan area and surrounding nonmetropolitan periphery,[29] indicating that migrants might be urbanizing but are left out of the urban gains from migration.

This study contributes to the literature on exclusionary urbanization by examining the findings from the migrant module of the recently completed the Center for the Advanced Study of India–National Capital Region (CASI–NCR) Survey. Comparing migrants and nonmigrants, the chapter describes the persisting axes of inequalities between the two groups and analyzes their differential spatial advantage[30] by measuring differences in infrastructure access and mapping population densities. The findings indicate that despite urbanization, major disparities exist between the two groups by gender, occupation, caste, and access to infrastructure. Migrants, particularly

Scheduled Caste/Scheduled Tribe (SC/ST) migrants, also tend to be spatially concentrated in areas which face a distinct disadvantage as measured by the lack of proper infrastructure.

Methodology

Defining Migration in the CASI–NCR Survey

The CASI–NCR Survey collected data on 5,477 households across 30 districts in the Delhi NCR. Household members are enumerated in a roster which contains information on a total of 24,693 individuals, of which our analysis includes 19,096 individuals aged 18 years or older. Three specific questions in the survey capture migration information: birth district and the district where the respondent presently resides, a reason for moving to the NCR, and a year of arrival to the NCR.

We define a respondent as a "migrant" using all three criteria, that is, a respondent is a migrant if their birth district is different than the district in which they presently reside, or if they report being born in Delhi but still provide a reason for moving to the NCR, or a year of arrival to the NCR. An NCR migrant is anyone who belongs to districts included in the NCR region. We define "migrant" households by both the migration status of the head of the household and whether any one member of the household is a migrant. While 20 percent of the households have heads of households who migrated, 60 percent of the households have at least one migrant. We use the former definition to conduct our household-level analyses.

Our analysis of migration is restricted only to in-migration to Delhi NCR, given the explicit focus of the survey on understanding urban processes within the NCR region. We also exclude less than 0.02 percent respondents for whom birth district information was missing from the data.

Using these criteria, 26.6 percent of the respondents are categorized as NCR migrants according to the census definition of migration. Of these, 3 percent (495 respondents) provide only a reason for moving to the NCR and 8.6 percent (1,322 respondents) only a year of arrival into the NCR despite choosing the option "born here" when responding to the survey question. We include these additional categories of respondents as migrants because of their high proportion in the data, in the main analyses. However, we also separately analyze these two categories and discuss the implications for their inclusion as migrants, given the historical roots of migration to Delhi.

Measuring Inequality

We hypothesize that if urbanization indeed blunts the effects of social structures and creates social mobility, then we should expect to see no socioeconomic differences between migrants and nonmigrants.

We test our hypothesis at the individual level by comparing differences between migrant and nonmigrant respondents by sex, occupation, and caste. We restrict our analysis of gender only to males and females because of the small sample sizes in the third category (three respondents only). The occupation variable had 0.41 percent missing data (n = 102) and 13 categories and was recoded (thematically) to seven more consistently sized categories. We test differences between categories using chi-square tests, with an alpha of 0.05 to reject our null hypothesis.

At the household level, we measure socioeconomic differences by the caste and migration status of the household. The caste variable had a high percentage of nonresponse, 15 percent of the households (n = 863), which did not report caste information, were excluded from the caste-specific analyses. Because STs only comprise 5.3 percent of the data, we combine the ST and SC categories for analysis. Although the survey does not directly ask respondents' income, several questions inquire about asset ownership in the home. These questions were constructed into an "amenities index" by Sircar[31] and are our proxy measure to test economic differences. To understand how differences vary across space, we perform this analysis by the state to which the household migrated (or the state in which a household was enumerated). Because there are more than two caste groups, we test mean differences in assets using a multifactorial ANOVA (analysis of variance) adjusted for the interaction between state, caste, and migration status. Post hoc, we test assumptions for normality by plotting residuals, checking for heteroskedasticity using Levene's test, and plotting our interaction effects using marginal analysis. All statistical tests are performed in Stata 15.0.[32]

Assessing Spatial Inequality

While these analyses capture socioeconomic disadvantage, our purpose is to go further and understand whether migrants face a spatial disadvantage too, which according to the literature would potentially limit their social mobility. Because migrants are often reported to live in informal settlements, we use two household-level measures as proxies for spatial disadvantage: approach road type and drainage type.

Because the survey also provides location information for each household, another way in which we assess spatial disadvantage is by mapping migrant households' density in Delhi NCR, to understand whether migrant households are spatially segregated, especially by caste. In the absence of total population data, we map migrant density using the Point Density tool in ArcGIS for Desktop v10.5.1,[33] which uses the total number of points that fall within a given neighborhood to calculate density and outputs a raster surface. For our analysis, we first separately map the migrant and nonmigrant points using the geographic coordinates of each household, and then use a 7-kilometer cell radius to compute a density surface. We then assess spatial clustering in our data by computing the global Moran's I index for each neighborhood using the Cluster and Outlier Analyst tool in ArcGIS. Because the bulk of our migrant clusters are located within the National Capital Territory (NCT) region, we then use the Municipal Corporation of Delhi's (MCD) data on property values across the city's zones to make exploratory inferences about migrants' spatial disadvantage as well.

Results

Sociodemographic Profile of the Sample

Table 5.1 compares the sociodemographic profiles of migrants[34] and nonmigrants included in the survey.

The socioeconomic profile of migrants in the CASI–NCR Survey closely mirrors what has been reported in previous surveys: migrants are generally poorer than nonmigrants as measured by mean assets ($p = 0.08$), overwhelmingly female (70 percent), urban (70 percent), move for marriage (64 percent), predominantly identify as Hindus (97 percent), and belong to the "general" (33.23 percent) or Other Backward Class or "OBC" (34 percent) categories.

Trends in Migration

Overall, the migration rates in our data (26.6 percent) are comparable to those reported by national surveys such as the Census of India, 2011[35] (37 percent) and National Sample Survey (NSS) 2007–08[36] (28.5 percent) and slightly higher than those reported by other studies (20.8 percent)[37]. Although the rate of female migration in our survey (70 percent) is comparable to the Census of India, 2011[38] (70 percent), our survey records a much higher proportion

Table 5.1   Characteristics of migrants and nonmigrants

Individual level	Nonmigrant (n = 10,249)	Migrant (n = 5,082)
Age in years (mean, SE)	38 (0.13)	45 (0.20)
Sex		
Female	62.37	29.73
Male	37.63	70.27
Occupation		
Domestic work	27.74	55.65
Unemployed	13.67	14.42
Private salaried	21.91	11.09
Own work	12.02	8
Government salaried	7.88	5.66
Casual wage labor	4.81	2.80
Student (or other)	11.98	2.38
State		
Delhi	58.36	68.02
Haryana	15.41	10.38
Rajasthan	3.06	1.87
UP	23.18	19.73
Household level	Nonmigrant (3,651)	Migrant (963)
Caste		
General	37.03	38.63
OBC	41.91	38.84
SC/ST	21.06	22.53
Drainage type		
Pucca (underground/covered)	91.4	86.6
Kuccha	8.34	12.92
No drainage	0.19	0.42
Approach road		
Motorable pucca	83.18	70.40
Motorable kuccha	4.74	5.92
Nonmotorable pucca	9.26	18.59
Nonmotorable kuccha	2.82	5.09
Assets (mean, SE)	0.05 (0.014)	−0.0004 (0.03)

Source: Author.

of migration for marriage, with a marriage migration rate of over 60 percent, compared to only 49 percent reported by the Census of India, 2011.[39]

Our study finds that overall rates of urban migration have decreased, with only 10 percent migrants arriving to Delhi NCR after 2010 compared to earlier time periods, a finding corroborated by Kundu and Saraswati[40] and Bhagat.[41] There is also a clear demographic shift in migration in recent decades, with the share of young (Figure 5.1a) and female (Figure 5.1b) migrants increasing in each decade.

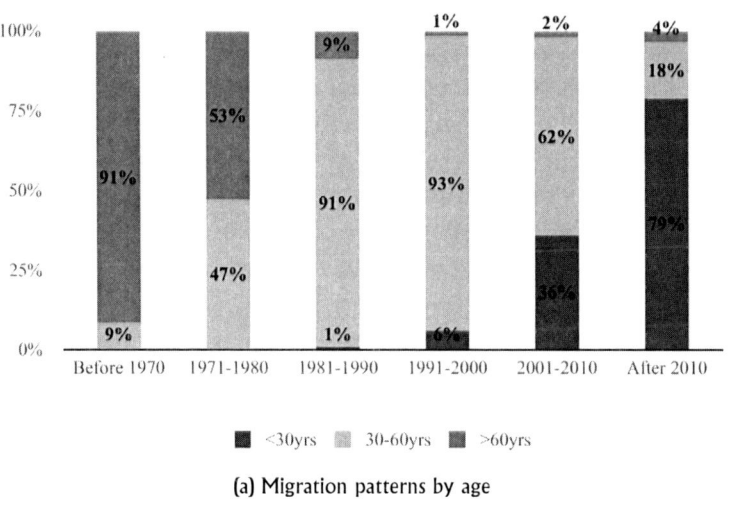

(a) Migration patterns by age

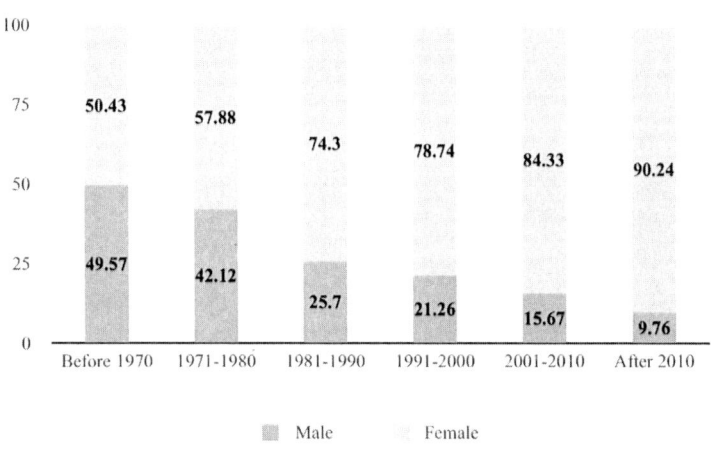

(b) Migration patterns by gender

Figure 5.1   Migration patterns

Source: Author.

A total of 20 percent households report having a household head who migrated to the NCR, comparable to 15 percent reported in the NSS.[42] At the state level, UP and Bihar remain the top migrant-sending states in each decade, along with Haryana, Rajasthan, and Punjab as the top five states where migrants come from.[43]

The Gendered Nature of Migration

Over the years, the survey records a gradual decrease in male migration and increase in female migration (Table 5.1). Although this is consistent with other reports of migration cited earlier, the reasons for migration continue to be gender specific—the overwhelming proportion of females migrate for marriage (80 percent) or for a household member's employment (7.43 percent), whereas male migration continues to be predominantly for employment (64.86 percent)—a finding which is true of every decade represented in the study. After 2010, however, among migrants who report moving for reasons other than marriage, the share of females (Figure 5.2a) moving for work increased and was 40 percent higher than their male counterparts (Figure 5.2b).

Labor Force Participation

Overall rates of work differ between migrant and nonmigrants, with unemployment being higher among migrant males by almost 5 percent and migrant females by 2.5 percent. Differences in labor force participation are even more pronounced by gender. Overall, more than 70 percent females (both migrants and nonmigrants) report attending to "domestic duties only." While the share of female migrants moving for work does increase after 2010, female migrants are still more likely to be unemployed ($p < 0.0001$) and perform a higher rate of domestic work compared to their nonmigrant counterparts ($p < 0.0001$) (Table 5.1). Interestingly, even among females who report moving specifically for employment or education, over 50 percent of them report engaging in domestic duties only and 21 percent are unemployed or seeking work.

Among males, migrants are more likely to be unemployed across all four states, Delhi, Haryana, Rajasthan and UP, perform "private work" at lower rates, and report doing more "own work" (Table 5.1). The proportion of casual wage labor performed across all states, except for Rajasthan, is similar, with the rate of casual wage labor higher by 13 percent points among migrants in the state.

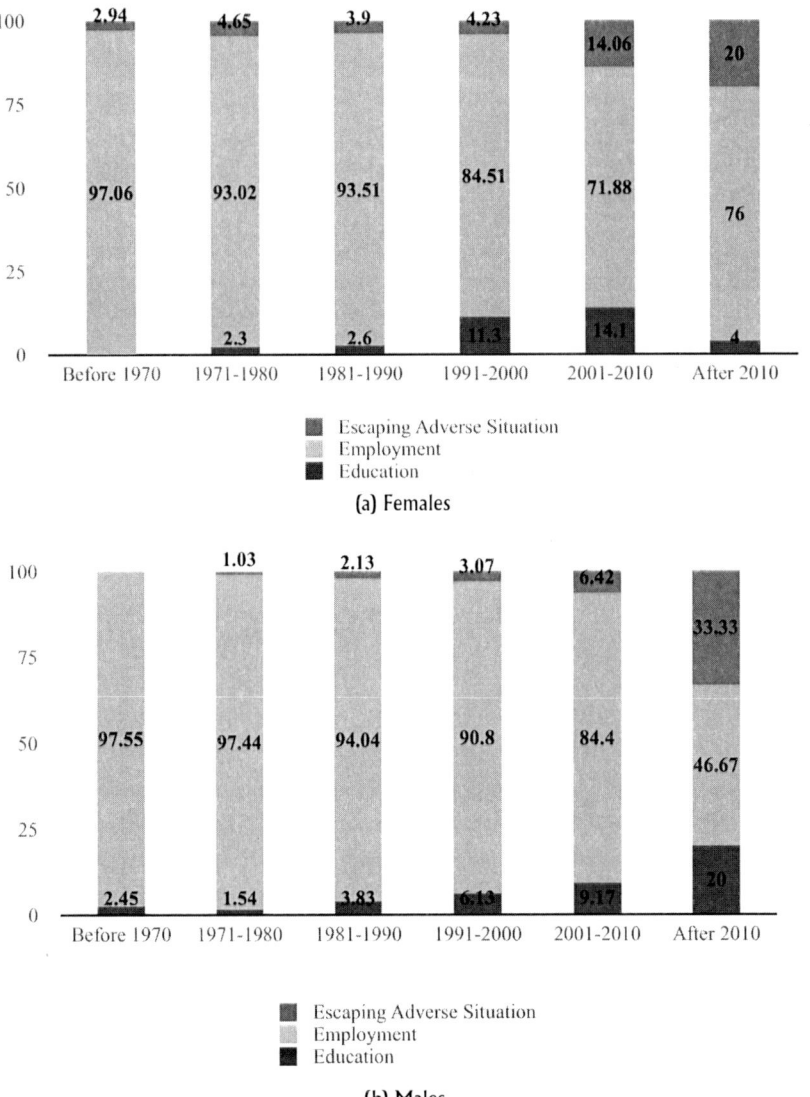

Figure 5.2   Reasons for moving other than marriage or household member's employment
Source: Author.

Inequalities by Caste

A total of 11 percent households in the survey are coded as migrant households. Overall, two-tailed t-tests for mean asset ownership show no significant differences between migrant and nonmigrant households (t = 1.34, p = 0.18).

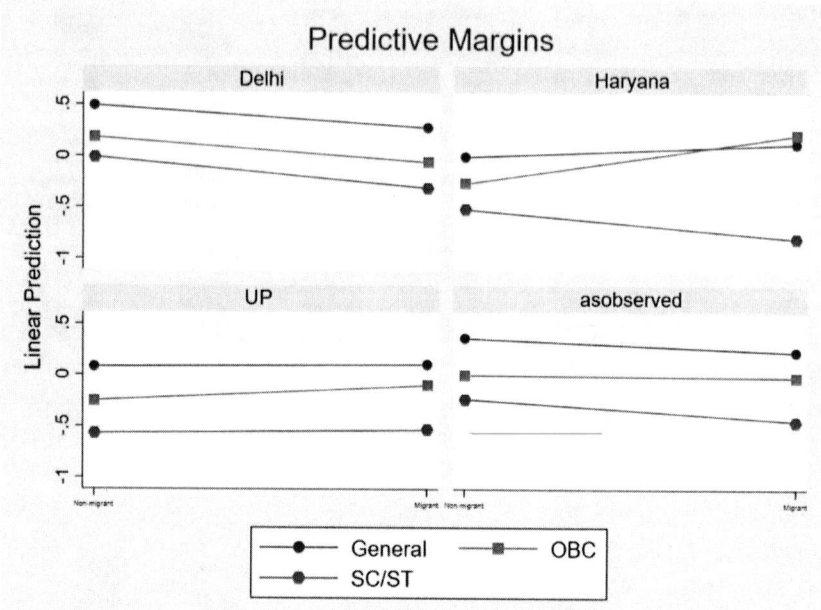

Figure 5.3 Asset ownership by state and migration status for different castes
Source: Author.

However, when we test group differences in mean assets by caste and the state of enumeration using a three-way factorial ANOVA including migration status, household caste, and state as covariates, we find caste (F[2,3233] = 37.83, p < 0.0001) and state[44] (F[3,3233] = 27.38, p < 0.0001) to be significant predictors of asset ownership. There is also a significant interaction between migration status and state (F[3,3233] = 8.06, p = 0.003), suggesting that neither caste nor state alone sufficiently predict asset ownership. Post hoc tests confirmed residuals were normally distributed and Levene's test for variance only approaching significance (p = 0.04).[45]

Figure 5.3. depicts the adjusted probabilities of asset ownership when comparing migrants to nonmigrants, showing that in each state (except for OBCs in Haryana), lower caste migrants generally are worse off economically.

Spatial Disadvantage

Despite the relatively small magnitude of difference in assets by migration status, chi-square tests show that migrants continue to have poorer access to infrastructure as measured by type of drainage (p < 0.0001) and approach road (p < 0.0001) (Table 5.1). When broken down by state, the proportion of SC/ST households with access to covered drains is equal, whether migrant or not, but the proportion of SC/ST households with no drainage is still higher among migrants by 7 percent points (p < 0.0001).

Figure 5.4 depicts the spatial distribution of the nonmigrant and migrant populations within the NCR region. Although the bulk of the migrant population resides within the boundaries of the NCT of Delhi, there are significant clusters of migrant populations (p < 0.0001) residing in the counter

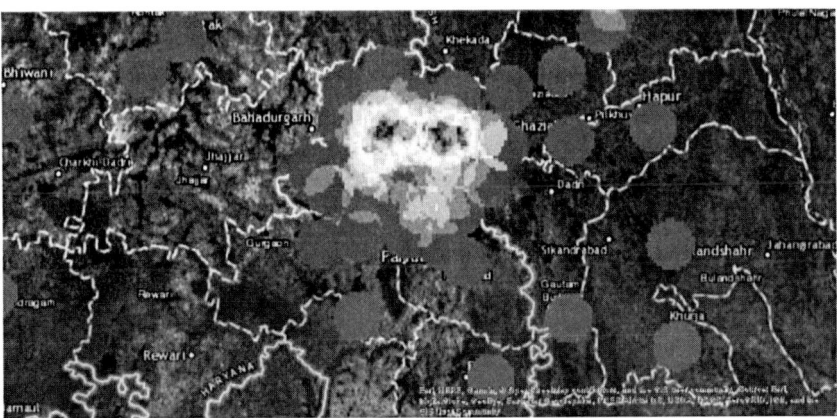

(a) Nonmigrant population

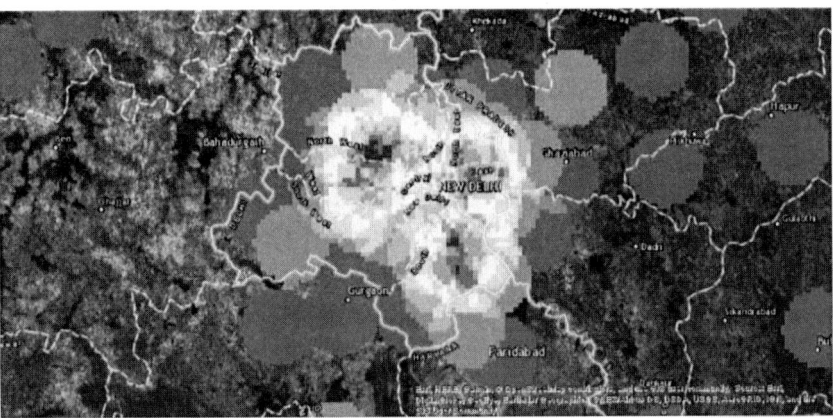

(b) Migrant population

Figure 5.4   Point density estimates of nonmigrant and migrant populations
Source: Author.

magnet areas within the NCR areas, predominantly Gurgaon, Faridabad, Panipat, Rohtak, and Bhiwani in Haryana, Ghaziabad, Noida, Meerut, and Bulandshahr in UP, and Alwar in Rajasthan.

While both migrant and nonmigrant households are concentrated in the northwest and eastern parts of the NCT region, migrant density is also high in the southeast region of the national capital. Overall, the bulk of the population density appears to be concentrated in northwest Delhi around Pehlad Pur and Bijapur village, and east Delhi around Maujpur, Madhu Vihar, Usman Pur, and Shanti Park areas. An additional cluster of migrants appears in southwest Delhi in the Okhla Industrial Area and Tughlakabad regions. Property value ranks of these areas provided by the MCD[46] depict that these colonies in the northwest areas are ranked as category H in circles, while in the southwest they are ranked from categories D to H.[47]

Discussion and Limitations

The purpose of this study was to understand whether urban migration has the effect of blunting the many documented inequalities that migrant populations routinely face in cities. We hypothesize that if indeed moving to urban areas alleviates the deep divisions that characterize social life in India, then urban migrants should be no different than nonmigrants socioeconomically. We measure these differences across gender, occupation, caste, and geographic space.

The first axis of inequality examined is gender. The study finds that reasons for migration continue to be an extremely gendered phenomenon, with women migrating at substantially higher rates for marriage or for a household member's employment, whereas men overwhelmingly move for employment. While female migration was limited in the 1990s, it accelerated drastically after the 2000s, becoming twice the rate of male migration in the same time period.[48] This acceleration is reported to be the result of an increase in the share of female migration for work. Our findings too indicate that the share of women moving for employment is greater than that of men after 2010, yet their workforce participation remains low.

Only 16.5 percent females in our survey report working outside the home. This number is even lower for migrant females who engage in higher proportions of domestic work and experience greater rates of unemployment compared to nonmigrant females. While studies on migration and gender report that marriage migration has a positive effect on female entry into the labor force and that marriage and work are not two mutually exclusive processes,[49] our data find that this is not the case. Among women who moved for marriage, only 10 percent report being in the workforce. While it is not possible to say from our data whether these females were in the labor force before marriage, the finding that such a high proportion who moved for marriage report attending to domestic duties only suggests that they could be falling through the cracks as their families urbanize. Although Tacoli and Satterwaithe argue that urban migration gives women a degree of independence and the ability to step out of the patriarchal mold,[50] Bhagat argues that patriarchal norms are instead transplanted from rural to urban areas through migration with little social reform.[51] The striking gender disparity in reasons for moving that we see in our data in the first place suggests that this might indeed be the case. It could also be that the data under-capture female workforce participation, similar to the NSS, which is also critiqued for rendering women's workforce participation invisible.[52]

The second axis of inequality examined is caste. Although there are no significant differences in asset ownership between migrants and nonmigrants, these differences become significant when caste and state are taken into account. Figure 5.3 shows that SC/STs in all states are likely to have lower assets. The effect is particularly pronounced in Delhi, compared to UP and Haryana. Delhi's level of urbanization is far greater than both these states and suggests that there is in fact a reinforcement of caste hierarchies in urban areas, as Mosse[53] and Olsen and Ramanamurthy[54] have also found.

Several scholars argue that in India, the caste system works against those who are at the lowest end of the totem pole and even when the ideological hold of caste disappears, there is limited possibility of vertical economic and social mobility.[55] Instead, Vaid argues that mobility for the lowest castes is primarily horizontal, from traditional caste occupations or agricultural labor in the village to insecure jobs at the lower end of India's vast informal economy.[56] Furthermore, while the upper castes may not be cushioned from the forces of downward mobility, those at the lower end of the caste hierarchy find it harder to move up the system.[57] That is, there is social continuity rather than social change.[58] This might also explain why caste alone has no effect on asset ownership.

It should be no surprise then that it is the interaction of migration and state, and not the caste, that predicts asset ownership. Abbas explains this effect based on the differential citizenship regime that he argues exists in India; wherein beyond just the failure of development, it is in fact the powerful duality between the native and the migrant in which the migrant experiences diminished citizenship and consequently poorer socioeconomic outcomes.[59]

Because of the staggering evidence linking social and spatial mobility, we also examine whether migrants experience a "spatial disadvantage." We infer spatial disadvantage by measuring the level of infrastructure (as measured by drain type and approach road) to which migrant households have access. Not surprisingly, migrant households have lower access to covered drainage, greater exposure to open drainage, and lower access to motorable *pucca* roads. The same disparities persist by caste, with SC/ST households (both migrant and nonmigrant) having far lower access to covered drainage or *pucca* roads. The findings are reiterated by Bhol[60] who examines access to toilets among SC/ST households in 15 different states across India. His study finds an interactive effect of caste and drainage in predicting access to toilets, concluding that access to basic goods such as a toilet is linked not only to economic factors but is also shaped by "social conditions, household behaviour, residential parameters and, most importantly, access to certain incentivizing public services."[61]

That caste continues to be a determinant of access to a basic human right in the 21st century is the sad reality of urban India. The segregation of groups by caste, as Vithayathil and Singh find in all metropolitan cities across India (namely, Mumbai, Delhi, Kolkata, Chennai, Bengaluru, Ahmedabad, and Hyderabad) and Dupont too substantiates in certain parts of Delhi,[62, 63] suggests that urbanization is not having its intended effect on weakening the hold of caste on urban Indian society. While spatial disadvantage no doubt translates to social disadvantage, Jodhka argues that there is a fundamental flaw in assuming that "economic development would inevitably convert caste-based inequalities across groups or communities into class-based differences among individuals."[64] He explains that "although old ideologies and traditional structures might disintegrate, the social and cultural prejudice associated with caste-based inequalities survives,"[65] and these prejudices then reproduce inequality through the differential diffusion of social and cultural capital, much like patriarchy does for gender.

While the findings of this study unequivocally point to the social, economic, and spatial exclusion of migrants from the benefits of urbanization, there are several limitations to our analyses. First, the survey measures migrants' socioeconomic and spatial conditions at a single point in time. Because there is no way to assess what migrants' conditions were prior to moving to Delhi NCR, it is difficult to understand the level of change they have experienced since migration. Although we do measure the length of migration and find it to be positively correlated with asset ownership ($r = 0.15$, $p < 0.0001$), we do not differentiate between migrants in our study temporally. This limits the inferences we can draw about the effects of urbanization on migration because there is ample documentation in the literature that not all migrants in India are equally vulnerable; permanent and semipermanent migrants are more likely to avail the full advantages of urban citizenship compared to temporary, often low-skilled migrants who are more vulnerable to urban exclusion.[66]

The first impetus of migration to Delhi was India's Partition. In our survey, a total of 11 percent migrants respond being born in Delhi while still providing a reason for migration or a year of arrival to the NCR. While their sociodemographic composition is no different from migrants defined as such by their place of birth, those who have been migrants for over 25 years have significantly higher asset ownership [mean (SE.) = 0.21 (0.03), $p < 0.0001$], compared to more recent migrants.[67] It could be that these are the families that moved to Delhi at the time of or soon after the Partition. Their relative wealth compared to more recent migrants could point to the "cumulative" effects of urbanization. Furthermore, the ambiguity between these respondents' self-perception as migrants and the fact that they do not fit into a neatly defined category of "migrant" open up additional possibilities to understand how migration narratives are imbibed and transmitted in a city such as Delhi where a bulk of the Partition migrants settled. Perhaps in the future, qualitative data collection with these migrants in our study could begin to uncover how histories of migration interact with urban processes more clearly. Ravinder Kaur's[68] work with Partition narratives, among others, finds that the Partition migrants successfully negotiate the terms of their citizenship and access to state services in Delhi by drawing upon these narratives, suggesting that histories of migration may also influence a migrant's economic prosperity in the long term.

Lastly, while there is substantial evidence that migrants are spatially concentrated to poorer neighborhoods in Delhi, our study does not pick up these effects. It is possible that this is an issue of scale and analyzing these data at the state or constituency levels is the wrong choice. Because assembly constituencies outside the NCT have relatively large areas, mapping population density at this scale has the effect of masking the local area variations that are otherwise documented to exist. The comparison of the migrant and nonmigrant clusters with the MCD data on Delhi's wards seems to indicate that there does exist a neighborhood disadvantage for the survey sample, owing to their low property value ranks. A further examination of these areas at the neighborhood level could highlight the differences between migrants and nonmigrants more clearly.

In conclusion, the CASI–NCR Survey data suggest that there exist clear axes of differentiation among migrants and nonmigrants in Delhi NCR. Not only do these differences exacerbate the existing socioeconomic inequalities in the rapidly urbanizing NCR landscape but also spur an "unbalanced spatial growth" in the NCR, selecting out very specific types of migrants to succeed in the sanitized global city while depriving the rest of their equal right to the city.

Appendix

Table 5A.1   Description of migrant population in CASI–NCR Survey

	Marriage (2,996)	Employment/ better opportunity (1,361)	Born here (296)	Education (224)	Escaping adverse situation/ other (66)
Sex					
Female	93.06	22.85	84.12	37.95	42.42
Male	6.94	77.15	15.88	62.05	57.58
*Caste**					
General	30.71	38.06	28.72	37.95	51.52
OBC	35.95	28.88	38.18	33.93	25.76
SC	14.49	15.06	15.2	13.84	7.58
ST	5.87	5.14	5.41	2.68	0
No response	12.98	12.86	13	11.61	15.15
Year of arrival to the NCR					
Before 1970	4.21	14.11	0	1.79	1.52
1971–1980	7.91	16.9	9.46	1.79	6.06
1981–1990	19.29	21.31	14.86	4.91	12.12
1991–2000	17.86	15.28	25.68	8.04	12.12
2001–2010	16.12	10.14	17.91	8.48	24.24
After 2010	9.48	2.42	21.96	3.13	22.73
No response	25.13	19.84	10.14	71.88	21.21
Occupation					
Domestic work	74.2	18.3	66.89	23.21	18.18
Unemployed	11.25	21.82	12.84	4.91	48.48
Private salaried	5.47	23	7.77	23.66	7.58

Contd

Table 5A.1 Contd

	Marriage (2,996)	Employment/ better opportunity (1,361)	Born here (296)	Education (224)	Escaping adverse situation/ other (66)
Own work	4.64	15.14	5.07	15.18	12.12
Government salaried	2.1	13.89	4.39	4.91	8
Casual wage labor	1.34	5.73	2.03	5.36	1.52
Student (or other)	1.0	2.13	1.01	22.77	4.55

Source: Author.

Notes: *Caste n = 4,309; for all other row variables, n = 4,946; column totals add up to 100 percent across categories for each variable.

Notes

1. Prachee Mishra, "Report of the Working Group on Migration," PRS Legislative Research, New Delhi, 2017.
2. P. Deshingkar and J. Farrington, "A Framework of Understanding Circular Migration," in *Circular Migration and Multilocational Livelihood Strategies in Rural India*, ed. P. Deshingkar and J. Farrington (New York: Oxford University Press, 2009), 1–36.
3. Rameez Abbas, "Internal Migration and Citizenship in India," *Journal of Ethnic and Migration Studies* 42, no. 1 (2016): 150–168.
4. Rachel Murphy, "Internal Migration and Rural Livelihood Diversification," in *The Elgar Companion to Development Studies*, ed. David Alexander Clark (Northampton, MA: Edward Elgar, 2006).
5. Priya Deshingkar, "Internal Migration, Poverty and Development in Asia: Including the Excluded through Partnerships and Improved Governance," *IDS Bulletin* 37, no. 3 (2006): 88–100.
6. Niranjan Sahoo, "India's Urbanisation Is Dangerously Exclusionary and Unequal," *Wire*, 2016.
7. M. S. A. Rao, *Urban Sociology in India: Reader and Source Book* (New Delhi: Orient Longman, 1974).
8. Robert E. Park, "The Urban Community as a Spatial Pattern and a Moral Order," in *The Urban Community*, ed. Ernest W. Burgess (Chicago: University of Chicago Press, 1926), 3–18; Louis Wirth, "Urbanism as a Way of Life," *American Journal of Sociology* 44, no. 1 (1938).
9. Ram B. Bhagat, "Migrants and Cities: New Partnerships to Manage Mobility," in *World Migration Report 2015* (Geneva: International Organization for Migration, 2015).

10. S. K. Mehta, "Patterns of Residence in Poona (India) by Income, Education, and Occupation (1937–65)," *American Journal of Sociology* 73, no. 4 (1968): 496–508; "Patterns of Residence in Poona, India, by Caste and Religion: 1822–1965," *Demography* 6, no. 4 (1969): 473–491.

11. S. Desai and A. Dubey, "Caste in 21st Century India: Competing Narratives," *Economic and Political Weekly* 46, no. 11 (2011): 40.

12. Pranav Sidhwani, "Spatial Inequalities in Big Indian Cities," *Economic and Political Weekly* L, no. 22 (2015): 55–62.

13. Jason Miklian and Niranjan Sahoo, "Supporting a More Inclusive and Responsive Urban India" (policy brief, Peace Research Institute Oslo, Norway, 2016).

14. Nandini Gooptu, "Economic Liberalization, Urban Politics and the Poor," in *Understanding India's New Political Economy: A Great Transformation?* ed. Sanjay Ruparelia et al. (Abingdon/New York: Routledge, 2011), 35–48.

15. Duncan Mcduie-Ra, *Northeast Migrants in Delhi: Race, Refuge and Retail* (Amsterdam: Amsterdam University Press, 2012), 68.

16. Neema Kudva, "The Everyday and the Episodic: The Spatial and Political Impacts of Urban Informality," *Environment and Planning A: Economy and Space* 41, no. 7 (July 2009): 1614–1628.

17. Mcduie-Ra, *Northeast Migrants in Delhi*, 66.

18. K. Menon-Sen, "Delhi and CWG2010: The Games behind the Games," *Journal of Asian Studies* 69, no. 3 (2010): 677–681.

19. Veronique Dupont, "Socio-spatial Differentiation and Residential Segregation in Delhi: A Question of Scale?" *Geoforum* 35, no. 2 (2004): 157–175.

20. Kudva, "The Everyday and the Episodic," 1619.

21. Gooptu, "Economic Liberalization, Urban Politics and the Poor."

22. H. Lefebvre, *The Production of Space* (Oxford: Blackwell, 1991), 410–411.

23. Park, "The Urban Community as a Spatial Pattern and a Moral Order," 10.

24. Dupont, "Socio-spatial Differentiation and Residential Segregation in Delhi."

25. B. S. Morgan, "Social Geography, Spatial Structure and Social Structure," *Geo Journal* 9 (1984).

26. NSSO (National Sample Survey Office), *Migration in India, 2007–2008*, (New Delhi: National Sample Survey Office, Ministry of Statistics and Programme Implementation, Government of India, 2010).

27. Yadlapalli S. Kusuma, Chandrakant S. Pandav, and Bontha V. Babu, "Socio-demographic Profile of Socioeconomically Disadvantaged Internal Migrants in Delhi," *Journal of Identity and Migration Studies* 8, no. 2 (2014): 37–50.

28. Laura B. Nolan, Priya Balasubramaniam, and Arundati Muralidharan, "Urban Poverty and Health Inequality in India" (Population Association of America, Boston, 2014), 1.

29. Debnath Mookherjee and Manie (H. S.) Geyer, "Urban Growth in the National Capital Region of India: Testing the Differential Urbanisation Model," *Tijdschrift voor economische en sociale geografie* 102 (2010): 88–99.

30. The term "spatial disadvantage" has long been used in urban studies to refer to the spatial inequalities that exist in the place of a person's residence and disadvantage them, either by compounding their social vulnerability (Rowland Atkinson and Keith Jacobs, "Damned by Place, Then by Politics: Spatial Disadvantage and the Housing Policy-Research Interface," *International Journal of Housing Policy* 10, no. 2 (2010): 155–171) or by restricting their social mobility through confinement in "spatial poverty traps" (Kate Bird, "Addressing Spatial Poverty Traps," *Chronic Poverty Advisory Network* [London: Overseas Development Institute, February 2019]).

31. See Chapter 2 of this volume by Nilanjan Sircar.

32. Stata Statistical Software: Release 15, StataCorp LLC, College Station, TX.

33. ArcGIS: Release 10.5.1, Esri, Redlands, CA.

34. For a within group description of migrants, see Table 5A.1.

35. Samarth Bansal, "45.36 Crore Indians Are Internal Migrants," *Hindu*, December 2, 2016.

36. NSSO, *Migration in India, 2007–2008*.

37. R. B. Bhagat and Soumya Mohanty, "Emerging Pattern of Urbanization and the Contribution of Migration in Urban Growth in India," *Asian Population Studies* 5, no. 1 (2009): 5–20.

38. Bansal, "45.36 Crore Indians Are Internal Migrants."

39. Ibid.

40. Amitabh Kundu and Lopamudra Ray Saraswati, "Migration and Exclusionary Urbanisation in India," *Economic and Political Weekly* 47, nos. 26–27 (2012): 219–227.

41. R. B. Bhagat, "Migration and Urban Transition in India: Implications for Development," in *United Nations Expert Group Meeting on Sustainable Cities, Human Mobility and International Migration* (New York: Population Division, Department of Economic and Social Affairs, United Nations Secretariat, 2017).

42. NSSO, *Migration in India, 2007–2008*.

43. Department of Economic Affairs, "India on the Move and Churning: New Evidence," in *Economic Survey 2016–17 Volume 1*, ed. Department of Economic Affairs (New Delhi: Ministry of Finance, Government of India, 2017), 264–277.

44. Rajasthan is excluded from these analyses due to a small sample size.

45. While unequal variances increase our chance of incorrectly rejecting our null hypothesis, because we know the embeddedness of caste in the social fabric in Haryana and Uttar Pradesh, it is important to include state in the model as well.

46. Municipal Corporation of Delhi, "MCD Zones in Delhi," map, MapmyIndia, available at http://app.mapmyindia.com/mcdApp/, accessed on July 28, 2020.

47. Circle rates range from category A (most well-off areas) to category H (poorest areas), and are used to assess land value and in loan calculations.

48. Department of Economic Affairs, "India on the Move and Churning."

49. Surjit S. Bhalla and Ravinder Kaur, "Labour Force Participation of Women in India: Some Facts, Some Queries," (working paper, London School of Economics Asia Research Center, London School of Economics, London, 2011).

50. Cecilia Tacoli and David Satterthwaite, "Editorial: Gender and Urban Change," *Environment and Urbanisation* 25, no. 1 (2013): 3–8.

51. Bhagat, "Migrants and Cities."

52. K. Shanthi, *"Female Labour Migration in India: Insights from NSSO Data* (Chennai: Madras School of Economics, 2006).

53. D. Mosse, "Brokered Livelihoods: Debt, Labour Migration and Development in Tribal Western India," *Journal of Development Studies* 38, no. 5 (2002): 59–88.

54. W. K. Olsen and R. V. Ramanamurthy, "Contract Labour and Bondage in Andhra Pradesh (India)," *Journal of Social and Political Thought* 1, no. 2 (2000): 1–27.

55. D. Vaid and A. Heath, "Unequal Opportunities: Class, Caste, and Social Mobility," in *Diversity and Change in Contemporary India*, ed. A. Heath and R. Jeffery (Oxford: Oxford University Press, 2010); S. Thorat and P. Attewell, "The Legacy of Social Exclusion: A Correspondence Study of Job Discrimination in India," *Economic and Political Weekly* 42, no. 41 (2007): 4141–4145.

56. D. Vaid, "Caste–Class Association in India: An Empirical Analysis," *Asian Survey* 52, no. 2 (2012): 395–422.

57. Ibid., 420.

58. S. Kumar, A. Heath, and O. Heath, "Determinants of 'Social Mobility in India'," *Economic and Political Weekly* 37, no. 29 (2002): 4096.

59. Abbas, "Internal Migration and Citizenship in India."

60. Aditya Bhol, "Horizontal and Vertical Inequalities Explaining Disparities in Access to Urban Sanitation: Evidence from the National Sample Survey of India" (working paper, New Delhi, Centre for Policy Research, 2018).

61. Ibid., 26.

62. Trina Vithayathil and Gayatri Singh, "Spaces of Discrimination: Residential Segregation in Indian Cities," *Economic and Political Weekly* 47, no. 37 (2012): 60–66.

63. Dupont, "Socio-spatial Differentiation and Residential Segregation in Delhi."

64. Surinder S. Jodhka, "Ascriptive Hierarchies: Caste and Its Reproduction in Contemporary India," *Current Sociology* 64, no. 2 (2015): 228–243.

65. Ibid.
66. Deshingkar, "Internal Migration, Poverty and Development in Asia."
67. For migrants whose length of migration was less than 25 years but more than 10 years, the mean score on the asset index was −0.03 (0.04) while for those who migrated less than 10 years ago, the mean score was 0.17 (0.03). These two groups were not significantly different from each other (p = 0.699).
68. Ravinder Kaur, *Since 1947: Partition Narratives among Punjabi Migrants of Delhi* (Oxford: Oxford University Press, 2007).

CHAPTER 6

Energy

Electrifying the Capital

Radhika Khosla

Introduction

India is at the cusp of an urban transition, predicted to be one of the largest in global history by 2050.[1] The implications of this transition are many—Indian cities will host 200 million more people by 2030—mostly starting from a low base of development who will demand modern fuels, appliances, air conditioners (ACs), and vehicles for improved quality of life. Demographically, at least 10 million people are expected to enter the Indian job market annually for the next two decades and urban areas will account for 75 percent of gross domestic product growth in the next 15 years.[2] In addition, two-thirds of India's buildings that will exist in 2030 have started to be built since 2010 onward.[3] Managing these urban transitions is a significant challenge in itself, one that is further complicated by the need to address their energy implications. In this chapter, I examine a significant driver of India's urban energy future—electricity demand in households—in the context of the National Capital Region (NCR).

Electricity use in Indian homes—for lights, ceiling fans, televisions, and refrigerators, among other appliances—has increased 50 times between 1971 and today,[4] even though India's per capita residential electricity consumption is less than a third of the world average.[5] Residential electricity now outpaces growth in the industrial, commercial, and agricultural sectors.[6] And India's residences, which avail of modern energy services such as cooling, clean cooking, lighting, and media access, are predicted to account for 85 percent of the country's floor space by 2050.[7] A combination of the residential growth, development needs, rising incomes, and the policy aimed to provide uninterrupted electricity to all homes by 2019 and is projected to increase electricity consumption by five to six times between 2014 and 2030.[8] Already, the residential sector used about 25 percent of the country's total current electricity consumption (with a 9 percent growth in 2015–2016)—and this was at a time when about a quarter of all households did not have an electricity connection and those who had used to face frequent power cuts.[9] The sheer scale of growth and the challenge of meeting the resulting energy needs in a sustainable manner pose unprecedented burdens on India's urban areas.

This burden is particularly salient to the NCR because Delhi, which forms the National Capital Territory (NCT) within the NCR, has the highest residential energy use in India.[10] In fact, one electrified household in Delhi consumes, on average, approximately the same average amount consumed by an electrified household in Germany.[11] This spike in Delhi's consumption is in part because of its population's ownership of high-energy-consuming appliances and the tariff subsidies provided. However, a detailed analysis on understanding the region's household consumption patterns and their drivers is limited.

Even at the country level, and in spite of the scale of current and future residential electricity use, there is little data publicly available on energy services apart from the data from the decennial census and the five-yearly National Sample Survey (NSS). Further, different studies, including different versions of the government's electricity planning document, the Electric Power Survey, predict dramatically different scenarios for the extent to which residential electricity use will grow.[12] This large variation stems from differing methods and assumptions—rooted in the lack of empirical data on how electricity is currently used in homes across the country.

These conditions provide the motivation for the research questions addressed in this chapter. In order to study changing residential electricity patterns in the NCR, the chapter focuses on three questions. First, how much electricity does a resident of the NCR consume? Second, what are the services that households use electricity for? And third, how is the ownership of appliances, to provide these services, changing with increasing incomes and the ability to consume more?

Shedding light on these questions could help inform future energy planning, the current ambiguity around which is a significant barrier to energy and climate policymaking. Inaccurate consumption forecasts can risk energy security, if demand is too high, or result in a series of stranded assets, if demand levels are low; both are issues of concern. And in either case, if unaddressed, rising residential electricity use will put serious constraints on already stretched national resources, posing serious social, local environmental, and climate change–related burdens.

Importantly, though, the scale of increased residential demand and the uncertainty in the extent to which it could increase make future electricity needs not only immense but also potentially malleable. This particular aspect of urban areas such as the NCR offers, perhaps counterintuitively, a potential advantage. The reason being that since most energy-intensive purchasing decisions are yet to be made by majority of the households, there is occasion to still shape electricity-consuming preferences and practices. Once invested in, these consumption patterns are difficult to reverse. The current ability of households to pick energy-conserving appliances is thus a distinctive window of opportunity to choose alternative pathways that do not compromise on needs, and yet also reduce the rate of energy and carbon uptake. But this opportunity is only as useful as the early decisions that households make. And its first step is understanding in detail how electricity is used today and the services that households seek the most.

The rest of this chapter aims to discuss these issues for the NCR. The chapter begins with providing an overview of electricity in the Delhi region, followed by an analysis that draws from the Center for the Advanced Study of India–National Capital Region (CASI–NCR) Survey, which is a representative sample of nearly 5,500 households of the NCR's population in 2017. Like other chapters in this book, the energy analysis often uses the "asset index" to indicate the ability of a household to consume. For the method and rationale for the asset index, see Chapter 2.

National Capital Territory's Electricity Landscape

In the summer of May 2016, the NCT of Delhi's peak demand hit a record 6,044 megawatts. This was more than the combined demand of cities such as Mumbai (3,700 megawatts) and Kolkata (2,100 megawatts). The peak demand in FY 2018–2019 was projected to be even higher at around 7,115 megawatts.[13] Compared with other parts of the country, Delhi consumes more electricity than all other states and it also uses more power than all the other metros put together. What is behind the city's electricity landscape?

Delhi's generation capacity is mainly from a mix of coal and gas, followed by hydropower (with a total of 7.5 gigawatts as of March 2015, shown in Figure 6.1).[14] However, the state finds itself in an ironic situation, as since 2015–2016, it has had the surplus availability of energy ranging from 30 to

33 percent, yet simultaneously, in terms of peak demand, it faces a shortfall of about 4–11 percent.[15] The mismatch is analogous with the larger electricity context in the country, where India is witnessing the curious phenomenon of surplus electricity capacity coexisting with millions unserved.[16] For the most part, these circumstances stem from the problematic state of the electricity distribution system, whose finances would further worsen if they provided power to the unserved.[17]

For the case of Delhi, specifically, electricity generation, transmission, and distribution is handled by the Delhi Vidyut Board.[18] The board was restructured in 2001 to comprise six successor entities and three private distribution companies (called BSES Rajdhani Power Limited, BSES Yamuna Power Limited, and Tata Power Delhi Distribution Limited).[19] This privatization brought in noticeable improvement in the infrastructure and quality of power delivery; thus, the aggregate technical and commercial loss levels in Delhi are now among the lowest in the country. At the same time though, privatization has also been met with roadblocks in the form of consumer protests over escalating tariffs and allegations of financial irregularity within the state's distribution companies.

On the policy end, Delhi plans to provide 24×7 power supply in anticipation of the state's growing electricity needs. Private distribution companies claim that ample arrangements are being made to source adequate electricity, such as via long-term power purchase agreements and banking arrangements with

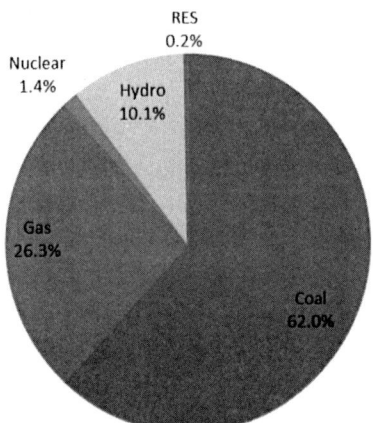

Figure 6.1   Generation capacity for Delhi, 2015

Source: Government of India and Government of Delhi, *24x7 Power for All: Delhi* (New Delhi: Government of India and Government of Delhi, June 2016), 7.

other states.[20] Distribution companies are also planning for additional power through central generating stations and renewable energy sources.[21] Solar energy in particular has been gaining prominence with the Aam Aadmi Party (AAP) government issuing the Delhi Solar Policy in June 2016, pegging Delhi's solar potential at 2,500 megawatts, given the city's over 300 days of annual sunshine. The targets specified under the policy are 1 gigawatt energy by 2020 and 2 gigawatts by 2025. This is certainly ambitious considering Delhi's solar rooftop-installed capacity of around 0.007 gigawatt as of August 2015.[22]

Along with the growing emphasis on solar rooftop projects within the city, a part of treating the complex electricity supply issue and the shortfall during peak demand is to manage needs from the demand side (Figure 6.2 shows the consumption profile for Delhi). The Delhi Electricity Regulatory Commission issued demand-side management regulations in 2014, with a mandate to bring about a reduction in energy consumption across residential, commercial, and industrial establishments. Tata Power, in particular, has taken a lead with the residential lighting, appliance replacement programs,[23] and an integrated auto-demand response program. These actions help distribution companies benefit from an offset in peak demand and the need to avoid buying expensive power then (between 3 pm and 5 pm in Delhi).[24]

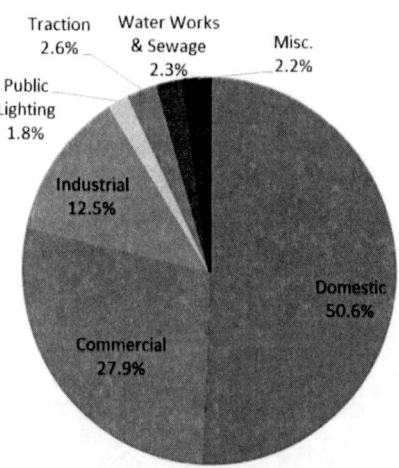

Consumption for Delhi 2015

Figure 6.2   Delhi power consumption profile, 2014–2015

Source: EE & REM (Energy Efficiency & Renewable Energy Management) Centre, *Initiatives & Achievements of Energy Efficiency & Renewable Energy Management Centre towards Energy Efficiency and Energy Conservation* (New Delhi: Department of Power, Government of National Capital Territory of Delhi, 2017), available at http://aeee.in/wp-content/uploads/2017/05/Power-Department-Delhi.pdf, accessed on September 2, 2020.

For the most part though, consumption-based metrics are difficult to implement. It is also not helpful that the current Delhi government's household electricity subsidy is among the most generous in the country, as the AAP government put in place large electricity subsidies for households in 2013, to compensate for the Delhi Electricity Regulatory Commission's tariff hikes in the immediately preceding years. The AAP government is, however, also taking some early steps toward promoting green energy, and given that electricity is on the election agenda in Delhi, it is likely that the nature of further innovations on renewables and reducing consumption will shape the region's electricity future.

How Much Electricity Do the National Capital Region Residents Consume?

It is clear that residential electricity use in India is rising, including in the high-consuming NCR region. However, while total consumption is an important metric, this section also unpacks how individuals within the aggregate consume electricity.

Figure 6.3 compares the NCR's per capita electricity use with recent per capita numbers from the literature on Delhi and India. It also shows estimates for other countries, the United States of America (USA) and China, to demonstrate the different contexts of developed and developing countries. The per capita electricity use for the NCR is calculated using the reported electricity bill per surveyed household (averaged to an annual amount), the number of people within that household, and using a tariff rate translation of INR 5 per kilowatt-hour of electricity (based on household consumption units and the current tariff slabs for Delhi,[25] Haryana,[26] and Uttar Pradesh (UP)).[27]

As the Figure 6.3 shows, an average person in an electrified USA household uses about 25 times the electricity of a person in an electrified home in India. By comparison, an average person in China uses about three times that of an average person per electrified household in India. Further, studies indicate that the difference in per capita consumption between India and China has increased significantly between 2001 and 2013, suggesting that the increase in per capita consumption has been much more severe in China than in India.[28]

Intra-country comparisons reveal analogously large differences. The electricity use per person based on the CASI–NCR Survey is broadly consistent with other statistics of Delhi, once again suggesting that Delhi or the NCT is the driver of the NCR energy story. The India average, on the other hand, is

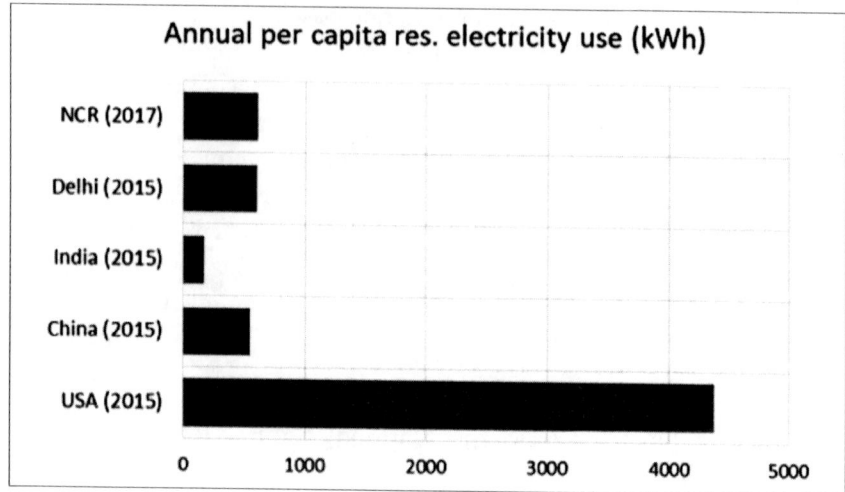

Figure 6.3   Comparisons of annual per capita residential electricity use
Sources: EIA, 2017; US Census Bureau, 2017; NBSC, 2017; NITI Aayog, 2017; CASI–NCR Survey, 2017.

3.5 times lower than the NCR number. Studies of other states that compose the NCR also have low consumption rates, closer to the average Indian number: Haryana at about 200 kilowatts-hour, and UP and Rajasthan at 100 kilowatts-hour, all annually in 2012.[29] The CASI–NCR Survey results demonstrate that in purely electricity terms, the NCR resident consumes the most: an amount that is continuing to rise and that will be mirrored by the rest of the county. In the next section, I examine what leads to this high consumption pattern.

What Drives the National Capital Region's High Energy Use?

To understand the NCR's high energy use, we break from the conventional planning emphasis on energy supplies and use the approach of examining how energy is consumed. We examine the energy services sought in the NCR by assessing the appliances owned by the population (Figure 6.4). We also contextualize and validate the results for the NCR from the CASI–NCR Survey by looking at similar appliance penetration numbers from other recent studies conducted for the Delhi region.

As Figure 6.4 shows, almost every house has a fan, closely followed by a television (TV). The studies in Figure 6.4 cover a five-year period between 2011 and 2017. The most recent of these, the CASI–NCR Survey, consistently shows the largest penetration rates of the appliances—across TV, fridge, AC,

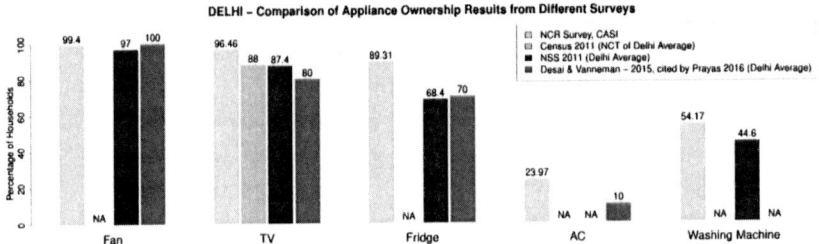

Figure 6.4 Comparison of appliance ownership results for Delhi from different studies

Source: Author.

and washing machine (and with a small exception for fans). In all cases, this increase is at minimum about 10 percent more for the 2017 results, with the most dramatic differences for fridges and ACs. It is likely that the 2017 NCR survey is capturing the rising appliance ownership over a few years. The comparison also demonstrates that while other appliance databases exist, none of them captures the range of appliances accounted for in the CASI–NCR Survey. This is especially important for energy intensive equipment such as fridges, ACs, and washing machines, which are increasingly prevalent within the NCR but which are not yet being captured by the census and/or the NSSO.

A next step to understand energy consumption is knowing the number of each appliance that households own. Based on the NCR data, we calculate the mode or the most commonly occurring number of appliances within the region (Table 6.1).

Two interesting characteristics of energy use in the NCR emerge from Table 6.1. First, Delhi's household appliance composition is different from other states with the addition of the washing machine prevalent in most homes. This likely has implications for higher electricity use in Delhi, and potentially for

Table 6.1 Mode appliance compositions in the NCR states

	Delhi	*Haryana*	*UP*	*Rajasthan*
Fans	2	2	2	1
Fridge	1	1	1	1
TV	1	1	1	1
Washing Machine	1	0	0	0
Water Purifier R/O	0	0	0	0
AC	0	0	0	0
Cooler	1	1	1	1

Source: Author.

the labor saved from washing clothes. Second, while an average home in the NCR typically has a cooler, they do not yet have an AC. This is true even in Delhi, which is considerably wealthier and the largest electricity consumer in the country. Also, while not represented graphically, the data also shows that 63 percent of households in the NCR have a two-wheeler while a smaller 17 percent have a car.

These trends of appliance ownership are also reflected when the data is categorized for *kuccha*/semi-*kuccha* (semipermanent) and *pucca* (permanent) homes. *Kuccha*/semi-*kuccha* homes, intuitively, have lower reported electricity bills than *pucca* homes, with reported numbers demonstrating a large difference of about 30 percent. All households, however, do not uniformly experience the estimate of a household's average monthly load. Indeed, different households own a different set of appliances, which is a function of their larger socioeconomic characteristics. Household income, stock of appliances, usage of appliances, family size, dwelling size, time spent out by the family members, and higher education level are reasons for varying electricity use.[30] The idea of an "average" household, thus, while valuable for making macro-estimates and central to informing policy, does also mask the variation across households.

Digging into the surveyed electricity data further allows us to examine the variation within the region. Using the reported bill, and the average price of electricity in the area of INR 5 per kilowatt-hour, Figure 6.5 shows the distribution of monthly electricity consumed by households. The figure demonstrates that there is much variation within the region. About 65 percent of the households consume less than 200 kilowatts-hour per month, after which

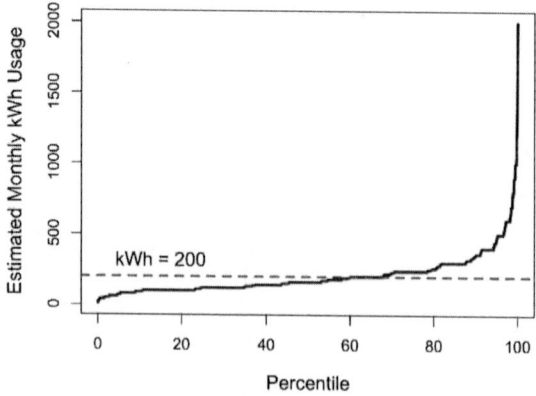

Figure 6.5   Calculated electricity consumption across the NCR
Source: Author.

consumption increases dramatically, with the top 20 percent homes consuming more than 300 kilowatts-hour per month that are spread across the long- and high-consuming tail of the distribution.

The intra-region variation is also seen when comparing the services used and appliances owned by households in the top 5 percent of the NCR, the top 5 percent of the NCT or Delhi, the top 5 percent of the non-NCT region of the NCR (parts of Haryana, Rajasthan, and UP surrounding Delhi), and then the bottom 10 percent of the NCR (Table 6.2).

It is striking that whether households occupy the top or the bottom 5 percent of the NCR—the two ends of a large spectrum—the only two appliances that are almost prevalent throughout are the fan and the TV. Between the top 5 percent of the NCT and the non-NCT regions, the NCT or Delhi shows subtle differences in lifestyle—more ACs than coolers, many more households with microwaves and water purifiers, and almost universal car ownership coupled with almost no three wheelers. In the same region though, the bottom 10 percent show almost no ownership of any of these appliances, with the exception of a TV, a fan, and a small fraction with a fridge.

The estimates for Delhi's consumption from the CASI–NCR Survey are broadly consistent with other estimates from the literature.[31] On an annual basis, the numbers suggest that Delhi's annual consumption (in 2017) is approximately twice the Indian average for household electricity use per electrified household in 2014. Further, Delhi's consumption in 2016 is of the same order of magnitude as Italy and Russia in 2014.[32]

Table 6.2 Intra-region appliance penetration rates in the NCR

Appliance	Top 5% of the NCR	Bottom 10% of the NCR	Top 5% of the NCT	Top 5% of the non–NCT
TV	98	90	99	98
Fan	100	98	99	100
Cooler	79	56	79	85
AC	93	0	96	86
Fridge	99	15	99	98
Microwave	77	5	82	41
Water purifier	92	4	96	55
Washing machine	95	0	95	95
Car	87	0	90	78
Three wheeler	21	7	17	21

Source: Author.

Changing Nature of Appliance Usage

The NCR is among the highest electricity-using parts of India, and as seen in the last section, there is much variation in consumption within this region. Which parts of the population are consuming more than others, and what are the additional appliances and energy services they seek? And as the population transitions toward further urbanization and higher levels of income, which appliances do they buy first? I examine the changing nature of appliance use by developing an "appliance ladder"—a metric which indicates how households buy more and different appliances as their ability to consume increases. The latter is indicated by the asset index, explained in Chapter 2 of this book in more detail.

The survey results tell us the most energy-intensive appliances used within the NCR region: the fridge, TV, washing machine, and devices that provide access to the internet (smartphones and Wi-Fi routers). As seen in Figure 6.6, almost every home, irrespective of where it ranks on the asset index, owns a TV. Based on this result, it is fair to say that a TV is among the first energy-intensive appliance that households buy. TVs are more ubiquitous than coolers and fridges, in spite of the hot-and-dry climate and peak summer temperatures of the region. This result aligns with the literature that shows that over the past few decades, TV viewing has become the most important leisure and entertainment activity for middle-class families.[33] The fridge

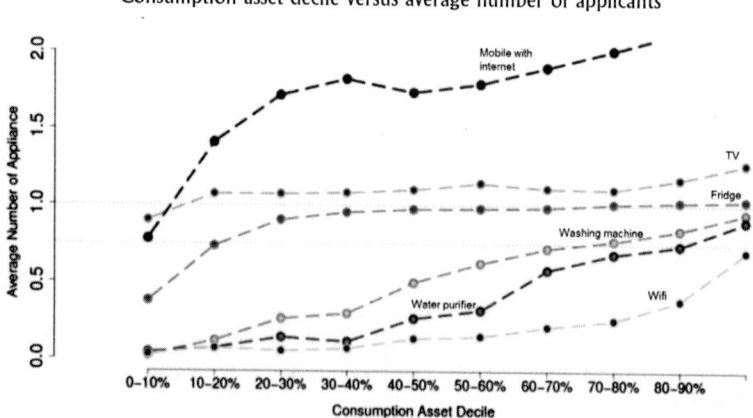

Figure 6.6   Energy-intensive and internet-accessed appliance ownership patterns in the NCR as a function of household asset index

Source: Author.

follows closely behind the TV, and by the 3rd decile, most households own one. While the ownership of a TV is ubiquitous across the country, owning a fridge, particularly in the lower 2nd and 3rd asset deciles, is particular to the NCR and the ability of its population to afford and consume more (see Chunekar, Dixit, and Varshney,[34] on fridge ownership patterns from other studies). Washing machines, on the other hand, follow the trend seen in other parts of the country, which is an increase in their ownership only at higher 7th–8th asset deciles.

Turning to internet access, which is increasingly seen as an indicator of development, the data shows that almost every household, irrespective of its asset rank, has access to the internet via a mobile phone. The number of phones per household increases as households move up the asset index, with a doubling by about the 5th decile. Wi-Fi routers, on the other hand, which are likely accompanied by computers, are seen only at the highest decile, and even at this level their penetration level is rather low.

Next, we examine the ownership of at least one cooling device per household, ranging from a fan, cooler to an AC (Figure 6.7). The data shows that while every household has a fan, only the top decile (at most) has an AC. The most prevalent cooling device continues to be the cooler, which households start acquiring as they enter the 4th decile.

The implications of the cooling appliances' ownership patterns could potentially be the most significant in determining the trajectory of the

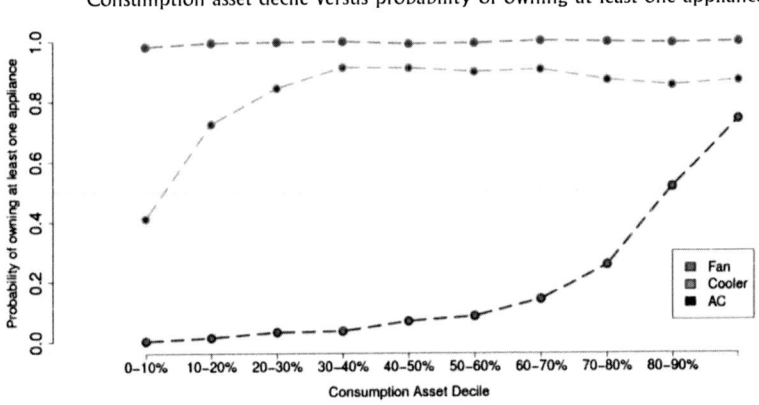

Consumption asset decile versus probability of owning at least one appliance

Figure 6.7   Cooling appliance ownership patterns in the NCR as a function of household asset index

Source: Author.

NCR's energy use. As income levels rise, the AC curve will increasingly mirror the current cooler curve in Figure 6.7. Furthermore, because the AC load (~1,500 watts) is an order of magnitude higher than that of a fan (~75 watts) or a cooler (~200 watts), the systemic effects of the resulting increased electricity demand and greenhouse gas emissions from AC use are predicted to be dramatic.[35]

The case of the NCR provides a preview of the changing nature of cooling for the rest of urban India. Delhi's cooling consumption is currently much more than other metros—one study shows that while in most metros the electricity demand during the night is lower than in the daytime (when power-intensive sectors such as industries, offices, and malls are closed)[36], in Delhi, peak demand for electricity is nearly the same during day and night in the summer months because of the city's AC use in middle-class homes. At the country level, currently, AC penetration is less than 10 percent in a country of 1.3 billion and where the impacts of rising temperature are particularly adverse. For the most part, the country is subject to extreme heat, with large areas of high relative humidity, and with a significant portion of the population with limited means for active space cooling. Simultaneously, the literature and market studies predict that India is at the cusp of an exponential growth in the AC market.[37] The impact on households of this AC penetration will be twofold—access to cooler indoor environments as the probability of extreme temperatures rises but also a marked increase in the household electricity bill, a systemic strain on the grid, and significant greenhouse gas emissions. By some estimates, room AC use is expected to add approximately 150 gigawatts to the peak demand by 2030—equivalent to 300 large power plants of 500 megawatts capacity each.[38] The social externalities are equally important, such as the asymmetrically distributed impacts of summer power outages which deny basic thermal comfort via fans to those that contribute least to peak AC-related demand.

It is perhaps fortunate that the lasting decisions about technologies and infrastructures, with analogous institutional structures and resulting consumption behaviors, have not yet all been made. Once such large capital investments are complete, the cost of switching to new infrastructure can often be too high. If end-use technologies with poor energy performance become the standard in yet-to-exist urban homes, they can lead to a series of path-dependent outcomes and lifestyles, which will make it difficult to reduce consumption for decades to come.

Looking Ahead: Energy in the NCR and Beyond

The provision of energy has long been central to India's development planning. In most cases, this has taken the form of generating and making available the supply of energy in the form of increased coal, gas, nuclear, renewables, and so on. The current energy plans highlight this trend: through a focus on coal (with a domestic production target of 1.5 billion tonness by 2020) and a growth in renewables (with aspirations to produce 175 gigawatts of renewable power by 2022). This view of energy planning with its supply-oriented solutions, however, is built around a narrative of chronic and ongoing energy scarcity. Specifically, it assumes constantly rising energy needs and a resulting pursuit of all available energy options—often without a complementary consideration of the uses to which the energy is put and the costs of procuring that energy. However, understanding demand is necessary for sensible supply-side planning, which is ultimately a function of future consumption and demand. But there does not exist yet a rigorous forecast of India's future grid size, and study projections range anywhere between 650 to 1,000 gigawatts.[39] More so, the traditional supply-dominated orientation has simply not been enough to fix the pathologies of Indian energy. The sector still suffers from inefficiencies and financial losses of electricity distribution companies in spite of increasing electricity production and a slew of policy targets. Notably, India's power sector is stuck in a unique paradox of energy surplus at the production plants and unmet demand at the consumer end—stemming from a systematic failure in understanding and planning for electricity demand.[40]

In this chapter, I recover some of the lesser recognized history of an alternative approach which focuses not only on how energy is supplied but also on how it is consumed. Such a narrative break was originally promoted in the mid-1980s in the work of Amulya Reddy who moved the conventional emphasis on "energy sources" to that of "energy services."[41] From this perspective, the objective of the energy system—and its supply and utilization activities—is to provide energy services such as lighting, comfortable indoor temperatures, refrigeration, transportation, and so on to achieve development outcomes.

This spotlight on energy services is particularly salient in the current context of the climate crisis, which is increasingly finding voice among citizens in Delhi and other cities in India and around the world. Indeed, any success toward the global temperature 2° Celsius target, laid out in the Paris Agreement to which most countries including India have signed on, is inextricably dependent on how actions toward this goal will filter down from nations to cities, households, and individuals.

As the Intergovernmental Panel on Climate Change 1.5°C Report states, there are only two pathways to achieve the global temperature target: (*a*) by drastically reducing global energy demand or (*b*) by the use of negative emission technologies (including bioenergy with carbon capture and storage) which reduce carbon dioxide concentration in the atmosphere. While the latter technologies are almost entirely in demonstration phase without being available at scale, the former option—reduction in energy demand—is both technologically feasible and cost effective. Taking forward these solutions, however, requires untangling the complex ways in which energy consumption is routinized in our daily lives, particularly in households—an examination of which is undertaken in this chapter. An understanding of the kind suggested in this work can play a key role in informing government initiatives focusing on energy demand through end-use energy-efficiency programs. While in many cities energy-efficiency and demand-based policies are already in play, to implement them systematically across first-time home and appliance owners requires a coordinated institutional effort to influence consumers at the point of purchase, ratcheting up energy-efficiency standards of appliances, and providing information about the benefits and lower lifetime costs. If strategically targeted across the core set of energy service technologies which households purchase, irrespective of household income levels, climate zones, and individual preferences, the growth in urban housing offers an important site for managing energy demand and climate mitigation.

Transformational changes, such as those suggested, will, however, require a broader conception of energy planning, which accounts for the linkages between energy supply and demand, and understanding how much is actually needed—by whom and when. Urban India will be at the heart of this consumption, yet, reshaping urban trajectories, to overcome existing, and often economically favorable, energy-intensive infrastructures is not trivial nor familiar. Such a shift in imagination will not be easy or automatic—especially because consumption patterns are embedded in a complex network of social institutions, practices, and norms. Yet, the time is ripe to revisit and recover the demand-side perspective on India's urban energy transition as a necessary complement to supply-side efforts. If unaddressed, this future demand will put serious constraints on already stretched national resources, posing social, local environmental, and climate change–related burdens. But if considered strategically, future urban consumption could enable more sustainable forms of development.

Notes

1. United Nations, *World Urbanization Prospects: The 2014 Revision* (New York: Department of Economic and Social Affairs, and Population Division, United Nations, 2014).

2. Press Information Bureau, "Need to Focus on Planning and Design for Sustainable and Clean Urban Mobility: Vice President," November 4, 2017, available at https://pib.gov.in/PressReleasePage.aspx?PRID=1508234, accessed on November 1, 2020; Rajguru Tandon, "India Needs 10 Million Jobs per Annum till 2030 to Counter Unemployment," *BW Businessworld*, February 26, 2018, available at http://businessworld.in/article/India-Needs-10-Million-Jobs-Per-Annum-Till-2030-To-Counter-Unemployment-/26-02-2018-141808, accessed on September 12, 2020.

3. Satish Kumar et al., "Developing an Energy Conservation Building Code Implementation Strategy in India" (American Council for an Energy-Efficient Economy, Washington, DC, 2010), available at https://aceee.org/files/proceedings/2010/data/papers/2174.pdf, accessed on September 12, 2020.

4. Radhika Khosla and Aditya Chunekar, "Plugging In-Residential Electricity in India" (Centre for Policy Research, New Delhi, and Prayas [Energy Group], Pune, December 2017), available at http://www.cprindia.org/research/reports/plugging-collection-insights-electricity-use-indian-homes, accessed on November 1, 2020.

5. Enerdata, "World Energy Council," May 2016, available at https://wec-indicators.enerdata.net/household-electricity-use.html, accessed on November 1, 2020.

6. Ministry of Statistics and Programme Implementation, *Energy Statistics 2017* (New Delhi: Ministry of Statistics and Programme Implementation, Government of India, March 2017), available at http://www.mospi.nic.in/sites/default/files/publication_reports/Energy_Statistics_2017r.pdf.pdf, accessed on November 1, 2020.

7. Global Buildings Performance Network (GBPN), *Residential Buildings in India: Energy Use Projections and Savings Potentials*, (Ahmedabad: GBPN and Centre for Environmental Planning and Technology [CEPT] University, September 2014), http://www.gbpn.org/sites/default/files/08.%20INDIA%20Baseline_TR_low.pdf.

8. Khosla and Chunekar, "Plugging In-Residential Electricity in India."

9. Ministry of Statistics and Programme Implementation, "Energy Statistics 2017" (2017); Saubhagya, website dashboard, available at http://saubhagya.gov.in/, accessed on November 1, 2020.

10. Central Electricity Authority (CEA), *General Review* (New Delhi: CEA, Ministry of Power, Government of India, 2012).

11. Enerdata, "World Energy Council."

12. Khosla and Chunekar, "Plugging In-Residential Electricity in India."

13. Government of India and Government of Delhi, *24x7 Power for All: Delhi* (New Delhi: Government of India and Government of Delhi, June 2016), 7, available at http://powermin.nic.in/sites/default/files/uploads/joint_initiative_of_govt_of_india_and_delhi.pdf, accessed on November 1, 2020.

14. CEA, *19th Electric Power Survey of India: Volume 1* (New Delhi: CEA, Ministry of Power, Government of India, January 2017), available at http://www.cea.nic.in/reports/others/planning/pslf/summary_19th_eps.pdf.

15. Government of India and Government of Delhi, *24x7 Power for All.*

16. CEA, *Load Generation Balance Report, 2015–16* (New Delhi: Ministry of Power, May 2015), available at http://www.indiaenvironmentportal.org.in/files/file/lgbr_report.pdf, accessed on September 8, 2020.

17. Ann Josey, Manabika Mandal, and Shantanu Dixit, *The Price of Plenty: Insights from 'Surplus' Power in Indian States* (Pune: Prayas [Energy Group], 2017).

18. The board serves all of Delhi except for the New Delhi Municipal Corporation and the cantonment areas.

19. The Energy and Resources Institute (TERI), *Public Private Partnership (PPP) in Electricity Distribution: Case Studies of Delhi and Odisha* (New Delhi: TERI, 2015), available at http://www.teriin.org/eventdocs/files/TERI-GSEP-PPP-in-Electricity-Distribution_Case-Studies.pdf.

20. *Times of India*, "Power Demand in Delhi Soars to All-India High," *Times of India*, June 6, 2017, available at https://timesofindia.indiatimes.com/city/delhi/power-demand-in-capital-soars-to-all-india-high/articleshow/59008303.cms, accessed on September 2, 2020.

21. Government of India and Government of Delhi, *24x7 Power for All.*

22. See http://ipgcl-ppcl.gov.in/documents/renewable/2016_05_19_2_Delhi_Solar_Policy.pdf, accessed on November 1, 2020.

23. Ibid., 7.

24. Ibid.

25. Bhanvi Arora, "Delhi Slashes Power Tariff ahead of Summer," *BloombergQuint*, 2018, available at https://www.bloombergquint.com/business/2018/03/28/delhi-slashes-power-tariff-ahead-of-summer.

26. *Hindustan Times*, "Power Tariff Hiked in Haryana," July 20, 2017, available at https://www.hindustantimes.com/india-news/power-tariff-hiked-in-haryana/story-aMPnjYGB9tmENHJ4waSEWN.html, accessed on September 12, 2020.

27. Press Trust of India (PTI), "Power Tariff Hiked in Uttar Pradesh, Opposition Cries Foul," *Mint*, November 30, 2017, available at https://www.livemint.com/Politics/tHl4a6LtiNHNH23Q5m9kKN/Power-tariff-hiked-in-Uttar-Pradesh-opposition-cries-foul.html.

28. Aditya Chunekar, Santanu Dixit, and Sapekshya Varshney, *Residential Electricity Consumption in India: What Do We Know?* (Pune: Prayas [Energy Group],

December 2016), available at http://www.prayaspune.org/peg/component/k2/item/download/709_95c95aa4a9ad64d4f944fc8dcd78000c.html.

29. Ibid.

30. Nidhi Tewathia, "Determinants of the Household Electricity Consumption: A Case Study of Delhi," *International Journal of Energy Economics and Policy* 4, no. 3 (2014): 337–348.

31. Chunekar, Dixit, and Varshney, *Residential Electricity Consumption in India*.

32. Enerdata, "World Energy Statistics: Energy Supply & Demand," 2018, available at https://www.enerdata.net/publications/world-energy-statistics-supply-and-demand.html, accessed on April 18, 2018.

33. Harold Wilhite, *Consumption and the Transformation of Everyday Life: A View from South India* (New York: Palgrave Macmillan, 2008).

34. Chunekar, Dixit, and Varshney, *Residential Electricity Consumption in India*.

35. Nihar Shah et al., *Cost-Benefit of Improving the Efficiency of Room Air Conditioners (Inverter and Fixed Speed) in India* (Berkeley, CA: Lawrence Berkeley National Lab, 2016).

36. Souparno Banerjee, "CSE Analysis of Delhi's Power Consumption Paints a Dark Picture," June 2015, available at http://www.cseindia.org/content/cse-analysis-delhis-power-consumption-paints-a-dark-picture.

37. Lucas W. Davis and Paul J. Gertler, "Contribution of Air Conditioning Adoption to Future Energy Use under Global Warming," *Proceedings of the National Academy of Sciences* 112, no. 19 (May 12, 2015): 5962–5967, available at https://doi.org/10.1073/pnas.1423558112.

38. Satish Kumar et al., "Thermal Comfort for All," (Alliance for an Energy Efficient Economy, New Delhi, September 2017), available at http://www.aeee.in/download-report-on-thermal-comfort-for-all/, accessed on November 1, 2020.

39. Navroz K. Dubash et al., "India's Energy and Emissions Future: A Synthesis of Recent Scenarios" (working paper, Initiative on Climate, Energy and Environment, Centre for Policy Research, New Delhi, September 2017).

40. Josey, Mandal, and Dixit, *The Price of Plenty*.

41. Amulya K. N. Reddy, "Energy Strategies for a Sustainable Development in India," (Conference on Global Collaboration on Sustainable Energy Development, Copenhagen, 1991), 11.

CHAPTER 7

Crime

Victimization in New Delhi

Insights from New Data

Milan Vaishnav and Matthew Lillehaugen*

Introduction

In recent years, concerns about public safety have grown in prominence in India's public discourse. An important catalyst in this regard was the tragic 2012 "Nirbhaya" gang rape in New Delhi, which captured headlines across India and around the world.[1] The gruesome facts of the case led to a popular outcry and the subsequent establishment of the Justice J. S. Verma Committee, which was given a mandate to recommend criminal law amendments that would hasten the prosecution—and enhance the punishment—of those accused of committing sexual assault against women.[2]

This popular reengagement with questions of public order and public safety has been mirrored by heightened rhetoric, if not decisive action, on the part of the Government of India. Since coming to power in May 2014, Prime Minister Narendra Modi has regularly highlighted improving public safety as an important priority for his government. For instance, in a 2015 address to law-enforcement officials, Prime Minister Modi discussed the need for a "flexible institutional framework" to ensure improved citizen–police engagement.[3] In 2017, NITI Aayog unveiled its "3-Year Action Agenda"—a medium-term

* The authors are grateful to project participants, especially Sanjoy Chakravorty, Devesh Kapur, and Neelanjan Sircar, for helpful comments. Vaishnav acknowledges financial support for this project from the Carnegie Corporation of New York. All errors are authors' own.

reform blueprint for economic and governance reforms. The roadmap contained a discussion of rule of law reform in which police modernization finds mention as a critical reform element.[4] The discourse on public safety, however, is not limited to elite circles. In the pivotal Uttar Pradesh (UP) assembly elections in the spring of 2017, Modi's Bharatiya Janata Party (BJP) made "restoring law and order" a central plank of its election campaign. In fact, one of its signature slogans for the campaign was *Na Goonda Raj, Na Bhrashtachar* ("No thug rule, no corruption").[5]

Against this backdrop of growing concern about public safety is the discouraging reality of the Indian police. Over the years, numerous studies have identified deep-seated infirmities that plague the performance of the police. Somewhat surprisingly—given the centrality of the police's role in any sovereign state and its well-documented weaknesses—the police remain a grossly understudied institution. One reason for this relative ignorance is poor data quality. This is a result of multiple factors, including official underreporting as well as a possible social stigma in reporting certain types of crimes.[6] This, however, is not a problem that is unique to India. The standard approach in countries around the world to circumvent shortcomings in official crime statistics is to undertake crime victimization surveys (CVSs), which could allow for better analysis of crime and police responsiveness.[7] In India, however, CVSs are neither institutionalized nor widely utilized.

This chapter reports on the findings of a crime victimization module embedded within a larger survey of urban life in the National Capital Region (NCR). In so doing, it adds to an emerging body of work experimenting with CVSs to study crime, public safety, and the police in India. In particular, this chapter has three objectives. First, it documents the survey results of actual crime victimization and the link between reported crime and perceptions of public safety. Second, it describes the strategies crime victims employ to address crimes committed against them or members of their household. Third and finally, it briefly studies the consequences of crime victimization. Here, building on an emerging literature exploring the connection between crime victimization and political participation, this chapter examines how victims and non-victims compare on several measures of political participation using voting and nonvoting measures.

Before we proceed, a few caveats are in order. First, the bulk of our analysis focuses not on the broader NCR, but the National Capital Territory (NCT) of Delhi itself. This is a decision borne out of necessity rather than choice. Overall, our sample contains relatively few households that have been victims of the limited types of crimes we examine. The overwhelming majority of these households are situated in the NCT, rather than outlying urban areas in the rest of the NCR. Although limiting the scope of our inquiry to Delhi does have its costs, it should be emphasized that Delhi is an important case to be studied in its own right. For the past five years, Delhi has recorded a crime rate that is more than double the national average among metropolitan cities.[8] Indeed, in common parlance, Delhi is often dubbed the "crime capital" of India because of the widespread perception that it is unsafe.

Second, because we are working with observational data, we cannot make strong causal claims with our data. Rather, we are motivated to explore and highlight patterns in the data that require further probing, including by using experimental or quasi-experimental techniques to identify causality. Third, we cannot rule out that the results of our analysis could be subject to some degree of social desirability bias. Such bias might result, for instance, in an underreporting of crime victimization if respondents fear disclosing details about their personal life. While this type of bias is certainly plausible, other CVSs report substantially higher victimization rates than what official crime statistics report, suggesting that respondents tend to be willing to admit to crime victimization, even if they did not go to the police. Further, the audit procedures built into the survey process give us some degree of confidence in the quality of the data with which we are working.[9] Finally, due to the nature of our sampling process, there may be segments of the population which were underrepresented in the data—particularly, the very wealthy and recent migrants.[10] With those caveats in mind, the trends reported and explanations proposed should, if nothing else, provide motivation to standardize and institutionalize CVSs in an effort to shed more light on a topic that has a direct effect on the lives of citizens across India.

Existing Literature

The existing literature on crime and public safety primarily focuses on two themes. The first examines the drivers of the police's weak institutional performance and possible reforms. Many of the concerns upon which this literature sheds light are not new, but this body of work highlights the deeply entrenched nature of the underlying issues. Since we lack the space to provide a comprehensive review of the literature on the Indian police, we instead highlight four stylized facts about its performance.

The first cardinal fact is that the police in contemporary India are the product of colonial design. The legislative framework under which the police operate to the present day is the Police Act of 1861. This colonial-era legislation established a police force designed not to prevent crime or carry out community policing, but rather to control unruly crowds of protestors and prevent local uprisings and riots.[11] Police norms and practices, dating back to the British Raj, continue to the present day. For instance, the rigid, two-tiered system of officers and beat cops—in which the latter have virtually zero chance of joining the former's ranks—is formally ingrained into the police's overall institutional ethos, leading to issues of poor morale, inefficiency, and corruption within the service.

Second, the police are inextricably linked to politics. Politicians regularly seek to use the police as a political instrument to protect their interests or punish those who oppose them. Political interference in the everyday functioning of the police is rife; the most visible manifestation is the abuse of discretion when it comes to the posting and transfer of police officials. As Bayley has written, the police in India "have become deeply involved in partisan politics: they are preoccupied with it, penetrated by it, and now participate individually and collectively in it."[12] Because law and order is a state subject, the police come under the jurisdiction of the state rather than the central government. More often than not, state chief ministers prefer to personally retain the home ministry portfolio because this allows them unfettered control of the instruments of state security.[13] Doing so not only affords them greater protection, it also could help neutralize their political opponents.

Third, accountability failures within the police force are widespread. For instance, the nongovernmental organization (NGO) Human Rights Watch has documented four abuses frequently committed by police in various parts of India: the failure to investigate crimes, arbitrary arrest and illegal detention, custodial torture, and extrajudicial killings.[14] As one Bangalore policeman told the NGO's investigators, "We do use some extralegal methods. You might disagree, but we cannot do all work by the book. Then the police would be completely ineffective."[15]

Last but not least, the police are plagued by serious shortfalls in capacity and financial resources.[16] Despite its image as a bloated "patronage democracy," India's police force is actually quite small relative to its population. India has the lowest number of police officers per capita of any of the Group of 20 (G-20) economies. Compounding this limited footprint is an endemically high vacancy rate, which currently stands around 25 percent.[17]

Taken together, as Jauregui puts it: the police in India are best conceived as a "provisional authority."[18] The police do not reflect a permanent sense of authority, but rather one that guarantees law and order on only a discretionary or *ad hoc* basis. The role of the police in such a system is not as the idealized, neutral arbiter of justice, but rather as another actor with its own interests and limitations that are intimately linked to the context in which they operate.

Over the decades, there have been innumerable white papers, task forces, and blue-ribbon commission reports recommending that the legislative framework and operational practices of the police be revamped.[19] Despite repeated calls for reform, most of the recommendations proffered by these expert committees have largely been consigned to the dustbin.[20] When it comes to the broader issue of public safety, however, it would be unfair to single out the police. The truth is that in India, the police are but one link in an anemic "rule of law" supply chain that includes the laws on the books, the lawmakers who make those laws, the courts that adjudicate disputes, and the prosecutors who bring charges.[21]

It is not only academics and experts who have commented on the failures of the police but citizens too have repeatedly voiced concerns. According to the 2013 State of Democracy in South Asia Survey, the police are the least-trusted nonelected institution in India. Just 16 percent of respondents stated that they have "high trust" in the police; only political parties fare worse.[22] According to the 2014 World Values Survey, the police also fare poorly when it comes to the trust citizens repose in them. Forty-nine percent of respondents in this survey have a "great deal" or "quite a lot" of trust in the police. To place this number in context, the corresponding values for the army, courts, and civil service were 82, 61, and 51 percent, respectively. Here too, political parties (at 34 percent) are one of the few entities to rank even worse.[23]

In recent years, scholars have adopted an experimental approach in studying the police by evaluating the relative effectiveness of various reform measures. For instance, Banerjee, Chattopadhyay, Duflo, Keniston, and Singh designed and implemented a randomized controlled trial (RCT) with the Rajasthan police that examined the impact of four discrete interventions on both the functioning of the police as well as perceptions about their conduct.[24] These interventions, which included placing community observers in police stations, freezing transfers of police staff, providing in-service training, and guaranteeing days off, had a mixed impact. Only the transfer freeze and additional training produced significant improvements in police effectiveness and public perception. Banerjee and his colleagues suspect that these interventions worked because they were top-down measures that did not require local implementation.

A second strand of the literature focuses on crime victimization and the act of reporting crimes. Prasad uses victim-reported crime data from the India Human Development Survey (IHDS) and compares that with official statistics recorded by the National Crime Records Bureau (NCRB), as documented in their annual *Crime in India* reports.[25] As Prasad notes, IHDS victimization rates were significantly larger than what government statistics have reported. Although the official statistics appear to understate the true crime rate, Prasad finds that the official statistics are not pure noise; once one takes into account possible confounding factors and regional differences, official crime rates are positively correlated with victim-reported crimes.

Similarly, Gupta reports on a similar study undertaken by comparing survey data from two waves of the National Family Health Surveys on violence against women with the official NCRB statistics.[26] Gupta's results point to serious underreporting of crimes against women: less than 1 percent of incidents of sexual violence by husbands, 1 percent of other violent incidents committed by other men, and just 2 percent of incidents of physical violence committed by husbands were reported to the police.[27]

A well-known paper by Iyer, Mishra, Mani, and Topalova uses a historical quirk in India's decentralization evolution to study the impact of women's political representation on crimes against women.[28] Exploiting the fact that states moved at different speeds to implement reservation for women in *panchayat* elections, the scholars assert that female representation had a positive impact on the number of documented crimes against women. While this sounds like a negative development, they—using a citizen survey in Rajasthan—confirm that the rise is driven by better reporting. Indeed, there is no discernible increase in other types of crimes as a result of female reservation.

Although CVSs have not been institutionalized in India, in recent years there have been a few examples of CVSs being undertaken by independent researchers focused on major metropolitan centers. In 2015, the Commonwealth Human Rights Initiative (CHRI) carried out a CVS in Delhi and Mumbai—what the organization claims was the first systematic study of crime victimization focused exclusively on either of these two metros.[29] The CHRI survey found that 13 and 15 percent of households in Delhi and Mumbai, respectively, were victims of one of seven types of crimes enumerated in the assessment between July 2014 and June 2015. Theft was the most commonly experienced crime, but the survey found that only half of total crimes committed were actually reported to police authorities. Sexual harassment, in particular, was highlighted as an offense that tends to stay under the radar; in Delhi, just 1 in 13 incidents (1 in 9 in Mumbai) were reported to the police.

In 2015–2016, the IDFC Institute carried out a similar survey in four large metro areas: Bangalore, Chennai, Delhi, and Mumbai.[30] This survey brought out stark differences across cities, with Delhi reporting the highest rates of crime across the board. For instance, 8 percent of Delhi households claimed they were victims of theft between October 2015 and September 2016, a rate twice as large as Mumbai and four times larger than either Bangalore or Chennai.[31] In all cities, however, crimes were severely underreported: only a fraction of victims approached the police, and only a fraction of this latter group successfully had a First Information Report (FIR)—an antecedent to charges being filed—recorded.

Our Survey

Within our broader survey on the political economy of urbanization in the NCR, we embedded a small module on crime and public safety. The module is divided into three parts. The first asks household respondents questions on perceived safety, including "What is the latest [time] you feel safe returning home alone at night?" In the "Results" section, we use this measure as an indicator of respondents' perceptions about public safety. The second part asks about crime victimization. Specifically, the survey asks household respondents: "Has any household member been victim to a crime in the last 5 years or since moving to NCR?" The survey collects responses on three types of crimes: theft outside the home, theft inside the home, and physical assault.[32] The third and final part of the module asks a series of questions about redressal or how victims responded to the criminal incident in question. These questions follow a decision tree that the research team designed in order to track the action respondents did or did not take (and, if not, why).

The decision tree proceeds as follows. After recording victimization data, the survey asks whether victims sought help from anyone and provides them with a list of options, including "Other," in which case victims were asked to specify what alternative option they pursued. For victims who chose to go to the police, the survey asks whether the police filed paperwork to register the offense. For those who did not go to the police (or who sought no help at all), the survey asks respondents why. All victims were also asked whether they had to pay any money in the course of redressal and whether they were satisfied with the outcome of their response to the crime. The survey separately asks respondents about their recent history of electoral participation, including voting in local body, state assembly, and parliamentary elections as well as their participation in various election-related activities. We utilize this set of questions to explore the link between victimization and political participation.

Overall, in our survey of 5,477 households, 5.5 percent of households reported being victims of one of our three types of crimes (theft inside the home, theft outside the home, and physical assault) in the past five years or since moving to the NCR.[33] The geographic variation in our data shows that the vast majority of crime being reported by survey respondents takes place in Delhi itself. The overall household victimization rate (across all three crime types) was 8 percent in Delhi and just 1 percent each in Haryana and UP. We picked up no reported crime in our sample of households in Rajasthan's NCR districts.[34] Due to the Delhi-centric nature of the victimization data, we restrict our attention to Delhi alone in analyses that follow, as that is where the bulk of our crime victims reside.

Delhi Context

When it comes to studying crime and public safety, Delhi is a geographic region of great relevance. Delhi's political status defies simple description. It is the nation's capital, the seat of the Delhi state government, and—along with Mumbai—one of India's two most populous metropolises.[35] Delhi also holds the dubious distinction of being widely perceived as a metropolis plagued by rampant crime. According to the 2017 edition of the annual *Crime in India* compilation issued by the NCRB (which covers incidents in calendar year 2016), Delhi reported the highest crime rate of any state in the union (974.9 violations of the Indian Penal Code [IPC] per 100,000 residents).[36] Unfortunately, Delhi also topped the league tables when it came to crimes against women and property offenses. What is especially disconcerting about the latter figure is that Delhi led the pack both in relative and absolute terms; it recorded 130,928 total property offenses, which is double the number recorded in Maharashtra—a state that is home to more than 115 million residents.[37]

Due to the well-known issues with official crime data, one should not necessarily put too much stock into these official figures. As a former senior police official has noted, total IPC violations in Delhi grew 250 percent in the three years from 2012 to 2014.[38] But this was likely the result of better reporting on account of the efforts of a new police commissioner rather than a statistical increase in the number of actual crimes. Having said that, the perception (if not the reality) still holds that Delhi deserves its appellation as the "Crime Capital" of India.

It is interesting to note that the Delhi Police appear to be far better equipped to tackle crime than many of their peers. According to 2016 data collected by the Ministry of Home Affairs' Bureau of Police Research and Development, Delhi boasted 347 civil police officers per 0.1 million population.[39] To put this in perspective, Haryana and UP—two of its neighbors—had only 154 and 78 police officers, respectively, while the all-India median stood at 121 officers per 0.1 million population.[40] Delhi also maintains a sizeable budgetary advantage over many of its counterparts. In 2016–2017, Delhi spent INR 2,731 per resident, three times the all-India ratio, four times the ratio in UP, and double the ratio in Haryana.[41] Some of these advantages are possibly illusory, however, on account of Delhi's designation as the nation's capital. According to government data, as much as 10 percent of Delhi's civil police force is deployed for VIP duty at any given time—representing a substantial drain on human resources available for day-to-day policing.[42]

In terms of overall governance structure, Delhi is something of an anomaly. Three distinct governance frameworks are relevant in Delhi today. At the lowest level, there are the five urban local bodies: New Delhi Municipal Council, Delhi Cantonment Board, North Delhi Municipal Corporation, South Delhi Municipal Corporation, and the East Delhi Municipal Corporation. Each has its own geographic jurisdiction, with the majority (nearly 95 percent of its area and 11 million of its residents) residing in an area governed by one of the three municipal corporations.[43] At the next level up, there is the state government of the NCT, which was established in 1992. The state government is headed by a chief minister and has a full-fledged legislative assembly, although both of these organs' powers are more limited than in other states. Finally, at the apex sits the union government, which of course calls New Delhi home. The union government is especially relevant to this chapter as it oversees law and order in Delhi; unlike other states, where the police are the responsibility of the state government, in Delhi they are accountable to the national government through the Ministry of Home Affairs, headed by the union home minister of India.

Results

In this section, we summarize the results of our analysis. We begin by looking at the relationship between perceptions and actual victimization and the correlates of being a victim. Next, we look at whether and how victims redress the crimes perpetrated against them, with special attention paid to the interaction between citizens and the police. In the final part of our inquiry, we look at the consequences of victimization. Here, following the literature, we focus one particular outcome of interest: political participation.

Safety Perceptions versus Reality

We begin by examining survey data on perceptions of public safety. The survey asks respondents the latest hour they feel safe returning home alone at night. Respondents were given a choice to answer "always safe," "always unsafe," or to list a specific time between 6 pm and 1 am. The vast majority of respondents answered "always safe" or "always unsafe," leaving us with a relatively small set of responses listing a specific hour or night. We combine those who answered with a specific time into a third category, "sometimes safe/unsafe."

On the whole, 56 percent of respondents claimed to always feel safe when returning home alone at night. When we look at how perceptions accord with actual crime victimization, we observe a mixed relationship. On the one hand, 46 percent of respondents from households that had been victimized reported that they always feel safe, compared to 57 percent from non-victim households. However, a slightly higher percentage of respondents from non-victim households claimed they always feel unsafe compared to

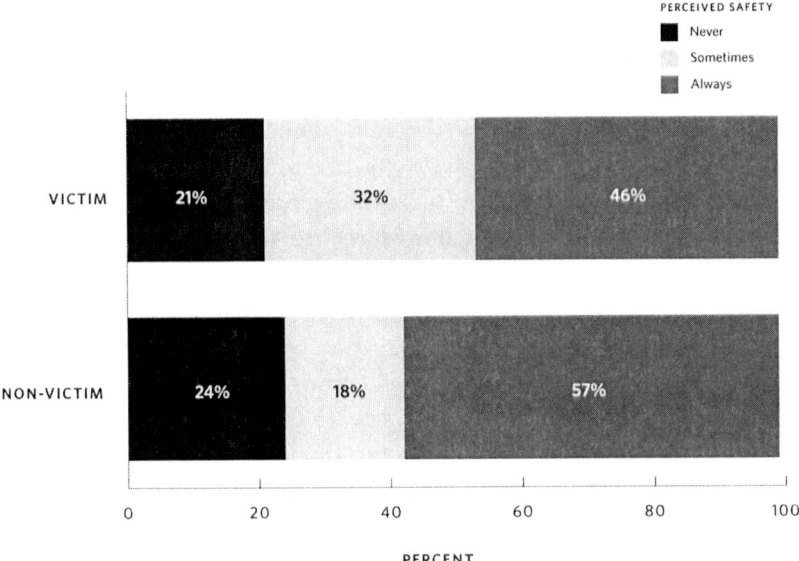

Figure 7.1   Perceptions of safely returning home at night
Source: Authors' calculations from the CASI–NCR Survey data.

victim households (24 versus 21 percent). Further, households with a crime victim selected the "sometimes safe/unsafe" category nearly twice as often as non-victim households (32 versus 18 percent). It may be that respondents from households that have been the victim of a crime have a more nuanced perspective on safety, but they might also just be more conscientious survey participants. Regardless, it appears that there is no clear directional correlation between actual experience as a crime victim and perceptions of public safety.

The results vary slightly when the sex of the respondent is considered, but the results generally follow the same pattern. Since our crime data are at the household level, we have no way of identifying the sex of the victim, so we lack individual-level data on the victims themselves (instead, we have households in which a member is a victim). For female respondents, the tendency to respond "always safe" dropped to 41 percent for victim households, but stood at 59 percent for non-victimized households. Male respondents displayed less variation between victimized and non-victimized households, with 52 percent and 56 percent reporting that they always feel safe, respectively.

Who Is a Victim?

The next step in our inquiry is to ask: who is a crime victim? We first examine the question by looking descriptively at two important dimensions: social identity and household amenities. We look at social identity through the prism of caste and religion by first disaggregating respondents by religion (Hindu, Muslim, and Other) and then further subdividing the Hindu respondents by broad caste category: General, Other Backward Classes (OBC), Scheduled Caste (SC), and Scheduled Tribe (ST). The ST respondents report the highest victimization rate (13 percent), followed by OBCs (11 percent) and Others (10 percent). Interestingly, SCs and Muslims report lower levels of victimization (8 and 7 percent, respectively), just marginally higher than what General Caste Hindus report (6 percent).

When we examine the data based on household amenities, it appears that victims are wealthier, on average, than non-victims. The median score on the amenities index for Delhi households across the entire sample is 0.17 (on a scale of –3 to 3).[44] Households that contain at least one victim of a crime possess median amenities of 0.29 while households containing no crime victims have a median amenity measure roughly equal to 0.16.

To look at these relationships more systematically, we run a linear probability model where the outcome variable is a binary measure of crime victimization.[45]

As regressors, we place identity and assets on the right-hand side along with a control for the size of household and the quality of the approach road (as a proxy for neighborhood). The results, contained in Figure 7.2, suggest that OBCs and STs (and SCs, to a lesser extent) are more likely to be victims compared to the reference category (General Caste). Compared to General Caste Hindus, OBCs, SCs, and STs are 4.6, 3.3, and 6.6 percent more likely to be victims, respectively. The former is significant with 99.9 percent confidence, while the latter two effects are significant at the 95 percent level. There is also a positive and significant coefficient on the assets measure while household size and road type ultimately end up as the strongest predictors.[46] A one-unit increase in our asset measure is associated with a 1.3 percent increase in the probability of the household having been victim to a crime (significant at the 95 percent level). Household size had a negative correlation with victimization, such that an increase of one member was associated with a 1.8 percent decrease in the

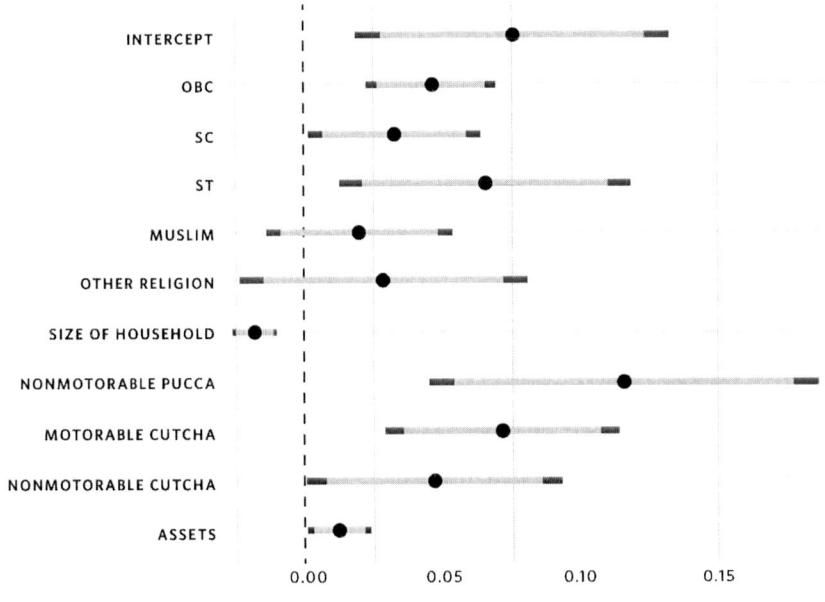

COEFFICIENT AND CONFIDENCE INTERVAL

Figure 7.2   Correlates of crime victimization

Source: Authors' calculations from the CASI–NCR Survey data.

Notes: The black circles reflect the coefficient estimates from a linear probability model where the outcome variable is a binary indicator of crime victimization. The dark and light gray bars reflect 90 and 95 percent confidence intervals, respectively.

probability of household victimization (significant at the 99.9 percent level). Roads, our proxy for neighborhood quality, measured the strongest effect: households on a motorable, *pucca* approach road having been 7.2 percent more likely to be victims than those on motorable, *kuccha* approach road (significant at the 99.9 percent level).[47]

Redressal

Next, we explore what action victims took, if they took any at all, in the aftermath of a crime. Nearly 85 percent of victims stated that they sought the help of someone after being victimized.[48] Because respondents were forced to select from one of the enumerated categories, we cannot rule out the possibility that they took help from multiple quarters. Instead, the data likely reflect who, in their view, the *primary* source of help was. Of those who sought help, the vast majority (over 87 percent) decided to seek help from the police. Roughly 11 percent of victims who sought help did so by seeking assistance from a neighbor. Few individuals claimed that they sought help from a relative, their *neta* (politician), *dada* (fixer), or some other party.

When we look at the nature of the crime, victims of theft outside the home were the most likely to seek help (94 percent), while assault (78 percent) and in-home theft (77 percent) victims were slightly less likely to seek help. When it comes to seeking help from the police, in particular, again victims of theft outside the home stand out: 87 percent approached the police compared to 69 and 60 percent for in-home theft and assault victims, respectively. While most victims approached the police, a small minority did not, and the survey asked them why they chose not to engage police authorities. We have grouped responses into three categories, with the modal answer being that they thought the "crime was not serious" enough (41 responses). This was followed by a range of responses (28 in all) grouped under the heading of "issues with the police" (fear, too costly, or too time consuming). A small number (a mere 6) chose not to go to the police because they were "influenced by others" who steered them elsewhere. Interestingly, 25 of these 41 individuals were assault victims who deemed the crimes perpetrated against them were not serious enough to warrant going to the police. To put this number in context, 25 individuals represent roughly one-quarter of our sample of assault victims. Obviously, we have a very small sample of respondents who sought help from someone other than the police, so these findings have to be taken with a grain of salt. Yet, these data raise an interesting question as to whether there is something about "assault" as a category for crime that is so broad that it tends to encompass crimes from the very petty to the very severe (thus making many victims less likely to think that their crime merited reporting).

In a multivariate regression framework, amenities again turn up as an extremely strong correlate of engaging the police (Figure 7.2). To place this in perspective, a one-unit increase in assets is linked to an 11 percent increase in seeking help from the police—a substantively large effect (this is significant with 99.9 percent confidence). In this model, no identity variable is significant. In the raw data, the median household asset measure is 0.29 (on our six-point scale). But for those who go to the police, it is 0.42, and for those who do not, it is –0.08.

For those who went to the police, the survey asked whether the police filed paperwork to register the offense. In practical terms, respondents understood by this that whether a police complaint and/or an FIR was registered.[49] While the former can be filed for either cognizable or non-cognizable offenses and has no required format, the latter is only utilized for the former and follows a standardized form.[50] Unfortunately, our data do not distinguish between the two. Of those who went to the police, a surprisingly large 84 percent claimed that the police registered their reported offenses. While the overall registration rates are quite high, there is some variation. Although respondents are more inclined to approach the police when they are victims of theft, they appear to have greatest success getting complaints/FIRs filed with assault cases. In these cases, paperwork was filed 94 percent of the time, compared to 83 percent for cases of theft outside the home and 76 percent for home theft.

This is a point of sharp contrast between our survey and previous ones and could be due to multiple factors. The most obvious is that our survey actually collected data on both FIRs and the less formal complaints, which could account for the difference. Future studies that effectively distinguish between the two will hopefully bring the much-needed clarity to these discussions. However, the discrepancy could also be the result of a policy change unveiled by the Delhi police commissioner in 2014, which called for the filing of FIRs in the instance of all "cognizable offences." Official reporting for all crimes in Delhi almost doubled from 2013 to 2014, the difference of which can be explained by the near tripling of reported street crimes.[51] Considering nearly half of the crimes reported in our survey occurred in the post-2013 era (and all of them would have been qualified as "street crime" by the commissioner's characterization), it is natural that those factors should contribute to higher registration rates. However, this leaves unexplained why the other CVSs, which took place post 2014, recorded such low FIR rates.

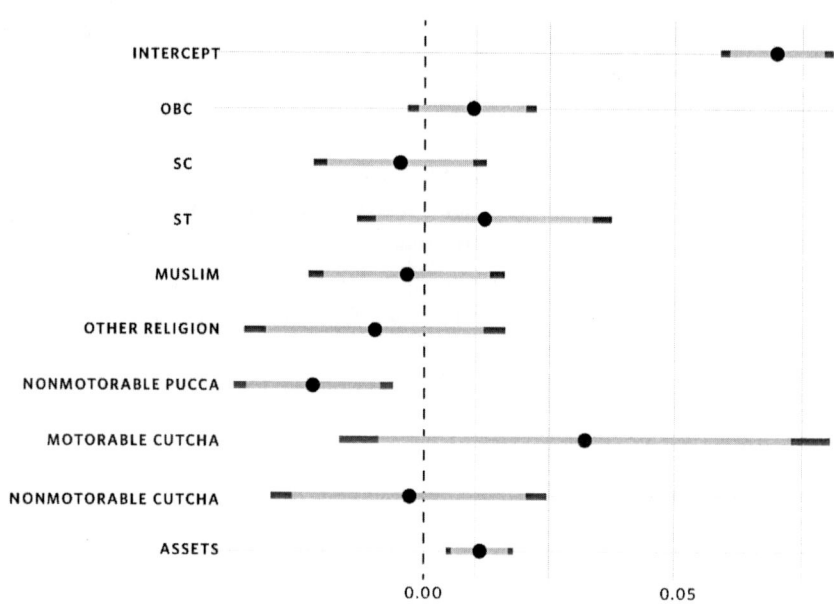

COEFFICIENT AND CONFIDENCE INTERVAL

Figure 7.3   Correlates of seeking help from the police

Source: Authors' calculations from the CASI–NCR Survey data.

Notes: The black circles reflect the coefficient estimates from a linear probability model where the outcome variable is a binary indicator of seeking help from the police. The dark and light gray bars reflect 90 and 95 percent confidence intervals, respectively.

Expenditure

The survey asks respondents whether households had to pay anything in the process of taking action to redress crimes committed against them. While these payments could involve bribe giving, they cannot simply be equated with bribery as the survey merely asked respondents how much money was spent on redressal, a question that could be interpreted in a variety of ways. Figure 7.4 contains two plots: the top panel (a) captures expenditure among those who did not go to the police, while the bottom panel (b) characterizes those who did. The big difference between (a) and (b) is the number of households reporting zero expenditure. Among those who did *not* go to the police, many of them did not have to spend any money. Overall, the median expenditure for those who circumvented the police was INR 2,500.[52] In contrast, it was commonplace for victims who approached the police to report at least some expenditure; the

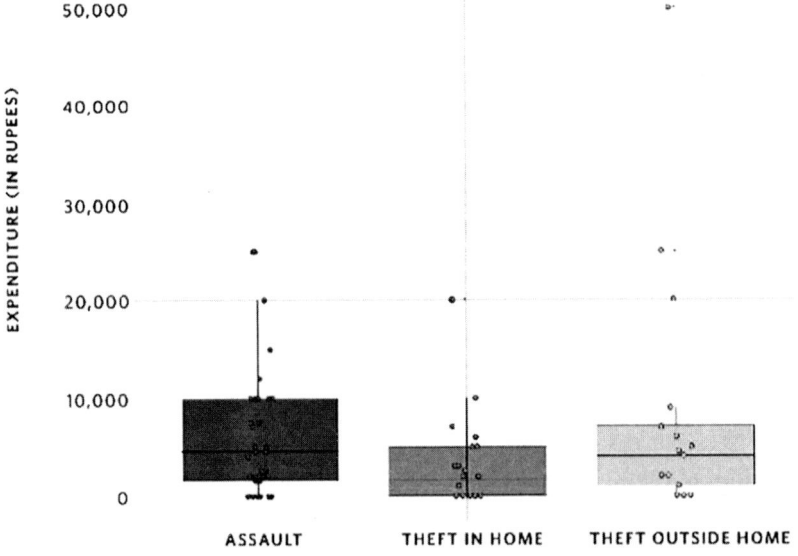

(A) HOUSEHOLDS THAT DID NOT ENGAGE THE POLICE

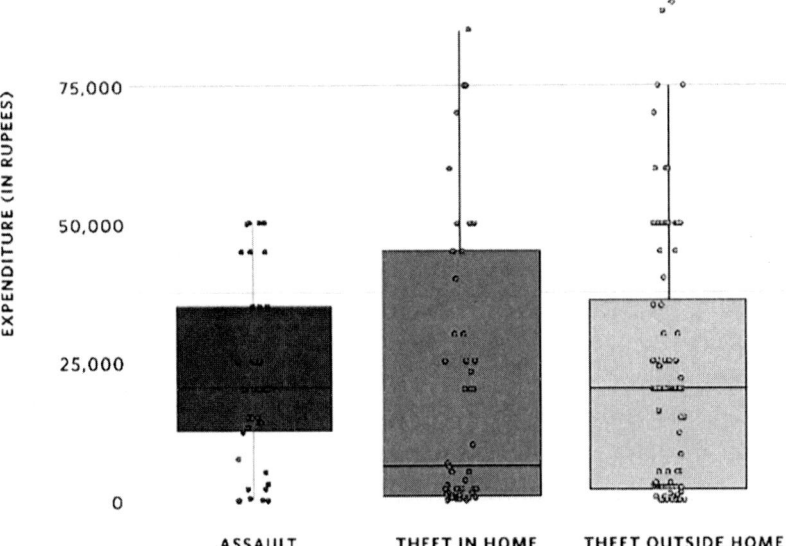

(B) HOUSEHOLDS THAT ENGAGED THE POLICE

Figure 7.4　Household expenditure based on action taken

Source: Authors' calculations from the CASI–NCR Survey data.

median payment across crime types was INR 20,000, substantially higher than what victims who avoided the police spent (Figure 7.4).

Satisfaction

The survey also asked respondents if they were satisfied with the response they received. When it comes to the police, measures of satisfaction broadly follow the trend seen with complaint/FIR success rates—albeit at a reduced level. In aggregate, one in two respondents (49 percent, to be exact) expressed satisfaction with their experience with the police. Assault victims are the most satisfied (61 percent), while theft outside home (46 percent) and home-theft (44 percent) victims are slightly less so. The reported satisfaction levels with nonpolice remedies are dramatically lower in comparison. Overall, only 29 percent of respondents who sought help from nonpolice actors state that they were satisfied with the response they received; the variation in satisfaction rates by crime type, however, mimic the variation in satisfaction with the police. We do not delve into them here because the number of household victims who chose a form of assistance other than the police was very small.

Consequences of Victimization

The final step in our inquiry is to explore the consequences of victimization. An older literature has traditionally held that victims of crime tend to be less trustful and more withdrawn than non-victims.[53] Although we do not know of studies that explicitly examine a negative link between victimization and political participation, studies have found that other negative shocks (such as job loss or divorce) do lead to lower participation.[54] Taking these two findings together, it is reasonable to hypothesize that victims should be less likely than non-victims to participate in politics on the assumption that victimization is an adverse personal shock that is likely to turn citizens inward and away from engaging politically. New work by Bateson, drawing on survey evidence from around the world, found the opposite: across all regions, there is a strong, positive link between victimization and political participation and engagement.[55] Bateson suggests that this association is a product of emotional and expressive factors—rather than a trauma-induced or purely instrumental response. As Bateson has written, "Victimization is always associated with decreases in the probability that an individual will have low levels of participation and engagement in politics, as well as increases in the probability that an individual will engage in high levels of political activity."[56]

Bateson's findings are in sync with a separate, but related, literature, examining war exposure on subsequent political activity. For instance, Bellows and Miguel found that individuals in Sierra Leone whose households experience more intense war-related violence were more likely to engage in civic and political forms of participation.[57] Blattman studied ex-combatants in Uganda and found a causal link between wartime violence and increased political engagement—although this relationship does not appear to extend to nonpolitical forms of social activity.[58] Similar findings are reported by Gilligan, Pasqaule, and Samii, who found that wartime violence in Nepal triggered increased levels of voting and community activism, a shift they attribute to heightened pro-social motivation.[59]

To explore possible links between political participation and victimization in the context of urban Delhi, we take advantage of two types of questions about political participation embedded in our larger survey. The first set asks household respondents whether they voted in the most recent municipal, state assembly, and national parliamentary elections. The second set asks respondents whether they participated in various electoral activities, namely, attending an election rally, campaigning door-to-door for a party or candidate, donating money to a campaign, fundraising on behalf of a campaign, and putting up campaign-related posters (Figure 7.5).

Crime victims, on average, appear to vote at higher rates than non-victims, irrespective of the level of the election. For instance, in local body elections, 82 percent of victims reported voting while 73 percent of non-victims did the same. However, when it comes to other forms of electoral participation, victims are *less* likely to participate. While 7.7 percent of non-victims said that they participated in at least one of the activities enumerated above, only 5.1 percent of victims partook in any nonvoting activities. Because we lack longitudinal data, these relationships should be treated as mere correlations. They do, however, raise an intriguing question of whether experience with victimization is likely to spur some kind of political participation over others. This is a question worthy of future research.

Comparing Our Results

How do our results compare to the official statistics and other crime victimization surveys? The assessment is not an easy one to make for a

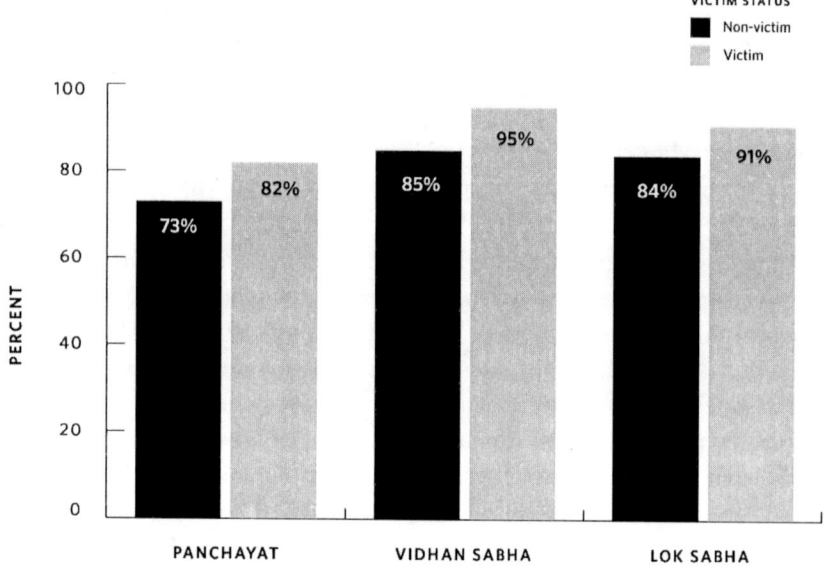

Figure 7.5 Victimization and voting habits
Source: Authors' calculations from the CASI–NCR Survey data.

number of reasons. First, different surveys ask about different types of crimes, occurring over different periods of time and in different urban geographies. For instance, the CHRI and IDFC Institute surveys ask respondents about crime victimization status within a discrete one-year period, while our survey asks about crimes committed in the "last five years or since moving to Delhi." Furthermore, these other surveys—unlike ours—relied on Delhi's police zones as their primary sampling unit. Second, other surveys "blow up" their survey data to create estimates of victimization at the city level. It is possible that this process of extrapolation could bias inferences. Finally, the sampling frame for our survey is the NCR as opposed to the NCT. We cannot confidently assert that the NCT numbers we examine are representative at the city level for the entire population.

With these caveats in mind, we nonetheless deem it worthwhile to look across surveys to search for commonalities and differences. To foster the most accurate comparison possible, we restrict the data to theft outside the home occurring in Delhi, which allows us to get as close as possible to an apples-to-apples assessment. The data reveal an interesting picture. Our data show that 4 percent of households were theft victims, smaller than what is reported by surveys conducted by either CHRI (10 percent) or the

IDFC Institute (8 percent), even before taking into account the time frames considered. On the other hand, the official statistics reported by the NCRB in the 2016 edition of their annual *Crime in India* report (the most recent edition publicly available at the time of writing) list a theft rate of 0.6 percent, which is smaller than what the three CVSs pick up.[60] Of course, we note that the official government number captures data on individuals, rather than households. Focusing narrowly on theft cases in Delhi, the victimization rates recorded in our survey are much lower than in the IDFC or CHRI surveys, but we report much higher rates of engagement with the police and complaint/FIR registration.

Our survey results suggest a police force that is more accessible and responsive than what is traditionally understood. Clearly, additional crime victimization surveys would be useful given the variation across surveys. For instance, there is a vast gap between the crime registration rates reported in our survey (84 percent) and what the FIR rates reported by CHRI (50 percent) or IDFC Institute (15 percent). Whether this is due to our broader definition (combining complaints and FIRs) or due to actual on-the-ground changes in recent years deserves further scrutiny. What is striking is that the FIR registration rates differ so starkly even between the CHRI and IDFC Institute surveys.

Implications for Survey-Based Approaches

Crime victimization surveys have the potential to teach us many things about the dynamics of crime, police–citizen interaction, and the effectiveness of the rule of law. However, one impediment to knowledge creation—not to mention policy impact—is a lack of standardization across surveys. In this section, we reflect on four principles we believe future studies of crime victimization in India should consider when designing CVSs.

First, different CVSs consider different types of crimes, and it is not always clear whether the crimes under study, even if superficially similar, are defined in the exact same manner. Obviously, this limits comparability. In the future, researchers might consider standardizing crime types to overcome this obstacle. A similar concern relates to differences between police complaints and FIRs. Ideally, surveys should ask questions about both milestones.

Second, the three CVSs described in the previous section (including ours) provide only snapshots of victimization in the cities they examine. This, combined with the lack of standardization, inhibits comparisons over time.

Looking ahead, we believe there is ample scope for longitudinal analyses that would measure victimization and citizen–state engagement on a periodic (say, annual) basis. Executing a repeated cross section or even a panel survey would give researchers and decision-makers some sense of changing trends.[61]

Third, future surveys should invest in a more systematic exploration of outcomes. Even if the police file an FIR on behalf of a complainant, is an arrest made? Is the alleged perpetrator prosecuted? In cases of theft, is the stolen good returned to the rightful owner? A deeper examination of how incidents are resolved (or not) would get us closer to the policy outcome we really care about—which is justice.

Finally, given the importance rightfully attached to crimes against women, researchers need to think much more carefully at the design stage as to how they might accurately capture gender-based crimes. This is especially important given the sensitivity of the issues at hand and prevalent social norms according to which women often are not able to respond to survey questions without a male family member answering on their behalf. While our survey recognized those difficulties and generally stayed away from such sensitive questions, these are important questions that must be addressed. To do so, future research must develop survey techniques that can adapt to social realities and address the issue of differences in intra-household experience and/or preferences.

Conclusion

Crime victimization surveys in India are neither broadly utilized nor institutionalized. This chapter reports on the findings of one attempt to study crime victims and their engagement with the police using data from a household survey in the NCR. Given the small sample sizes, we restrict the bulk of our analysis to households residing in the NCT, where the prevalence of crime is the greatest. Even then, the numbers themselves should be treated with caution. Our analysis of the data suggests four main takeaways.

First, roughly 8 percent of households in the NCT contain at least one member who has been a victim of assault, home theft, or theft outside the home, either in the last five years or since moving to the NCR. When we restrict our attention to theft outside the home, this figure is smaller than what comparable surveys report but larger than the official figures gathered by the government. There is no clear relationship between actual crime victimization and perceptions of public safety, when the latter is measured by beliefs about public safety while returning home at night.

Second, identity and assets are strong correlates of crime victimization and, to a lesser extent, one's subsequent decision to approach the police. While better-off households are more likely to be crime victims and to subsequently engage the police, identity appears to only influence crime victimization—with STs and OBCs more likely to be victims than General Caste Hindus. Due to the small sample sizes, these demographic differences should be treated as a first cut.

Third, the vast majority of households who have been victimized report engaging the police. Our data suggest much higher police engagement and crime registration rates than comparable surveys. According to our data, theft victims, in particular, were inclined to seek help from the police. However, theft victims did not report the highest crime registration rates— that designation belonged instead to assault victims. Registering a crime, however, does not appear to come free: households reported much higher spending if they sought the help of the police. Despite the higher costs, households reported being much more satisfied with the response if that response involved the police than if it did not.

Finally, the survey finds suggestive evidence of a link between crime participation and some forms of political participation. Households that were victimized by crime report higher rates of voting in recent elections but slightly *lower* rates of political participation when it comes to practices other than voting (such as taking part in political campaigns). These results (especially the latter) should be treated with caution but will hopefully inspire further examination of the topic.

Our findings raise several other questions which deserve further research. To begin, if households are genuinely getting FIRs filed at such high rates, what follow-up actions have the police taken to bring their criminal complaint to its logical end? While victims report being much more satisfied with their chosen recourse when they turned to the police authorities rather than nonpolice forms of intermediation, future work could explore what actually happens to the cases once FIRs are registered. How many criminals, for instance, are actually charged and later convicted?

A second area worthy of deeper exploration is the apparent identity-based patterns of victimization. If STs and OBCs report higher victimization rates, on average, is this due to spatial settlement patterns? Or might there be other factors that lead to higher reported crime rates among these two communities? Further, why do identity issues seem to matter less when it comes to seeking help from the police? Are there underlying social or structural reasons within the police force which might account for this? Or does the discrepancy arise from phenomena outside of our data, such as the severity of the crime?

Finally, a third area where future work is needed is on the consequences of crime victimization. This chapter briefly explores the link between victimization and political participation—through voting and other nonvoting activities—but what about other forms of civic or community engagement? Are victims more active in civic life as a consequence of their past experience with crime or have they, instead, withdrawn? These and other questions deserve much closer scrutiny as CVSs gain a foothold in the Indian context.

Notes

1. Heather Timmons and Sruthi Gottipati, "Woman Dies after a Gang Rape That Galvanized India," *New York Times*, December 28, 2012; Amy Kazmin, "Portrait: 'Nirbhaya'," *Financial Times*, December 12, 2013.
2. Anviti Chaturvedi, *Police Reforms in India* (New Delhi: PRS Legislative Research, 2017).
3. Press Information Bureau, "PM Addresses Conference of Directors General of Police," December 20, 2015, available at http://pib.nic.in/newsite/PrintRelease. aspx?relid=133628, accessed on November 7, 2017.
4. NITI (National Institution for Transforming India) Aayog, *India: Three Year Action Agenda, 2017–18 to 2019–20* (New Delhi: NITI Aayog, Government of India, 2017).
5. Subhashis Mittra, "High Octane Politics Hallmark of 2017 in Uttar Pradesh," *Outlook*, December 19, 2017, available at https://www.outlookindia.com/ newsscroll/high-octane-politics-hallmark-of-2017-in-uttar-pradesh/1212510, accessed on April 6, 2018.
6. Government of India's Committee on Crime Statistics, convened by the Ministry of Statistics and Programme Implementation (2012), asserted that India's crime statistics are plagued by significant underreporting for a variety of reasons, ranging from negative attitudes toward the police to a belief that certain crimes are not serious enough to warrant reporting. See Basant Rath, "Let's Not Take India's Crime Statistics Seriously," *Wire*, December 4, 2017, available at, https://thewire.in/government/ncrb-crime-statistics-india, accessed on April 6, 2018.
7. Renuka Sane, "For a True Picture of Crime and Public Safety," *Business Standard*, October 5, 2016.
8. Monika Vij, "Geographical Perspective of Crime in Delhi," in *Sustainable Smart Cities in India: Challenges and Future Perspectives*, ed. Poonam Sharma

and Swati Rajput (Cham, Switzerland: Springer, 2017), 731–754. According to Vij, Delhi occupies the top spot when it comes to nearly all violent crimes, when judged on a per capita basis. Furthermore, Delhi has topped this list for five consecutive years.

9. See "Statistical Appendix."

10. Ibid.

11. Arvind Verma, "The Police in India: Design, Performance, and Accountability," in *Public Institutions in India: Performance and Design*, ed. Devesh Kapur and Pratap Bhanu Mehta (New Delhi: Oxford University Press, 2005): 194–257.

12. David H. Bayley, "The Police and Political Order in India," *Asian Survey* 23, no. 4 (April 1983): 484.

13. In the National Capital Territory (NCT) of Delhi, the police are actually under the jurisdiction of the Union Ministry of Home Affairs, as opposed to the Delhi state government. At times—especially when partisan alignment between the center and state is missing—this has also led to calls of political interference by Delhi officials who believe the central government is working against them.

14. Human Rights Watch, *Broken System: Dysfunction, Abuse, and Impunity in the Indian Police* (New York: Human Rights Watch).

15. Ibid., 10.

16. Chaturvedi, *Police Reforms in India*.

17. Devesh Kapur and Milan Vaishnav, "Strengthening Rule of Law," in *Getting India Back on Track: An Action Agenda for Reform*, ed. Bibek Debroy, Ashley J. Tellis, and Reece Trevor (Washington, DC: Carnegie Endowment for International Peace, 2014), 247–263. As of January 2017, state police forces had a 22-percent vacancy rate according to government data on police organizations. See Bureau of Police Research and Development, *Data on Police Organizations* (New Delhi: Bureau of Police Research and Development, Ministry of Home Affairs, Government of India, 2017), available at http://www.bprd.nic.in/WriteReadData/userfiles/file/databook2017.pdf, accessed on April 5, 2018.

18. Beatrice Jauregui, *Provisional Authority: Police, Order, and Security in India* (Chicago: University of Chicago Press, 2016).

19. For instance, the Second Administrative Reforms Commission (2007), constituted under the United Progressive Alliance government, issued a detailed report on "public order" with an exhaustive list of recommendations—many of which were culled from previous police reform commissions. See Second Administrative Reforms Commission, *Fifth Report: Public Order* (New Delhi: Second Administrative Reforms Commission, Government of India, 2007).

20. Vappala Balachandran, *Keeping India Safe: The Dilemma of Internal Security* (New Delhi: HarperCollins India, 2017).

21. Kapur and Vaishnav, "Strengthening Rule of Law."

22. Lokniti, *Democracy in India: A Citizens' Perspective* (New Delhi: Centre for the Study of Developing Societies, 2013).

23. Data from the World Values Survey can be accessed online at http://www. worldvaluessurvey.org/wvs.jsp.

24. Abhijit Banerjee, Raghabendra Chattopadhyay, Esther Duflo, Daniel Keniston, and Nina Singh, "Improving Police Performance in Rajasthan, India: Experimental Evidence on Incentives, Managerial Autonomy, and Training" (Working Paper No. 17912, National Bureau of Economic Research, November 2014).

25. Kislaya Prasad, "A Comparison of Victim-Reported and Police-Recorded Crime in India," *Economic and Political Weekly* 48, no. 33 (August 17, 2013): 47–53. Data from the India Human Development Survey can be found online at https://ihds.umd.edu/. Crime statistics from the annual *Crime in India* reports are compiled by the National Crime Records Bureau (NCRB), which is an agency of the Ministry of Home Affairs. The 2016 *Crime in India* report can be found at http://ncrb.gov.in/.

26. Aashish Gupta, "Reporting and Incidence of Violence against Women in India" (working paper, Research Institute for Compassionate Economics, September 25, 2014).

27. Under Indian law, marital rape is not considered a criminal offense. As a result, it is difficult to accurately assess the degree to which sexual violence perpetrated by husbands against their wives is actually "under-reported" to police authorities. See Monica Sarkar, "Marital Rape: Why Is It Legal in India?" *CNN*, March 9, 2015, available at https://www.cnn.com/2015/03/05/ asia/marital-rape-india/index.html, accessed on April 4, 2018.

28. Lakshmi Iyer, Prachi Mishra, Anandi Mani, and Petia Topalova, "The Power of Political Voice: Women's Political Representation and Crime in India," *American Economic Journal: Applied Economics* 4, no. 4 (2012): 165–193.

29. Commonwealth Human Rights Initiative, *Crime Victimisation and Safety Perception: A Public Survey of Delhi and Mumbai* (New Delhi: Commonwealth Human Rights Initiative, 2015).

30. IDFC Institute, *Safety Trends and Reporting of Crime (SATARC)* (Mumbai: IDFC Institute, 2016).

31. The IDFC Institute surveyed 6,187 households in Delhi.

32. Given the high rates of gender-based violence in Delhi, we would have liked to have included more detailed questions on crimes that specifically impact women. Unfortunately, we were constrained both in resources and in space on the survey instrument.

33. Note that, "or since moving to NCR" was interpreted by some respondents to include a time frame that was much greater than five years. As a result, the data contain some crimes dating back over a decade.

34. The data cover a small number—147 to be exact—of households in Rajasthan.

35. While Mumbai was still the largest metropolis in India at the time of the 2011 Census, United Nations estimates suggest that, as of 2016, the urban agglomeration of Delhi is larger than that of Mumbai (26.5 million versus 21.4 million). That gap is expected to grow even larger by 2030. See United Nations, "The World's Cities in 2016," *Data Booklet*, available at http://www.un.org/en/development/desa/population/publications/pdf/urbanization/the_worlds_cities_in_2016_data_booklet.pdf, accessed on April 9, 2018.

36. NCRB, *Crime in India 2016: Statistics* (New Delhi: NCRB, 2017), available at https://ncrb.gov.in/sites/default/files/Crime%20in%20India%20-%202016%20Complete%20PDF%20291117.pdf, accessed on November 1, 2020.

37. Ibid.

38. Rath, "Let's Not Take India's Crime Statistics Seriously."

39. Bureau of Police Research and Development, *Data on Police Organizations* (New Delhi: Bureau of Police Research and Development, 2017), 42, available at http://www.bprd.nic.in/WriteReadData/userfiles/file/databook2017.pdf.

40. Ibid.

41. Authors' calculations based on data from ibid.

42. Ibid; see also Neeraj Chauhan, "3 Cops to Protect Each VIP but Just 1 for Every 663 Common Man," *Times of India*, September 18, 2017.

43. Cities of Delhi, "The Intersection of Governments in Delhi," (policy brief, Centre for Policy Research, New Delhi, April 2015), available at http://cprindia.org/sites/default/files/policy-briefs/The-Intersection-of-Governments-in-Delhi.pdf, accessed on April 6, 2018.

44. The household amenities measure is explained in greater detail in Chapter 2 by Neelanjan Sircar.

45. We also ran logistic models and received nearly identical results. Thus, for simplicity, we will limit our attention to the linear model in this chapter.

46. That being said, our models have limited predictive power since the overwhelming majority of respondents—irrespective of identity or assets—reported not having been victims.

47. Note that the levels of significance for the non-motorable approach roads are somewhat weaker when considering the difference relative to motorable *pucca* road. If motorable *kuccha* road is selected as the reference, however, their effects are much more pronounced.

48. In a small number of cases, households reported being victims of multiple crimes. Technically, the data in this and the following two sections of the chapter take the individual crime incident as the unit of analysis.

49. Although the survey instrument was originally designed to ask about the filing of a First Information Report (FIR), the question was open to some interpretation in the field. As a result, we are unable to distinguish between an FIR and police complaint.

50. In the case of a cognizable offence, a police officer has the authority to make an arrest without a warrant and to initiate an investigation without a court's permission. In the case of a non-cognizable case, a police officer can neither make an arrest without a warrant nor commence an investigation without first obtaining a court order.

51. Taj Hassan, "Crime in Delhi," *Delhi Police Annual Review 2014*, December 8, 2014, available at http://www.delhipolice.nic.in/Crime_in_Delhi.pdf, accessed on April 6, 2018.

52. Even if we ignore the zero values, the median expenditure only rises to around INR 5,000.

53. See, for instance, the discussion contained in Regina Bateson, "Crime Victimization and Political Participation," *American Political Science Review* 106, no. 3 (August 2012): 570–587.

54. Holger Lutz Kern, "The Political Consequences of Transitions out of Marriage in Great Britain," *Electoral Studies* 29, no. 2 (2010): 249–258; Steven J. Rosenstone, "Economic Adversity and Voter Turnout," *American Political Science Review* 26, no. 1 (1982): 25–46.

55. Bateson, "Crime Victimization and Political Participation."

56. Ibid., 575.

57. John Bellows and Edward Miguel, "War and Local Collective Action in Sierra Leone," *Journal of Public Economics* 93, nos. 11–12 (2009): 1144–1157.

58. Christopher Blattman, "From Violence to Voting: War and Political Participation in Uganda," *American Political Science Review* 103, no. 2 (May 2009): 231–247.

59. Michael J. Gilligan, Benjamin J. Pasquale, and Cyrus Samii, "Civil War and Social Cohesion: Lab-in-the-Field Evidence from Nepal," *American Journal of Political Science* 58, no. 3 (July 2014): 604–619.

60. NCRB, *Crime in India 2016*, 25.

61. Units of analysis are also an important source of variation: some surveys ask questions of individual respondents and others ask questions of households.

PART 2

Social and Political Change Overview

Does dynamic urbanization in the National Capital Region (NCR) engender social and political change? As discussed in the Introduction, the principle that urbanization leads to social change is almost viewed as a "law" of social science in the West. The literature in India has been more circumspect. When one considers the structural social inequalities imposed by India's caste system and gender biases imposed by a deeply pervasive patriarchy, phenomena that still very much exist in India's cities, it is easy to see why scholars of India have not picked up these Western frameworks with alacrity. But just because social inequalities remain pervasive does not mean that urbanization is inconsequential for social behavior. The answer, as our chapters in this part of the volume show, is more complicated. The social and political gains from NCR's urbanization are highly uneven.

Community and State

The first part of this volume characterized life in the NCR at the metropolitan scale, with an explicit focus on the "spatial inequalities"—in terms of caste, wealth, and access to infrastructure and public services—that characterize the region. By looking at quantitative data across the breadth of the NCR, we were able to develop a deeper understanding of various social and economic inequalities across the expanse of the region and how they are interconnected. If the first part of this volume focused on the breadth of the NCR, the second part focuses on details about its *residents*—in particular, how urbanization affects households and the societies in which they live. We find it useful to think about this part of the volume as analyzing how life in the NCR structures interactions within and across communities, as well as with the state.

The first set of questions we ask are about communities. By this, we mean the role that urban conditions in the NCR play in breaking "traditional" community structures that limit interactions and mobilities across caste, religion, and gender. Do the changing patterns of spatial location highlighted in the first part of the volume change the way in which people from different caste or religious groups interact with each other? Are there "new" communities formed by these changing patterns of spatial location? To what extent are women in the NCR afforded greater educational opportunities, and is this reflected in the job market? Do women have the opportunity to marry outside of their caste and religious groups?

The next set of questions we ask are about the state. By this, we mean the ways in which citizens make demands on the state through formal and informal channels and how this impacts policy discourses. How successful are residents in using informal intermediaries to get grievances addressed by the state? What are the demographic and ideological factors that have led to rise of the Aam Aadmi Party (AAP) in Delhi, and what are its implications for Delhi's future politics? As air pollution in the NCR becomes a major problem, how is policy discourse on the matter shaped?

Our aim in this part of the volume was to generate a methodologically and intellectually diverse approach to understand the societal changes in the NCR. Here, we cover changes in gender outcomes and marriage practices (Chapters 9 and 10), changes in caste and religious conservatism and the creation of communities across caste and class (Chapters 8 and 11), as well as how citizens interface with the state in politics and policy (Chapters 12, 13, and 14).

Whereas the first part of this volume relied heavily on the Center for the Advanced Study of India–National Capital Region (CASI–NCR) Survey to provide general empirical characterizations of the NCR, the sources in this part of the volume are more diverse. The goal here was to put some of the findings of the CASI–NCR Survey on social and political change (or lack thereof) in discussion with scholars working with different methodological approaches. Of the seven chapters in this part of the volume, four use the CASI–NCR Survey while the three others use ethnographic methods, historical analysis, and survey analysis (of another survey).

Chapters in This Part

In Chapter 8, Sumitra Badrinathan and Devesh Kapur provide a wide-ranging theoretical discussion of the potential role of urbanization in Indian cities and social change. The fundamental claim is that urbanization changes patterns of interaction, education levels, and economic well-being, all of which induce certain behavioral changes that are reflected in the weakening of caste and religious practices and diminishing of regressive gender norms, as well as increased political participation. They test the implications of the theory using novel data from the CASI–NCR Survey on "commensality," that is, who is willing to eat together with whom. The authors show that the strongest predictor of breaking down caste and religious barriers in food practices—which are very resilient in Delhi (and surely more so, therefore, in the rest of India)—is economic status. They find similar wealth effects on willingness to let women eat with men (for migrants) and on voter turnout. The findings in this chapter are stark and depressing. Wealth is about more than money, it also structures how people live in the city—their interactions, occupations, and education. Insofar as urbanization unleashes greater earning power (as the rising urban–rural wage gap in India suggests) and modes of earning that are not tied to traditional village work, we may have some room for qualified optimism of the impacts of urbanization on breaking down various modes of social conservatism. But, in India, it is likely to be a long and slow process.

Taking this argument to its logical next step, in Chapter 9 Megan Reed investigates marriage practices in the NCR. Marriage is well known to be the most conservative of Indian institutions, where caste, religion, and class all structure who can marry whom in arranged matches. The results in Chapter 9 are even more disappointing than in Chapter 8. Less than 1 in 20 respondents supports marriages outside of or between castes, classes, linguistic groups, or religious identities. As one might expect, marriage outside of social class and linguistic group is marginally more acceptable than marriage outside of caste and religion (especially religion). Within these very low rates of social approval, some patterns do emerge. Reed documents that those respondents from wealthier households and those from a younger generation perceive greater social acceptance of marriage outside of their group (but by small margins). Taking Chapters 8 and 9 together also sheds light on the kinds of practices that might be quicker to change in urban environments (eating practices) and those that are harder to change (marriage). Once again, we reiterate that these claims are not about aggregate levels of conservative practices in cities (which are prevalent in the NCR) but the dynamics and the possibility of change.

Taking the findings on marriage as a starting point, Chapter 10 by Deepaboli Chatterjee, Babu Lal, and Rimjhim Saxena investigates the education and job opportunities for young working age women in the NCR. The key finding (using the CASI–NCR Survey data) with respect to education is that while women in older cohorts were less educated (by large margins) than their male counterparts, in the youngest cohort women are *more* educated than their male counterparts. However, this increase in women's education does not seem to have a strong impact on their participation in the labor force, with much of the female sample reporting that it is soon married and at home after finishing studies. A small sliver of women enters the highest skilled occupations, but those women with sufficient wealth at home are conspicuously missing from the labor market. This combination of data leads the authors to suggest that education is being used more as a signal for the "marriage market" and not the job market. In short, women with higher educational outcomes are more likely to marry into well-off families rather than enter the labor force. Social mobility, if it can be called that, comes through marrying into better-off households for women rather than through entering the job market in better and more well-paying work.

Chapter 11 by Sanjay Srivastava comments on the emergence of new communities in the NCR from an ethnographic lens. The value of this lens is to understand social transformations of space that cannot be readily picked by a large quantitative survey approach. Using a detailed study of two localities—a high-income private corporation controlled colony in Gurgaon and a now-demolished slum on the banks of the Yamuna river—he explores how communities are constructed through changing relations with the state, the economy, and other residents. He analyzes these dynamics and the construction of urban space through the idea of "post-nationalism" which is "the articulation of the nationalist emotion with the robust desires engendered through new practices of consumerism and their associated cultures of privatization and individuation." One of the core aspects of the post-nationalist movement is the reimagining of a state that is viewed as sympathetic to the middle classes instead of the poor, on the one hand, and subservient to private capital, on the other. Through his analysis of corporation-controlled DLF City, Srivastava chronicles how such corporation-controlled colonies resist traditional state control by building new communities through "citizen groups" that act as a forum between the colony's residents and the corporation that controls them. By contrast, in the slum of Nangla Matchi, where residents need state supports but often lack the formal identity proof to receive them, residents must rely on communities built on the kindness of neighbors and informal intermediaries to navigate the state.

It is this latter observation, of a community built on informal intermediaries, that forms the basis of the analysis in Chapter 12 by Neelanjan Sircar. The last three chapters of this volume, 12–14, explore the politics and planning in its various forms in the NCR. Sircar conceptualizes the role of informal intermediaries—middlemen or *dalals* in common parlance—as emanating from the interplay between two private markets. The first market is of intermediaries themselves who compete to bolster their reputation in the community. The second market is one of citizens who are wealthy enough to afford the private provision of public services such as trash collection and electricity (much like what Srivastava observes in DLF City). These two markets in turn shape the kinds of demands citizens make on the system and who the intermediaries are willing to help. In particular, because informal intermediaries are not elected, they need not build a large coalition of supporters; rather, they focus on the most important and well-off citizens to bolster their reputation. Indeed, Sircar's analysis of the CASI–NCR Survey finds that intermediaries are far more willing to address the grievances of the wealthy, and that frees the wealthy themselves to focus their concerns on heavy infrastructure such as roads and street lighting (as they can privately acquire most public services). The empirical implication of this state affairs is that the poor are much less likely to have their grievances, which are more likely to focus on state-provided public services, addressed satisfactorily. And this implies that there is significant under-provision of civic services to the poor.

Chapter 13 by Adnan Farooqui shifts the focus from informal politics to the formal arena. He analyzes the dramatic rise of the AAP in Delhi's political landscape. The chapter proved to be deeply perceptive, as the chapter was authored before AAP's romp in the 2020 Delhi Election (where it won 62 of 70 seats). Analyzing election post-poll data provided by Lokniti at the Centre for the Study of Developing Societies, Farooqui traces the rise of the AAP to two important social changes in the region. First, as has occurred through much of the country, the Congress began a period of steady decline from the mid to late 2000s onward, culminating with the rise of the AAP in the 2013 election. In the aftermath, many former Congress supporters switched support to the AAP, forming a significant reservoir of support. Second, as the NCR has been a growing destination for migrants from "Purvanchal," the states of Uttar Pradesh and Bihar, the Purvanchali migrant vote began to become pivotal in Delhi electoral politics. Farooqui shows how the AAP constructed a base of Dalits, Sikhs, and Purvanchali voters to develop a formidable bloc of support (although recent results suggest that some of the Purvanchali vote may be going to the Bharatiya Janata Party).

In the final chapter of the volume, Awadhendra Sharan applies a historical lens to understand the various discourses toward air pollution and clean air starting with the early 1900s. The early discourses focused on "smoke" produced from industrial development and burning of biomass fuels at home. In the more recent past, concerns have moved toward the impact of the incineration of trash to the impact of fireworks during Diwali. Now, as Delhi fashions itself as a modern world city, the extraordinary levels of air pollution have become an embarrassment. We chose to end this volume with this chapter as it encapsulates the various debates we have seen in Delhi over time, from issues that were very much parochial to concerns that animate discussion beyond its borders. As these last two chapters show, the ever-shifting composition of urban space and the social demographics that comprise the region are reflected in the newest political and policy discourses.

CHAPTER 8

Religion, Caste, Class, Politics
How Urbanization Affects Social Interactions and Political Behaviors

Sumitra Badrinathan and Devesh Kapur

Introduction

What are the impacts of urbanization on social identities and social cleavages in India? It is now widely accepted that urbanization is as much a social process—transforming behavior, culture, and social institutions over time—as it is an economic and spatial process. Urbanization transforms core societal organizations such as the family, the nature and density of social interactions, the nature of work and diversity of occupations, and individual freedoms and personal autonomy. Cities are sites of social change that offer possibilities for social mobility by disrupting the social stratifications of rural societies. While the degree and rate of urbanization in India is contested, there are multiple questions on the country's urban future, ranging from the drivers and pace of this urbanization, settlement type, and economic foundations. However, the question of the impacts of urbanization on social identities, attitudes, and hierarchies has not been widely explored.

Severe social cleavages—caste and class, region and religion, gender and generational—continue to characterize Indian society. Discussions and analysis of these cleavages have occurred against a backdrop of an India that was overwhelmingly rural. But as India rapidly urbanizes, these social cleavages are likely to evolve. While some might attenuate, others could amplify and yet others may well transform. What factors might influence this evolution and what mechanisms might shape urbanization's effects on social identities? In India's case, how are these mechanisms likely to evolve? Our analysis of data from the National Capital Region (NCR) offers some insights into these questions.

We argue that at least some social cleavages are blunted through the processes of urbanization. Urban areas tend to have more heterogeneous populations resulting in greater exposure to nontraditional attitudes. This greater exposure has the potential to attenuate inter-household cleavages based on caste and religion and intra-household cleavages based on gender. Our results suggest that increases in wealth increase social interactions across different social groups, which might thereby soften caste- and religion-based cleavages. However, a wealth increase in and of itself does not have a similar liberalizing effect on gender norms. But while wealth can blur caste- and religion-based hierarchies, we find that migrant status has the opposite effect, in that migrants are significantly less likely to break down traditional barriers in intergroup interactions. In discussing these findings, we highlight that our results are mediated by neighborhood effects, especially housing segregation. While migrants are less likely to interact with other caste and religion groups, our data demonstrates that the most common reason cited for lack of interaction is the absence of family or friends of other religions and castes. Our conclusions underscore the challenges in measuring the impacts of urbanization given cross-sectional data and the difficulties in establishing causality in the relationships we measure.

Urbanization and Social Change: What Does the Literature Tell Us?

Since the mid-nineteenth century, the consequences of urbanization and its concomitants—the dissolution of the village community, the rise of the city together with industrialization—have been much debated by social theorists. The German sociologist Ferdinand Tonnies proposed that social life in villages was *gemeinschaft*—a community united by ties of kinship and neighborhood, underpinned by a common language and traditions, and an interdependent economy based on land. In contrast, urban life was *gesellschaft*, characterized by individualism, and beliefs were a result of indirect and impersonal interactions. In his famous essay in 1903, "The Metropolis and Mental Life," another German sociologist Georg Simmel argued that in contrast to the dominance of feelings and emotions that characterize rural life, the stimuli of urban life make urban residents more calculating and rational, where interpersonal relationships are mediated more through the impersonal means of money.

The society-wide transformations intrinsic to urbanization have been recognized in the long-standing debates on village life in rural India—and by implication the effects of urbanization on India's social stratification. In the mid-nineteenth century, Karl Marx had commented,

> we must not forget that these idyllic village-communities [in India], inoffensive though they may appear, had always been the solid foundation of Oriental despotism, that they restrained the human mind within the smallest possible compass, making it the unresisting tool of superstition, enslaving it beneath traditional rules, depriving it of all grandeur and historical energies.[1]

Prior to independence, Mahatma Gandhi, an advocate of the advantages of community-oriented village life, famously remarked that "the soul of India lives in its villages." In contrast, B. R. Ambedkar, the principal architect of the Indian Constitution, argued: "What is a village but a sink of localism, a den of ignorance, narrow mindedness and communalism?" As a Dalit, Ambedkar was painfully aware of the degrading effects of ascriptive social identities in rural India, where everyone's social identity was known and inescapable. He believed that the very anonymity of urbanization offered escape routes and pathways to social mobility by attenuating spatially specific social identities, whether through greater social interaction in public spaces such as markets and transportation systems or in labor markets.[2]

The broad conclusion from these works was that urbanization would lead to the development of individual identities over (or at the cost of) group identities. The high population densities of urban areas increase the opportunities that residents have for face-to-face interaction, and city size further increases the diversity of interactions. Further, to the extent that urban areas have more heterogeneous populations, the resulting greater exposure to nontraditional attitudes, behaviors, and lifestyles could make urban residents more tolerant than their rural counterparts. But such outcomes are by no means guaranteed. Segregated neighborhoods, along with economic and political competition, might well sharpen social cleavages and amplify intolerance.

The most obvious aspect of urbanization that affects traditional social hierarchies is its effect on occupations and employment. As the economic base of urban societies becomes nonagricultural, new and different occupations emerge and employment moves from the informal to the formal sector. In India, the lack of historical correspondence of these occupations with a specific caste and relatively more formal contractual arrangements in labor markets are likely to affect social cleavages (notably caste). Historically, the key mechanisms of the intergenerational replication of caste have been occupation and marriage. The modern urban economy, however, generates new occupations that may well have a correspondence with class but not caste (at least as historically determined). A bus or car driver or fast-food delivery person may have a modest income with few social protections, but there may no longer exist a strict correlation of occupations with specific castes. Hence, the greater diversity of occupations in a large and growing urban economy is likely to weaken the historic link between caste and occupation.

The economic base of urban areas rests on industry, commerce, and services. Economic interests can provide a form of "bridging" social capital, in contrast to the "bonding" social capital that emanates from belonging to specific ethnic and religious groups. In the last two centuries, industrialization was the key driver of urbanization, as populations moved from rural areas to find work in factories. These wage earners—often employed in terrible working conditions—gradually coalesced as a class, which Marx identified as the proletariat. The growth of class consciousness with common solidarities cuts across the local identities that migrants had carried from their villages. The rise of labor unions to fight for their members' common interests forged labor solidarities that enabled the formation of new labor-based social identities.

This was the case in many Indian cities as well from the late nineteenth to the late twentieth centuries—labor streamed in to work in cotton and textile mills in cities such as Ahmedabad, Surat, Mumbai, and Kanpur; or jute mills in Calcutta; or after independence in heavy engineering as in Ranchi; and in the new steel mill townships such as Durgapur, Bhilai, Bokaro, or Rourkela until about the mid-1970s. An example of the link between industrialization, unions, and communally integrated associational life is Hindu–Muslim relations in Indian cities. The decline of large textile mills in cities such as Ahmedabad and Mumbai in the 1970s and 1980s has been cited as a factor in the weakening of interethnic engagement, rendering informal sector workers easy prey for politicians who sought to polarize people along communal lines for electoral advantage.[3]

Labor markets in India have witnessed large changes in recent decades. Most employment in urban India is now in services and in small firms or is self-employed, conditions that make it harder to organize labor worldwide. The exception is white-collar unions in the public sector, especially in public administration and the financial sector (in particular, public sector banks). But as the public sector gradually retreats from commercial activities, this is an unlikely site for building solidarities across social cleavages in the foreseeable future. In principle, employment in public administration could be sites of intermixing, but in most cases, lower-level public sector jobs are deeply nativist and reservations have often made them sites of resentment and animosity rather than spaces for building social bonds. Indeed, with formal sector jobs at a premium, growth in urban jobs will take place largely in the informal sector, through self-employment, small entrepreneurship, or household support services. The effects of these trends in urban employment on social cleavages remain poorly understood.

Commerce provides another channel that binds communities, especially when it provides complementary, nonreplicable services. Gains from economic exchange were key to building communal harmony between Hindus and Muslims in the port cities of western India.[4] In today's world, this implies that when commerce embeds different communities in supply chains, the ensuing engagement can build and strengthen bonds of trust and economic interest. Standalone or parallel and competitive services do not create such bonds and may indeed align sectarian political interests with economic incentives to reduce competition, as has been observed in incidents of targeted violence directed at minority-owned businesses.

If the distinctive economic base of urban areas provides possibilities for more liminal social identities through industry and commerce, it is also the petri dish of a distinctive social group—the middle class. The Indian middle class has expanded hand in hand with India's burgeoning urbanization. The political and social consequences of this expansion will depend on the economic and social base of the middle class and resulting attitudes and policy preferences. Its collective self-identity will also depend on the degree of heterogeneity within this class, given that there are marked differences in income, education, and cultural and social capital between the lower and upper middle classes as well as between those in metropolitan cities and small towns. Whether the middle class is more likely to emerge as a progressive actor or as a reactionary force, and how this might vary across social and political issues, is an open question.[5]

But perhaps, the possibilities of the transformative impact of urbanization on social identities would appear more salient in the case of migrants (especially rural–urban and interregional) and intergenerational changes in identities, particularly in the case of large urban agglomerations. However, the effects of migration on social identities can be mixed. Migrants from rural areas form nonfamilial ties in urban destinations, which compete with family ties in the place of origin. First-generation migrants, while embedded in a new urban environment, continue to identify and to maintain close relationships with their rural households and kinship groups. Their lower education and incomes and weak cultural capital mean that even if they may have a strong desire to be integrated into urban life, with weaker rights to full citizenship in the city, they are often marginalized. Internal migrants experience a lesser citizenship status and curtailed citizenship rights partly because of their impoverishment and weak and venal urban governance structures, but also because they are migrants per se.[6]

At first glance, the discrimination suffered by migrants from India's Northeast to cities such as Delhi and Bengaluru or of north Indian migrants (especially Muslims) to Mumbai appears to provide a pessimistic prognosis about urbanization's impact on social cleavages. However, despite an often-unfriendly metropolis, with time migrants have become active contributors to the vibrancy of these cities and have incrementally forced the city to acknowledge them as Indians, even as they still largely live within their own communities.[7]

The example of the spatial stratification of migrant communities is a reminder that it is not urbanization per se but the varying urbanization processes unfolding in India that will affect the trajectory and degree of change in social identities and the intensity of social cleavages. Housing patterns are a good example. Slums standing alongside opulent gated communities exemplify graded citizenship, but the former, in particular, are sites of coexistence of multiple communities, living cheek by jowl.[8] On the other hand, middle-class housing complexes with selection criteria that, for example, proscribe nonvegetarians, will inevitably exclude certain social groups and end up reinforcing rather than attenuating the prejudices and biases prevalent in the Indian society.

It is also likely that the size of a city will matter for new forms of social identities to emerge. The degree of anonymity and the ranges and types of economic activity vary with city size. A female migrant from India's Northeast is visible today in service sector occupations in Delhi or Bengaluru, but those occupations are simply absent in small-town India for women, let alone those from the Northeast. Consequently, we might expect different effects in the National Capital Territory (NCT) from the towns that constitute the NCR (excluding Gurugram and Noida).

Characteristics of the Urban Population and Behavioral Outcomes

In this chapter, we undertake the task of delineating the effects of urban processes on social behavior and attitudes. The sociological and political science literature examined in the previous section underscores the impacts of urbanization in cultivating individual identities over group identities, such that region-specific or area-specific attitudes that migrants hold are attenuated in urban settings. As a result, our expectation is that social cleavages are blunted through the processes of urbanization. We posit that as urban areas have more heterogeneous populations resulting in greater exposure to nontraditional attitudes, urbanization will attenuate inter-household hierarchies on the basis of religion and caste. Further as gender is one of India's most salient social cleavages, the ways in which urbanization will affect gender-based attitudes rests on increasing female labor force participation, which in turn might depend on factors such as access to safe modes of public transportation and public services such as policing.

The argument that urbanization and the underlying processes associated with it result in social change begs the question of what constitutes social change. The social concomitants of the transition from rural to urban life are multiple. This chapter examines social change on two dimensions: first, intra-household change, in particular, changing attitudes toward gender-based activity *within the household* and second, inter-household change, that is, social change as measured by changes in attitudes and prejudices *between social groups*, specifically across religious and caste-based cleavages.

Figure 8.1 summarizes the argument of our chapter. We posit that urbanization leads to changes in social attitudes and behavior. Urban populations are generally more educated, are wealthier, and have more diverse occupations. They also have a larger presence of migrants. These characteristics in turn shape social behavior across the urban population, manifest in consumption behavior and eating habits. One measure of this behavioral change is commensality—the act of eating together. "Breaking bread together," so to speak, is a very basic indicator of communal bonds (or lack thereof). Does urbanization increase commensality across caste and religious cleavages? We also analyze attitudinal changes within households, specifically urbanization's effects on strong gender norms that adversely affect women.

Urbanization is also likely to affect political behavior. Urban areas have a large middle class whose political preferences could be very different from farmers and, as a result, traditional voting patterns prevalent in rural areas may break down. Furthermore, since urban voters are more educated and wealthier, modes of political participation, such as activism and protests, may also change. However, these behavioral changes might be different for migrants who might still vote in the places where they have migrated from.

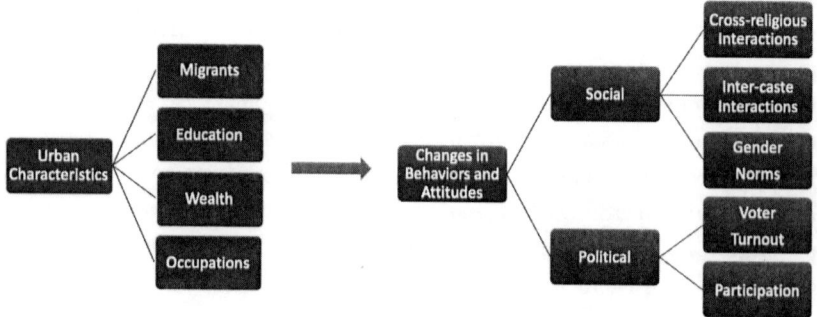

Figure 8.1 Urbanization's effects on social and political attitudes and behavior
Source: Authors.

In this chapter, we are particularly interested in understanding whether the political behavior of migrants is distinct from nonmigrants.

The outcome of interest in this study is respondent attitudes toward social change. What factors drive intergroup and intra-household variation on these social attitudes? We hypothesize that attitude changes are brought about by the mechanism of urbanization, but are primarily shaped by its characteristics of migration, education, wealth, and occupation. To begin, urbanization drives migration. Urban areas have more heterogeneous populations, resulting in greater exposure to nontraditional attitudes, behaviors, and lifestyles, which in turn could make urban residents more tolerant than their rural counterparts, thereby affecting social attitudes of migrants. The effect of heterogeneous urban neighborhoods, however, is likely to be more pronounced for those who have moved to the city from outside versus those who have been in the city for all their life. In this regard, we expect different attitudes on social cleavages among migrants as compared to the populations they are drawn from, especially in the case of rural to urban migrants.

Second, education is often seen as a way to shape attitudes in young minds. But while educational opportunities and access are greater in urban areas, the content of education—much harder to capture in surveys—can be as important as the level of education, with the latter affecting job opportunities and incomes, and thereby attitudes indirectly.

Lastly, we also expect wealth and occupations to play an important role in predicting attitudes. One of the most obvious aspects of urbanization is that the economic base shifts from agriculture to a wide variety of other occupations. This change is usually accompanied by higher incomes that are less volatile and have access to more social protections such as better health care. Thus, as people are more educated and earn more, it is intuitive that the combination of an urban setting with occupations that lead to a better standard of living, greater contact with more heterogeneous populations, and exposure to media might lead to changes in social attitudes. While both migration and wealth have an independent effect on social attitudes, the interactive effect of migration coupled with increases in income and wealth is likely to be even greater.

Given the difficulties of measuring income from household surveys, in this study, we do not measure respondents' incomes directly. Instead, we proxy for income with an index measuring household assets; this index is a continuous scale running from –3 to 3, where 3 represents the upper bound on household assets. Migration is a binary measure in our analyses, indicating whether the respondent migrated from out of the NCR region or not.

Results

Characteristics of the National Capital Region Population (I): Education

In India, inequalities in educational attainment are manifest across social groups. However, in a giant metro such as the NCR, a strong marker of education attainment is migrant status. A significantly greater proportion of migrants in our sample are uneducated as compared to nonmigrants. As the level of education increases, the gap between migrants and nonmigrants first reduces and then keeps increasing. For instance, there is no significant difference in the proportion of migrants and nonmigrants who report that they have a 5th grade through 9th grade education. However, a significantly higher proportion of nonmigrants have a 12th grade education, a bachelor's equivalent degree, and a master's equivalent degree (Table 8.1).

Another social cleavage affecting education attainment is gender. When we compare the education level of men and women in the sample, we see that differences in education are marked toward the tails (and especially the lower

Table 8.1   Education of migrants and nonmigrants in NCR (in percentage)

	Uneducated	5th grade pass	6th–8th grades	9th–10th grades	11th–12th grades	Bachelor's	Master's and beyond
Migrant	21.24	9.85	12.47	20.55	15.70	15.47	4.69
Nonmigrant	11.26	6.51	10.87	18.39	20.01	24.83	8.09

Source: Authors.

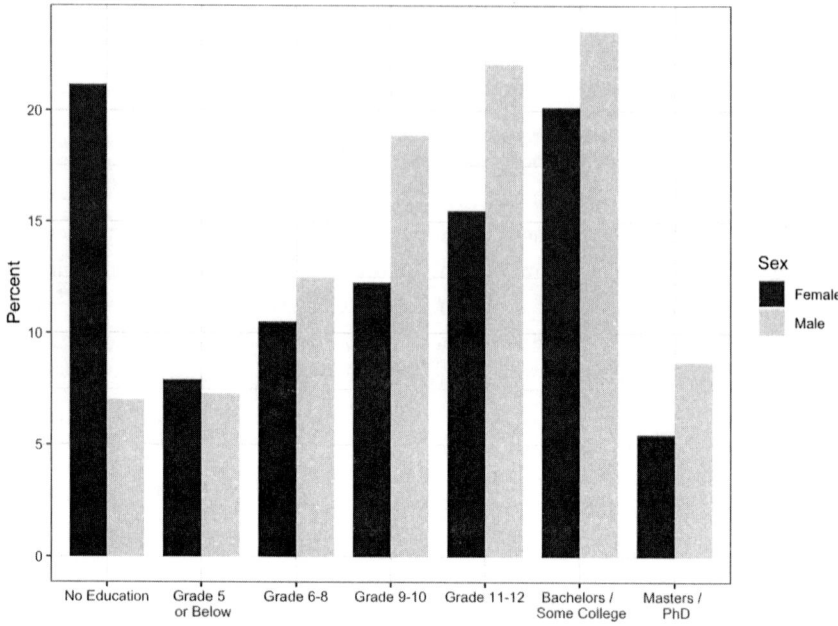

Figure 8.2   Level of education by sex
Source: Authors.

tail) but are less stark in the center of the educational distribution. In Figure 8.2, a significantly higher number of women report having no education as compared to men. The difference is reduced as the level of education keeps increasing. However, a significantly higher proportion of men have 12th grade, bachelor's, and master's degrees (Figure 8.2).

Characteristics of the National Capital Region Population (II): Occupations

Another mechanism of urbanization's effects on social change is through occupational change. We analyze how jobs are distributed within castes. In our survey, we asked respondents their primary jobs and classified their answers into four categories. High-skilled jobs are those in which respondents are legislators, senior officials, professionals, and managers. Medium-skilled jobs are those in which respondents are technicians and associate professionals, clerks, service workers, and in manufacturing. Low-skilled jobs are those where respondents are in agriculture, fishery, craft and related trades, and elementary occupations. Our fourth category is that of a housewife, which we use as a

Table 8.2   Percentage of caste breakdown by job category

	Upper caste	OBC	SC/Dalit	ST	Herfindahl index
High-skilled jobs	42.42	35.15	8.78	3.63	3,125
Medium-skilled jobs	33.92	33.24	14.03	5.72	2,485
Low-skilled jobs	27.22	32.37	17.47	7.73	2,154
Housewives	32.64	36.29	13.03	5.33	2,581

Source: Authors.

baseline for comparison, because we expect there to be small differences in caste-based concentration in the housewife category, as this occupation cuts across social categories.

In Table 8.2, we compute the proportion of each caste in each of the four job categories. We find that in high-skilled jobs, upper castes are represented 10 percentage points more as compared to the baseline housewife category. As job skill decreases, the concentration of upper-caste respondents in those jobs also declines. In contrast, for Scheduled Caste/Schedule Tribe (SC/ST) groups, the concentration of these castes increases as job skill declines. We do not see much variation across job categories for Other Backward Classes (OBCs). In order to better measure the share that each caste holds in each job category, we compute the Herfindahl Index (a widely used measure of concentration) for each job category to capture the concentration of castes within each of the four job categories. The index ranges from 0 to 10,000, with higher numbers indicating more concentration. As compared to the baseline of 2,581 for the category of housewife, we see that the Herfindahl score for medium-skilled and low-skilled jobs is lower, indicating comparatively less caste concentration in lower-skilled job categories. In contrast, high-skilled jobs have the highest Herfindahl score, showing a greater caste concentration.

Behavioral Effects across the National Capital Region Population: Consumption

Our survey data shows that a large number of households possess a range of assets which would have been inconceivable for most Indian households a few decades ago. Intellectuals tend to sniff at consumption. For Marx, consumption was a "commodity fetish" induced by capitalism; for Weber it was instrumental rather than as a social action carrying meaning in itself. But consumption creates new identities, from individual self-regard to citizen consumer—and of course, new markers of status. As Weber recognized, the ability to possess consumer goods is an important means of marking social status in any society. While structural changes in an economy create the economic foundations of mass consumption, it is also affected by (and itself influences) individual changes in values, attitudes, and behavior that result in something distinct—a consumer culture. Consumption has been a tool for self-assertion by the socially marginalized. In her classic work on consumption in the United States of America, Lizabeth Cohen argued that "For social groups not otherwise well represented, in particular women and African Americans, identification as consumers offered a new opportunity to make claims on those wielding public and private power in American society."[9]

In recent years, a growing body of literature within consumer culture theory has sought to examine how consumers rework and transform symbolic meanings encoded in marketer-generated materials (for example, advertisements, brands, retail settings) or material goods to manifest their particular personal and social circumstances and further their identity. This work argues that consumption and the marketplace have become preeminent sources of symbolic resources through which people, including those who lack resources to participate in the market as full-fledged consumers, construct narratives of identity, enacting and personalizing cultural scripts that align their identities with the structural imperatives of a consumer-driven global economy. A broad historical view links the rise of consumer culture with the modern creation of a "choosing self" (according to Don Slater)[10] in which identity shifts from a fixed set of characteristics determined by birth and ascription to a reflexive, ongoing, individual project shaped by appearance and performance.

In India, consumption for socially marginalized groups like Dalits—from clothes to foods—was severely proscribed. Thus, consumption of items is not only restricted to an objective usefulness but also its signaling value in social interactions across groups with distinctive social identities. Khamis, Prakash, and Siddique find differences in consumption of items in India that signal "visible consumption" across social groups that is consistent with the status signaling nature of the consumption items.[11] For instance, OBCs spend 8 percent more on visible consumption than high-caste groups (and this higher spending of OBC households on visible consumption is diverted from education spending). Similarly, Punarjit Roychowdhury finds that lower-status social groups in India spend more on conspicuous goods in order to overtake the ones who are further up the social ladder in the contest for social status.[12] But this, in turn, strengthens the incentives for those higher in the

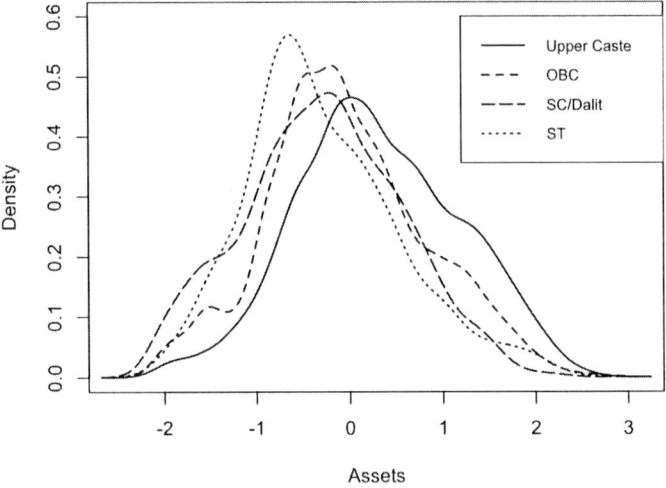

Figure 8.3   Distribution of assets by caste
Source: Authors.

social hierarchy to acquire even more conspicuous goods in order to defend their social status. Thus, while status competition leads everyone to increase spending on conspicuous goods, any gain in status is cancelled out by the similarly increased expenditure of others.

What does the evidence in the NCR tell us in this regard? Figure 8.3 plots the distribution of assets by caste. We can observe a clear overlap in distributions. While the upper-caste asset distribution is more centered and the ST asset distribution is to the left, there is a large overlap in the area under the curve for all four caste groups. This demonstrates that although there may be significant differences in mean assets between caste groups, there is considerable heterogeneity in assets within caste groups. Indeed, the spread of the distribution of household assets *within* caste groups is greater than that *between* caste groups. Whether this might result in a weakening of caste-based identification and its replacement with consumption- and class-based identities is an open question.

Intergroup Behavioral Effects: Commensality

Commensality—eating and drinking at the same table—is a fundamental social activity, which creates and cements relationships.[13] Commensality has been "the root of all caste distinction"[14] and Appadurai has argued that food consumption practices act as "the semiotic instrument of Hindu ideas of rank and distance."[15] Social strictures, evidenced for instance in the practice of untouchability that forbade eating any cooked foods that had even been touched by Dalits, led to strict boundaries that fueled practices of inclusion and exclusion, strengthening or weakening existing social cleavages. Ambedkar had highlighted the importance of interdining in breaking down caste barriers, when he argued:

> You are right in holding that Caste will cease to be an operative farce only when inter-dining and inter-marriage have become matters of common course. You have located the source of the disease. But is your prescription the right prescription for the disease? Ask yourselves this question; Why is it that a large majority of Hindus do not inter-dine and do not inter-marry? Why is it that your cause is not popular? There can be only one answer to this question and it is that inter-dining and inter-marriage are repugnant to the beliefs and dogmas which the Hindus regard as sacred.[16]

Indian media still highlight numerous stories of discrimination and violence around food practices, especially in rural India. In urban India, the growth of restaurants and the growing practice of eating out (and ordering in) is breaking down the strictures of food purity and pollution. The Irani cafes in Mumbai, for instance, provided affordable eateries in a city that had lacked public places to eat and drink and played a part in breaking some of Mumbai's social and religious restrictions. "An Irani café was the sort of place you could go eat whether you were an upper-caste Hindu or a Muslim, and not care who's on the table next to you, and not care who served you."[17]

What does the NCR data tell us about this practice in urban India? Although there has been scholarly attention devoted to banquets and feasts for religious, political, or ritualistic purposes, few studies have concentrated on commensality as a quotidian practice and its implications for cross-group interactions. We attempt to do so through a range of questions to assess intergroup dining or commensality as an indicator for social interactions.

We first analyze the role of commensality as an important tool in forging personal and group identities by examining whether respondents have eaten in any nonrelatives' homes. We supplement that with a question on whether, in the past year, any nonrelative has eaten in the respondent's home. We pose these questions to respondents by religion, in order to obtain answers stratified by whether the respondent was Hindu, Muslim, or Sikh. Figure 8.4 plots the responses to these questions. We see that while most respondents say that they have not eaten in a nonrelative's home in the past year, the percentage of respondents who say they have eaten in nonrelative's home is greater for Muslim respondents as compared to Hindu respondents, and is the highest for Sikh respondents (Figure 8.4).

Following this, conditional on whether the respondents said that nonrelatives ate at their home or that they ate at nonrelatives' homes, we determine the religious make-up of the interactions. The idea behind asking questions about the religion of the respondents' guests is to establish whether the behavior of commensality can lead to the softening of cleavages in urban areas. Muslim respondents were asked if any of the people they had eaten with were Hindu or Sikh, and Hindu respondents were asked if any of the people they had eaten with were Muslim or Sikh. Similarly, Sikh respondents were asked about the religion of the nonrelatives they had eaten with. If there are cross-cleavage ties in commensality, it is possible that urbanization is playing a role, especially in contrast to rural India.

However, when these cross-cleavage interactions do not exist, we seek to understand why. Hence, we asked respondents for the reasons why they have not shared a meal with people from other religions. Figure 8.5 plots the percentage

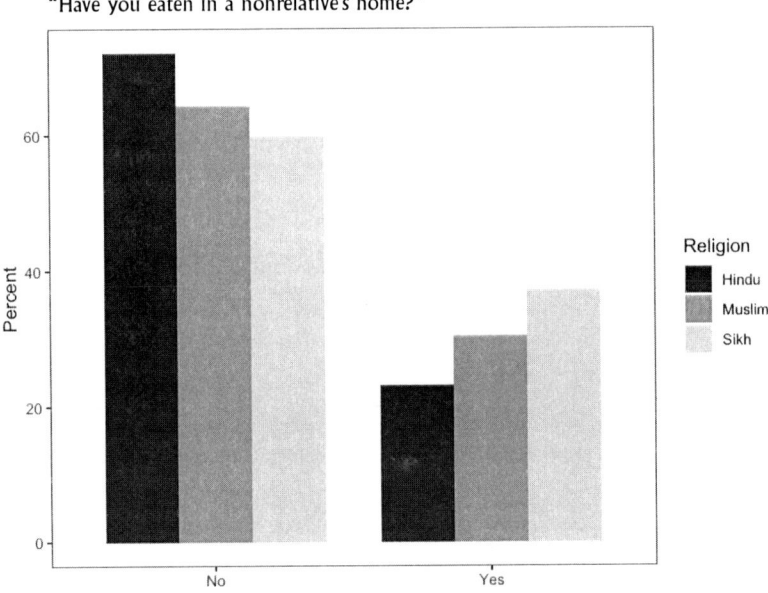

Figure 8.4   Percentage of respondents who have eaten in a nonrelative's home
Source: Authors.

for each reason that Hindu respondents said was salient in determining whether or not they had shared a meal with someone of another religion. We see that for Hindus, the primary reason for not having shared a meal with a Muslim is because they did not have friends or family from that religion. However, more than a third of the Hindu respondents are either uncomfortable or have purity concerns. Although we might expect urban centers to attenuate the effects of such segregation, they are likely to be mediated by other variables such as education, wealth, migrant status, and the social composition of neighborhoods and workplaces, which we examine later in this chapter (the results for Muslim and Sikh respondents are similar).

Commensality is likely to be affected not just by religion but also by caste. Our survey measured attitudes toward lower castes by asking whether SCs/STs would be invited over for a meal to the respondents' homes. In another section of the survey, we also asked how respondents perceive the caste breakdown of their neighborhoods. Specifically, we tried to understand whether respondents believed that they were living in a segregated or nonsegregated neighborhood and how this might shape patterns and frequencies of interactions. On the question of whether they would invite an SC/ST person home for a meal, while 57 percent of the sample said they would invite an SC/ST person home for a meal, the remaining 43 percent stated they would not.

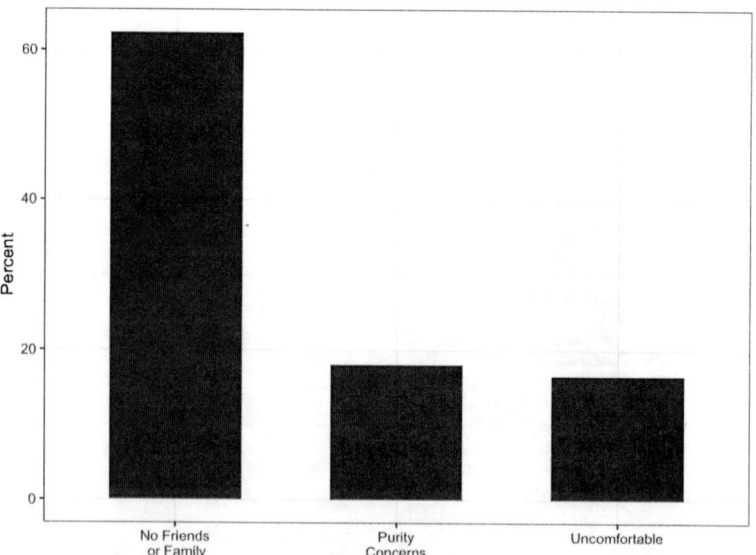

Figure 8.5   Reasons Hindu respondents provide for not sharing a meal with a Muslim
Source: Authors.

On further analysis, it appears that there are strong wealth effects underlying these commensality results. In examining how respondents at different levels of assets answer whether they have eaten at a nonrelative's home in the past year, we find that among Hindu respondents the mean assets for those who answered in the affirmative to this question is 0.33, a much higher asset value than the sample average of 0. On the other hand, however, Hindu respondents who did not answer in the affirmative to this question had an asset mean of –0.07, placing them below the sample asset average. The mean assets for Hindus who have eaten at a nonrelative's home in the past month is significantly higher than the mean assets for Hindus who have not eaten at a nonrelative's home.

The difference in asset means follows the same direction for Muslim respondents. Muslim respondents who ate at a nonrelative's home in the past month are significantly wealthier than those who have not eaten at a nonrelative's home in the past month. However, it is interesting to note the average asset values for the Muslim respondents who said they have eaten at a nonrelative's home is significantly lower (average of 0) compared to Hindus who reported the same. Thus, a respondent's wealth is a good predictor of within-group commensality. However, it is essential to point out how religious subgroups are significantly different in terms of baseline assets themselves. This is exemplified by Sikh respondents in the sample. In this subgroup, we did not find significant differences in assets for those who provided "Yes" versus "No" responses to the question of whether one has eaten at a nonrelative's home. Sikh respondents who said they have eaten at a nonrelative's home have an average asset level of 0.72, significantly greater than the Hindu average of 0.33, underlining the greater wealth of Sikh respondents in the sample.

When we look at answers to the question of whether any nonrelative was invited to a respondent's home in the past year, the results are similar. The differences in mean assets between those who responded in the affirmative and those who did not were significantly different for Hindu and Muslim respondents but were not different from each other for Sikh respondents. Figure 8.6 plots predicted probabilities (based on logistic regression models) of eating at nonrelatives' homes and of inviting nonrelatives over as a function of assets.

From Figure 8.6, it is evident that there is a positive, monotonic relationship between eating at a nonrelative's home and assets, in that as assets increase, the predicted probability of eating at a nonrelative's home increases significantly, but only for Hindu and Muslim respondents. The same pattern is observed when graphing the predicted probability of inviting a nonrelative over for a meal. At lower income levels, having people over for a meal depends not just

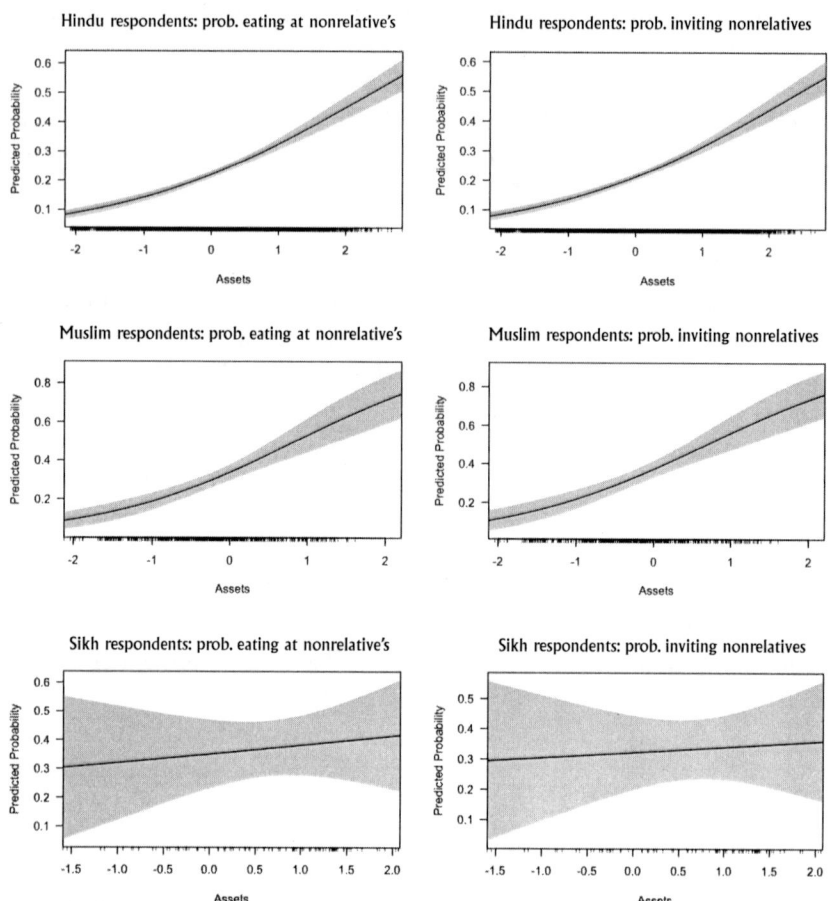

Figure 8.6 Probability of eating at a nonrelative's home by assets (*left panel*) and probability of inviting a nonrelative by assets (*right panel*)

Source: Authors.

on willingness but also on financial means. This is most evident among Hindu and Muslim respondents, but considerably less among Sikhs.

However, the relationship between assets and cross-religious eating did not hold for Sikh respondents; in their case, the likelihood of inviting or eating at homes of people of other religions was not correlated with wealth. One reason this might be the case is that this religious group is also the richest in our respondent sample. It is possible that the effects of income and wealth are more manifest at lower levels where the financial capacity to invite someone for a meal can be a binding constraint. At higher levels, preference rather than capacity becomes the driver. If so, greater income in urban areas (compared to rural areas), rather than different preferences per se, might increase cross-religious interactions and perhaps induce dynamic effects on preferences over medium and long term.

The predicted probabilities in Figure 8.7 demonstrate this result. Derived from logistic regression models, Figure 8.7 shows a positive, monotonic relationship between assets and the probability of cross-religious eating behavior.[18] Nonetheless, as discussed earlier, the most frequently cited reason for not engaging in cross-religious interaction was the paucity of family or friends of the other religion. It is precisely this segregated nature of interaction that we expect an inclusive urbanization to weaken but that is likely to be shaped by how segregated they are, which we examine later in this chapter.

In addition to cross-religious interactions through commensality, we also examined commensality across caste, specifically whether one would invite an SC/ST person over for a meal. Here too, we find a significant relationship between increasing assets and the likelihood of inviting an SC/ST person for a meal. Thus, urbanization appears to be at least blunting the sharp edges of caste-based cleavages in multiple ways, with increasing incomes as one mechanism. We consequently see a reduction in the barriers toward interacting with different castes as wealth increases. Thus, so far, it would appear that increasing wealth can soften caste-based and religion-based cleavages which could make urban residents more tolerant (or at least less intolerant) than their rural counterparts, albeit not necessarily so.

How do these results differ for migrants? One might expect migrants to form nonfamilial ties in urban settings. In this regard, being a migrant should

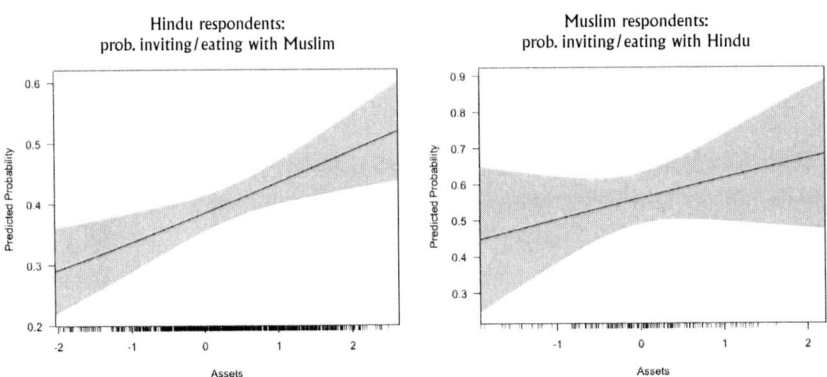

Figure 8.7   Cross-religious interaction through commensality
Source: Authors.

have a positive relationship with cross-religious interactions and eating habits, in that respondents who are migrants should have a higher likelihood of having eaten at a nonrelative's home or having invited a nonrelative for a meal. On the other hand, rural migrants or those from small towns bring with them embedded social norms which might blunt intergroup interactions. The latter effect seems to prevail in our data. We find that being a migrant has a negative effect on cross-religious interactions. Specifically, when respondents were asked whether they have eaten at a nonrelative's home, our results primarily show that being a migrant is associated with a lower likelihood of doing so. When broken up by religion, Hindu migrants are significantly less likely to have eaten at a nonrelative's home, as are Muslim migrants, relative to nonmigrants. We do not see an effect of migrant status on the likelihood of cross-religious interaction for Sikh migrants.

Responses to the question of whether any nonrelatives were invited mirror the above result. Being a migrant has a significant negative effect on inviting nonrelatives, for both Hindu and Muslim migrants, but we see no effect on Sikh migrants. A further survey question asked respondents whether they have invited their neighbors to their home. Here too, we find that being a migrant leads to a decrease in the likelihood of inviting a neighbor over for a meal.

There might be three possible reasons why migration has an effect contrary to that of assets. First, it is likely that migrants are poorer and simply cannot afford to invite nonrelatives or visit others' homes. Second, migrants' social norms and inherent attitudes may dictate the way they interact in an urban setting. While migrants, especially those from rural areas, may form new ties in urban settings, the norms they bring with them are likely to be "sticky" and resilient to change. A change in attitudes might come with their children as they assimilate in their urban milieu. Third, migrants may not have neighbors they are familiar with or established networks that allow them access to crosscutting social groups.

We find that migrants in our sample are indeed significantly poorer than nonmigrants, and hence their wealth might motivate a lower level of interaction with nonrelatives. We examine the last factor—neighborhoods and networks— through two survey questions. We asked respondents whether they interact with their neighbors, and if so, how frequently. A second question asked respondents their perceptions of the social make-up of their neighborhoods. Specifically, they were asked whether they perceive all the people in their neighborhood to be of the same religion as them, most of the same religion, some, or none. This question was aimed at understanding the perception of segregation in urban neighborhoods. For migrants, especially, moving to a new city and living in a neighborhood that is diverse might mean a lack of networks or connections, implying fewer interactions. In order to study neighborhood segregation and migration, we ask respondents whether they believe their neighbors are of the same religion as them. That is, we measure the respondent's perception of segregation or diversity.

Although we do not find that migrants perceive that they live in more segregated neighborhoods as compared to nonmigrants, we do find that their interactions with nonrelatives is a function of their perception of segregation in their neighborhoods. Specifically, as migrants perceive that their neighborhood is more diverse, that is, as fewer of their neighbors are of the same religion as them, there is a significant decrease in respondents saying that they interacted with a neighbor over a meal.

We further ask respondents whether any of the people they have invited or visited have been of a different religion. Specifically, we asked if Muslims ate at or invited Hindus and vice versa. Although we do not find a difference in interaction of this kind between migrants and nonmigrants, we do find a positive effect of perception of segregation. When respondents perceive that they live in a less segregated and diverse neighborhood, they are also significantly more likely to indicate that they have interacted with a neighbor of a different religion. The probability of cross-religious interaction increases in more diverse neighborhoods, although that does not imply increases in commensality.

One might expect that in a mega metropolis such as the NCR, migrants will come from different states and will have different religious and caste backgrounds. These varied backgrounds produce the very social heterogeneity that should result in attenuating—perhaps in the long run—strong local identities, at least of rural migrants. In the case of caste-based cleavages, when we examined whether respondents would invite an SC/ST person over for a meal, we did not find that being a migrant has an effect. Thus, the differential responses to this question do not depend on whether the respondent migrated to the NCR. This contrasts with the effect of wealth, where we see a positive relationship. Interestingly, although migration produces a negative effect on cross-religious interactions, wealth produces a positive effect. This raises the possibility of interaction effects between migration and assets leading to differential behaviors. We explore this question later in this chapter.

Intragroup Behavioral Effects: Gender

The principal attitudinal and behavioral change within households that might be affected by urbanization is that affecting women. To measure social changes within households, we look at responses to the question of whether men eat before women in the house. In rural India, patriarchal practices dictate customs within the family, including eating habits. When the women of a village sit down to eat, it is usually after the rest of the family has finished its meal, the men first, the children next, and themselves last. Although this has been a common practice in many rural households, our goal in the survey was to determine whether urbanization weakens this pattern. Figure 8.8 provides a preliminary breakdown of the responses to this question. Respondents predominantly answered "No" to this question, with about 37 percent of the sample saying that men ate before women in the home.

What factors might explain this result? We first examine the impact of assets on intra-household behavior. We run logit regressions with assets as a continuous independent variable and find that an increase in the level of assets does not have any relationship with the way in which this question was answered. Thus, it appears that gender-based cleavages, with regard specially to eating behaviors in the family, are not affected by wealth. This contrasts with the positive and significant effect that wealth had on intergroup attitudes. We next examine the relationship that migration has on intra-household behavior. As with wealth, we find that the effect of migration does not raise or lower

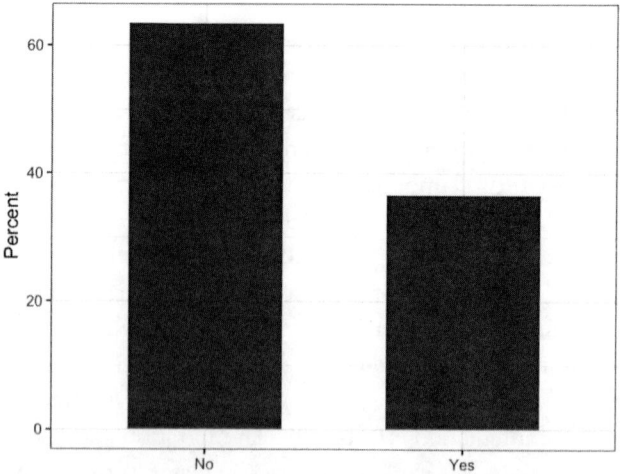

Figure 8.8   Responses to "Do men eat before women in your household?"
Source: Authors.

gender cleavages in the home. Specifically, when asked whether men eat before women in the family, responses did not differ based on whether respondents were migrants or not.

Thus, we do not see a main effect of either assets or migration on responses to whether men eat before women. However, it is plausible to believe that migration affects social change at different levels of assets. To test this relationship, we examine the marginal effect of migration on intra-household change, that is, the effect of being a migrant versus a nonmigrant at different levels of assets.

We run a logit model interacting both assets and migration, and find that when respondents have assets at level 0 (or average), being a migrant has a positive effect, that is, a higher likelihood of saying that men eat before women, again attesting to norm resilience among migrants. When the respondent is not a migrant, an increase in assets has a significantly negative effect, that is, a lower likelihood of saying that men eat before women. Figure 8.9 plots the interaction between assets and migration on the predicted probability of answering in the affirmative to the question of whether men eat before women. At higher levels of assets, migrant respondents are more likely to say that men eat before women. In other words, at higher assets, migration does not attenuate

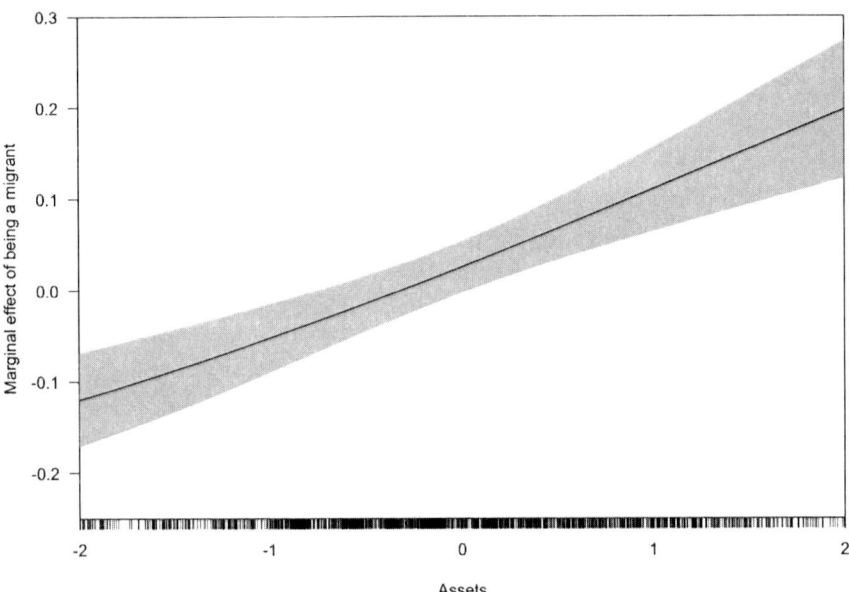

Figure 8.9   Marginal effect of being a migrant on gender attitudes—by assets
Source: Authors.

gender cleavages in the home. Conversely, at lower levels of assets, migrant respondents are less likely to say that men eat before women.

Split by gender of respondent, these findings provide interesting results. In migrant households, a significantly higher percentage of women (42 percent) say that men eat before women, whereas in nonmigrant households, somewhat fewer (36 percent) women say the same. The number of men saying that men eat before women is lower than that of women and the difference between migrant and nonmigrant households remains, though it is reversed in the case of men: 25 percent of migrant men say that men eat before women and 35 percent of nonmigrant men say the same.

Because our measure of intra-household change is based on gender differences, it is interesting to analyze how respondents of different genders answered this question. We find that as compared to men, women are more likely to say that men eat before women in their family. Our results show that 33 percent of men said that men eat before women as compared to 40 percent of women who said the same, highlighting differential baseline perceptions about household norms held by both genders.

Additionally, we examined generational effects on intra-household norms. For this, we divided our sample into respondents between ages 18 and 30, respondents between ages 30 and 60, and respondents above 60. We find, however, that age does not influence whether one is more' or less likely to respond in a certain way to the question of whether men eat before women. The idea that younger cohorts have more progressive gender norms, at least as per this limited question, does not seem to be evident.

Behavioral Changes: Political Attitudes and Behaviors

As discussed earlier, urbanization leads to the emergence of a middle class. Is this middle class likely to be more or less engaged in political activity? Drawing on the lower voter turnout in cities as compared with rural areas in the last two general elections in India, many scholars (like Ahuja and Chhibber) cite India's growing middle class in cities as the reason for lower electoral turnout.[19] This idea of "middle class apathy" was challenged by Kumar and Banerjee, who demonstrate based on the National Election Studies data from 2009 and 2014 that contrary to popular claims, there is a positive relationship between electoral participation and economic class.[20] They find that voter turnout in big cities among the middle class and richer sections is much higher than among lower income populations.

We test the relationship between wealth (as measured by our asset index) and political turnout in our sample. Although we do not have an objective indicator of what it means to be middle class, we can use the asset index as a proxy for respondent wealth. To approximate a middle class in our sample, we first drop the wealthiest 5 percent of our sample. Next, we drop the poorest 5 percent of the sample (this restricts the asset index from –1.5 to 1.5).

In Figure 8.10, we plot the reported turnout at the national level by assets. We find that the lowest 5 percent of the asset index report only a 78 percent turnout, as compared to 90 percent for the wealthiest of the sample (upper middle class) and 85 percent for the lower middle class that remains. Thus, voter turnout does increase as assets increase, corroborating Kumar and Banerjee that the economically poor classes vote in significantly lower numbers in urban cities. Middle class apathy compared to the poor is not in evidence in our findings.

Kapur, Sircar, and Vaishnav point toward education as being an important variable in one's self-conception of middle class.[21] In this regard, we check whether the education level of respondents can predict their turnout. We find, however, that education level is unrelated to self-reported turnout in our sample. In other words, people who have a college degree are just as likely

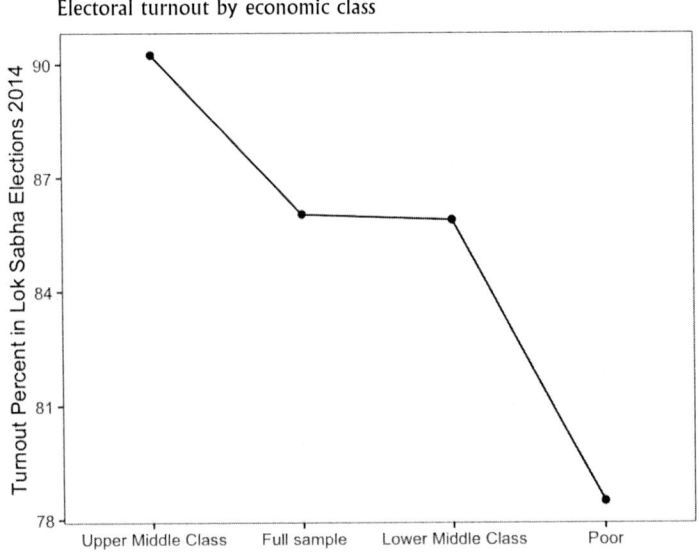

Figure 8.10   Self-reported voter turnout by assets
Source: Authors.

to vote as compared to uneducated people. Thus, education does not seem to affect propensity to vote, although wealth and assets have a significant effect.[22]

Although voter turnout is affected by assets, we do not find that other common predictors affect turnout. Particularly, religion and caste are unrelated to turnout level in our sample, as is education. However, one other variable that negatively affects turnout is migration. We find that migrants are significantly less likely to turn out to vote at all levels irrespective of their assets, which may be because they vote in their place of origin, rather than at the destination.

Apart from turnout, our survey asks respondents about other forms of political participation, such as taking part in an electoral rally or a protest or a door-to-door campaign. Again, we find a positive effect of assets in that greater wealth is associated with increases in participation in political activities such as protests, rallies, and door-to-door political campaigns.[23]

Conclusion

Indian society has been marked by intense social cleavages and deeply conservative attitudes with regards to caste, gender, and religion. These attitudes were rooted in an India that was largely rural. Is urbanization likely to change some of these attitudes? If so, which ones and at what pace?

The empirical evidence on social attitudes from the NCR survey offers some clues as to what we might expect. An important finding is that wealth has a significant and positive effect in increasing intergroup interactions, which might in the long run increase tolerance. Conversely, migration has a negative effect in forging intergroup relationships, both because migrants are less wealthy and cannot afford to invite other people over as well as the nature of their physical (neighborhood) settings which reduce the likelihood of cross-group social interactions. Our data indicates that the frequency of interaction with neighbors is highest when neighborhoods are less segregated. While this seems obvious, it highlights how the nature of urbanization, such as the evolution of neighborhoods, matters and the reality that the social norms that migrants bring with them are likely to attenuate only over generations.

However, wealth does not have a significant effect in leading to more positive intra-household social change on gender (at least on the dimension that we measure). Wealth also affects political participation, with turnout increasing with increasing assets. Lastly, with regard to caste, we find overlapping asset distributions for the four main caste groups, indicating that the possible emergence of new urban-based class interests, especially the emergence of a middle class among all caste groups. While there is still a concentration of upper-caste respondents in high-skilled jobs, here too we find an emerging occupational overlap across castes.

An important weakness in interpreting our findings is that we have no baseline to compare our results with, either within the NCR over time or with rural India. These findings indicate that while social change is taking place, the degree is not particularly striking. Given the tenacity of India's social institutions, this is not especially surprising. Nonetheless, it raises questions about the larger social implications of India's rapid growth and urbanization. While out-marriage has remained extremely stable at 5 percent over the half-century from 1950 to 2000 in rural India, it has increased over time in the urban data—at least in Mumbai for which comparable data is available over the same period. It was even lower than 5 percent, somewhere between 2 and 4 percent, prior to economic liberalization, but then increased steeply in the 1990s to 12 percent in the 1995–2000 period.[24] While Mumbai is hardly representative of urban India, it does point to what might occur if urbanization is yoked to economic dynamism.

Another limitation we face is that the very nature of urbanization makes it difficult to causally identify the impact of urban processes such as migration on outcomes. Even if exposure to more heterogeneous populations in urban areas might expose migrants to more intergroup social interactions, we cannot rule out that the migrants who choose to move to urban areas are self-selected, that is, they are relatively more open than their counterparts who choose to remain in rural settings.

In the stylized pathways of economic development, rapid economic growth leads to a structural transformation of the economy from agriculture to industry to services, with the latter two stages coinciding with increasing urbanization and a move from informal to formal employment. But India's "precocious developmental model" has defied these stylized facts.[25] India's annual growth of urban population was highest in the 1971–1981 decade (3.83 percent), albeit from a low base. It dropped to 3.09 percent in 1981–1991 and then further to 2.74 percent in the 1991–2001 decade, while marginally recovering to 2.76 percent in the most recent decade of 2001–2011. Since India grew most rapidly in this period, the weak correlation between India's economic growth and urbanization is puzzling.

Low rates of urban growth have coincided with low rural–urban migration, despite the less than happy story of India's farm sector. The census figures on migration suggest that the share of net rural–urban migration in urban population growth has been around 20–22 percent for the past three decades, again weakly correlated with growth. The low level of rural–urban migration differs markedly from the trends observed in China and other East Asian and Southeast Asian economies where rural–urban migration has played an important disruptive and transformative role in urbanization and economic growth. The link between the growth of manufacturing and urbanization, in turn driving rural–urban migration, has been one of the stylized facts of development. However, rural India now produces more from manufacturing than urban India.[26]

The causal arrow between economic growth and social change ran through urbanization, with the movement to industrial and formal sector employment playing a critical role. The weakness of both these processes means that other mechanisms—housing and neighborhoods, public spaces, consumption patterns, and political beliefs in urban India—are likely to play a greater role, but how exactly is not yet clear. But a more recent mechanism is likely to play a more positive role.

The exponential growth of new food-ordering technologies is inexorably weakening the strictures on food purity and pollution. For instance, by late 2019 Zomato was delivering 1.3 million orders a day from about 150,000 odd restaurants across India. It is estimated that within a decade, about 200 million people in India will be ordering food online, on average at least once a week. The millions of people in urban India ordering the food are favoring taste, convenience, and costs over who cooks the food and who delivers it. That will not necessarily make them more tolerant. But it will surely undermine one of the pillars of the caste order.

Notes

1. Karl Marx, "The British Rule in India", *New-York Daily Tribune*, June 25, 1853.
2. Elijah Anderson, *The Cosmopolitan Canopy: Race and Civility in Everyday Life* (New York: W. W. Norton & Company, 2011); Rakesh Mohan, *Work, Wages, and Welfare in a Developing, Metropolis: Consequences of Growth in Bogota, Colombia* (New York: Oxford University Press, 1987).
3. Ashutosh Varshney, *Ethnic Conflict and Civic Life: Hindus and Muslims in India* (Yale University Press, 2003).
4. Saumitra Jha, "Trade, Institutions, and Ethnic Tolerance: Evidence from South Asia," *American Political Science Review* 107, no. 4 (2013): 806–832.
5. Devesh Kapur, "The Middle Class in India: A Social Formation or Political Actor?" in *Political Power and Social Theory*, ed. Julian Go (Emerald Group

Publishing Limited, 2010), 143–169; Devesh Kapur, Neelanjan Sircar, and Milan Vaishnav, "The Importance of Being Middle Class in India," in *The New Middle Class in India and Brazil—Green Perspectives?* ed. Axel Harneit-Sievers and Dawid Danilo Bartelt (New Delhi: Academic Foundation, 2017).

6. Rameez Abbas, "Internal Migration and Citizenship in India," *Journal of Ethnic and Migration Studies* 42, no. 1 (2016): 150–168.

7. Duncan McDuie-Ra, *Northeast Migrants in Delhi: Race, Refuge and Retail* (Amsterdam: Amsterdam University Press, 2012).

8. Adam M. Auerbach, "Clients and Communities: The Political Economy of Party Network Organization and Development in India's Urban Slums," *World Politics* 68, no. 1 (2016): 111–148.

9. Lizabeth Cohen, "A Consumers' Republic: The Politics of Mass Consumption in Postwar America," *Journal of Consumer Research* 31, no. 1 (2004): 236–239.

10. Don Slater, *Consumer Culture and Modernity* (Cambridge, UK: Polity, 1997).

11. Melanie Khamis, Nishith Prakash, and Zahra Siddique, "Consumption and Social Identity: Evidence from India," *Journal of Economic Behavior and Organization* 83, no. 3 (2012): 353–371.

12. Punarjit Roychowdhury, "Visible Inequality, Status Competition, and Conspicuous Consumption: Evidence from Rural India," *Oxford Economic Papers* 69, no. 1 (2016): 36–54.

13. S. Kerner, C. Chou, and M. Warmind, "Methodological and Definitional Issues in the Archaeology of Food," *Commensality: From Everyday Food to Feast* (London and New York: Bloomsbury, 2015), 89–98.

14. Conlon's work of 1977 mentioned in V. Iversen and P. S. Raghavendra, "What the Signboard Hides: Food, Caste and Employability in Small South Indian Eating Places," *Contributions to Indian Sociology* 40, no. 3 (2006): 311–341.

15. A. Appadurai, "Gastro-politics in Hindu South Asia," *American Ethnologist* 8, no. 3 (1981): 494–511, esp. p. 497.

16. B. R. Ambedkar, *Annihilation of Caste* (Lahore: printed by the author, 1936).

17. Supriya Nair, quoted in Benjamin Parkin, "Boman Kohinoor, Mumbai Restaurateur, 1922–2019," *Financial Times*, October 10, 2019.

18. Logistic regression models help to determine the relationship between two or more variables by predicting the likelihood of the outcome of a dependent variable on the basis of one or more predictor variables. In this case, we present results that demonstrate the likelihood of eating or inviting a nonrelative for a meal on the basis of predictor variables such as assets.

19. Amit Ahuja and Pradeep Chhibber, "Why the Poor Vote in India: 'If I Don't Vote, I am Dead to the State'," *Studies in Comparative International Development* 47, no. 4 (2012): 389–410.

20. Sanjay Kumar and Souradeep Banerjee, "Low Levels of Electoral Participation in Metropolitan Cities," *Economic and Political Weekly* 52, no. 45 (2017): 82–86.

21. Kapur, Sircar, and Vaishnav, "The Importance of Being Middle Class in India."
22. It is important to note that the self-reported turnout in our sample is much higher than the actual average turnout levels in India. Although we suspect that the reporting of higher numbers is due to social desirability bias, our trends of decreasing participation by assets reinforce theoretical expectations on electoral turnout.
23. We additionally checked whether assets affected how people vote. We find a positive effect of assets on voting for the Bharatiya Janata Party (BJP), indicating that BJP affiliation increases with the wealthy portion of the sample. We further find that on controlling for assets and migration status, the level of education has a positive effect on BJP support. Specifically, those who reported that they have at least a bachelor's degree are more likely to support the BJP. Migrant status has no effect on vote choice, though the religion of the respondent affects political affiliation, with Muslim respondents indicating significantly less support for the BJP.
24. Kaivan Munshi, "Caste and the Indian Economy," *Journal of Economic Literature* 57, no. 4 (2019): 781–834.
25. Arvind Subramanian, "India's Economy a Precocious Growth Model," *BusinessLine*, April 10, 2015, available at https://www.thehindubusinessline. com/economy/policy/indias-economy-a-precocious-growth-model-arvind-subramanian/article22498153.ece, accessed on August 2, 2020.
26. The *Annual Survey of Industries* data reaffirm these trends, showing a decline in manufacturing employment from its urban share of 67.2 percent in 2001–2002 to 59.2 percent in 2014–2015 as plants in the formal sector are moving away from urban and into rural locations, while the informal sector is moving from rural to urban locations.

CHAPTER 9

Marriage
When, to Whom, and How People Get Married

Megan N. Reed

Marriage serves as the foundation for family life. This social institution can be found in all societies, though its character varies across cultures. An exploration of when, to whom, and how individuals marry can reveal important insights about how a society is structured. The age at which people marry and the method of selecting a partner may reflect gender and generational power dynamics in the family. Social rules about who one can marry are one way that groups construct social boundaries. These boundaries may be defined by religion, ethnicity, race, caste, linguistic group, social class, or some other characteristics. Marriage, therefore, plays an important role in reproducing patterns of social inequality and social distinction across generations. It is for these reasons that social scientists often study marriage and changes in marriage practices as a window through which to examine changing social structure and values.

In India, marriage is nearly universal. Only 1 percent of women and 2 percent of men will have never married by age 45–49.[1] Divorce and remarriage are also relatively rare, so, for most Indians, marriage only happens once in their lifetime. Weddings are often central to the plotline in Bollywood cinema and, in real life, they are the single most costly and important event in an average Indian's life.[2] However, there is reason to believe that marriage has been changing over the past few generations, especially in terms of when, to whom, and how Indians marry. India has undergone rapid economic and political change, an expansion of access to education and increased globalization. This has led to increased urbanization, the nuclearization of families, and changes in the nature of work, with more Indians employed in the non-farm sector.[3]

Despite these large social shifts, there remains a debate in the literature about whether Indian marriages are also changing.

Early theories of family change predicted a global convergence in family form across different societies. According to this perspective, as countries developed, urbanized, industrialized, and expanded education, their families and marriage behaviors would begin to look more like those in the West.[4] Families were expected to delay marriage and adopt self-choice in partner selection. Overall, researchers in this tradition emphasize the role of economic factors in shaping the family. They argue that many aspects of Indian marriage systems, such as arranged marriage and early age at marriage, are incompatible with the conditions of "modern" life in industrialized societies. Many researchers have anticipated a link between urbanization and marital change.[5] Other structural changes such as increased education, female labor force participation, and overall women's empowerment have been linked to changes in marriage behaviors in empirical studies.[6]

Another theoretical perspective emphasizes the global spread of ideas about the ideal family or marriage. Arland Thorton and others emphasize the ideational factors causing family change as normative beliefs about "the modern family" spread from the West to the developing world through schools, colonialism, travel, mass media, missionaries, international development aid, and other mechanisms.[7] These normative beliefs include the idea that marriages should be self-arranged and that intermarriage is good for society. There is some evidence that exposure to and endorsement of these ideas, often called "developmental idealism" by social scientists, is associated with changing marriage behaviors.[8] A related literature emphasizes the role of globalization and mass media leading to the spread of "Western" values such as individualism and companionate "love marriage."[9] This literature often focuses on the changing depictions of family, marriage, and love in Bollywood cinema as a sign of changing social norms.

It is likely that both structural and ideational factors are at play in changing the way Indians think about marriage. However, it remains unclear just how important any of these factors are in changing marriage patterns because there is insufficient evidence that marriage patterns are, indeed, changing in India. This chapter will describe new findings on marriage patterns from the Center for the Advanced Study of India–National Capital Region (CASI–NCR) Survey conducted in 2015–2016 and contextualize these findings with other data sources. Respondents were asked to not only report details about their own marriage but also to recall details about their parents' marriage and their expectation for the marriages of the next generation in their family. This retrospective and prospective data provides a unique opportunity to examine intergenerational change and continuity in marriage practices within the same family using a cross-sectional data set. The CASI–NCR Survey, drawn from a random sample of voters, is representative of the National Capital Territory (NCT) of Delhi and the adjacent districts of Haryana, Uttar Pradesh, and Rajasthan which form the NCR.

This chapter will show that many marriage practices in the Delhi NCR are, in fact, changing. These changes include an increasing age at marriage and expanded involvement of individuals in their own partner selection, though not necessarily self-arranged or "love marriages." Rather, most of the increased involvement is through, what is sometimes called "joint-arranged" marriages, where young people play a role in selecting their marriage partner within the structure of the arranged marriage system. Other aspects of marriage, on the other hand, are more resistant to change such as attitudes toward intermarriage. The chapter begins with a discussion of changing patterns of when residents of the NCR marry. The second section addresses the question of who one can marry. It documents attitudes toward and incidences of intermarriage by caste, religion, language, and social class. The final section answers how people get married. This section documents marital arrangement patterns, from arranged to "love marriage," across three generations.

When to Get Married?

National survey data has documented a pattern of rising age at marriage for both men and women in India. The mean age at first marriage is 19 for women and 24.5 for men who were aged 25–49 when surveyed in 2015–2016.[10] This is an increase from a decade ago when the mean age at marriage was 17.2 and 22.6 for women and men, respectively. There are many possible explanations for these changes. Delays may occur while children are completing higher levels of education than in the past or because it takes parents longer to save money for the dowry or wedding expenses, which have been increasing.[11] The mean age at marriage is significantly higher in urban areas. Urban women married nearly two years later than rural women, though this gap has been decreasing over time.[12]

Another significant factor is the decline in child marriage. Marriage before the legal age remains common in some areas of the country and within some communities but is rapidly losing social acceptability. The passage of the

Prohibition of Child Marriage Act 2006 signaled a move toward enhanced punishment of those who facilitate marriages below the legal age (18 for women and 21 for men). In 2015–2016, 29 percent of women and 20 percent of men aged 20–24 married before the legal age.[13] In the older cohort of individuals aged 45–49, the early marriage rate was much higher at 46 percent for women and 29 percent for men.

The CASI–NCR Survey provides a unique opportunity to explore patterns of age at marriage across marriage cohorts and generations in the Delhi region. Respondents were asked not only about their own age at marriage but also about the marriage ages of their parents. They were also asked about the expected age at marriage for boys and girls in their household today.

About a fifth of the respondents, voters randomly drawn from the voting lists, were unmarried at the time of the survey. Of those who were married, the average male respondent reported marrying at 23.6 while the average female respondent reported marrying at 21. The percentage of male and female respondents who married before their respective legal marriage ages were 21.7 and 13.8, respectively. For women married in the 1980s, the mean age at marriage was 20.8 and 30.3 percent of women were married before 18. For the female respondents most recently married in the 2010s (up to 2016 when the survey was completed), the mean age at marriage had increased to 22.6 with only 1.6 percent of women reporting that they had married before 18.

The survey also collected data about the age at which the respondent's parents married. The mean age at marriage for the fathers and mothers of respondents was 22.8 and 20.1, respectively. Only 25.2 percent of respondents reported that their mothers married before the legal age and 35.3 percent reported that their fathers married before the legal age. The question asked when the respondents' parents married was not necessarily their parents' age at first marriage. While remarriage is not especially common in India, it could be partly to blame for the high mean ages reported by respondents. Unfortunately, there was also a high rate of nonresponse to this question. Close to half (44.6 percent) of the respondents said that they did not know their parents' age at marriage. A further 10.6 percent refused to give an answer. Given the growing taboo around child marriage, it is probable that many who did not report their parents' marriage ages were unwilling to admit that their parents had a child marriage.

Respondents were also asked about their expectations for the next generation. The mean expected age at marriage for boys in the household was 24.6, with 3.4 percent of households expecting a marriage before the legal age. The mean age for girls in the household was 22, with only 0.5 percent of households expecting a marriage before the legal age. Very early marriage appears to have fallen out of fashion as child marriage becomes increasingly criminalized by the Indian state.

Respondents from wealthier households report a slightly higher expected marriage age. For example, the poorest quintile of respondents expected girls to marry, on average, at 21.5, whereas the wealthiest expected their girls to marry at 22.9. A higher level of education was also associated with higher expected age at marriage for girls. Those with a bachelor's degree or higher, on average, expected girls to marry at age 22.4. Respondents in Delhi NCT had a higher expected age at marriage than those living in other parts of the NCR, but this difference could be explained entirely by the wealth differences. Migrants to the NCR region from other parts of India reported a slightly lower expected age at marriage for women but again, this difference could be explained entirely by wealth and education. Overall, there is much less variation in expected age at marriage than there was for observed age of marriage of respondents. Half of respondents expect girls to marry between ages 21 and 23 and boys to marry between ages 23 and 25. This suggests that there has been significant convergence in society around when is the "right" time to marry.

Who to Marry?

In *Annihilation of Caste*, B. R. Ambedkar wrote:

> Fusion of blood can alone create the feeling of being kith and kin, and unless this feeling of kinship, of being kindred, becomes paramount, the separatist feeling—the feeling of being aliens—created by Caste will not vanish. Where society is already well-knit by other ties, marriage is an ordinary incident of life. But where society is cut asunder, marriage as a binding force becomes a matter of urgent necessity. The real remedy for breaking Caste is inter-marriage.[14]

Over 80 years after Ambedkar wrote these famous words, his dream of caste integration through marriage remains unrealized. Caste endogamy, the practice of marrying within one's caste, remains pervasive. National estimates of the rate of intercaste marriage range from around 5 to 11 percent.[15] Religious endogamy rates are estimated to be even higher with very few marriages crossing the Hindu-Muslim boundary. A related concept is homogamy, the term used to describe when people marry others of similar status to themselves. Across all societies, marriages tend to be homogamous as individuals usually marry someone of similar social class, education, age, and other status characteristics.

Sociologists have long recognized that marriage patterns can illuminate boundaries of social groups. It is through excluding certain types of individuals from their potential marriage pool that a group defines its boundaries. In this sense, marriage patterns reflect a set of preferences for in-group members, whether the group is defined by caste, language, social class, or some other characteristics. These patterns of excluding dissimilar individuals lead to sharp boundaries between social groups and results in a phenomenon which sociologists call "social closure." Crossing these social barriers may have serious and even deadly consequences as the case of honor killings reveal. The recent "Love Jihad campaign" is built on social anxieties about the possibility of marriage boundaries eroding. However, for most, marrying within one's social group is relatively easy because people generally prefer associating with people like themselves. Furthermore, in India, caste endogamy fosters caste-based social networks which remain important in schooling and career outcomes.[16]

Some have argued that the increasing diversity of India's urban centers generates more opportunities for marriages which cross group barriers. Ambedkar argued that cities were better for Dalits (those formerly known as Untouchables) because it was in the metropolis that they could escape the localism of caste in exchange for the anonymity of urban life. Recent research suggests that the decoupling of caste from socioeconomic status has led to a rise in the importance of class in defining the marriage pool in India and possibly a decrease in the centrality of caste.[17] The expansion of access to the internet brought the rise of online matrimonial sites, especially in urban areas, which allow individuals to extend their marriage partner search beyond their local social network. These trends would suggest that the opportunity for intermarriage might be increasing in urban India. Whether preferences are changing, however, remains to be seen.

So far, empirical investigations have failed to identify any evidence that intermarriage is more common in urban areas. Allendorf and Pandian found that intercaste marriage was no more prevalent in urban areas than in rural areas.[18] They also document that most self-arranged marriages were endogamous, revealing that caste-based preferences dominate even outside of arranged marriage. Using data from three online matrimonial sites in India, Ahuja and Ostermann tested their participants' willingness to consider a potential groom from a different caste.[19] They found that 70.7 percent of Scheduled Caste (Dalit) and 53.9 percent of upper-caste (groups which historically benefitted from high ritual status) women were willing to consider a groom profile from another caste. Importantly, individuals were willing to consider an intercaste marriage only if it was consistent with upward social mobility (in terms of class), though study participants remained unwilling to consider the request of Dalit grooms.[20] Ahuja and Ostermann's research suggests that the role of social class in marriage partner selection may be growing in importance. It also suggests that willingness to consider a non-endogamous spouse may be much larger than the actual patterns of intermarriage reveal.

Attitudes toward Intermarriage

The CASI–NCR Survey is the first to collect data on attitudes toward caste-, religion-, language-, and class-based intermarriage. In keeping with the emphasis on intergenerational change, the survey collected this data for two different generations in the household. First, respondents were asked if, during the time of their own marriage, it was acceptable in their family for a girl to marry a man from a different religion, *jati* (caste), language, or from a poorer family. Then, they were asked if, in their opinion, it would be acceptable for a girl from their household today to marry outside of their religion, caste, language, or into a poorer family. The questions were worded in a way to capture what people perceived to be acceptable to their family, not necessarily their own personal beliefs toward intermarriage. The survey also collected data on incidences of intermarriage in the households surveyed in two ways: first, by asking respondents to report whether any immediate family members had an intermarriage and second, by collecting data on the caste and religion of the heads of households and their spouses. This data provides the most extensive picture yet of intermarriage in the Delhi NCR.

Support for all kinds of intermarriage was extremely low in both generations of the households surveyed. However, support for intermarriage was statistically higher for the youngest generation for all forms of intermarriage, as shown in Figure 9.1. It is important to remember that the acceptability rates are not the personal attitudes of individual respondents but the perceived social acceptability, which might explain why the rates are so low. The vast majority of respondents felt that intermarriage would not be accepted in their family, revealing the strength of social barriers to integration, even in urban India.

Examination of the data reveals some heterogeneity by the type of intermarriage and respondent characteristics. The data suggests that support for intercaste and interlinguistic marriages may be growing at a slightly faster rate than for marriages which cross religion or class borders. Interreligious marriage appears to be the least acceptable. Hindus and Muslims report similar

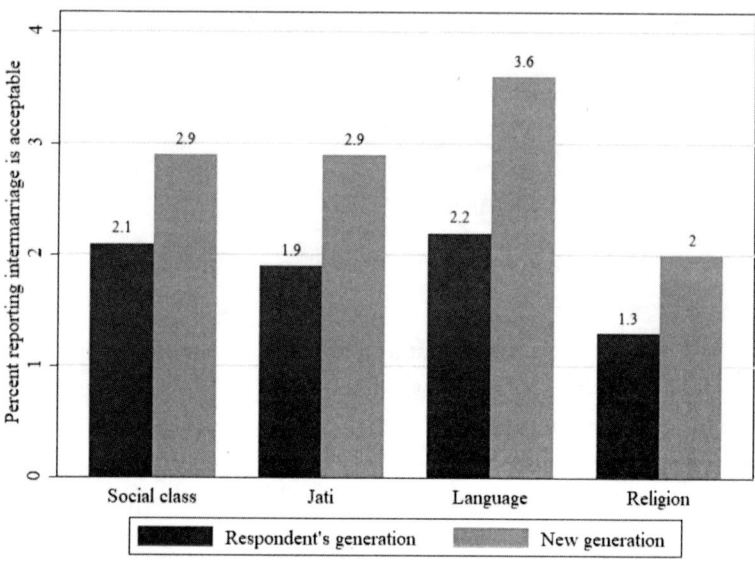

Figure 9.1   Percentage of respondents reporting that intermarriage is/was acceptable by type and in which generation
Source: Author.

rates of acceptability for all types of intermarriage. Sikhs, on the other hand, are significantly more likely to report that all forms of intermarriage would be acceptable in their family. The Sikh community is a true outlier in their attitudes toward integration with other groups. Among Sikhs, 6.3 percent reported that interreligious marriage would be acceptable for girls from their household, and 11.5 percent reported that intercaste marriage would be acceptable. Dalits were also slightly more likely to report that intermarriage is acceptable in their family. Their willingness to marry outside of the community extends beyond caste barriers to other forms of intermarriage, such as religion and class. Wealth appeared to play a role in how families think about intermarriage. As Figure 9.2 shows, the acceptability of intermarriages of all kinds increases with wealth, as measured in assets ownership. Figure 9.2 also reveals differences in the patterns across different types of intermarriage. Social acceptability for interreligious marriage remains low regardless of wealth. On the other hand, approval of interlinguistic and intercaste marriages increases dramatically with wealth.

However, the single most important factor explaining the acceptability of intermarriage was geographic location. Outside of the Delhi NCT, acceptability of intermarriage of all forms was nearly nonexistent. Interestingly, migrants

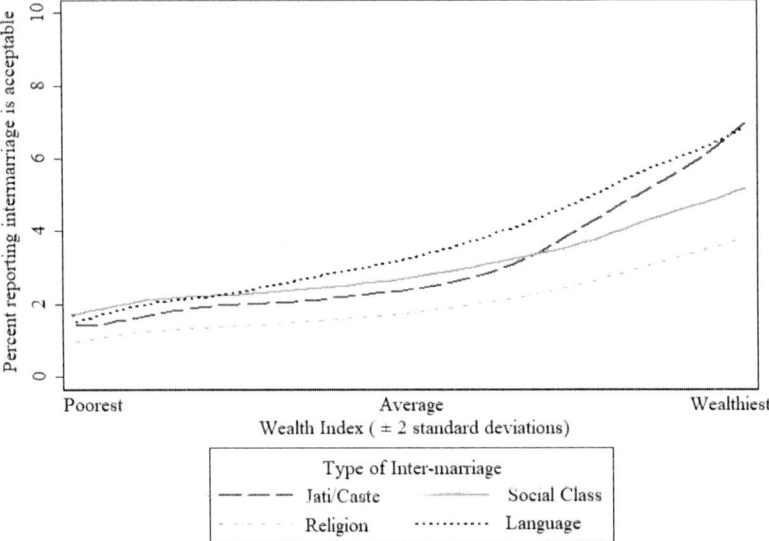

Figure 9.2   Percentage of respondents reporting that intermarriage is acceptable by type and household wealth
Source: Author.

and rural-born respondents were not necessarily less likely to report that intermarriage was acceptable.

Intermarriage of any kind remains highly taboo in the NCR. Almost no households reported that it would be acceptable if a girl wanted to marry outside of her religion, caste, social class, or language group. Data from respondents revealed that it was only in small pockets in the urban core in the NCT where intermarriage would not be met with disapproval, particularly in the wealthiest and Sikh neighborhoods.

Incidences of Intermarriage

Given the taboo on intermarriage reported by respondents, it is not surprising that few reported instances of intermarriage in their family. Less than 1 percent of respondents reported that anyone in their immediate family (parents, siblings, or children) had an intermarriage of any kind. It is likely that there was a high response bias on this question. Respondents may withhold information about a family member's intermarriage because of the stigma associated with breaching group boundaries.

Data was also collected about the respondent and their spouse to identify interreligious and intercaste marriages. Only 28 (0.5 percent) households were headed by a couple in an interreligious marriage. Half of those households were Hindu–Sikh interreligious marriages. However, it should be noted that some interreligious marriages might be accompanied by a religious conversion of one of the spouses.

The caste data on the head of household and spouse revealed 209 (4.4 percent) intercaste marriages, defined as crossing the four broad categories of upper caste, intermediate caste, Dalit, and Adivasi. Intermediate castes are defined as those whose status falls between the privileged upper-caste category and those in marginalized Dalit or Adivasi (indigenous or tribal) groups. Most of those in the intermediate castes are designated Other Backward Classes (OBCs) by the Government of India because of their educational and social underdevelopment. There are likely more intercaste marriages if caste was compared at the individual *jati*-level, rather than across the broad categories. It is important to note that around 13 percent of respondents did not give information about their caste. The most common caste mix reported in a marriage was between intermediate castes and upper castes, but this is to be expected since the intermediate castes are numerically dominant. In upper caste and intermediate caste marriages, it was much more common for the husband to be upper caste. This could occur because women face stronger barriers to marrying "lower" than men. Dalits and Adivasis were the most likely to be in an intercaste marriage and intermediate castes were the least likely. Among Dalit men, 6.9 percent who were the head of the household were in an intercaste marriage compared to 2.6 percent of intermediate-caste men. Households headed by an intercaste couple were slightly wealthier, matching with observations above that intermarriage is slightly more likely to be acceptable in wealthier households.

Intermarriage is often viewed as a marker of social inclusiveness.[21] It is this type of social inclusiveness that Ambedkar sought when he called for intermarriage to promote "the feeling of being kith and kin." However, data from the Delhi NCR reveals that strong barriers remain to intermarriage by caste, religion, class, and language. Support for intermarriage, particularly by caste and language, has been increasing slightly over the past two generations, yet rates of intermarriage remain low. Support for intermarriage is highest in the wealthiest communities of the NCT. It is possible that the spread of economic development and urbanization may weaken taboos against intermarriage, especially if fewer people define themselves primarily through their ascribed identities of caste, ethnicity/language, and religion. However, such changes, were they to occur, could include a corresponding increase in the importance of social class in sorting on the marriage market as wealth and education become the key factors in defining social position.

How to Find a Spouse?

Parent-arranged marriages have historically been the most common form of partner selection in India. Arranged marriage is built into the kinship structure of India where the joint family system gives significant authority to family elders.[22] It was also the dominant form of marriage in many other Asian countries as well, but sharp declines in the prevalence of arranged marriages have been documented in China, Indonesia, Japan, Malaysia, Sri Lanka, Kyrgyzstan, Nepal, Taiwan, and Togo.[23] India has been slower to show patterns of arranged marriage decline.

There is significant debate about why arranged marriage might decline. Some argue that the practice is incompatible with the conditions of modern life in industrialized societies.[24] This may be due to the emphasis on individualism, the impracticality of large joint family living, or the breakdown of the traditional age hierarchy in "modern" societies. As skill and education become increasingly important markers of status, age-based power hierarchies, which are essential to the arranged marriage system, may be challenged. Increased time spent in school, employment away from the home, and residence in large urban areas increase the contact that young people have with nonrelatives, which has been shown to have an association with the adoption of self-choice marriages.[25]

With the growing importance of individualism comes a greater valuation of love and choice in marriage. Depictions of love and "love marriages" are common in popular mass media, especially Bollywood cinema and music. This, some have speculated, may inevitably lead to an erosion of traditional arranged marriage.[26] Some scholars emphasize the role of globalization and the spread of ideas or beliefs about what constitutes "the modern family" as a major factor in marriage change.[27] In the Darjeeling Hills, a region where elopements have become quite common, interview respondents reported that love marriages were "inherently good" and more likely to be successful, in their opinion.[28] Increased education, technological change, and "foreign influence" were reasons given by respondents in the Darjeeling Hills for the move away from arranged marriage.[29]

Using data from the India Human Development Surveys (IHDS), Allendorf and Pandian published an overview of recent trends and patterns in arranged marriage in India. They conclude that "the practice of arranged marriage is shifting rather than declining.... Rather than displacing their parents in the decision process, young women joined their parents in choosing husbands."[30] Self-choice marriages comprised less than 10 percent of all marriages in India during the 2000s, though this is a small increase from previous marriage cohorts. The scholars document the rise of the "joint-arranged" marriage, where children are consulted by their parents in arranging the marriage. By the 2000s, joint selection was the dominant marriage form in India, comprising two-thirds of all marriages.[31] Parent-arranged marriages were least common in urban areas, especially in the six largest metro regions. In metro regions, the proportion of joint-arranged marriages increased across marriage cohorts; however, self-arranged marriages were no more common in urban areas than in villages.[32]

Patterns across Generations in the National Capital Region

The CASI–NCR Survey collected data on marital arrangement type across three generations in each household surveyed. Respondents were asked who arranged their parents' marriage, their own marriage, and who they expect will arrange the marriage of boys and girls in their household today. The survey also collected data on the use of matrimonial websites and attitudes toward *roka* (engagement) rituals. This data gives a unique picture of how and why marriage practices change between generations of the same family. The data distinguished between different types of "joint-arranged" marriages, giving us more granularity than the IHDS data permits. Respondents could distinguish between (*a*) parents selecting a spouse and seeking the approval of the choice from the child and (*b*) children selecting their partner and then seeking the approval of their parents for the match.

The majority of married respondents were not involved in the selection of their marriage partner. As shown in Figure 9.3, 82.3 percent of respondents had parent-arranged marriages and 16.8 percent were consulted for their approval of the parents' selection. Only 0.8 percent of respondents said that they were the sole or primary decision-maker of who they would marry. Comparing respondents from different marriage cohorts reveals that change has been very gradual over time in the NCR. Of the respondents who were married in the 1980s, 87.8 percent of them had parent-arranged marriages. By the most recent

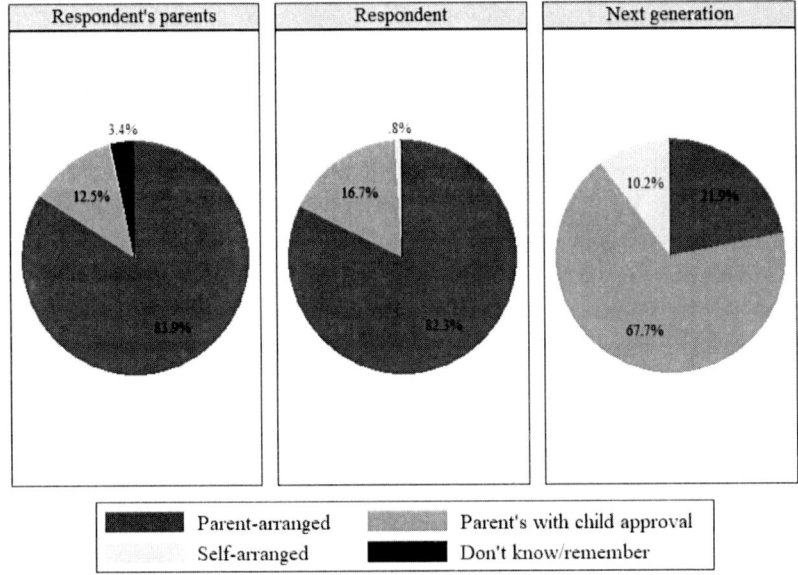

Figure 9.3   Changes in spousal choice across three generations
Source: Author.

marriage cohort in the 2010s (up to 2016), the percentage of respondents who had parent-arranged marriages had reduced to 75.8 percent. Comparing the NCR data with the national trends analyzed by Allendorf and Pandian shows the rate of change has been much slower in the NCR region compared to the nation as a whole. Further, the relative share of marriages which are arranged only by parents is much higher in the NCR region than the national average across all marriage cohorts.

The patterns for respondents' parents generally follow that of the respondents, as shown in Figure 9.3. A small number (3.4 percent) of respondents reported that they did not know or remember how their parents' marriage was arranged. The similarity in the overall patterns of marriage between the two generations hides important intergenerational changes. Only 7.3 percent of respondents reported that they had more involvement in selecting their partner compared to their parents' marriage, whereas 6.6 percent reported a decrease in control relative to their parents' generation. The rest of the respondents had the same type of marriage arrangement as their parents. The patterns reveal changes occurring in both directions but a high level of persistence in traditions across generations.

The largest changes occurred in respondents' reported expectation for who would arrange marriages today. They were asked their expectations for boys and girls separately, and there was a statistical difference in how respondents answered, granting slightly more decision-making power to boys than girls. The modal response was that young people today would have joint parent-arranged marriage where their parents select the partner but seek their child's approval before the match is fixed. Joint-arranged marriage was endorsed by 66.7 percent of respondents for girls and 67.7 percent of respondents when describing their expectations for boys.

About 10 percent of respondents expected their young family members to be the sole or primary decision-maker for their own spouse. This category was a combination of several different options in the survey. The majority of the 10 percent who endorsed self-arranged marriage selected the option "child chooses as long as the family approves." This response could also be considered a form of joint-arranged marriage, but here it is considered as "self-arranged" because the spousal search is explicitly led by the child rather than the parent. Less than 0.5 percent endorse the option of "love marriage" demonstrating that the term still carries a strong taboo. A small number of respondents selected the option "the family would look only if the child could not find a partner on their own."

Most respondents (62 percent) expect that young people today will have greater say in their spouse selection than previous generations. However, 20.9 percent of respondents reported that they do not expect a move away from the kind of parent-arranged marriages that they had. The dramatic change across generations should be taken with a few notes of caution. Respondents' report of expectation may not necessarily reflect how marriages will actually take place. Recalling that over 75 percent of respondents who were married in the six years prior to the survey report had parent-arranged marriages, it is possible that some respondents may exaggerate their expectation of social change between generations due to a social desirability bias which leads them to think that joint- or self-arranged marriages are a more "correct" answer.

As documented in the national trends, joint-arranged marriages have become the dominant form of marriage arrangement with strictly parent-arranged marriages slowly falling out of fashion. However, the survey data separates joint-arranged marriages which are led by parents from those which are led by the children themselves, unlike the IHDS, thus revealing that most joint-arranged marriages are led by the parents. In these joint-arranged marriages, children are allowed to veto choices made by the parents. A much smaller proportion of marriages follow the opposite pattern, with children selecting a partner and seeking the approval of parents. Almost no respondents endorsed a system where parents played no role in selecting a spouse. This data confirms that arranged marriage is far from retreating in Indian society. Rather, it is taking new forms which allow for greater involvement of individuals in their own partner selection while still giving parents a significant role.

Predictors of Joint– and Self–Arranged Marriages

Figure 9.4 displays the relationship between wealth, measured in assets ownership, and reported expectation of marital arrangement type for girls. Middle-class (defined by wealth) respondents were the most likely to expect a parent-only arranged marriage. Expectation of joint-arranged marriages increased both as wealth increased and as it decreased. Interestingly, expectation of self-arranged marriages was relatively flat across the wealth spectrum with a small bump among poorer (but not the poorest) households. Though wealthier individuals were less likely to expect parent-arranged marriages in their household, they were not necessarily more likely to expect self-arranged marriages. In fact, in regression analysis controlling for other characteristics, wealth was associated with a decreased likelihood of expecting self-arranged

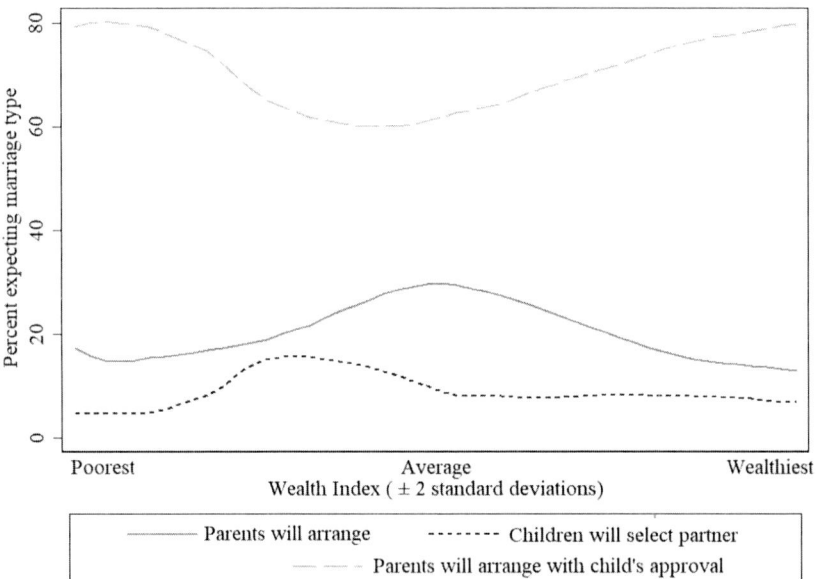

Figure 9.4   Expected marital arrangement type for girls by wealth
Source: Author.

marriage. Examination of the relationship between the respondent's marriage and wealth revealed that higher wealth predicted parent-only arranged marriage.

Respondents with at least higher secondary-level education were more likely to expect girls in their family to have a self-arranged marriage. This supports the developmental idealism hypothesis, which argues that exposure to educational settings may increase the likelihood of valuing Western-style family norms. Overall, however, education, while important, did not appear to be the central factor in explaining the trends in marital arrangement.

Like wealth, region of residence in the NCR was a significant factor explaining marital arrangement type. The modal expectation for Delhi NCT residents was joint-arranged marriage led by the parent. In fact, the NCT residents were less likely to expect both a parent-only arranged marriage and a self-arranged marriage. About one-tenth (10.6 percent) of respondents who lived outside of the NCT said that they expected girls in their family to have a self-arranged marriage compared to only 9.7 percent of residents of the NCT. Surveyed residents of the NCR region of Haryana had the most liberal expectations for girl's marriage with 14.2 percent of them expecting girls to have a self-arranged marriage.

Migrant status or rural origins explain some of the patterns of expectation. Respondents who were born in rural areas were slightly less likely to expect girls in their family to have a self-arranged marriage. Older migrants from earlier marriage cohorts have a higher likelihood of reporting that they had a parent-arranged marriage than nonmigrants. However, in the more recent marriage cohorts, there is convergence between migrants and nonmigrants. No difference between migrants and nonmigrants in marital arrangement was found in the most recent marriage cohorts. This could be because the sociodemographic characteristics of migrants have changed over time, with migrants looking more like the existing population of the NCR than in the past.

Figure 9.5 displays the relationship between attitudes toward intermarriage and expected marriage type for girls. Overall, families which expected children to be involved in spousal choice were slightly more open to intermarriage of all forms; however, the rates of acceptability remain low. There was little difference in acceptability of intermarriage between the joint-arranged and self-arranged marriages. Individuals who themselves had an intercaste marriage were no more likely to report that intermarriage would be acceptable for young people today in their family than those who did not have an intercaste marriage.

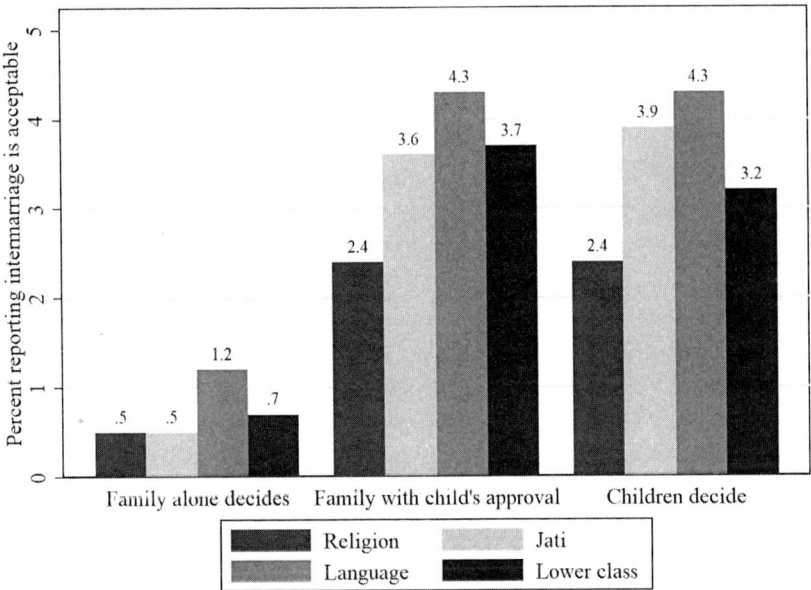

Figure 9.5   Percentage who say intermarriage is acceptable by type of intermarriage and expected marriage type for girls in the family

Source: Author.

Roka *Ceremonies*

Roka is a term used for a ceremony, often weeks or months before the marriage, where the families officially announce they have finalized the match for their son and daughter. The ceremonies are sometimes elaborate and involve an exchange of gifts between the families. These types of ceremonies, which are a form of engagement or *sagai*, have been growing in popularity in north India. Respondents to the CASI–NCR Survey were asked about *roka* because this practice has received limited attention in the literature and there is anecdotal evidence that *roka*s open a period of courtship for the couple as they get to know each other before their marriage. In that sense, *roka*s may contribute to Indian marriages beginning to look more like marriages in the West where the marriage is preceded by a trial period of dating for the couple.

Respondents were asked if they thought *roka* was a desirable practice. Almost two-thirds (65.4 percent) of respondents found it desirable, whereas 23.1 percent did not. A further 11.5 percent of respondents either did not know about the practice of *roka* or did not know how they felt about it. Those who liked the idea of *roka* reported that the *roka* should occur, on average, 6.5 weeks before the wedding.

Popularity of *roka* was similar across families of different wealth or education levels, but the practice was significantly more favored in the Delhi NCT compared to other areas in the region. *Roka* appeared to be more popular in communities where children are involved in selecting their own spouse. A very large share (87.7 percent) of those who expected self-arranged marital arrangement thought that *roka* was a desirable practice compared to 75.4 percent of those who expected a joint-arranged marriage and 25.1 percent who expected a parent-arranged marriage. A larger proportion of those who anticipated parent-arranged marriages reported that they did not know about or have an opinion about the practice of *roka*.

There was evidence that families are using *roka* to test out the marriage. Almost half (48.5 percent) of respondents reported that it was desirable to break the *roka* if it became clear that the marriage would be unhappy. A quarter (25.2 percent) of respondents said that they did not know or have an opinion about breaking a *roka*. However, *roka* was viewed differently by families depending upon the type of marital arrangement expected in their household. Those who anticipated self-arranged marriage in their family were significantly less likely to say that breaking *roka* was desirable even if it meant avoiding an unhappy marriage compared to those who anticipated parent-led marital arrangements. This suggests that self-arranged engagements may be more difficult to break, perhaps because the betrothed presumably already know each other well and are expected to have already decided that the match is favorable. Interestingly, wealth was significantly associated with attitudes toward breaking a *roka*, especially for those who anticipated self-arranged marriage. The wealthier the individual, as measured in assets ownership, the more likely they were to say that breaking a *roka* was a desirable outcome if it meant avoiding an unhappy marriage. This may be because of more permissive attitudes among the wealthy or because wealthy individuals are more cautious about entering marriage due to concerns about legal trouble related to combining economic assets or inheritance.

Matrimonial Websites

Online matrimonial websites have changed the way that individuals search for spouses. These websites allow individuals to broaden their search outside of their personal networks. Only 5.5 percent of respondents to the CASI–

NCR Survey reported that some online matrimonial sites had been used in their partner search. When asked about whether they expected it to be used by family members in the future, only 4.3 percent said yes but 11.8 percent reported that they were not sure if it would be used or not. Other research has found that, despite the use of online resources, many individuals end up finding a partner through their social network and not online.[33] It remains unclear how influential these resources become in the future marriage markets; however, the evidence from the CASI–NCR Survey suggests that they play only a marginal role.

Conclusion

This chapter answered important questions of when, to whom, and how individuals get married in the NCR. Factors such as wealth and specific location within the NCR were found to be especially important in explaining patterns of marriage. Overall, the data points to a rising age at marriage and modification of the practice of arranged marriage to incorporate the views of young people into marriage decision-making. However, these changes are happening alongside the continued importance of caste, religion, linguistic group, and social class in defining the pool of acceptable marriage partners.

The data revealed an increasing mean age at marriage across marriage cohorts and strong consensus on when children these days "should" get married. Much of the change was driven by the growing taboo against child marriages. Residing in the NCT, wealth, and education were associated with higher ages at marriage.

Very few respondents reported that intermarriage, whether by caste, religion, language, or class, would be accepted in their family. However, there was a small increase between the respondents' generation and their reported expectation of the acceptability of intermarriage for the next generation. The most important factor in predicting if a respondent would report that intermarriage was acceptable in their family was whether the household resided in the heart of the NCR—in the city of Delhi itself. In fact, it was only in the Delhi NCT that some respondents reported that intermarriage was acceptable. Wealth was also an important predictor of acceptability of intermarriage. Wealthier individuals were especially more accepting of intercaste and interlinguistic marriages.

Two-thirds of respondents anticipate the next generation of their family to play a larger role in selecting their spouse. While few respondents reported an expectation for "love marriages," a growing number expected boys and girls today to play a role in their partner selection. This involvement ranged from allowing children to veto partner options identified by parents to letting children select their own spouse with parental approval. Again, wealth and region of residence emerged as important factors explaining the trends, but the wealthiest and the NCT residents were not the most open to self-arranged marriage. Instead, wealthier households and those that resided in the NCT were more likely to endorse the joint-arranged marriage system. Middle-class households (as defined by asset ownership) were the most likely to endorse parent-only arranged marriages. Few families in the NCR accept the idea of self-arranged marriage, though the practice was slightly more common among the more educated and those residing in the Haryana side of the NCR.

Comparison of the CASI–NCR Survey to national trends reveals that the capital city has been much slower to change its marriage norms. The NCR region remains more "conservative" in dimensions such as arranged marriage than other large metros. However, within the NCR region, residence in the NCT was associated with higher ages at marriage, more acceptability of intermarriage, and less endorsement of parent-arranged marriage. Some, but not all, of these regional patterns could be explained by the higher levels of wealth and education in the capital suggesting that the urban environment does matter. Interestingly, migrant status and rural origins did not emerge as primary predictors of marriage behaviors. This suggests that migrants to the NCR are either selected to be more like native Delhiites or that they adapt their marriage behaviors to match the norms in the city.

Families in the NCR have incorporated changes to their marriage behaviors such as delaying marriage and allowing children to help select their partner, while, at the same time, resisting inclusiveness in partner options. These changes are more than just demographic trends; they reflect changes in the way that families think about marriage. Residents of the NCR region are delaying marriage until both partners have completed some education and reached adulthood. When it is finally time for marriage, parents are letting their children take part in the marriage arrangement process. This suggests that families increasingly value love and personal compatibility between spouses. It also reveals a shift toward increased autonomy for young people, especially in terms of key life decisions like marriage. Overall, time will tell if the new marriage patterns which emerge will look like those in Western industrialized countries or if they take on their own, uniquely Indian, identity.

Notes

1. International Institute for Population Sciences (IIPS) and ICF, *National Family Health Survey (NFHS-4), 2015–16: India* (Mumbai: IIPS, Ministry fo Health and Family Welfare, December 2017), available at https://dhsprogram.com/pubs/pdf/FR339/FR339.pdf, accessed on October 5, 2020.
2. Francis Bloch, Vijayendra Rao, and Sonalde Desai, "Wedding Celebrations as Conspicuous Consumption: Signaling Social Status in Rural India," *Journal of Human Resources* 39, no. 3 (2004): 675.
3. Saritha Nair Niranjan and T. K. Roy, "A Socio-demographic Analysis of the Size and Structure of the Family in India," *Journal of Comparative Family Studies* 36, no. 4 (2005): 623–651; Shirish Sankhe et al., "India's Urban Awakening: Building Inclusive Cities, Sustaining Economic Growth," McKinsey & Company, 2010.
4. William J. Goode, *The Family*, second edn (Englewood Cliff, NJ: Prentice-Hall, 1982).
5. Lauren A. Corwin, "Caste, Class and the Love-Marriage: Social Change in India," *Journal of Marriage and Family* 39, no. 4 (1977): 823–831.
6. B. R. Ambedkar, *Annihilation of Caste* (Lahore: printed by the author, 1936); Amit Ahuja and Susan L. Ostermann, "Crossing Caste Boundaries in the Modern Indian Marriage Market," *Studies in Comparative International Development* 51, no. 3 (2015): 365–387; Corwin, "Caste, Class and the Love-Marriage: Social Change in India."
7. Arland Thornton, *Reading History Sideways: The Fallacy and Enduring Impact of the Developmental Paradigm on Family Life* (Chicago: University of Chicago Press, 2005).
8. Ibid.
9. Keera Allendorf and Arland Thornton, "Caste and Choice : The Influence of Developmental Idealism on Marriage Behavior," *American Journal of Sociology* 121, no. 1 (2015): 243–287.
10. International Institute for Population Sciences (IIPS) and ICF, *National Family Health Survey (NFHS-4), 2015–16*.
11. Siwan Anderson, "The Economics of Dowry and Brideprice," *Journal of Economic Perspectives* 21, no. 4 (2007): 151–174.
12. International Institute for Population Sciences (IIPS) and ICF, *National Family Health Survey (NFHS-4), 2015–16*.
13. Ibid.
14. Ambedkar, *Annihilation of Caste*.
15. Srinivas Goli, Deepti Singh, and T. V. Sekhar, "Exploring the Myth of Mixed Marriages in India: Evidence from a Nation-Wide Survey," *Journal of Comparative Family Studies* 44, no. 2 (2013): 193–206.

16. Kaivan Munshi and Mark Rosenzweig, "Traditional Institutions Meet the Modern World: Caste, Gender, and Schooling Choice in a Globalizing Economy," *American Economic Review* 96, no. 4 (2006): 1225–1252.

17. Ahuja and Ostermann, "Crossing Caste Boundaries in the Modern Indian Marriage Market."

18. Keera Allendorf and Roshan K. Pandian, "The Decline of Arranged Marriage? Marital Change and Continuity in India," *Population and Development Review* 42, no. 3 (2016): 435–464.

19. Ahuja and Ostermann, "Crossing Caste Boundaries in the Modern Indian Marriage Market."

20. Ibid.

21. Matthijs Kalmijn, "Intermarriage and Homogamy: Causes, Patterns, Trends," *Annual Review of Sociology* 24, no. 1 (1998): 395–421.

22. Irawati Karve, *Kinship Organization in India*, third edn (Bombay: Asia Publishing House, 1968).

23. Allendorf and Pandian, "The Decline of Arranged Marriage?"

24. Goode, *The Family*.

25. Allendorf and Thornton, "Caste and Choice."

26. Patricia Uberoi, *Freedom and Destiny: Gender, Family, and Popular Culture in India* (New Delhi: Oxford University Press, 2006).

27. Thornton, *Reading History Sideways*.

28. Keera Allendorf, "Schemas of Marital Change: From Arranged Marriages to Eloping for Love," *Journal of Marriage and Family* 75, no. 2 (2013): 453–469.

29. Ibid.

30. Allendorf and Pandian, "The Decline of Arranged Marriage?" 457.

31. Ibid.

32. Ibid.

33. Abhijit Banerjee, Esther Duflo, Maitreesh Ghatak, and Jeanne Lafortune, "Marry for What? Caste and Mate Selection in Modern India," *American Economic Journal: Microeconomics* 5, no. 2 (2013): 33–72.

CHAPTER 10

Education

Understanding the Gender Gap in Education and Employment

Deepaboli Chatterjee, Babu Lal, and Rimjhim Saxena

Introduction

Women have historically lagged behind their male counterparts in educational attainment. This gender gap in education has produced greater gender disparities on a host of social and economic indicators. Not only does the gender gap in education generate big differences in employability and wages for men and women but also affects a number of "non-market" outcomes as well. As Schultz[1] and McMahon[2] have shown, the benefits stemming from greater education show up in the form of reduced family size, improved health status, and better childcare, as well as increased political awareness and efficiency in home production.

These concerns are recognized by the Indian government, as the recent *beti bachao, beti padhao* (save the girl child, educate the girl child) campaign shows. Indeed, data have consistently shown major economic benefits in educating females. P. Duraisamy,[3] for instance, in his comparison of prevailing Indian education trends in the decade of 1983–1994 shows how investment in women's education generates higher economic returns, particularly at the middle, lower-secondary, and higher-secondary levels.

The hard work has paid off. Existing data show that females have largely caught up to men in educational attainment and, in the case of Delhi, surpassed them. According to the census, the proportion of females in higher education has been increasing consistently over time—from 13 girls enrolled for every 100 boys in 1950 to 58 girls for every 100 boys in 2000–2001 and finally to 88

Table 10.1 Gross enrollment ratio (GER) in Delhi and across India, selected education levels

Gender–region/education level	Across India		Delhi	
	Boys	Girls	Boys	Girls
Secondary	79.16	80.97	103.213	111.27
Higher secondary	55.95	56.41	73.25	83.6
Higher education	26	24.5	42.8	48.4

Source: Authors' calculations from government data in parliamentary questions.

Note: The GER is the ratio of the number of actual enrolled students at a particular education level and the projected children of an age group who should be enrolled at that education level. Since there can be students above the official school age of a particular education level enrolled at that level, the GER ratio can go above 100 percent.

girls for every 100 boys in 2016–2017. Table 10.1 describes this convergence of girls in education using the current gross enrollment ratio (GER) measured in percentage for boys and girls at different levels of education at an all-India level versus the capital region of Delhi.

While the GER has been increasing at the secondary level, higher-secondary level and in higher education across India, Delhi fares unusually well when compared to India as a whole—girls have higher enrollment ratios than boys at all levels of education. Yet these educational gains have not translated into jobs for women. In fact, things have gone in the other direction. A report by the International Labor Organization shows that female labor force participation in India dropped from 35 percent in 1990 to 27 percent in 2014. The gender gap in labor force participation in 2014 was 53 percentage points, which is among the biggest gender gaps in the world. This has happened even though per capita income has been rising in India, especially since the 1990s onward and, as shown above, the GER for girls has been increasing as well. As the working age population of India swells and possibly creates the so-called "demographic dividend," it is imperative to integrate women into the Indian workforce. Integrating sufficiently educated working age women has the capacity to generate significant economic growth (not to mention a host of other social benefits).

This chapter delves into the data characterizing the educational attainment and employment of females in the National Capital Region (NCR) in and around Delhi. This region is among the wealthiest and fastest growing in India and one that most Indians associate with social mobility. It is, thus, a natural place to understand the extent of social mobility available to women in India.

Intergenerational increases in educational outcomes, that is, the educational attainment of a child versus his or her parents', remains one of the best measures of social mobility. Yet, typically, this is difficult to characterize due to a lack of data on the educational status of parents and children in the same household. The Center for the Advanced Study of India (CASI)–NCR Survey of nearly 5,500 households and 25,000 individuals in the NCR yields a sample of 2,504 children and their parents in tandem with their educational statuses in the youngest cohort (ages 21–30), allowing for a careful documentation of educational attainment of females in the region. Furthermore, the large sample of households and individuals in this one region allows for nuanced analysis of prevailing conditions in the labor market.

These data allow for an investigation of the education–employment linkage for females in the NCR in detail. This chapter demonstrates that while the growth in educational attainment for females in the NCR has been impressive, these educational gains have not translated well to the labor market. In fact, even at a high level of education, women's participation in the labor force remains poor. In order to understand the lack of an education–employment linkage for females, we argue that greater education of females yields returns on the "marriage market,"[4] with more educated women marrying into wealthier households rather than entering the labor market. This creates significant distortions in the economy, where the most educated women from the wealthiest households, precisely whom one would expect to be the most productive workers, enter the workforce at very low rates.

Educational Attainment in the National Capital Region

The CASI–NCR Survey captures information on the educational status and demographic information of each member of a surveyed household. The religious affiliation of the population captured in the data set is predominantly of Hindus (85.98 percent), followed by Muslims (10.91 percent), Sikhs (2.09 percent), Christians (0.29 percent), Jains (0.4 percent), Buddhists (0.04 percent), and others (0.29 percent) which very closely aligns with the religious composition of Delhi's population as captured by the 2011 Census data.[5] The caste composition is led by the category "other backward class," followed by General, Scheduled Caste, and Scheduled Tribe. The sample is representative with 55 percent males and 45 percent females, similar to 2011 Census gender composition of Delhi with 54 percent males and 46 percent females.

The schooling system in India classifies schooling years using milestones—primary, upper-primary, secondary, and higher-secondary schools. Educational attainment of each individual in the CASI–NCR data set has been reclassified in seven levels corresponding to the Indian system. The levels are: illiterate; less than 5th pass (primary school incomplete); 5th pass (primary school complete); 8th pass (upper-primary school complete); 10th pass (secondary school complete); 12th pass (higher-secondary school complete and diploma holders); and graduates and above (college complete, including postgraduates and doctorates).

With a data set comprising of individuals of all ages, those under the age of 21 have been specifically discarded from the analysis to account for those who, at least in principle, could plausibly have been graduates (the final category). This prevents biases in measurement due to those children still in school at lower educational levels, for whom we cannot make inferences about future educational attainment. According to the Department of School Education and Literacy,[6] the average age for completing the 12th standard in India lies in the 16–18 age bracket, while individuals in the age group of 18–23 are most likely to be enrolled in some form of higher education.

Age Cohorts

The amount of importance each generation has given to education has changed through time, especially with respect to gender. It is, therefore, crucial to see how educational achievement has changed for both genders, captured by the survey in the NCR. At the age of 25, 45.6 percent individuals were graduates as compared to 30.2 percent at the age of 35, 21 percent at the age of 45, and 20 percent at the age of 55. This data shows huge progress in the educational attainment in the Delhi NCR in the last few decades.

In order to understand how educational attainment changes in the population over time, the data are grouped into age "cohorts" of 21–30, 31–40, 41–50, and 51–60. Figure 10.1 captures the age effect by gender in cohorts to understand the spread of education across different generations. While there are more illiterate women than men in all the four age cohorts, not only does the total proportion of illiterate individuals go down on moving from older generations (51–60 years) to younger generations (21–30 years) but the gap between males and females also reduces significantly. An increase in the average level of education for each group is observed, with a higher proportion

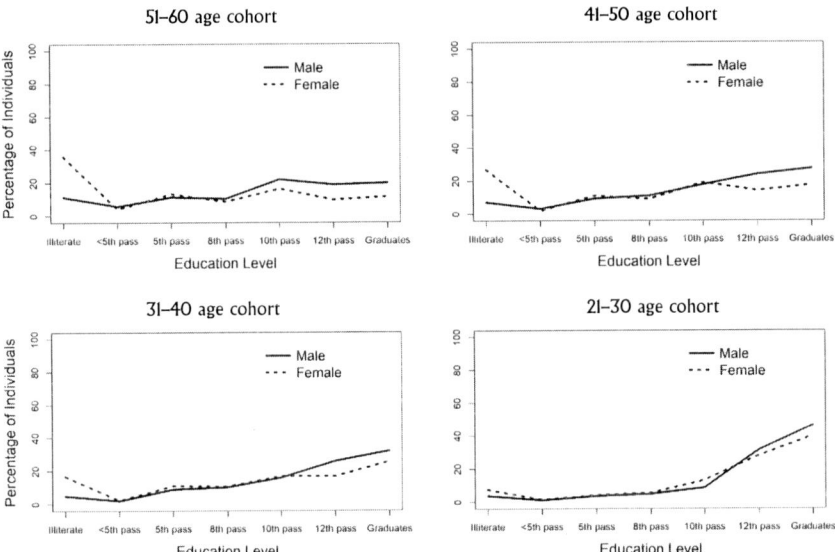

Figure 10.1 The gender gap in educational attainment by age cohort
Source: Authors' calculations from the CASI–NCR Survey data.

of individuals completing their schooling and higher education as one moves from the older age cohorts to the younger age cohorts. Convergence between the genders is also observed at the "bottom" of the spectrum with the proportion of illiterate women and men converging over time.

These results tally with the government statistics we have shown for comparison, with an increasing number of individuals, especially women, entering higher education over time. The results also echo those from a recent study by Runu Bhakta[7] on consumption expenditure analysis using the National Sample Survey data that show that the gender gap in educational attainment in India has reduced over the years.

Comparison with Parent's Educational Attainment

Parents are known to play a crucial role in determining the health and education levels of children and, thus, their future occupations and incomes on attaining adulthood. Indeed, the sociodemographic characteristics of parents are known to be highly predictive of future education, employability, and income.[8] For this reason, we analyzed the educational outcomes of children as compared to their parents. The extent to which children attain formal education beyond the levels reached by their parents is a natural measure of social mobility across generations—what is referred to as "intergenerational mobility."[9] These intergenerational effects magnify the benefits arising from government investment in education, as it continues to benefit successive generations.[10]

To understand the basis of the growth in educational attainment across age-groups, it is important to look at the parental background of these individuals. In particular, it is important to trace if the growth in educational attainment is limited to children of highly educated parents in previous generations or if educational attainment is truly growing across a broad swathe of the population.

Across age cohorts

The CASI–NCR Survey collected information of each of the members of the household in relation to the respondent of the survey and head of the household. To explore intergenerational mobility, we analyzed a data set of parent–child pairs for individuals over the age of 21 with both mother and father alive and within the household.

This study is the first of its kind to quantify the link between parents' levels of education and the educational level of children in the Delhi NCR metropolitan area. To understand how gender differences play out in this context, the probability of being a graduate for an individual was explored across different age cohorts as a function of the father's education level. The mean level of education for all fathers in this data set was 10th pass; hence, the top panel in Figure 10.2 describes the probability of an individual being at least a graduate with a father having a below-average level of education, while the bottom panel describes the probability with a father having an above-average level of education.

Regardless of the father's level of education, the percentage of male graduates remains largely constant across age cohorts. However, the percentage of female graduates sees a secular increase of over 20 percentage points. In fact, the percentage of female graduates surpasses the percentage of male graduates in both panels in the 21–30 age cohort. A similar comparison with the mother's education level produced nearly identical results, although it is important to note that the increase in percentage of female graduates was more pronounced

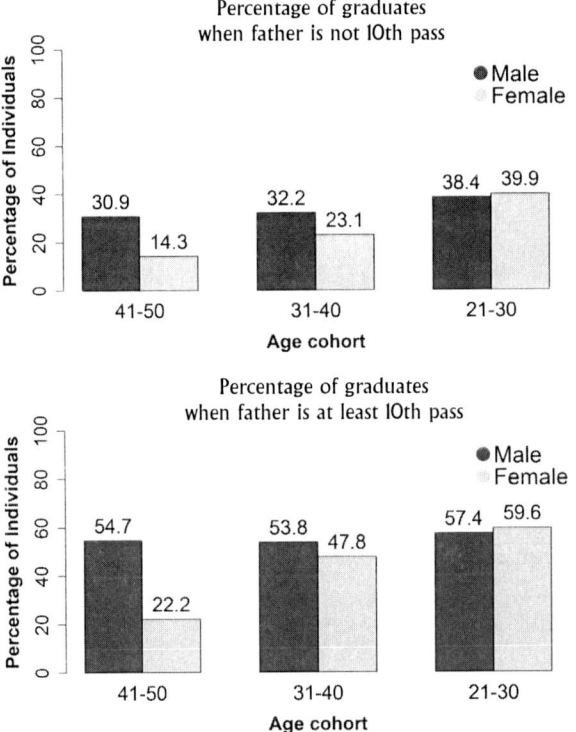

Figure I0.2 Gender differences in the proportion of graduates by their fathers' levels of education
Source: Authors' calculations from the CASI–NCR Survey data.

when compared to mother's education level (with about a 45 percentage points increase in female graduates in 21–30 age cohort as compared to the 41–50 age cohort for mothers who were at least 10th pass).

21–30 age group

To understand the scale of the social mobility in the NCR today, characteristics of the youngest cohort (age 21–30) were explored in detail. In this cohort, there are 2,504 parent–child pairs. This cohort has a rather high number of individuals with an uneducated mother (33 percent), while the median level of education for the father was 12th pass. Due to low levels of mother's education, over 85 percent of the cohort reported a higher level of education

Educational attainment when the mother is illiterate

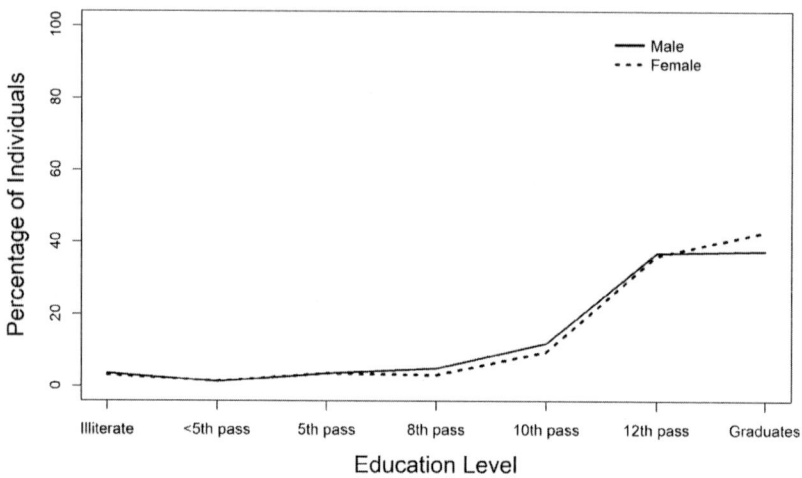

Figure 10.3   Gender gap in educational attainment for those with uneducated mothers, ages 21–30

Source: Authors' calculations from the CASI–NCR Survey data.

than their mothers, while over 65 percent of the cohort reported a higher level of education as compared to their fathers.

To demonstrate the very high social mobility in the NCR, Figure 10.3 displays the educational attainment of individuals in the 21–30 age cohort with uneducated mothers. The highest proportion of the cohort is located in the graduates (and above) category followed by the 12th pass (and diploma course) category. In fact, a higher percentage of females are in the graduates (and above) category than men, affirming the extraordinary social mobility of females in the NCR (in educational terms). Furthermore, the fact that such high levels of educational attainment are achieved for individuals with uneducated mothers attests to the breadth of this social mobility.

A similar analysis using individuals with uneducated fathers shows that the highest percentage of males are located in the graduates (and above) category, closely followed by the 12th pass category, while females are most heavily clustered in the 12th pass category, followed by the graduates (and above) category. Figures 10.2 and 10.3 together highlight the fact that the number of females graduating has been rising consistently with every age cohort and shows that this increase is fairly universal in nature.

The Education–Occupation Link for Women

In principle, greater educational attainment should positively impact an individual's employability in two ways. First, it should qualify the individual to do a greater range of jobs, so that the individual has a higher probability of employment. Second, it should endow the individual with greater skills, so that the individual should be able to obtain higher-skilled employment. In short, education should make individuals more employable. At the same time, there exist social pressures, patriarchal norms, and infrastructural concerns (that may make it unsafe for women to travel great distances outside the home) that hinder a woman's opportunities to take a job. Accordingly, this section explores the linkages between greater educational attainment and labor market outcomes for women.

According to the 2011 Census, 50 percent of India's population is below the age of 25 years and over 65 percent individuals are below the age of 35 years, making India a young country with a large and growing working population—a condition that is supposed to generate a "demographic dividend." With such a significant proportion of the population of working age, countries are often purported to make great leaps in economic development in this period, especially given a significant increase in educational attainment.[11] If there were less gender discrimination, one would expect that the closing of the gender gap in education would yield significant employment generation for women.

Using the information available in the data set on the industries, the individuals in our sample were employed in, their designation and the nature of work they engaged in, occupation was divided into five skill levels according to the 2004 National Classification of Occupations[12] as follows:

1. Skill Level I: elementary operations
2. Skill Level II: plant and machinery operators and assemblers, craft and related trade workers, skilled agricultural and fishery workers, service workers, shop and market sales workers, and clerks
3. Skill Level III: associate professionals
4. Skill Level IV: professionals
5. Skill Level V: legislators, senior officials, and managers

For the purpose of this analysis, three separate categories have also been included—namely, unemployed individuals, that is, those who are actively looking for a job, housewives, and students. Looking at the occupation distribution across age cohorts, shown in Figure 10.4, without including any

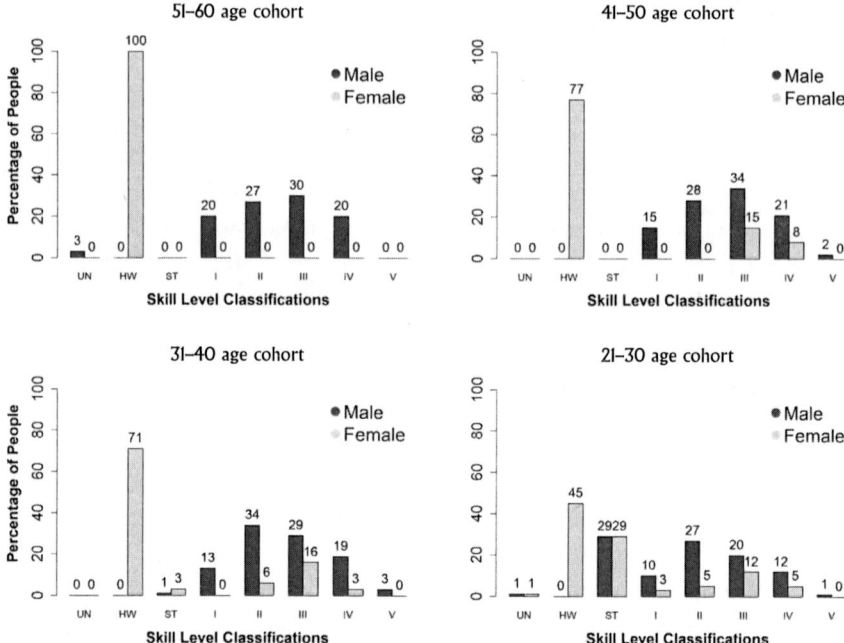

Figure 10.4   Gender differences in occupational status by age cohort
Source: Authors' calculations from the CASI–NCR Survey data.
Note: UN, HW, ST stand for unemployed individuals, that is, those who are actively looking for a job, housewives, and students, respectively.

education filter gives an idea of how the labor force is distributed for different age groups across genders. The 51–60 age cohort fails to capture any working woman, with 100 percent of these women reporting that they are housewives. A marked departure from the employment outcomes of this cohort is observed in the percentage of women who are a part of the paid labor market, which starts growing in the younger age cohorts of 41–50, 31–40, and 21–30.

In the age cohort of 21–30, the proportion of male and female students is the same at 29.3 percent. While working men are mostly clustered in Level II, followed by Levels III and IV, working women are predominantly located in Level III, followed by Levels II and IV. A 45.1 percent of the women in this age group identified as housewives. It is interesting to note that working women in this data set are mostly clustered at skill-based Levels III and IV across all age cohorts and very few of them are concentrated near Level I, implying most of these women are either in well-paying white-collar jobs or they do not enter the labor market at all. This also reiterates the idea that rising education tends to be associated with stronger preferences for white-collar jobs.[13]

But higher levels of education alone are not enough to explain the greater concentration of women in white-collar jobs (conditional on entering the labor force). Given similar levels of education between men and women, without any distortions one would expect to see similar skill distributions between men and women in the labor market. However, many lower-skilled professions, such as construction labor, are often viewed as inappropriate for women. Thus, the distribution of jobs for women is likely a function of both preferences for certain jobs and the constraints imposed by a highly patriarchal society on the appropriateness of the profession.

Returns to Higher Education

The youngest age cohort (21–30) is clustered in higher education and the percentage of graduates has been increasing through the decades. An analysis of the employment outcomes of this cohort helps understand the role that increasing educational attainment has had on job market outcomes.

Paid labor market returns

While graduate men are distributed across all skill levels, graduate women are clustered around higher skill levels. This is consistent with the idea that women are only willing or allowed to undertake sufficiently high-status jobs. This might be due to many reasons such as scarcity of jobs suitable for women, preference for men in the labor market for certain types of jobs, lower wages for women, poor working conditions, security concerns, or the social stigma associated with women working outside the home.[14,15]

Figure 10.5 compares the employment status between men and women for the age cohort of 21–30, using a statistical technique called locally estimated scatterplot smoothing (LOESS) to model the probability that an individual who is a college graduate has a job given his or her household's economic condition. The horizontal axis shows the asset index, a measure of household wealth that is described in earlier chapters. The comparison is restricted to graduates because, at least in principle, this is the most employable group in the population.

Figure 10.5 demonstrates that almost all the male graduates in this age cohort are employed, although the skill levels (I–V) vary greatly. On the other

Gender disparity in labor force

Graduate individuals in 21–30 age cohort

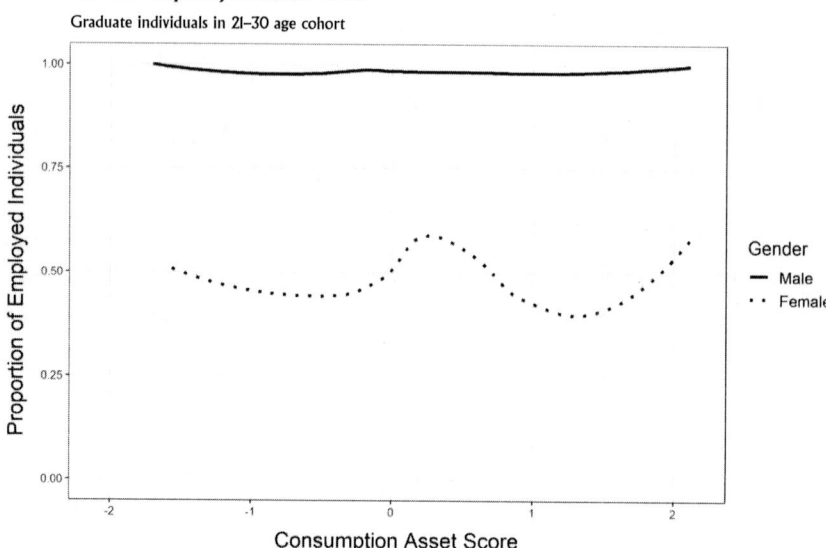

Figure 10.5   Gender gap in the labor force by wealth of the household
Source: Authors' calculations from the CASI–NCR Survey data.

hand, only half of all graduate women are employed. Most importantly, there is no discernible positive or negative relationship between economic wealth and woman's ability to enter the labor market for the women who are graduates.

This is a somewhat surprising result. Traditional economic models imply that the willingness of women to enter the labor force should be impacted by "income effects." On the one hand, as the household wealth increases, the incentive for women to enter the labor force should decrease suggesting a negative relationship between household economic wealth and female labor force participation. On the other hand, wealthier households can invest more heavily in their women members in ways that may boost their employability (for example, by investing in education, healthcare, and/or safe modes of transport).[16] Nonetheless, one should exercise some caution interpreting this data, as they are based on cross-sectional data on cohorts rather than data over time.

Marriage market returns

If women's entry into the labor force (among those highly qualified to enter into it) is not responsive to household wealth, then what mediates women's entry into the labor force? One conjecture is that women's education is more valuable in the "marriage market"—the phenomenon of more educated women marrying into more well-off households due to the higher status attached to these women. More precisely, Behrman, Foster, Rosenzweig, and Vashishtha[17] have argued that the demand for educated wives increases if the labor market returns to men's education increases. The positive relationship between household wealth and educational status is a standard feature of social data, as it is here (not shown), but usually the claim is that people who come from greater household wealth are more likely to become educated. While this is still likely to be true in India, the marriage market claim makes the reverse argument—women with higher education are likely to find themselves marrying into wealthier households (irrespective of personal earnings).

But why should a greater household preference for educated females necessarily dampen labor force participation? It is because, for many households, education for women is associated with status and not productivity. To understand this point, it is important to delve into the sets of behaviors considered "appropriate" for women. Patriarchal norms dictate that it is typically inappropriate to leave the home for work, significantly restricting the set of income-generating activities available to even highly educated females. Unlike rural Indian households, many of which are living at subsistence levels, the woman's income is not required for the household to survive.[18, 19] In such a scenario, even the poorest of households in the NCR (which are still reasonably well-off by all-India standards) may choose to forego a woman's income for propriety.

To explore the dynamics between the productivity gains from education and the role of household wealth in employability, Figure 10.6 analyzes women in the age cohort of 21–30. The left panel of Figure 10.6 displays the proportions of women that are housewives and employed among graduates while the right panel displays the proportions of women that are housewives and employed among nongraduates. Two important trends emerge from Figure 10.6. Unlike for graduates, the rate of employment for female nongraduates is increasing in the wealth of the household. Furthermore, graduates are consistently employed at a higher rate than nongraduates (with the employment rate of nongraduates converging to that of graduates only at the highest wealth levels).

These two facts taken together imply that there is a positive relationship between household wealth and female labor force participation, as well as a positive relationship with educational attainment. But these dynamics also point to something troubling. Women hit a ceiling in terms of the probability

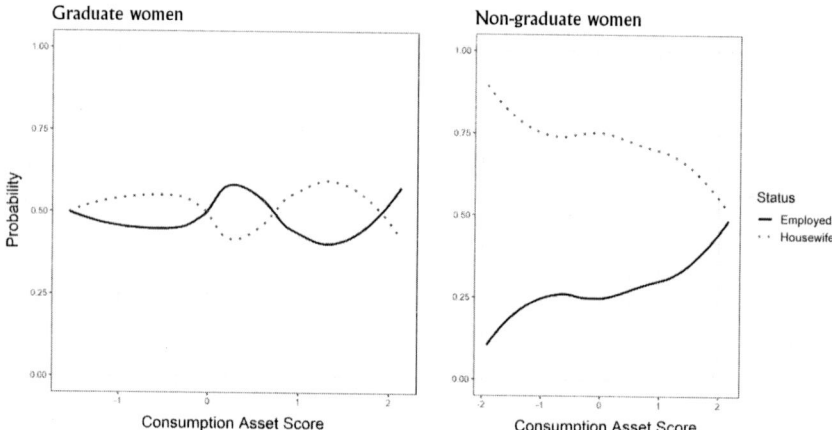

Figure 10.6   Comparison of graduate and nongraduate women in labor force participation
Source: Authors' calculations from the CASI-NCR Survey data.

of being in the labor force at around 50 percent; graduate women hit the ceiling immediately, while nongraduate women only hit the ceiling at the highest wealth levels. In this sense, wealth and education are "substitutes" for each other in engendering employment. That is, there is a ceiling on employment for precisely those women who are likely to be the most productive in the labor force in terms of education and underlying household wealth.

Conclusion

The goal of this study was to understand trends in women's education in the Delhi NCR as well as how they relate to women's labor force participation. While the gender gap in education is closing all across India, the Delhi NCR is particularly noteworthy in this regard: the gender gap has largely closed in the region, and by many measures of educational attainment, women are outperforming their male counterparts. Unfortunately, as shown in some detail here, the region's exemplary performance on education has not effectively translated to women's labor force participation.

There is some existing theory to help make sense of poor female labor force participation in this context. Claudia Goldin[20] hypothesized that female's labor participation follows a "U-shaped" curve with respect to economic development. Indeed, there is quite a bit of empirical evidence for this phenomenon. Goldin hypothesized that women's labor force participation should be the lowest in lower-middle- and middle-income countries (such as India) because while women are gaining in social status, the jobs they are offered are not commensurate to their status. This is still the most widely accepted explanation for this empirical phenomenon, but the data presented here seem to present an alternative explanation for low women's participation in the labor force.

The data in this chapter suggest that the highest-status women (in terms of education and household wealth) are also the women who participate the most in the labor force. Rather, the problem seems to be that larger environmental and structural issues—lack of safe transport outside of home and judgement about the propriety of women leaving the home—generate a hard ceiling on how many women are able to enter the workforce. This also explains why educational attainment of women can be increasing while labor force participation is decreasing. The existence of a marriage market, where women that are more educated are viewed as higher status deserving of "better" marriages, creates perverse incentives to educate women.

It is often assumed by looking at the "U-shaped" curve that as countries develop economically, the issues of low female labor force participation will sort themselves out. But the reverse may be true, countries may fail to develop economically if they cannot harness the power of women in their labor force. In the coming years, India will face enormous challenges in generating a sufficiently skilled workforce to sustain and enhance economic growth. India seeks to reap the benefits of a "demographic dividend" during a period over which a very large share of the population will be of working age due to recently increasing life expectancies and lower fertility rates. This increased labor force has the ability to provide a big push to economic well-being and development in India, but lagging educational and health outcomes threaten to prevent the labor force from acquiring sufficient skills to unlock these potential gains.

More to the point, without serious intervention, poor integration of women into the skilled labor force will likely attenuate the positive impacts of India's demographic dividend. International Monetary Fund Chief Christine Lagarde has described the tremendous positive effects that would accrue to India's economy by integrating women into the labor force, claiming that India's gross domestic product will grow by 27 percent if female workers in the economy increase to the same extent to that of men.[21]

The situation may seem unpromising, but there are reasons to be more optimistic. As the education data on age cohorts show, the closing of the gender gap on education is a very recent phenomenon. Social change can occur very rapidly, and similar rapid changes may occur in employment with the correct investments in female labor force participation. For instance, the Delhi metro has been lauded for providing relatively safe transport until a fairly late hour across much of the NCR. A recent study,[22] for instance, found that the Delhi metro was impactful in allowing young women to attend colleges far away from home in the Delhi region. These sorts of investments have had a large impact in allowing women greater choice in education, and it stands to reason that similar impacts on labor force participation may be seen in the future.

While India has witnessed convergence in educational attainment for girls and boys over the past couple of decades, the analysis presented in this chapter hints at greater challenges for similar convergence in the arena of employment opportunities. The inability to integrate the most educated women into the labor force has pernicious effects on the economy, as the country is unable to use its most productive workers. It is an issue that demands immediate attention—the inability to translate educational gains for women into employment gains would have severe consequences for the aspirations of a rapidly developing India.

Notes

1. T. Paul Schultz, "Educational Investments and Returns," in *Handbook of Development Economics*, ed. H. Chenery and T. N. Srinivasan (New York: Elsevier Science, 1988), 543–630.
2. Walter W. McMahon, "Consumption Benefits of Education," in *International Encyclopedia of Economics of Education*, ed. T. Husen and T. N. Postlethwaite (Oxford: Elsevier Science, 1985), 982–985.
3. P. Duraisamy, "Changes in Returns to Education in India, 1983–94: By Gender, Age-Cohort and Location," *Economics of Education Review* 21, no. 6 (2001): 609–622.
4. "Marriage market" here refers to an alternative to enter the paid labor market as a return to investment on education, which is influenced by strong cultural and social norms.
5. Census 2011 India, "Delhi Religion Census 2011," religion data—population of Hindus/Muslims/Sikhs/Christians, available at https://www.census2011. co.in/data/religion/state/7-delhi.html, accessed on February 10, 2019.
6. Department of School Education and Literacy, *Educational Statistics at a Glance: 2016* (rep. no.; New Delhi: Department of School Education and Literacy, Ministry of Human Resource Development, Government of India, 2016), available at http://mhrd.gov.in/sites/upload_files/mhrd/files/statistics/ ESG2016_0.pdf, accessed on August 2, 2020.

7. Runu Bhakta, "Educational Attainment of Young Adults in India: Measures, Trends & Determinants" (Working Paper No. 34, Indira Gandhi Institute of Development Research, Mumbai, 2015).

8. Jere R. Behrman and Mark R. Rosenzweig, "Does Increasing Women's Schooling Raise the Schooling of the Next Generation?" *American Economic Review* 92 (2002): 323–334.

9. It is also the best measure we have of social mobility in a context in which verifiable information on individual income is unavailable.

10. Sang Yoon (Tim) Lee, Nicholas Roys, and Ananth Seshadri, The Causal Effect of Parents' Education on Children's Earnings, mimeo, March 2015.

11. David E. Bloom, David Canning, and Jaypee Sevilla, *The Demographic Dividend: A New Perspective on the Economic Consequences of Population Change* (Santa Monica, CA: Rand, 2003).

12. The list of occupations is available at http://www.icssrdataservice.in/datarepository/index.php/catalog/2/download/47, accessed on February 10, 2019.

13. S. Desai, A. Dubey, B. L. Joshi, M. Sen, A. Shariff, and R. Vanneman, *Human Development in India: Challenges for a Society in Transition* (New Delhi: Oxford University Press, 2010).

14. E. Boserup, *Women's Role in Economic Development* (London: Earthscan, 1970).

15. M. B. Das and S. Desai, *Why Are Educated Women Less Likely to Be Employed in India? Testing Competing Hypotheses*, Social Protection Discussion Paper Series, vol. 313 (Washington, DC: World Bank, 2003).

16. E. K. Fletcher, R. Pande, and C. T. Moore, "Women and Work in India: Descriptive Evidence and a Review of Potential Policies" (CID Faculty Working Paper No. 339, December 2017).

17. J. R. Behrman, A. D. Foster, M. R. Rosenzweig, and P. Vashishtha, "Women's Schooling, Home Teaching, and Economic Growth" *Journal of Political Economy* 107, no. 4 (1999): 682–714.

18. M. Kohara, "Is the Full-Time Housewife a Symbol of a Wealthy Family?" *Japanese Economy* 34, no. 4 (2007): 25–56.

19. S. Klasen and J. Pieters, "What Explains the Stagnation of Female Labor Force Participation in Urban India?" (working paper, Policy Research Working Papers, World Bank, 2015).

20. C. Goldin, "The U-Shaped Female Labor Force Function in Economic Development and Economic History," in *Investment in Women's Human Capital and Economic Development*, ed. T. Paul Schultz (Chicago: University of Chicago Press, 1995), 61–90.

21. Press Trust of India, "Gender Parity in Workforce Can Boost India's GDP by 27%," *Economic Times*, September 6, 2015.

22. Girija Borker, "Safety First: Perceived Risk of Street Harassment and Educational Choices of Women" (working paper, Department of Economics, Brown University, 2017).

CHAPTER 11

Spatial Politics

Sociality, Transparency, and Ideas of Community in Delhi and Gurgaon

Sanjay Srivastava*

Introduction

This chapter seeks to explore certain ideas around corruption, transparency, and community as they emanate from two different socioeconomic contexts. The first of these concerns the middle-class locality of what I will call New Gurgaon. In particular, my focus is on the privately developed DLF City—built by the Delhi Land and Finance (DLF) company—located in the district of Gurgaon that borders Delhi. Gurgaon is in the state of Haryana, located immediately south of the national capital, and a part of the National Capital Region (NCR). According to one report, the areas falling under the recently (2008) constituted Municipal Corporation of Gurgaon (MCG) (that includes DLF City as well as several other privately developed residential enclaves) contains around 1.2 million persons. However, residents' groups (known locally as the residents' welfare associations or RWAs) dispute this estimate, claiming the true figure to be closer to 2 million. RWAs suggested that the actual figure had been suppressed so that the "corrupt" corporation did not have to provision for the actual number of residents.

The second context of my discussion is the now demolished slum locality of Nangla Matchi ("Nangla") that, till 2006, lay on the western banks of

---

* Parts of this chapter have been adapted from Sanjay Srivastava, *Entangled Urbanism: Slum, Gated Community and Shopping Mall in Delhi and Gurgaon* (New Delhi: Oxford University Press, 2015).

the Yamuna river that flows through Delhi. The locality, established in the late 1970s, was demolished between 2006 and 2007 to make way for an urban "beautification" program connected to the preparation for the 2010 Commonwealth Games.

My aim in this discussion is to think about some of the key aspects of urbanization and what they tell us about ideas of citizenship, relations with the state, and notions of community across different class fractions. The ideas that link the two quite different socioeconomic contexts I will discuss here are those of "transparency," corruption, faking, and morality.

With regard to the discussion that concerns DLF City, I will work on my discussion through a specific concept that I refer to as "post-nationalism." This concept, I suggest, illuminates crucial contexts of new forms of urbanism in India as well as changing relationships between the state and middle-class citizens. It also, I further argue, allows us an entry into understanding ideas regarding corruption and transparency among specific class fractions.

Before I get to post-nationalism, however, it is important to historicize the social and political landscape of the NCR in order to locate the processes of its sociopolitical present as a *specific* case of urbanism. That is to say, that while urbanization may be a "planetary"[1] phenomenon, discussions based around "modular" urbanism provide little purchase on the trajectories on the lives of cities as spaces produced through *unique* combinations of historical processes. The broader theoretical framework I wish to deploy—post-nationalism—requires a detour through the materiality of recent history: those multiple operations by citizens, private capital, and the state that have direct bearing on the making of natural topographies into social ones; that juncture where "land" becomes place and opens itself to the kinds of theorizations I seek to discuss.

Land into Place

The tangled skein of the colonial politics of land provides the first rung of the story through which we might seek to understand the specificity of the NCR. The colonial government established the Delhi Improvement Trust (DIT) in 1937 in order to "de-congest" parts of the old, walled city. As a consequence, the DIT promulgated the Delhi-Ajmeri Gate Slum Clearance Scheme in 1938. Beyond its putative mandate of "slum clearance," the founding of the DIT set in motion a series of bureaucratic and political operations on land whose social consequences continue to resonate in the postcolonial present. The most significant of these is the absolute monopoly over land-related activities granted to the trust. The background to the DIT's monopolistic powers lay in the control the state exercised over vast tracts of *nazul* lands, namely, "the Delhi Crown lands denoting property which has descended to Government either as successor of former Government or by escheat, in absence of heirs to legal owners."[2]

The legal fiction of *nazul* lands served, in effect, to consolidate colonial control of land through prohibiting all private real estate activity, unless routed through the trust. The Land Acquisition Act of 1894 (amended twice before it was replaced with a new law in 2013)[3] was a fundamental legal tool deployed by the DIT to consolidate its power and lock out private players. The trust was superseded by the Delhi Development Authority (DDA) in 1957; however, the postcolonial nation-state was not about to overturn the power over land enjoyed by the DDA's predecessor. For, the ordinance of 1955 that led to the establishment of the new authority incorporated just as sweeping a vision of state control over land as that put in place by the colonial government. In the DDA's wake, the state established itself "as the sole agency legally authorized to develop and dispose off land [and] ... left little, or no role for the private land developer."[4]

The historic nature of the state as a land monopolist[5] in the city-state of Delhi has had specific consequences in a region—Delhi and the broader NCR— where the mixture of party-political activity, private capital maneuvering and assertions by citizens' rights groups has produced a prolix urban landscape. Most specifically, as I will discuss in the next section on "post-nationalism," it concerns—what might be referred to as—a "restructuring" of the state in terms of its historical relationship to different class fractions as well as private capital. And the politics of urban spaces is at the heart of this state of play.

I will now briefly reflect upon one other contiguous context to build the case for the specificity of the Delhi region (a term I invoke as a synonym to the NCR), before moving on to the main arguments of this chapter. It further lays the groundwork for the discussion of the later sections.

Given the historic hold of the state over land within Delhi, two specific processes are of particular import: the rise of direct negotiations between the state and the city's residents in order to garner particular rights over land and the efflorescence of private real estate activity just beyond the borders of the city into other parts of the NCR beyond Delhi. I will discuss the former here while detailing the latter in a separate section since it forms a crucial part of the discussion of this chapter.

The rise of middle-class citizens' rights groups, their keenness to engage the state on a variety of urban issues and the alacrity with which the state seeks to not only respond but also actively encourage the relationship, forms one of the most striking aspects of the politics of urbanism in Delhi. A particularly salient example of this is the *bhagidari* ("Cooperation") scheme introduced by the Congress in Delhi under erstwhile Chief Minister Sheila Dikshit. Initiated in 2001 (and terminated in 2013 when the party lost power), the program brought together representatives of RWAs, market traders' associations (MTAs), and key government officials at periodically organized workshops as well as regular monthly meetings. The meetings and workshops were intended to reimagine the city as a space of cooperative endeavor, one where "citizens" play an active role in formulating and implementing urban policies, and the state responds through "transparent" mechanisms of urban governance.[6]

Though the program was imagined as a decentralization of urban governance, the grounds for *bhagidari* were actually prepared through the overweening reach of the state over matters of land. It is for this reason that the state—as I discuss in the next section—has become very significant, if not the exclusive, focus of a restructuring such that relatively powerful urban bodies (such as those that represent of middle-class residents) seek not only to gain new access to it but also deny access to others. Hence, under the *bhagidari* scheme—participation within which was limited to RWAs that were registered with the registrar of cooperatives—one of the most consistent demands was to forcefully demolish localities inhabited by the poor and to relocate these to the edges of the city. A significant background to the new relationship between middle-class citizens and the state is the concurrently changing relationship between private capital and both the previous entities. In the next section, I provide a more detailed discussion of this relationship—which is new in as much as the Nehruvian postcolonial nation-state explicitly defined its most significant role as association with the nation's marginalized citizens—and the consequences for urban policy.

It is the historically sequestered nature of the state—segregated from the functioning of various markets—that, I suggest, is the context of the current tumult where the nature of the state and its *legitimate* role in issues of social and economic justice are sought to be changed *along* with attempts to force it to engage with the market. That is to say that, ironically, it is the lack of past experience with the market that is the grounds for the rejection of the state *in toto*. These peculiarities, writ large upon the physical and symbolic terrains of Delhi NCR make the region a study in the *specifics* of the relationships between the state, private capital, and citizens. It is this aspect that the next section seeks to theorize through the notion of post-nationalism.

Post-Nationalism

Through "post-nationalism," I seek to focus upon the changing nature of the relationship between citizens and the state in order to present the relationship as a complex site of new attitudes toward consumption and private capital.

The term does *not* mean to imply that the nation-state is insignificant as a context of analysis or that we now live in a (what has been referred to as a) "post-patriotic" age where the most significant units of analysis are certain "postnational social formations"[7]—such as non-governmental organizations (NGOs)—that putatively problematize nationalist and statist perspectives. Further, my deployment is also different from another recent usage where it is used as an exhortation to develop thinking beyond the nation-state.[8] Post-nationalism, as deployed here, is the articulation of the nationalist emotion with the robust desires engendered through *new practices of consumerism and their associated cultures of privatization and individuation*. The term seeks to capture the "national" emotion at a time *beyond* the era of classic nationalism that came at the end of colonial rule. The "post" in post-nationalism refers not to the end of nationalism, but to its life when it enters into *explicit* dialogue with ideas of privatization of erstwhile public-funded activities and consumerism as a way of life.

A fruitful way of approaching the topic—and providing concrete illustrative examples—is through a brief exploration of the contemporary politics of urban spaces in Delhi. In 1999, soon after being elected to office, Delhi's erstwhile Chief Minister Sheila Dikshit "called for an active participation of Residents Welfare Associations in governance." The rationale for this was the "failure" of "civic agencies" to carry out their normal tasks. The chief minister's secretary noted that the call to actively involve RWAs in urban governance heralded a new era, marking as it did "the first step towards a responsive management of the city."[9] Positing a distinction between the state and the community, the secretary further noted that the "failure" of "civic agencies"—including their corrupt practices—meant that "it's really time for the community to be given direct control of managing the affairs of the city."[10] Subsequently, the government decided to "empower" RWAs to "take certain decisions on their own." It was proposed that they be given control over the management of resources such as parks, community halls, parking places, sanitation facilities, and local roads. A more direct relationship between the state and RWAs was also mooted through the idea of joint surveys of "encroached" land—that is, land that had been "illegally" occupied, usually by slum-dwellers—with the possibility that all illegal structures would "then be demolished in a non-discriminatory manner." Finally, it was proposed that RWAs be allowed to impose fines on government agencies which failed to carry out their assigned tasks.

In 2005, the Delhi state government announced that it would raise the electricity tariff by 10 percent. The Delhi Residents Welfare Association Joint Front (RWAJF) was formed in the same year in order to protest against the measure. The front consisted of 195 separate member RWAs from around the city. The increase in power rates for domestic consumers was the second one since the state-owned electricity body was "unbundled" in June 2002 as part of power sector "reforms." As a result, three privately owned companies secured contracts for electricity distribution.[11]

There was vigorous protest over the price rise and, in addition to the RWAJF, NGOs, such as People's Action, and another group known as Campaign Against Power Tariff Hike joined the campaign. Individual RWAs asked their members to refuse payment of the extra amount, while the RWAJF lobbied the government and organized citywide protests. The protests gained wide coverage in both the print and electronic media, and, echoing Gandhian anti-colonial strategies, the organizers were reported to have deployed "the ideas of 'civil disobedience' and 'people's power'."[12] Indeed, the parallels sought to be drawn between the Gandhian anti-colonial movement and the present times were even more explicit with the convener of the RWAJF referring to the protests as "non-violent Satyagraha."[13] Satyagrah, made up of two words satya (truth) and agrah (insistence), was used by Mahatma Gandhi to refer nonviolent resistance in his struggle against colonial rule. Eventually, the Delhi government backed down and the price rise was shelved. According to Sanjay Kaul, president of the People's Action NGO, the success of the protest heralded the making of a "middle-class revolution."[14] Kaul is one of many who had rediscovered and deployed anti-colonial vocabulary on behalf of the "people" at a time when the colonial era itself had become part of the sphere of mass consumption. In the wake of the 2011 anti-corruption movement led by social worker Anna Hazare, yoga guru Swami Ramdev invoked "Gandhi in calling for a 'satyagrah' against corruption'."[15]

The circulation of the ideas of "civil disobedience," satyagrah, and "revolution" and the consolidation of the notion of a "people" contesting the state occur in a context that might be called post-national. By this, I mean a situation where the original moral frisson of these terms—provided by anti-colonial sentiment—no longer holds. Indeed, in an era of post-Nehruvian economic liberalization characterized by consumerist modernity,[16] the moral universe of the anti-colonial struggle is no longer part of popular public discourse. At a time of post-nationalism, the "colonial ambience" is, in fact, an important part of popular marketing strategies.

Within this new context, the earlier emphases on the ethics of "saving" and delayed gratification for the "national good"[17]—that were indispensable ideological accompaniments to "civil disobedience" and *satyagrah* and also sought to foreground the significance of production of industrial goods and capacities that characterized the Nehruvian era—do not find any resonance in contemporary popular discourses on the role of the state. As I have noted earlier, the term post-national does *not* mean to imply that the nation-state is insignificant as a context of analysis. Rather, it refers to the new ways in which the nation-state relates to capital and the contexts within which it relates to different fractions of citizens. Hence, for example, in relation to the changing relationship between the state and the middle classes, the actions of the RWAs indicate an era of the "gentrification" and "re-spatialization" of the state[18] such that the consumer-citizen becomes the key focus of policy debates. This is a significant shift from the ideologies of the Nehruvian-era developmentalist state that succeeded the colonial one, with the poor as its key focus.[19]

A brief comment is required regarding my use of the term post-nationalism, given that there is another that has wide currency and might be said to describe the same set of social and economic circumstances. This is "neo-liberalism."[20] While I cannot dwell on this aspect in any great detail, the key point I wish to make is that this term "is unable to account for the specific *national* histories that transform into postnational ones."[21] As well, its deployment assumes that there is a "universal neoliberal moment"[22] that allows for a "global" view. As Terry Flew points out, the

> debate about neoliberalism as *one of a number of competing ideas about the organization of capitalist economies and societies* has been largely overwhelmed by those arguments that present neoliberalism as the ascendant ideology of global capitalism, so that the world is seen as being, or becoming, more and more neoliberal in its institutional structure and policy choices.[23]

My use of "post-nationalism" seeks to avoid the "too-easy application of models of capitalism and neoliberalism that obscure the variety of local experience."[24] In particular, the term seeks to capture the nuances of local histories—of capital and its cultural and economic fields—that are specific to the region by virtue of the necessary jaggedness of the every day in different parts of the world.

Particularized regional histories apart, there are other reasons too why we should be wary of "global" histories of capitalism that do not account for the analytical limitations of the term. A great deal "of the usage of the term," Flew also suggests, "is intellectually unsustainable, particularly where it functions as an all-purpose denunciatory category or where it is simply invoked as 'the way things are'"[25] and that "it largely functions as a rhetorical trope, where the meaning is already known to those who would be interested in the topic in question."[26]

A significant aspect of the post-national moment in India is the process of rethinking the state[27] such that it is increasingly imagined as a "friend" of the *middle classes*. The postcolonial state in India has most significantly been imagined as a benefactor of the poor, with "development" as its most significant policy focus. Indeed, the development focus of the state has been a defining feature of perceptions of postcoloniality itself.[28] The developmentalist state has also been perceived as anti-consumption. The RWA activities such as those discussed earlier have become sites for the reformulation of these historically well-entrenched notions of the state and its relationships with different class fractions. These neighborhood and city-level activities unfold in tandem with the broad national thrust toward "de-regulating" the economy,[29] including a shrinking public sector and easy loans for consumer purchases. It is this that I refer to as characteristic of post-nationalism.

One of the most significant ways in which the post-national moment resonates within the politics of urban space concerns the repositioning of the language of anti-colonial nationalism from the national sphere to the suburban one. This, in turn, also indexes the move from the idea of the "national" family to the nuclear (gated) one, and, the translation of the notion of nationalist solidarity to (middle) class solidarity. And though I am unable to discuss it fully here, there is also in all this, a process of redefinition of the idea of the "ordinary person." That is, as the nature of the state changes from a developmentalist to a post-developmentalist one, the idea of the most natural subject of the state—the ordinary person—is also undergoing change. The discussion that follows builds upon a great deal of recent scholarship that has outlined the connection between the growth of "new middle-classes," the consolidation of cultures of consumerism, and the making of new selves in the non-Western world.[30]

Creating DLF City: State Control to Consumerist Utopia

The DLF company was established in 1946 by a civil servant, Chaudhury Raghvendra Singh. By the mid-1950s, the DLF corporation had developed around 22 new suburbs in Delhi. The key aspect of DLF's business strategy was its ability to both surmount as well as manipulate the extraordinary layers of land and planning regulations instituted by the colonial state and later, the postcolonial one. The *soi-disant* dreams of an alternative spatial modernity—marked by advertisements that showed swimming pools and buxom beauties, lakes and carefree couples, flower-bedecked roads, and their patrician crowds—came to end, however, in 1957. For, following a highly critical report of an inquiry into the functioning of the DIT published in 1951, the postcolonial state established the DDA in 1957. The new Authority, as noted earlier, became a land monopolist.

On April 21, 1980, the DLF corporation gained the first license for acquiring around 170 acres of land in the village of Chakkarpur in Gurgaon district. Work on developing the site as a residential and commercial locality started soon after.[31] From the early 1980s, then, the company began to acquire land in Gurgaon and by the mid-1980s, it had accumulated some 3,500 acres—much of it on credit, with promises to pay later—and was ready to transform the rural hinterland into, as its publicity later proclaimed, the "Millennium City."

Within a period of some three decades, fields of green have turned into spaces of global commerce and habitation, in turn fueled by changes in the Indian economy since the mid-1990s. One of the most significant of these—spurred by new urbanism and constituting a fundamental stimulant to consumerist activity—has been the rapid expansion of the private banking sector and the relative ease of obtaining home loans. Aggressive market forays by both state owned and new private entrants (including foreign banks) sought to target "young and highly educated professionals who began their careers through the 1980s, [but] could not afford to own their own homes."[32]

As this section suggests, contemporary, private real estate developments in India are a prime site for the making of the citizen-consumer. And that the current phase of middle-class "activism," in the shape of RWAs, also owes much to urban spatial transformations initiated by companies such as DLF, which gained ground in the wake of economic liberalization policies put in train by the Congress party through its New Industrial Policy in 1991.

Spaces of Consumerism

Gated communities such as those in Gurgaon are being constructed across several Indian cities, and such topographical transformations are accompanied by broader discursive shifts regarding family life, state, nation, and citizenship.[33] That is to say, the spatial transformations that characterize new urbanism are also contexts of discourses about a new self. In this case, ideas of the entrepreneurial self[34]—ensconced within spaces made by entrepreneurial urbanism—help to consolidate attitudes toward consumerism as self-making. In this context, gated communities in India have also created specific relationships that cohere around what might be called "the morality of the market."[35] Post-nationalism, where the relationship between the state and the middle classes is undergoing change and new discourses about the morality of the market are, of course, linked contexts.

In order to illustrate the specificity of the present, it may be useful to refer to a counterpoint to my discussion. This can be found by contrasting the mammoth urban transformations currently underway in the contexts described above with another similar experiment during the mid-twentieth century, namely, the construction of "steel towns" by the postcolonial state. A comparison between contemporary—private—spatial transformations and mid-twentieth century state-sponsored ones points to significant shifts in the imagination that conjures the "ideal" citizen and his/her relationship with the state. It also tells us something about the changing nature of thinking on consumerism and self-making.

From the late 1950s, the Indian state undertook construction of a number of industrial townships in different—usually economically underdeveloped—areas of the country that were intended to be "exemplary national spaces of the new India."[36] Located within the larger framework of centralized economic development (most significantly manifested through the Soviet-inspired Five-Year Plans for economic development), the townships were the state's attempts at *postcolonial* modernity where the modern citizen would work and live in an environment that "proclaimed the birth of the sovereign nation."[37]

Most significantly, the postcolonial nationalist project of producing modern citizens within steel towns related to external spaces—such as town planning, streetscape, and design of shopping spaces—through which residents were expected to pass through. Surrounded by well-delineated areas for industrial activity, "shops, schools, parks, and entertainment centres,"[38] the citizen was to absorb the spatial geometry, transforming it into personal discipline across a number of areas of social life such as democratic engagement, secular belief, and industrial work practice. Discourses of transformation surrounding the contemporary gated community, on the other hand, shift the focus to internal spaces. So, gated communities are presented as effecting transformations that significantly relate to *domestic* (kitchens, dining areas, bedrooms, and so on) aspects of urban living. Intimate spaces are more directly addressed, locating, as it were, the domestic sphere as the indispensable grounds for the making of a global Indian modernity. The internal life of the household is one that is populated by goods and commodities, and it is these that are imagined to determine contemporary subjectivity. So, whereas steel towns established relationships between the individual and the nation-state through seeking to locate the former within the symbolic and concrete infrastructure of the latter, gated enclaves produce relationships between individuals and commodities. In this way, the public exhibition of intimate spaces indexes an era where contemporary dreams of modernity are inextricably linked to cultures of consumerism. Hence, gated enclaves posit a model of *post-national* citizenship that constitutes a particular gloss on the relationship between the state and its citizens in the backdrop of transnational consumerist modernity.

Post-National Citizens and the Morality of the Market

The gathering belief in the morality of the market relates to the idea that the state is inherently corrupt and that an incorruptible middle-class community— the "ordinary" people—can only be produced through the processes of capital. I would like to illustrate this through reference to a context where private capital actively produces its own citizens—consumer-citizens—such that the idea that there exist separate and autonomous spheres of the state, citizens, and capital becomes untenable. What we are left with, in fact, is a "simulacra"[39] of separate spheres.

Despite official regulations, the process of handing over privately developed localities in Gurgaon to the MCG has been slow and erratic, and many aspects of their functioning continue to be in the hands of the companies that built them. This is a context for the relationship between citizens (in the shape of RWAs), the state, and the private capital, DLF.

In 1996, some residents of DLF City combined to form the Qutub Enclave Residents' Welfare Association (QERWA). One of its most consistent demands had been that, as per official regulations, the DLF corporation hands over its townships to the government. The QERWA mounted a considerable agitation over this issue. It filed court cases, petitioned the government, and even put up candidates—without success—in state assembly elections. In the early 2000s, another RWA—known as the DLF City RWA—appeared on the scene. This is an umbrella body which claims affiliation from many individual RWAs in DLF City. An office holder of the QERWA (the older body) described the situation to me as follows:

> DLF did not want to hand over its townships to the government and the government is not interested either: for as long as DLF has control, it can arbitrarily continue to use the land within its areas as it pleases by changing original planning agreements. So, it can build a commercial building on a plot that was earlier indicated on planning documents as a community centre or a medical dispensary. The government does not wish to change anything because of the massive amounts of under the table money that it gets from private developers. If these localities were to be handed over to the Municipal Corporation of Gurgaon, it would be more difficult to make money. It is easier to make money from the private sector.

The DLF City RWA (the new body) was, in fact, created by the DLF corporation to counter what it perceived to be an association of residents (the QERWA) that was hostile to its interests. The DLF-sponsored RWA has a comfortable air-conditioned office in the same building as many of DLF's corporate offices in DLF City. A QERWA office holder told me that in the early 2000s, DLF initiated moves that led the Haryana government appointing an administrator to oversee its affairs and that it currently lies dormant. The DLF-sponsored association, on the other hand, appears to be flourishing. It is headed by retired corporate executive and primarily acts (as the head told me) "as a bridge between DLF and the residents of DLF City." The DLF corporation has, in this way, reconfigured the relationship between the state and the market in order to produce a non-state version of the civic sphere, which, simultaneously, grows out of the collaboration with the state; it has created its own citizens' group—and a private citizenry—through sponsoring the DLF City RWA. This too is an aspect of post-national urbanism where the idea and the body of the active citizen is produced not through political processes and debates over rights and responsibilities, but through a relationship between the state, the corporate sector, and urban real estate markets.

In recent years, the state has tried to exert in its "stateness"[40] through the formation of the MCG in 2008, and this aspect forms the final rung of this story on the relationship between the state, citizens, and private capital in a time of post-nationalism and consumerist modernity. In many of its own areas, the MCG is not able to levy any house tax as, through a confusing and complicated arrangement, private developers have not handed over ownership of their localities to the state.[41] Here, companies such as DLF levy a "maintenance" charge upon residents of "their" areas, and residents refuse to pay the state any house tax. An official of the DLF City RWA (which is sponsored by the DLF corporation) informed me that residents do not want the MCG to "take over" the private townships as there was far greater trust in the administrative abilities of the private sector than the state. The state government, he added, is "corrupt and corruptible." And, he said, DLF has an interest in looking after its older localities since it is building new township and wants to maintain "brand equity," not wanting its existing product to be sullied through poor state administration. That is why, he added, DLF will continue to carefully tend to its already constructed townships rather than risk shoddy state and corrupt activity in urban maintenance.

To Fake Is to Make: Duplicity, Intimacy, and Community

This section presents a discussion on a part of the NCR that is dramatically different than described earlier. It seeks to present another, quite different, model of relationships between corruption, ideas of community, and the state. I do this in order to foreground the multiple narratives of contemporary urban life that—in this case through the trope of corruption—say something about older as well as emerging forms of urban sociality.

During the period of my fieldwork at the *basti* (slum) of Nangla Matchi ("Nangla"), situated on the western banks of the Yamuna river in central Delhi, everyone wanted identity (ID) cards. For the urban poor, proof of identity is necessary for access to a variety of goods and services that are provided by the state. However, in order to obtain an official ID card of any kind, one needs to provide evidence of permanent or long-term residence in the city, a particularly difficult task for a population whose life strategies are tied to passage and movement. The effort that is required to secure appropriate documents is not only surrounded by anxieties and apprehensions but also relates to specific strategies of making the acquisitions.

I would like to focus here upon the ways in which senses of community, neighborliness, and trust permeated the acts and narratives of faking and corruption at Nangla. These include ideas of *tariqa* or etiquette or protocol and the necessity of exploiting one's own in order to provide care against the arbitrary callousness of outsiders. At Nangla too, just as in DLF City, the state is perceived as corrupt and arbitrary. However, here, the strategies of dealing with the situation are dramatically different and produce different narratives.

Tariqa *and Norms*

One day as I sat around the local mosque with Shahid Ansari, a Nangla resident in his seventies, several people carrying different pieces of paper approached him to ask about their "case." These included "cases" concerning the issue of ration cards, voter's identity cards, "Below Poverty Line" (BPL) cards, and several other kinds of documents. One man was accompanied by Raj Kumar, a low-level government official of the Municipal Corporation of Delhi (MCD), who was in charge of various government schemes in the locality. The man wanted Ansari to put his signature on an application form. Raj Kumar also urged Ansari to sign the document. But Ansari exclaimed, "come later—illegal work can't be done in broad daylight!" "Illegal" has an interesting position here: it is publicly mentioned as such, and is allocated a particular time for when it can be carried out, rather than rejected out of hand as beyond the pale. However, more significantly, though it is a regular part of life at Nangla, it is also a potentially dangerous activity: if caught, counterfeiting can incur a wide range of serious penalties. Acts of counterfeiting involve an entire chain of participants—middle men, procurers, information-gatherers, transferees of "originals," and beneficiaries, for example—and carry risks of disrupting closely established links within neighborhoods and settlements. Hence, the most admired members of the community are those—such as Ansari—who possess the capacity to do "illegal work" in a proper manner, minimizing or eliminating the risk of damage to community life. But not only this, the "proper" conduct of "illegal work" also ensures the life of the community: it is the grounds upon which everyday life—food, education, health, employment, and residence—is based.

Soon after the above episode, Ansari was approached by a young woman who asked about her "form" that she had asked Ansari to complete. "I'll take back my twenty rupees," she said, "unless I get the card immediately." Ansari turned to me and said that he was deeply offended by these comments. Then, addressing the woman, he told her that her "work" would not now be done since "even though we are neighbours, you don't trust me to do your illegal work properly!" A friend of Ansari joined the discussion and told me that this was all *bachpana* (childishness): "Look at all the effort that goes into getting all this work done," he said, "and all these people can talk about is rupees twenty-thirty." "What about all those young men," he continued, pointing to a group of locals, "who are helping to verify and fill up the forms. They are educated, their parents have spent huge amounts in educating them, yet they give of their time freely." Another man now approached our group and asked Ansari to help him fill in the identity application form. "Go to that other place," he was ordered, meaning the house of a local leader of a rival faction to that of Ansari's. A bystander offered to complete the form. "Let's see you if you can!" Ansari shouted. An elderly man sitting next to us now spoke up: "You don't only need education but also a *tariqa* [method, etiquette]. After all, the engineer makes the plan, but it's an illiterate *mazdoor* [laborer] who executes it. You need *tariqa*!" Ansari then turned to the supplicant: "There are forty-five columns to be filled up," he said, "miss a single one and the form is invalidated!" The government, according to Ansari, has a *gupt* (secret) system of coding and the slightest mistake in filling up a form could mean permanent denial of housing and other rights. The man quietly withdrew.

Why does one need *tariqa* to be corrupt in a corrupt world? *Tariqa* and trust make a community in the face of arbitrary and apparently secret rules and regulations that must be engaged with on their own terms. *Tariqa* and trust ensure that even though the well-being of the community depends on mimicking the arbitrariness and dishonesty of the state, this does not translate into the community becoming *like* the state. But how does *tariqa* ensure that corruption at the local level ensure that the community does not become like the state? Let me explain through another example.

Neighbors with the Kindest Cuts

I met Mohammad Islam in 2008 through Nangla resident Rakesh Kumar. Mohammad Islam was Rakesh's friend and had lived at Nangla Matchi before it was demolished. Following government policy, he had been allotted an alternative plot of land in the locality of Savda Ghevda but did not move there as he did not have the funds to build a house. Savda Ghevda is on the northern border of Delhi and approximately 40 kilometers away from the Nangla Matchi area. Rakesh had developed a flourishing real estate business once he moved to Savda Ghevda.

Islam told me that Rakesh had lent him INR 40,000 for treatment of a serious illness and had told him that he could return it whenever he was able. However, after some months, he realized that he would not be able to pay

Rakesh back the money, so he offered him his Savda Ghevda plot as payment in kind. Rakesh, Islam added, told him that he would "take" the land, and that whenever Islam had the money, he could return it and take back "his" property. Since Islam was unable to sign his name, he put his thumb impressions on "some papers," handing over the land to Rakesh. The land did not legally belong to Rakesh, and under government regulations, it was a criminal offense to sell it. However, given the latter's experience as a real estate dealer, he drew up a fake "agreement" between Islam and himself stating that the former had borrowed money from him and had offered his land as collateral. Then, sometime later, Rakesh obtained all of Islam's documents that proved his ownership of the land and altered this information, inserting his own name instead. This was done with Islam's knowledge: "I have complete trust in him," Islam repeated several times to me. A few months later, Islam told Rakesh that, given the ongoing expenditure on his medication and his general state of penury, he was now certain that he would not be able to pay back the money and hence, Rakesh should consider the Savda Ghevda land his own.

Rakesh told me that he always tried to convince ex-Nangla residents not to sell their land, even if it meant some hardship in the short term, such as having to commute long distances to their work and disruption in their children's schooling, and that "if they held on for a while, things would get better." However, if they were going to sell, Rakesh said, "they might as well sell to someone like me who they can trust, I will never betray them." Having "sold" the land to Rakesh, Mohammad Islam's troubles multiplied. He was forced to live about two hours from his place of work in an "unauthorized" settlement, having to change three buses to and from work. Sometime later, he borrowed money on the informal market to buy a plot of land near where he now lives but lost it all as it turned out that the real estate agent had actually sold off government land. And yet, Islam could hardly stop singing Rakesh's praises. "I can't tell you how kind Rakesh has been to me," he told me. "He is one of the kindest people I know."

Islam's take on his miseries is instructive. Rakesh exploited his neighbor's extremely vulnerable economic condition to purloin his sole asset, exposing him to further exploitation and ongoing wretchedness. And yet, Rakesh's "trustworthy" operations in the counterfeit real estate market—that appear to have left Islam permanently disadvantaged—struck Islam as a deepening of neighborly bonds and a fulfillment of community obligations; to be made predictably wretched by one's "own" is, nevertheless, deliverance from the arbitrary havoc of outsiders. Islam's comfort in the depredation of intimates leads us, once again, to the question of norms.

At the heart of Islam's attitude toward Rakesh is his belief that unlike "outsiders," Rakesh's exploitative behavior is based upon certain norms and the etiquette of neighborliness, which, in turn, will secure a degraded package of "benefits" that may not otherwise be forthcoming. These are the norms of community life in a hostile and arbitrary urban environment. Indeed, the range of strategies utilized by the urban poor when dealing with the state—pretending to have political and bureaucratic as well as underworld connections, for example—are expressions of their understanding of the arbitrariness of the state. Under such conditions of life, it is imperative to rely upon those who would convert the capricious economies of faking and counterfeiting into some minimal advantage through the bedrock of neighborliness and community feeling. Indeed, the cultures of faking make community possible.

The state, the understanding goes, has no norms and this is evidenced by the arbitrariness of its procedures that its subjects encounter: secret and, hence, inscrutable. But even as one counters the state through mimicked procedures, it is important to not become the state, to remain of "the people," and that requires *tariqa*, etiquette. It is here also that particular kinds of neighborly bonds take shape when neighbors "help" each other, in the manner that Rakesh sought to assist Mohammad Islam by transferring the latter's property in his own name thorough counterfeit means. It was his duty; it is preferable to be preyed upon by one's own rather than be left to the mercies of the depredatory state. In the former case, the bonds of intimacy are strengthened as well as ensuring a result in one's favor.

Conclusion

This chapter has focused upon the specificity of the contexts in which people reflect upon ideas regarding community through the notions of corruption and transparency; it has sought to reflect upon local circumstances that—though located in the crucible of capital—cannot be captured through generalized theories of capitalism. Both DLF's residents and those of Nangla Matchi think the state to be corrupt. However, in the former case, the idea of the honorable (and honest) community is linked to producing community life and citizenry through the processes of the market. This, in principle at least, does away with the idea of different social and political categories and contexts that interrogate each other. The question which then remains is this: if private capital produces categories of citizens, then how does one differentiate between private and public interests? And how does one define the concept of corruption?

In Nangla Matchi, on the other hand, the perceived corruption of the state produces a chain of localized illegalities, which are seen to strengthen community bonds, and the most admired are those who have the *tariqa* to guide the community through proper application of the illegalities. Here, the "community" interrogates the state, mimics it, and yet does not become it. We require "local" histories of capital, rather than succumb to the seductions of "global" analyses that might derive from usage of the term "neo-liberal" in order to more carefully interrogate relationships between broader socioeconomic processes and the quotidian procedures of urban existence. So, while the residents of Nangla Matchi are subject to vigorous processes of contemporary capital—land transfer from the poor to the well-off, for example—they do not themselves, in turn, convert into the "enterprising" subject of neoliberalism.[42] However, the residents of DLF City display behavior that might more reasonably be said to approximate entrepreneurialism as a way of life; long-standing histories of local lives and the manner in which they articulate with broader processes (those of capital and the "capitalization" of the state, say) have a great deal to tell us about the tumult of the present.

Through the trope of "corruption," my key aim in this chapter has been to explore the making of community life in the city as it emerges out of changing relations between the state, private capital, and "citizens." These relations form the crucible within which urban lives are being transformed. For an anthropologist, they also point to ways in which large-scale processes and entities—"capital," "the state"—might become sites of ethnographic inquiries regarding the quotidian city.

Notes

1. Neil Brenner, ed., *Implosions/Explosions: Towards a Study of Planetary Urbanization* (Berlin: Jovis, 2014).
2. Uma Prasad Thapliyal, *Gazetteer of Rural Delhi* (Delhi: Delhi Administration, 1987), 127.
3. Sanjoy Chakravorty, *The Price of Land: Acquistion, Conflict, Consequence* (New Delhi: Oxford University Press, 2013).
4. Suneetha Dasappa Kacker, "The DDA and the Idea of Delhi," in *The Idea of Delhi*, ed. Romi Khosla (Mumbai: Marg, 2005), 72.
5. See also Chakravorty's clear-sighted analysis of the role of the state on land issues on a national level since the Independence in Sanjoy Chakravorty, *The Price of Land*. The colonial model established and perpetuated in Delhi has had far-reaching consequences.

6. *Bhagidari Report* (New Delhi: Bhagidari Cell, Government of NCT of Delhi, 2001).

7. Arjun Appadurai, "Patriotism and Its Futures," *Public Culture* 11 (1993): 411.

8. M. de Alwis, S. Deshpande, P. Jeganathan, M. John, N. Menon, A. Nigam, and S. A. Zaidi, "The Postnational Condition," *Economic and Political Weekly* 44, no. 10 (2009): 35.

9. Abhilasha Ojha, "RWAs Will Soon Have Direct Control over Sanitation and Community Halls," *Indian Express*, January 12, 1999, available at www.indianexpress.com/res/ple/ie/daily/19991201, accessed on December 11, 2007.

10. Ibid.

11. Arman Sethi, "The Price of Reforms," *Frontline* 22, no. 19 (September 10–23, 2005): 5.

12. Ibid.

13. Tanvi Sirari, "Civil Uprisings in Contemporary India" (Working Paper No. 161, Centre for Civil Society, New Delhi, 2006), 5.

14. Ibid., emphasis added.

15. Jacob Copeman and Aya Ikegame, "Guru Logics," *HAA: Journal of Ethnographic Theory* 2, no. 1 (2012): 318.

16. William Mazzarella, *Shoveling Smoke: Advertising and Globalization in Contemporary India* (Durham, NC: Duke University Press, 2003); Leela Fernandes, *India's New Middle Class: Democratic Politics in an Era of Economic Reform* (Minneapolis, MN: University of Minnesota Press, 2006); Filippo Osella and Caroline Osella, "Muslim Entrepreneurs in Public Life between India and the Gulf: Making Good and Doing Good," *Journal of the Royal Anthropological Institute* 15, no. s1 (2009): S202–221.

17. Srirupa Roy, *Beyond Belief: India and the Politics of Postcolonial Nationalism* (Durham and London: Duke University Press, 2007).

18. D. Asher Ghertner, "Gentrifying the State, Gentrifying Participation: Elite Governance Programs in Delhi," *International Journal of Urban and Regional Research* 35, no. 3 (2011): 526.

19. Akhil Gupta, *Postcolonial Development: Agriculture in the Making of Modern India* (Durham, NC: Duke University Press).

20. Aiwa Ong, *Neoliberalism as Exception: Mutations in Citizenship and Sovereignty* (Durham, NC: Duke University Press, 2006); David Harvey, *A Brief History of Neoliberalism* (New York: Oxford University Press, 2005).

21. Sanjay Srivastava, "Divine Markets: Post-nationalism, Religion and Moral Consumption in India," in *Religion and the Morality of Markets*, ed. Filippo Osella and Daromir Rudnyckyj (Cambridge: Cambridge University Press, 2017), 99.

22. Ibid.

23. Terry Flew, "Six Theories of Neoliberalism," *Thesis Eleven* 122, no. 1 (2014): 49–71. Emphasis added.

24. Daniel Mains, "Neoliberal Times: Progress, Boredom, and Shame among Young Men in Urban Ethiopia," *American Ethnologist* 34, no. 4 (2007): 660.

25. Flew, "Six Theories," 51.

26. Ibid., 52.

27. Sangeeta Kamat, "Deconstructing the Rhetoric of Decentralization: The State in Education Reform," *Current Issues Comparative Education* 2, no. 2 (2002): 110–119.

28. Partha Chatterjee, *The Nation and Its Fragments. Colonial and Postcolonial Histories* (Princeton, NJ: Princeton University Press, 1993); Gupta, *Postcolonial Development.*

29. Steve Derné, *Globalization on the Ground: New Media and the Transformation of Culture, Class, and Gender in India* (New Delhi: Sage Publications, 2008); Atulan Guha, "Labour Market Flexibility: An Empirical Inquiry into Neoliberal Propositions," *Economic and Political Weekly* 44, no. 9 (2009): 45–52.

30. Amita Baviskar and Raka Ray, eds., *Elite and Everyman: The Cultural Politics of the Indian Middle Classes* (New Delhi: Routledge, 2011); Christiane Brosius, *India's Middle-Class: New Forms of Urban Leisure, Prosperity and Consumption* (New Delhi: Routledge, 2010); Mark Liechty, Carla Freeman, and Rachel Heiman, eds., *The Global Middle Classes: Theorizing through Ethnography* (Santa Fe: School of Advanced Research Press, 2012); Sandhya Krishnan and Neeraj Hatekar, "Rise of the New Middle Class in India and Its Changing Structure," *Economic and Poliitcal Weekly* 52, no. 22 (2017): 40–48.

31. Letter from DLF to the Haryana Town and Country Planning Department, dated June 24, 1981, in possession of the author.

32. Tarun Khanna, *Billions of Entrepreneurs: How China and India are Reshaping their Futures* (Boston, MA: Harvard Business Press, 2007), 107.

33. See Karina Landman and Martin Schönteich, "Urban Fortresses: Gated Communities as a Reaction to Crime," *African Security Review* 1, no. 4 (2002): 73–85 for South Africa; Choon-Piew Pow, "Securing the 'Civilised' Enclaves: Gated Communities and the Moral Geographies of Exclusion in (Post-) Socialist Shanghai," *Urban Studies* 44, no. 8 (2007): 1539–1558 for China; and Şerife Geniş, "Producing Elite Localities: The Rise of Gated Communities in Istanbul," *Urban Studies* 44, no. 4 (2007): 771–798 for Turkey.

34. Nandini Gooptu, *Enterprise Culture in Neoliberal India: Studies in Youth, Class, Work and Media* (London: Routledge, 2013).

35. Filippo Osella and Daromir Rudnyckyj, eds., *Religion and the Morality of Markets* (Cambridge: Cambridge University Press, 2017).

36. Roy, *Beyond Belief,* 134.

37. Ibid., 138.

38. Ibid., 142.

39. Jean Baudrillard, "Simulacra and Simulations," in *Jean Baudrillard. Selected Writings,* ed. Mark Poster (Stanford, CA: Stanford University Press, 1988).

40. Philip Abrams, "Notes on the Difficulty of Studying the State," *Journal of Historical Sociology* 1, no. (1988): 58–89; Karina Landman and Martin Schönteich, "Urban Fortresses: Gated Communities as a Reaction to Crime," *African Security Review* 1, no. 4 (2010): 73–85.

41. This process has been unfolding in fits and starts, and the following excerpt from a news report from January 2018 presents a representative picture: "Missed deadlines and slow process for taking charge of privately developed colonies by the Municipal Corporation of Gurugram (MCG) has become a cause for worry for the residents of Sushant Lok." See Dhananjay Jha, "MCG Takeover of Sushant Lok in Gurgaon in a Limbo Even after Four Months," *Hindustan Times*, January 9, 2018, available at https://www.hindustantimes.com/gurgaon/mcg-takeover-of-sushant-lok-in-gurgaon-in-a-limbo-even-after-four-months/story-LqXxtggBllnhLw2i0AdcCN.html, accessed on March 12, 2018.

42. Gooptu, *Enterprise Culture in Neoliberal India*.

CHAPTER 12

Politicians and *Netas*
The Politics of Grievance and Political Intermediation

Neelanjan Sircar

Introduction

In 1985, the late Prime Minister Rajiv Gandhi claimed, "Of every rupee spent by the government, only 17 paise reached the intended beneficiary."[1] Indeed, even the most basic services and infrastructure, from water to garbage collection to roads, are routinely under-provided to Indian citizens. There are myriad reasons for this poor delivery of goods from the state—among other things, a sheer lack of funds, weak bureaucratic capacity to deliver benefits, and outright corruption.

But whatever may be the reasons for the poor performance of the Indian state, the inability of the state to deliver on its promises obliges citizens to use "informal routes" to extract what they have been promised from the state. In a hot, arid climate such as that of Delhi, potable water is at a premium, and the taps often run dry in any number of Delhi's colonies. In such situations, citizens of the colony leverage their local contacts—who themselves typically have political and bureaucratic connections—to put pressure on the state to restore water provision.[2] Of course, when water access is restored in the colony, it is typically taken away from another colony, one with "less connected" local contacts.[3] When the state fails to meet expectations, citizens of urban India, such as those described in the previous paragraph, must pursue redressal of their "grievances" through such local contacts.[4]

The local contacts used by citizens are "intermediaries," although in common parlance they may be called *dalals* (middlemen), *samaj sewaks* (social workers), fixers,[5] *netas* (leaders), brokers, influencers, or many other names. The name is not important. What is important is that these "informal" intermediaries fundamentally mediate access between the state and its citizens.[6] Because intermediaries are so crucial to the last mile delivery of services, infrastructure, and benefits to citizens, they effectively choose the winners and losers in state provision.[7] This naturally engenders inequality in state provision to citizens. Intermediaries may be endowed with different levels of skill and connections, or they simply be more attached and responsive to certain citizens, leaving those without regular access to high-quality intermediaries largely excluded from the largesse of the state.[8]

Concerns about poor state delivery and the inequality of state access, which are certainly not just restricted to India, sparked off a period of "democratic decentralization" in the 1990s that reached other countries such as Bangladesh, Brazil, Ivory Coast, Ghana, and South Africa.[9] The goal was to implement free and fair local elections to decrease the "distance" between elected politicians and their constituents, to whom politicians should be accountable. That is, where the state lacks the capacity to efficiently target its citizens, locally accountable leaders should be better at this task because they have more direct access to their constituents. If an elected leader is to shirk or underperform in his/her responsibilities, citizens may simply vote out the politician.

This democratic decentralization principle was applied unevenly in India. In rural India, the 73rd amendment to the Indian constitution provided for elected local village governments or *panchayats*. A *panchayat* ward member is typically elected at the level of a polling booth, and there is approximately one *panchayat* ward member for every 315 rural citizens.[10] The 74th amendment to the Indian constitution instituted a similar electoral decentralization to urban local bodies (ULBs) to elect municipal ward councillors. But these urban, elected politicians do not have the same proximity to their constituents as *panchayat* ward members. In Delhi, for instance, the municipal wards contained 70,000 residents on average according to the 2011 Indian Census. In practical terms, this means that India's rural citizens have the opportunity to directly raise grievances with a politician who is held accountable to them through elections.[11] By contrast, the sheer distance between citizens and elected politician in urban India obliges those who live in Indian cities to often use intermediaries to address their grievances. This is to say nothing of the differences in expectations of services between urban and rural citizens.

In the voluminous political science literature on intermediaries, there is surprisingly little effort in understanding how the structural and institutional context affects the behavior and function of these informal actors. Because the Indian urban context can be differentiated from its rural context, in both the nature of the grievances raised and the local administrative and political structures, a study of Indian cities offers the opportunity to nuance our understanding of intermediation. This study is the first large-scale study of informal intermediaries at the scale of Indian urban agglomeration, thereby providing an analysis over a level of social and spatial variation that one can rarely bring to such an important issue. In order to make large-scale claims, this study develops a framework to understand the impact of political intermediation through the interplay of two markets, the market for intermediaries themselves and the market for privately provided civic services such as water and garbage collection. Such a theoretical framework privileges the role of citizens' incentives and choice, both in whether to raise a grievance and the manner of the grievance. This deviates from the dominant literature in political science, which argues that citizens exercise little choice due to political patronage and clientelism.[12]

This chapter analyzes the use and performance of intermediaries in the National Capital Region (NCR)—the large urban region surrounding Delhi—using the Center for the Advanced Study of India (CASI)–NCR Survey of 5,477 households. As argued earlier, understanding the availability, approachability, and responsiveness of urban intermediaries is crucial to understand the quality and the inequality in state provision of promised goods and services. As India's most rapidly growing urban region, an analysis of political intermediation in the NCR affords the opportunity to understand the intricacies of state access over a complex and highly varied urban terrain.

The core finding of this chapter is that intermediation disproportionately benefits the wealthiest households in the NCR, as intermediaries are the most responsive to their grievances. This occurs because, absent any mechanism to hold intermediaries accountable, intermediaries target the wealthiest households to bolster their social position. These wealthy households typically have the money to purchase water, electricity, and garbage collection on the private market—unlike the urban poor. Thus, while the urban poor demand civic services from the state, a bias in targeting the wealthy leads to significant under-provision of urban civic services.

Markets for Intermediaries and Civic Services

Intermediaries are not charity workers; mediating access to the state is a vocation. Indeed, it is often the most lucrative vocation—as intermediaries trade their ability to get things done and to reach citizens to extract rents from the system. More precisely, because intermediaries provide access to state benefits to regular citizens, they will often request some compensation from citizens (anything from money to a vote for a particular politician). Similarly, political elites and parties often recruit intermediaries due to their influence over citizens, offering them compensation or political positions.

The space of intermediaries is usually an unregulated, highly competitive *market*, as these intermediaries aggressively compete with each other to increase their scale of local influence.[13] In short, if there is an opportunity to extract rents by mediating access between the state and citizens, someone is likely to show up to fulfill this role.

Naturally, the market for intermediaries follows certain rules of supply and demand. We expect intermediaries to be available to citizens if three "scope conditions" are met. First, there must be a demand for their services; that is, the state does not supply certain services or goods and these require informal routes to the state. Second, intermediaries must have sufficient "ability" and connections to do their job; this means that, in addition to building connections to politicians and bureaucrats, intermediaries must possess detailed knowledge of the complexities of India's state—its norms, laws that govern it, and responsibilities of each state actor. Finally, and perhaps most importantly, it must be sufficiently lucrative for intermediaries to enter the market. This means citizens being assisted either must be wealthy enough, and willing to pay enough, or must be willing to trade something valuable (for example, votes) for services rendered by an intermediary.

Availability and Approachability of Intermediaries

The intermediaries that enter the market may be quite diverse. They may differ in experience, strength of party affiliation, religious and caste identity, and many other attributes. Yet, because the *price* that intermediaries can demand/extract from citizens is a function of their connections and abilities, effective intermediaries are likely to be distinguished in status terms—higher caste, more educated, powerful families. For the vast majority of these intermediaries, their ability to extract is directly related to their own abilities, not anointed by higher political actors.[14] As such, intermediaries can trade their scale of influence locally for financial benefits or political positions with higher-level political elites. Because multiple parties and political actors likely vie for the influence wielded by intermediaries, these intermediaries can regularly renegotiate their agreements and contracts with higher-level political actors.[15] In short, most intermediaries may behave such as mercenaries, although typically they are referred to on the ground (quite euphemistically) as *samaj sewak*s (social workers). That is not to say that political parties do not enter the market, with committed party workers on the ground, but typically these party workers and social workers compete side-by-side in the same market for intermediaries.[16]

Nonetheless, it would be incorrect to assume that the citizens are served equally even if intermediaries are not stable agents of political parties. In many contexts, an intermediary must hook on to *some* political party that can direct resources toward him/her—and these parties are more likely to cater to grievances from certain identity groups and social classes. A citizen will approach an intermediary if he/she believes there is a sufficient chance of grievance redressal, that is, the perceived benefits of approaching the intermediary outweigh the costs of doing so. Certain individuals will find the price of an intermediary prohibitive for the quality of the service being provided due to an inability to procure resources from higher-level political actors, and will thus choose not to approach the intermediary. Accordingly, one should expect those social groups with poorer political representation at the highest levels to be least likely to approach intermediaries.

Until this point, nothing in our discussion of intermediaries is unique to the urban Indian context; indeed, previous work has found a vibrant market for informal intermediaries in villages in the Indian state of Bihar.[17] But urban areas differ from rural areas in two important ways. First, the sorts of grievances raised by urban citizens are likely to be different from those raised by rural citizens, owing to different expectations of services and infrastructure provided by the state (for example, garbage collection, sewage), and different patterns of social relations between urban citizens and rural migrants creating greater pressures for the state to ease movement across the city (and to do so safely). Second, as discussed in the Introduction of this chapter, the structure of institutions in urban India is quite different from that of rural India. In rural India, the closest elected representative is the *panchayat* ward member, who typically interacts with each of his/her constituents on a personal basis.

Table 12.1   To whom are grievances framed?

	State Capacity	
	Low	High
Low	Informal Intermediaries	Political Representatives
High	The State	The State

Source: Author.

The constituencies of the most local elected representatives in urban India are far too large for this sort of personal interaction. Thus, in urban India, intermediaries must fill in for political representatives in ways that are not demanded in rural India.

Elections, Intermediaries, and Responsiveness

When the state is unable (or perhaps unwilling) to effectively and efficiently deliver benefits to its citizens, the state is said to be lacking in "capacity." In such situations, when citizens cannot directly go to the state, citizens must find avenues to register and redress grievances with poor delivery of benefits. The natural avenue for grievances is the local political representative.[18] When there is sufficient democratic decentralization, the local political representative knows each of his/her own constituents, and the citizens can directly reach the political representative. This is the situation in rural India, where *panchayat ward members* are elected by and accountable to a small number of citizens (there is one ward member for approximately 340 citizens in rural India). Abstractly, citizens will be reliant on informal intermediaries where the reach of the state is weak and where there is little local political representation—this is exactly the situation in urban India. The two-by-two table (Table 12.1) displays to whom the citizen frames grievances with the state.

The person or institution to whom grievances are framed in turn structures biases in the distribution of benefits. To the extent that state has strong capacity, and can directly act on grievances from citizens, the distribution is likely to be fair (in the sense that it conforms to the rules laid out for distribution, not that the rules themselves are fair). The introduction of politics in distribution also introduces biases in the recipients of benefits—but there are differences in biases emanating from elected representatives and informal intermediaries.

In free-and-fair elections, a candidate must procure the support of a "minimum winning coalition," which is guaranteed to be a large proportion of the constituency. This structures the actions of the elected representative in important ways. He/she must make broad-based appeals since he or she will be held to account by elections. Furthermore, the wealth of the household being assisted by the elected representative makes little difference, as the vote of each voter counts the same, irrespective of the personal characteristics of the voter. In fact, although there are likely to be political biases, there is ample evidence that elected representatives are likely to assist the *poorest* households disproportionately.[19]

The situation for informal intermediaries is different. Because elections do not determine social position for informal intermediaries, households are differentiated, as the intermediary prefers to hold sway over the highest-status households in the area since this maximizes the extent of his/her influence. Under such a scenario, one expects that intermediaries will be disproportionately responsive to the wealthiest households, the opposite of the rural electoral scenario. Because urban India broadly has intermediaries of this informal, unelected variety, one expects that the pattern of urban intermediation disproportionately cater to the interests of wealthiest households. This generates inequalities in the access to state resources, where the poor disproportionately lose out.

Market for Civic Services and Grievances

One can broadly categorize the set of public goods demanded by citizens as "excludable" or "non-excludable."[20] Excludable goods are those such as electricity and water that can be targeted to particular households while excluding surrounding households. Non-excludable goods are typically heavy infrastructure such as roads and street lighting that cannot easily exclude surrounding households. The category of excludable public goods are available for private provision. Historically, it was very difficult to privately provide health care or water, as can be seen in, for instance, the British case.[21] In these situations, there was public demand from all citizens for operational civic services that benefited poor and wealthy households alike. As technology has progressed, citizens have become adept in crafting private solutions to avail of excludable public goods and civic services.

When the state is inefficient in delivering what it has promised to its citizens, the costs to citizens, particularly in terms of time and quality of provision, of recouping these services and goods from the state may not be worth it. For those with sufficient wealth, it may be easier to *privately* purchase these public goods. In the NCR, and in most developing world urban contexts, there is also a vibrant market for public goods that can be privately provided. Electricity can be provided through generators at the cost of petrol, water can be provided through purchasing potable water from private providers, and there are many private vendors for garbage collection. In short, for a set of basic civic services, the *wealthy* can simply opt for private provision rather than raising grievances with the state. By contrast, the poor, who cannot afford to privately provide all of these public goods, must raise grievances with the state for basic civic services.[22]

On the other hand, non-excludable public goods, largely heavy infrastructure, are purely the domain of the state for all citizens.[23] The state is responsible for upgradation and maintenance of heavy infrastructure such as roads or street lighting which cannot be reasonably paid for by households, and one should expect even wealthy households to raise grievances on such matters.[24] Thus, one should expect poorer households to disproportionately approach intermediaries with grievances around civic services, while one should expect wealthier households to approach intermediaries with grievances around heavy infrastructure. It is also worth noting that the sorts of political connections required to change road or lighting infrastructure (the types of decisions that are highly politicized in any urban context and require the assent of many party and bureaucratic actors) are likely to reside disproportionately with party workers. Accordingly, one should expect the wealthy to approach political/ party workers at higher rates.

Hypotheses

The empirical predictions of intermediary behavior and grievance redressal result from the interaction between two markets, the market for intermediaries and the market for private provision of civic services. From the previous discussion, we can discern two clear hypotheses for urban Indian contexts, especially as they relate to the wealth of the household.

H1. Poverty and civic services: The poorer the household, the more likely it is to express grievances with civic services being provided by the state. The wealthier the household, the more likely it is to express grievances with heavy infrastructure being provided by the state.

H2. Wealth and responsiveness: The wealthier the household, the more likely an intermediary is to be responsive to its grievances.

Data

At the outset, it should be noted that any measurement of informal leadership is necessarily complicated. Unlike formal or well-defined roles, there is no objective way to characterize the "universe" of informal intermediaries. Rather than trying to identify all plausible intermediaries, the CASI–NCR Survey adopted a citizen-side approach to identify these individuals. After much piloting of the survey, we determined that the most natural way to ask for intermediaries was to ask respondents to report about *ilake mein neta* (local area leaders). To avoid confusion, we will continue to refer to this character as an intermediary in the remainder of this chapter.

Respondents were asked successively about the availability of an intermediary, the approachability of the intermediary, and the effectiveness of the intermediary in solving a problem. In order to make the survey questions more tangible, and to avoid certain types of response biases, respondents were asked about their personal experiences. Concretely, respondents were asked a sequence of questions:

1. Availability: Can you give the name(s) of intermediary/intermediaries in this area who solve disputes or other local problems?
2. Approachability: Have you ever approached the named intermediary/ intermediaries with an issue? What was the issue?
3. Responsiveness: Was the intermediary/intermediaries able to resolve the issue?

The sequential nature of these questions structures response in important ways. First, given how the questions are asked, it is not possible to answer the following question unless the previous question has been answered in the affirmative. For instance, it is impossible to answer a question about whether one has approached the named intermediary if no such intermediary has been named or if the intermediary effectively resolved an issue if no issue was raised with the intermediary. The advantage of this structure is that it allows the researcher to model not only the absolute probability, for instance, an individual approaches an intermediary, but also the *conditional* probabilities, for example, the probability of an individual approaching an intermediary given that an intermediary is available to him/her. This structure of questions, thus, helps disentangle the extent to which availability, approachability, or responsiveness of intermediaries can explain biases in intermediation for citizens.

Once respondents gave the name of an intermediary, the survey asked the respondent to provide demographic details of the intermediary, namely, caste, religion, role in the community/occupation, state of birth, and party of affiliation. When cross-referenced with data on the household of the respondent, this data provides a characterization of the *relationship* between intermediaries and citizens, especially in terms of demographic factors.

Availability

In this section, we report the relative availability of intermediaries, and the relationship between citizens and their available intermediaries. As discussed

previously, first and foremost, the availability of intermediaries on the ground
signals a rent-seeking opportunity (that is, opportunity to extract from the
system) because the state is not sufficiently providing promised goods and
services on the ground. Based on the geography of the NCR, one should
expect that as one moves away from the core of the urban zone, the reliance
on intermediaries for access to the state grows.[25] This is because one should
expect the penetration of the state to be greatest in the urban core of a city,
especially with regard to electricity and water.

   All told, 75 percent of 5,477 respondents named at least one intermediary
(but only 5 named more than one intermediary). This suggests that the
prevalence of intermediaries is quite high. While the fact that most respondents
only named one intermediary may suggest that there is not much of a local
market for intermediaries, our observations in the field suggest that respondents
only named the person(s) that they are likely to approach with grievances as
opposed to the entire population of intermediaries. Figure 12.1 shows that the
availability of intermediaries grows as one moves from the Delhi to the main
suburbs of Faridabad, Ghaziabad, Gurgaon, and Noida to the "outskirts" (the
areas in the NCR further from Delhi than the aforementioned suburbs). This
provides further evidence that the supply of intermediaries do in fact respond
to "market-like" incentives.

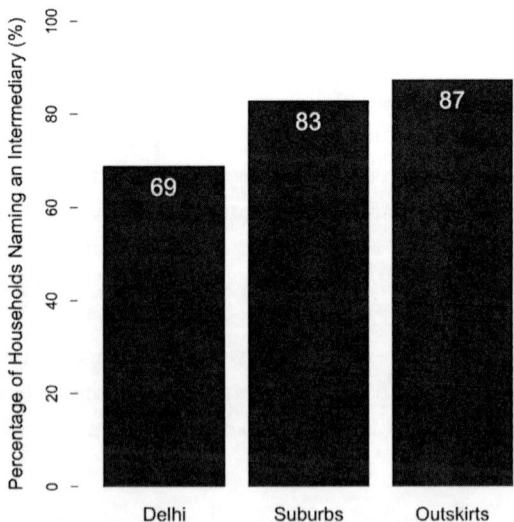

Figure 12.1   Core–periphery dynamics in intermediary availability
Source: Author.

The CASI–NCR Survey asked respondents to report the named intermediary's "position" in the community, from property dealer to strongman, to social worker, and to party/political worker. In our sample, approximately 58 percent of the named intermediaries were viewed as "social workers," with 36 percent being viewed as "party workers" (and only 6 percent were given some other designation). This provides evidence that the vast majority of the intermediaries are not viewed as entrenched partisan actors. This is consistent with the idea that a large number of intermediaries act as mercenaries, allying themselves with local political elites, which has been observed in other work on India and around the world.[26] It is worth noting that even though citizens typically did not see their intermediaries as entrenched partisan actors, they nevertheless believed their intermediaries had currently aligned themselves to one party or another—96 percent of the named intermediaries could be associated with a particular political party.

In line with the recent work on intermediaries in India, the data suggest that intermediaries are of "higher status" than the population at large because these are precisely the individuals that are most effective at mobilizing contacts in the state.[27] This generates demographic biases in the population, as these individuals are more likely from upper castes, more likely Hindus, and more likely born in the state in which they are residing—which is verified in Table 12.2.

Naturally, one might ask the extent to which these biases extend to the availability of intermediaries. A conservative view might be that the availability of intermediaries is identity-specific and sorted by religion and caste. That is, because of the strength of religious and caste ties, largely Muslim intermediaries are available to Muslims, Scheduled Caste (SC) intermediaries to SCs, and so on.

Figure 12.2 reports the relationship between the identity of the respondent's head of household and the identity of the available intermediary. The first panel shows the relationship over four broad caste classifications: General,

Table 12.2 Differences in characteristics between intermediaries and the overall population (in percentage)

	Intermediaries	Overall population (NCR)
Hindu	92	87
Upper caste	57	37
Born in the state of residence	94	88

Source: Author.

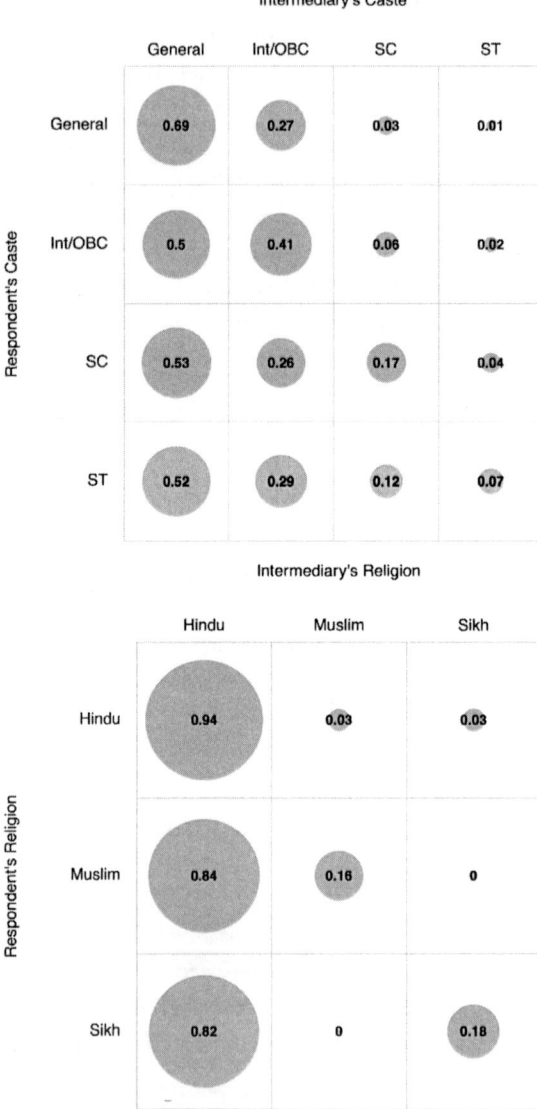

Figure 12.2   Relationship between the identities of the household and the intermediary
Source: Author.

Notes: (a) This figure displays the relative association between the castes of the respondent households and the castes of the intermediaries. The numbers refer to the proportion of intermediaries of the caste groups named in the columns, given that the household is from the caste groups named in the rows. (b) This figure displays the relative association between the religion of the respondent household and the religion of the intermediary. The numbers refer to the proportion of intermediaries of the religious groups named in the columns, given that the household is from the religious groups named in the rows.

intermediate/Other Backward Class (int./OBC), SC, and Scheduled Tribe (ST). The second panel shows the relationship for populations from the three major religions in the sample: Hindu, Muslim, and Sikh. In the correlation plot, the area of the circle is proportional to the probability a household from a particular identity group has an intermediary of a particular identity available. For instance, a General Caste household has 0.69 probability of having a General Caste intermediary available and a 0.03 probability of having an SC intermediary available. Conversely, a Muslim household has a 0.16 probability of having a Muslim intermediary available and a 0.84 probability of having a Hindu intermediary available.

A simple inspection of Figure 12.2 reveals little evidence for identity-specific availability of intermediaries. While there is some evidence of caste and religious sorting (for example, a Muslim citizen is more likely to have a Muslim intermediary available than a Hindu or Sikh citizen), the vast majority of citizens have access to intermediaries with "higher status" identities. Indeed, as Table 12.2 shows, Muslim citizens are more likely to have a Hindu intermediary available and SC citizens are more likely to have an upper-caste intermediary available. This lends further credence to the argument that an intermediary enters less on the basis of existing social ties on the ground and more on the basis of the capacity to mediate access between state and citizen.

Approachability and Grievances

In this section, we describe the social dynamics in approaching an intermediary and the grievances raised therein. We consider the probability of approaching an intermediary given that such an intermediary is available (that is, named by the respondent). All told, 22 percent of the respondents have approached the intermediary named previously by the respondent.

One should interpret the numbers around approachability with some caution. There are many reasons as to why a citizen may choose not to approach the intermediary in addition to the reasons described earlier in the chapter. Perhaps the citizen is genuinely satisfied with the provision of services and infrastructure and has no major grievance to raise with the state. Or maybe there are mitigating circumstances that make the cost of approaching the intermediary very high, for example, inability to take time off work. Finally, it is plausible that citizens do not approach an intermediary because other means of resolving the issue are available to them, such as government contacts or the ability to resolve the issue through private means. Nonetheless, the fact that more than one in five of our respondents have approached the named intermediary suggests that this is a major route for addressing grievances to the state.

Just because an intermediary is available to a citizen does not mean that he or she will be approached with a grievance. While there can be many reasons to approach (or not) an intermediary, one can assume that a citizen will only approach the intermediary when the perceived benefits of doing so outweigh costs. The costs of approaching may include opportunity cost of following up with the intermediary to more direct financial costs. The perceived benefits are related to expected likelihood of grievance redressal. A naive calculation of the rate at which an intermediary addresses a grievance is flawed because those who perceive that their grievances will remain unaddressed will also refuse to pay the price to approach an intermediary. For these reasons, an analysis of biases in approach rates is important for an analysis of intermediation. We characterize these biases by the caste and religious identity of the household and by the wealth of the household.

Figure 12.3 displays the demographic biases in approaching intermediaries by identity group (the caste groupings are coded for Hindus, Sikhs, and Christians, while the Muslims are coded as a separate identity group). We find that General Caste and SC citizens approach intermediaries at higher rates. Perhaps, this is owing to identity bases of the powerful parties in the region. For instance, western Uttar Pradesh (a large portion of the NCR) is

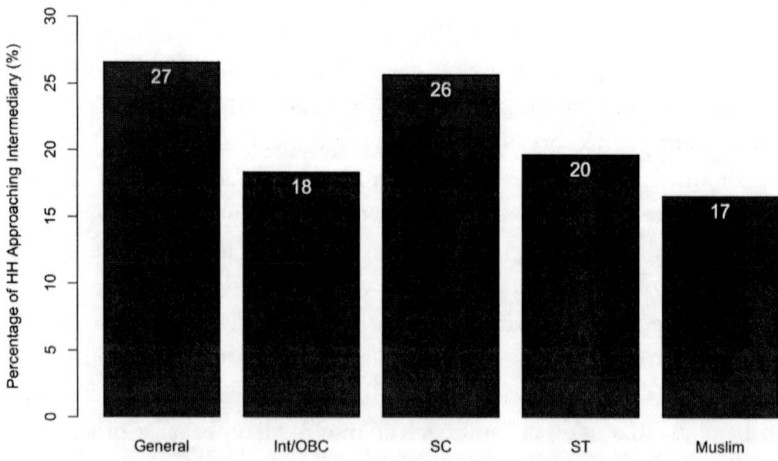

Figure 12.3   Intermediary approach rates by caste and religion
Source: Author.

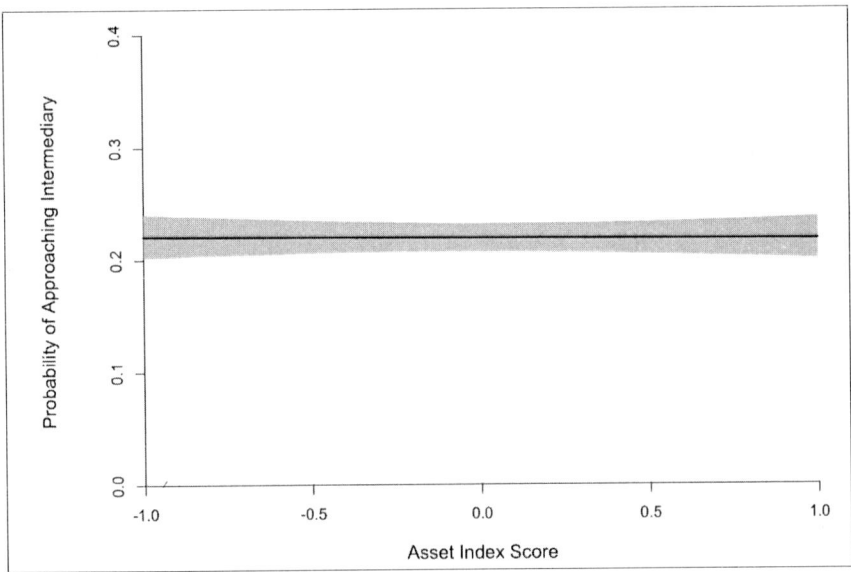

Figure 12.4   Intermediary approachability by household wealth

Source: Author.

Notes: This figure displays the estimated probability of approaching a named intermediary as a function of the asset index. The estimates come from a bivariate binary logistic regression, with 95 percent predictive intervals. No discernible relationship is noticeable.

seen as a stronghold for the upper caste–dominated Bharatiya Janata Party (BJP) and the SC-dominated Bahujan Samaj Party (BSP). Given the relative political mobilization of SC and General Caste populations in the region, on the margin they may reasonably expect greater responsiveness from the system. Figure 12.4 displays the probability of a household approaching a named intermediary as a function of wealth (measured by the amenities index) according to a bivariate logistic regression. There are no discernible economic wealth effects on approach rates to intermediaries, which stands to reason as parties do not explicitly mobilize on economic class terms.[28]

Grievances

Once respondents mentioned that they had previously approached the named intermediary, they were asked about the grievances for which they sought redressal. The grievances were dominated by civic services (43 percent), heavy infrastructural issues (36 percent), and with security issues (6 percent) lagging behind. A smattering of other issues constituted the remaining 15 percent of grievances. The CASI–NCR Survey did not deeply probe the grievance of concern; however, respondents took heavy infrastructure to mean upgradation of physical infrastructure such as road construction, street lighting, and so on while civic services were understood to mean those things that require greater personnel or a government decision for effective delivery such as garbage collection, electricity, and water.[29]

In order to make sense of the social dynamics of grievance, we analyzed how these grievances change as a function of economic wealth using a series of bivariate logistic regressions, as there is little variation in grievances by identity.[30] We remind the reader that the first major hypothesis of the market-driven framework developed in this chapter is that the wealthy should disproportionately demand heavy infrastructure, while the poor should demand civic services (because they cannot easily opt in to the private market for these services). Figure 12.5 confirms the first hypothesis. On the poorer end of the asset index (a value of –1 corresponds to approximately the 10th percentile), a grievance for civic services is almost twice as likely as a grievance for heavy infrastructure. On the wealthier end of the amenities index (a value of 1 corresponds to approximately the 85th percentile), a grievance for heavy infrastructure is more likely than a grievance for civic amenities. Interestingly, security emerges as a discernible grievance for the wealthier populations, even though one might argue that the poor bear the brunt of a bad safety situation. Consistent with these grievances, Figure 12.6 shows that the wealthy are increasingly likely to approach party workers (political leaders), who are more connected to the parties in power and can more easily deliver heavy infrastructure, while the poor are far more likely to reach out to social workers.

Responsiveness

Of course, the politics of grievance redressal is fundamentally about who can successfully solve citizens' problems. In order to understand intermediary responsiveness, we coded whether the respondent believed the issue was resolved by the intermediary (conditional on having approached the intermediary) and measured the probability of the issue being resolved by the intermediary. All told, a remarkable 54 percent of respondents believed that the intermediary had resolved the issue, conditional on having been approached. But, as we have discussed earlier in this chapter, this number is likely driven by selection effects—one is unlikely to approach an intermediary if the intermediary is unlikely to resolve the issue.

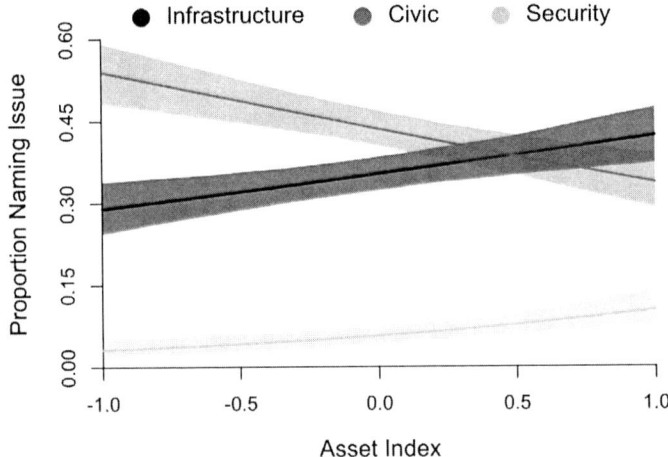

Figure 12.5 Grievances by economic wealth

Source: Author.

Notes: The graph displays the estimated probability of raising a grievance related to infrastructure, civic services, and safety, respectively, as a function of the asset index. The estimates come from a bivariate binary logistic regression, with 95 percent predictive intervals. Poorer households disproportionately raise grievances about civic services, while wealthier households disproportionately raise grievances about infrastructure.

To get a sense of the social dynamics of intermediary responsiveness, we model the probability of having an issue resolved by the intermediary as a function of a household's asset index score with a bivariate logistic regression (we note, once again, there are no clear identity-based dynamics in responsiveness). Our second hypothesis suggests that intermediaries should be most responsive to the grievances of the wealthiest households because they are most important to an intermediary's social position. Figure 12.7 demonstrates a striking relationship between the wealth of a household and the probability of having an issue resolved by the intermediary. At an asset score value of –1 (approximately the 10th percentile), the issue is predicted to be resolved about 38 percent of the time, and at an asset score value of 1 (approximately the 85th percentile), the issue is predicted to be resolved about 70 percent of the time. In short, the wealthy in our sample have their issues resolved for the vast majority of the time, and the poor in our sample are unable to resolve their issues for the vast majority of the time.

At first blush, this result is somewhat confounding. If the poor are so unlikely to have their issues resolved, why approach the intermediary at all? Indeed, we showed that identity groups which were not targeted by the

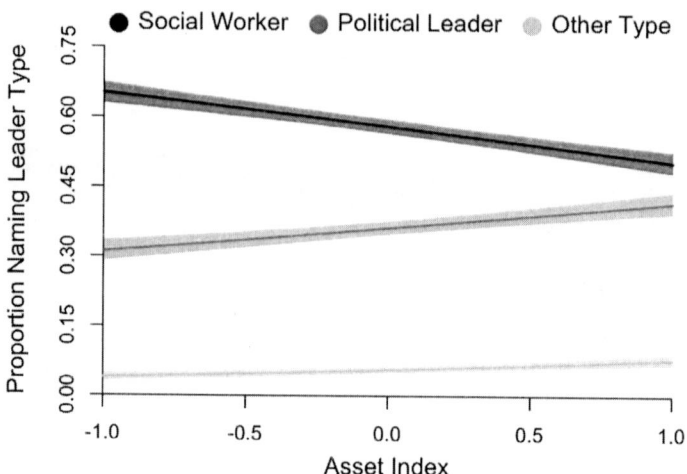

Figure 12.6   Type of intermediary named by household wealth

Source: Author.

Notes: The figure displays the estimated probability of naming an intermediary, as a function of the asset index, from the following three categories: social worker, political leader (party worker), and other type. The estimates come from a bivariate binary logistic regression, with 95 percent predictive intervals. Poorer households disproportionately name social workers, while wealthier households name party workers at a much higher rate. Combined with different issues raised as grievances, this shows the pattern of grievance from wealthier households is quite different from that of poorer households.

political parties were less likely to approach an intermediary, this was not true for economic wealth. A possible answer lies in the interplay between the two markets we discussed at the beginning of this chapter. Because the poor simply cannot privately purchase a great many civic services, they are obliged to seek them from the state. At the same time, without any electoral pressure or other accountability mechanisms, urban intermediaries are likely to be less responsive to the needs of the poor.[31] Thus, while the poor may have to pay the same price for intermediaries in financial or other costs as the wealthy, they may be less likely to reap benefits from the political intermediation system. Thus, even with intermediaries to address state weakness, there is likely to be a significant under-provision of services to the poor.

Concluding Thoughts

This chapter has attempted to make large-scale empirical claims about urban political intermediation in India using a framework that considers the

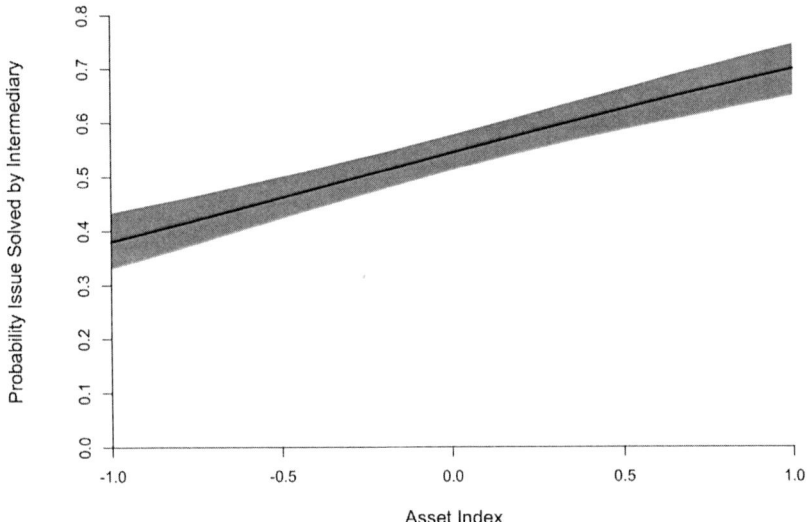

Figure 12.7   Intermediary responsiveness by household wealth

Source: Author.

Notes: This figure displays the estimated probability of having a grievance satisfactorily addressed as a function of the asset index. The estimates come from a bivariate binary logistic regression, with 95 percent predictive intervals. Wealthier households are significantly more likely to have their grievances satisfactorily addressed.

interplay between the market for intermediaries and the market for privately provided public services. As the data show, this is a system, in the absence of electoral or state regulation, that disadvantages the poor. Because the poor disproportionately demand civic services, while informal intermediaries disproportionately respond to the wealthy, there is under-provision of urban civic services. As we conclude this chapter, it is useful to reflect on political intermediation in market terms.

State weakness provides opportunities for a population of entrepreneurs to become intermediaries to extract rents from the system. At the same time, these intermediaries provide a valuable service, as many citizens would have little access to state benefits without political intermediation. So, how might we evaluate the aggregate impact of intermediaries on social welfare? In the short term, it can be said that intermediaries provide a service (albeit an exclusive one in the case of the NCR) and, therefore, have a positive welfare impact on the system. On the other hand, the need to extract rents from the system makes intermediaries complicit in a system of corruption and non-transparency as intermediaries have an economic incentive in keeping citizens beholden to them. Thus, while intermediaries can be said to help mitigate the problems of state weakness, they can also be seen as the cause of it.

In the case of the NCR, the problems of urban political intermediation are compounded by the fact that there is no accountability mechanism, such as *panchayat* elections, with the citizenry. This necessarily obliges intermediaries to cater to the most powerful, high-status individuals in society because they are the most crucial for the social standing of intermediaries. While local elections mitigate these issues somewhat, as elections engender greater targeting to the poor, they also lead to a whole new set of problems in political biases.[32] Given the similarity of urban institutional and political structures across India, there are reasons to believe these concerns extend across urban India.

In general, the study of political intermediation in India has suffered from artificial distinctions between social workers, party workers, local *panchayat* leaders, and so on, even when they compete with each other to a great extent. A market perspective on political intermediation that accounts for all plausible political actors provides a more realistic canvas over which to understand how citizens address state weakness and make grievances against the state. At the same time, a perspective that only understands grievance redressal through political intermediation is woefully inadequate. Even the data in this chapter show that only about a fifth of all citizens approached an intermediary. Citizens likely use all manner of actors and strategies to cope with a weak state, from bureaucratic actors to neighbors and local shopkeepers.

The approach undertaken in this chapter allows us to understand variation in grievances and the behavior at a macro-urban scale. As the study of urban political intermediation grows, it will be necessary to develop a deeper understanding of the conditions under which citizens seek assistance from intermediaries. But as this volume demonstrates in so many ways, this is not a question that can be answered in isolation from its context. Greater Delhi and the NCR are subject to unique patterns in spatial inequality and segregation, social mores, and caste behavior. These are all factors that fundamentally shape how citizens seek to redress their grievances and even the types of grievances they bring to the table. While this chapter sheds light on some of the grievance redressal processes in the NCR, more nuanced investigation is necessary. The ability to raise a grievance with the state and to have it judged fairly should be a fundamental right of any urban citizen. In a city that is growing as rapidly and haphazardly as Delhi, it is also the only chance most citizens have to secure a stable life in the city. It is for these reasons we require a sustained and thorough research agenda on the "politics of grievance."

Notes

1. Santosh K. Joy, "Rahul Echoes Rajiv Gandhi's Comments on Public Funds," *Rediff News,* January 17, 2008, available at http://www.rediff.com/news/2008/jan/17rahul.htm, accessed on December 30, 2018.

2. Kriti Seth, "Water Problems in a South Delhi Slum: Challenges of Access, Usage and Awareness," Accountability Initiative, Centre for Policy Research, May 18, 2017, available at https://accountabilityindia.in/pa-series-180517, accessed on December 30, 2018.

3. Lisa Björkman, *Pipe Politics, Contested Waters: Embedded Infrastructures of Millennial Mumbai* (Durham, NC: Duke University Press, 2015). For a detailed discussion about the urban negotiations around water, from city bureaucracy to engineers and intermediaries, see recent work by Lisa Björkman on the issue in the Indian city of Mumbai.

4. Gabrielle Kruks-Wisner, *Claiming the State: Active Citizenship and Social Welfare in Rural India* (Cambridge: Cambridge University Press, 2018). Recently, work by Gabrielle Kruks-Wisner has focused on understanding how citizens make claims upon the state in rural India. This is a highly applicable framework for making sense of how citizens seek to deal with local problems in urban India.

5. James Manor, "Small-Time Political Fixers in India's States: Towel over Armpit," *Asian Survey* 40, no. 5 (2000): 816–835. This classic article provides a vivid picture of the ground-level actors that are required to solve everyday problems. In many ways, the discussion in this chapter is a natural extension of this work.

6. Kanchan Chandra, *Why Ethnic Parties Succeed: Patronage and Ethnic Headcounts in India* (New York: Cambridge University Press, 2004). Susan C. Stokes, "Perverse Accountability: A Formal Model of Machine Politics with Evidence from Argentina," *American Political Science Review* 99, no. 3 (August 2005): 315–325. Much of the prominent political science literature, starting with Stokes' seminal work, has focused on how intermediaries are used to secure votes for a clientelistic party. The focus in this chapter is simply on how intermediaries are used to make grievances on the state, not its implications for vote choice. This relationship between material exchange and votes has been described by Kanchan Chandra in her characterization of the Indian political system as a "patronage democracy." It is worth noting, however, that Chandra's discussion is focused on higher-level political representatives, and not local intermediaries.

7. Ward Berenschot, "Political Fixers and India's Patronage Democracy," in *Patronage as Politics in South Asia*, ed. Anastasia Piliavsky (Cambridge, UK: Cambridge University Press, 2014). Ward Berenschot describes the role of urban intermediaries, who may themselves not be beholden to any party, in the context of Indian democracy and clientelistic exchange.

8. Much of the literature describes these forms of exchanges through the lens of "clientelism" or "patronage." A fundamental feature of this framework is the lack of choice for citizens in addressing grievances. By understanding intermediaries as part of a more competitive process, and by drawing upon recent work on India, the framework in this chapter seeks to unsettle this traditional narrative.

9. Patrick Heller, "Moving the State: The Politics of Democratic Decentralization in Kerala, South Africa, and Porto Alegre," *Politics and Society* 29, no. 1 (2001): 131–163.

10. This approximation is based on data provided from the 2011 Indian Census (and its count of the rural population) and data provided by the Ministry of Panchayati Raj on the number of elected representatives in the *gram panchayat* (2008 is the latest year available).

11. Jennifer Bussell, *Clients and Constituents: Political Responsiveness in Patronage Democracies* (New York: Oxford University Press, 2019). This recent work by Jennifer Bussell shows that citizens often seek out higher-level representatives (who serve the constituency more generally) when there is poor representation among the most local intermediaries and leaders.

12. Stokes, "Perverse Accountability". Stokes describes a system in which machine (clientelistic) parties hold voters accountable and restrict their choice, rather than the standard model of democratic accountability. "The Argentine evidence, then, on the whole supports the theoretical finding that perverse accountability—the ability of parties to monitor constituents' votes, reward them for their support and punish them for defection—is what sustains machine politics" (p. 325).

13. Simon Chauchard and Neelanjan Sircar, "Courting Votes without Party Agents: Political Competition and Partisan Networks in Rural India" (working paper, 2018). See http://www.simonchauchard.com/wp-content/uploads/2014/02/politicalbrokerage_022618.pdf, accessed on 26 October, 2020.

14. Anirudh Krishna, "Politics in the Middle: Mediating Relationships between the Citizens and the State in Rural North India," in *Patrons, Clients, and Policies*, ed. Herbert Kitschelt and Steven Wilkinson (New York: Cambridge University Press, 2007).

15. Alisha C. Holland and Brian Palmer-Rubin, "Beyond the Machine: Clientelist Brokers and Interest Organizations in Latin America," *Comparative Political Studies* 48, no. 9 (2015): 1186–1223; Horacio Larreguy, Cesar Montiel, and Pablo Querubin, "Political Brokers: Partisans or Agents? Evidence from the Mexican Teacher's Union," *American Journal of Political Science* 61, no. 4 (2017): 877–891. There is disagreement on this matter in the Latin American cases, which is responsible for much of the literature on intermediaries in political science. Holland and Palmer-Rubin find that intermediaries consistently renegotiate their positions with the political parties, while Larreguy, Montiel, and Querubin argue that intermediaries are driven by partisan attachment.

16. Adam Michael Auerbach, "Clients and Communities: The Political Economy of Party Network Organization and Development in India's Urban Slums," *World Politics* 68, no. 1 (2016): 111–148; Adam Michael Auerbach and Tariq Thachil, "How Clients Select Brokers: Competition and Choice in India's Slums," *American Political Science Review* 112, no. 4 (2018): 775–791. Adam Auerbach has shown the importance of urban brokers connecting to party networks in slums. In later work, with Tariq Thachil, he demonstrates that brokers fundamentally distinguish themselves in *quality* or the ability to deliver and not by partisan or ethnic affiliation.

17. Neelanjan Sircar and Simon Chauchard, "Beyond Coethnicity: Political Influencers in Ethnically Diverse Societies" (manuscript, 2018). See http://www.simonchauchard.com/wp-content/uploads/2014/02/Sircar-Chauchard_031518.pdf, accessed on 26 October, 2020.

18. Gabrielle Kruks-Wisner, *Claiming the State: Active Citizenship and Social Welfare in Rural India* (Cambridge: Cambridge University Press, 2018).

19. Mark Schneider and Neelanjan Sircar, "Whose Side Are You On? Identifying Distributive Preferences of Local Politicians in India," Unpublished, 2020.

20. Note that here we are deviating from convention and theorizing these terms at the level of a locality or neighborhood, not at the level of a polity or an electoral constituency.

21. Alessandro Lizzeri and Nicola Persico, "Why Did the Elites Extend the Suffrage? Democracy and the Scope of Government, with an Application to Britain's 'Age of Reform'," *Quarterly Journal of Economics* 119, no. 2 (2004): 707–765. In Britain, for instance, health crises of the 1800s became a concern for citizens across social classes, so there was a demand for all-encompassing health-care reform.

22. Theodore Bergstrom, Lawrence Blume, and Hal Varian, "On the Private Provision of Public Goods," *Journal of Public Economics* 29 (1986): 25–49. This is a fairly general result in game theory. When wealth is concentrated in a few elites, these elites choose to privately provide public goods. As the wealth distribution equalizes, government-provided public goods "crowd out" such private provision.

23. The theoretical differentiation may be challenging to apply in empirical terms. While laying down electricity lines may be heavy infrastructure, the provision of electricity in and of itself is a civic service. A similar differentiation exists between laying infrastructure to provide piped water, as opposed to the provision of water. In the mind of the average Indian citizen, something the government technically has the capacity to provide and can choose to provide based on existing infrastructure, such as trash collection, water, or electricity, is a civic service. If physical infrastructure, such as a road, a pipe, an electricity line, and so on must be built, then this moves beyond a demand for civic services (even if the infrastructure would be necessary to provide the service).

24. From a theoretical perspective, two variables are at play here. First, the amount that would be required from voluntary contributions to pay for the construction and maintenance of these goods is prohibitively high. Second, the private contributors to a good cannot be compensated with greater provision of the good, as with electricity or water.

25. This is most evident in the manner in which housing has been built in these areas. In Delhi, the government, for example, through the Delhi Development Authority (DDA), is responsible for a significant amount of housing development and construction. In Delhi's suburbs, such as Gurgaon and Noida, much of this development has been outsourced to private actors such as DLF Limited.

26. Susan C. Stokes et al., *Brokers, Voters, and Clientelism: The Puzzle of Distributive Politics* (New York: Cambridge University Press, 2013).

27. Chauchard and Sircar, "Courting Votes without Party Agents."

28. We note that in our analyses there are no discernible differences in approachability across regions, so a region-wise analysis of approachability is omitted in this chapter.

29. Heavy infrastructure and civic services are not cleanly separable, as in principle the government could lay pipes for water or invest in a new transformer for electricity. But in common parlance and lived experience the delivery of water and electricity are seen largely to be distribution problems that require, for example, providing sufficient water tankers or preventing blackouts (load sheddings).

30. There are some differences in grievances by identity groups, but a larger regression that controls for economic wealth shows that these differences are primarily driven by the relative wealth of different social groups. Accordingly, we only present the results based on the asset index here.

31. One may naturally counter that responsiveness to the wealthy may be a function of different demands or different types of intermediaries, but further analyses show the results are robust to such complications.

32. Schneider and Sircar, "Whose Side Are You On?"

CHAPTER 13

Political Parties

The Emergence of the Aam Aadmi Party and the Changing Contours of the Party System

Adnan Farooqui

In the 2015 election for the Delhi Legislative Assembly, the Aam Aadmi Party (AAP) stunningly won 67 of the 70 seats. The Bharatiya Janata Party (BJP) won the remaining three seats. The Indian National Congress (INC), which had held power for 15 continuous years from 1998 to 2013 under Chief Minister Sheila Dixit, did not win a single seat. The emergence of the AAP as a disruptor in stable two-party system, and its critique of political class and marginalization of citizen voices in the political sphere, has to be located in the wider changes which have come about in India's social and political landscape in general and Delhi in particular. In Delhi, the AAP dislodged the incumbent Congress party from power and relegated it to political margins in the city-state. However, at the federal level, it has failed to project itself as a viable political alternative.

The significance of the AAP lay in the fact that it brought the agenda of social and political transformation, akin to social democratic experiments in the Scandinavian countries, to the political center stage, albeit fleetingly, as the India Against Corruption (IAC) movement transformed itself into a political party.[1] The formation of the AAP and its early success in galvanizing support across class categories was believed to be a resolution of the dilemma often faced by civil society movements. Previous movements led by civil society had failed to resolve class differences due to their inability to build a network cutting across class divides.[2] As an offshoot of the hugely popular IAC movement, the AAP succeeded in providing a common platform to disparate sections of the urban poor and middle class and managed to stitch a broad-based social coalition cutting across social and economic categories. Patrick Heller characterizes the IAC movement as belonging to the category of counterpower movements, with an express agenda of challenging the status quo by mobilizing civil society as a "counterpower."[3] He argues that their most significant contribution has been to bring the issue of participatory governance, accountability, and transparency to the political limelight.

This chapter investigates the political fortunes of the AAP since its emergence in 2012, its meteoric rise, and swinging political fortunes. It is divided into six sections. The first looks at the constitutional position of the Delhi Legislative Assembly historically to understand the tussle between the present AAP government and the center. The second section traces the political competition up to 2008 to understand the backdrop against which the AAP emerged, in what was for long believed to be a stable two-party system. The third section analyses the 2013 assembly elections and the debut of the AAP on Delhi's political scene and the reasons behind its failure in the subsequent parliamentary election. The fourth section is focused on the 2015 assembly election and analyses the AAP's phenomenal success and subsequent reversal in its fortunes. In the fifth section, I draw some conclusions about what these elections reveal about politics in Delhi. These analyses make extensive use of the Lokniti–Centre for the Study of Developing Societies (CSDS) pre- and post-election survey data for the 2013 and 2015 assembly elections. In the final section, I briefly analyze the outcome of the assembly elections of February 2020—the AAP's big win and its violent aftermath.

Special Constitutional Status

The Delhi Legislative Assembly was constituted in 1952 with a Council of Ministers under the Government of Part C States Act 1951. In 1956, Delhi ceased to be a Part C state and became a union territory administered directly by the president of India, in line with the recommendations of the State Reorganisation Commission. In lieu of an elected government, a provision was made, through the Delhi Municipal Corporation Act 1957, to constitute a municipal corporation for Delhi through direct elections.[4]

The Delhi Metropolitan Council (DMC) was set up by the Delhi Administration Act 1966 on the basis of the recommendations of the Administrative Reform Commission. It consisted of 61 members, of which 56 were directly elected by the Delhi electorate from single member constituencies.[5] The remaining five seats were filled through nominations by the central government. The DMC, therefore, became the highest elected body of Delhi, with a restricted mandate to act as the deliberative wing of the Delhi administration with recommendatory authority. It remained, at best, a compromise solution between a representative body with legislative and financial powers and administration by the president through the office of the lieutenant governor. The chief executive councillor was the leader of the house and was appointed by the president of India with a mandate to assist and advise the lieutenant governor.

However, the DMC suffered from certain drawbacks. Chief among them was the fact that its function was principally deliberative, with no legislative power. Its advice was not binding on the lieutenant governor. The Constitution (69th Amendment) Act 1991 was the result of the sustained pressure and demand, across the political spectrum, for a full-fledged state assembly with a Council of Ministers to aid and advise the lieutenant governor. The supplementary legislation passed by the parliament, the Government of National Capital Territory of Delhi Act 1991, provided for the framing of rules, procedures and conduct of the legislative assembly. Delhi at present has a legislative assembly and a Council of Ministers with a chief minister as the head of the government.[6]

The total strength of the assembly is 70, with 12 seats reserved for Scheduled Castes. Though the assembly can frame laws with respect to all the matters included in the State List or in the Concurrent List, crucial matters related to public order, police, and land have been kept outside the purview of the state assembly and are administered through the lieutenant governor of Delhi. Though severely constrained in its administrative functioning, compared with other full-fledged states, this is a considerable improvement over the earlier setup when as many as nine subjects were outside the purview of the 1952 State Assembly under the Government of Part C States Act. Though it ceased to be a union territory in 1992 and became a semi-state, the elected Delhi government still does not have the powers of a full-fledged state.

Party Politics in Delhi–National Capital Territory

Overview, 1951–2008

Delhi's politics for long was dominated by national parties, with the top two contenders, the Congress and the Bhartiya Jan Sangh/Bharatiya Janata Party (BJS)/(BJP), cornering a majority of seats in both parliamentary and state assembly elections. The smaller parties and independents remained at best marginal players.

The Congress support base in Delhi from the onset was broader compared with the BJS/BJP. Though the social profile of the average Congress and BJS/BJP supporter was nearly identical, the BJS/BJP were thought to be more elitist, at least, socially and economically, compared to the Congress. For instance, the BJP/BJS consolidated their base among the first wave of migrants from west Punjab, along with the trading communities, and was certainly elitist when it came to the caste base of the party.[7] However, the Congress party too was able to stake its claim on a section among the Punjabi refugees and the trading class, along with its core support base comprising of peasant communities, Dalits, and Muslims. This remained the case till the 1993 assembly elections in the newly constituted National Capital Territory (NCT) of Delhi.[8]

The BJP was able to secure a majority with 49 seats and form a government after the assembly election held in 1993. The Congress, which was in power in the DMC elected in 1983, performed poorly, winning only 14 seats. The Janata Dal (JD) and independent candidates took four and three seats, respectively. In the election to the legislative assembly held in 1998, the Congress was able to win primarily due to anti-incumbency, compounded by incessant factionalism in the BJP (exemplified by the rule of three chief ministers in a span of five years). In the three successive elections held in 1998, 2003, and 2008, the Congress under the leadership of Sheila Dixit was able to win the assembly elections, albeit with a reduced seat and vote share in 2008 (Table 13.1). Their lost vote share was not matched by a corresponding rise in the BJP's vote share, which remained stable. In order to understand the emergence of the AAP in 2013 as a third pole in Delhi politics, it is necessary to dissect the 2008 Assembly Election verdict.

Before doing that, it is useful to understand the social and geographical profile of the assembly constituencies and the city's political landscape. According to the Lokniti–CSDS profile of the assembly constituencies in Delhi (Table 13.2), the constituencies have been classified under three regions—periphery, city, and trans-Yamuna—with 16, 38, and 16 seats, respectively. There are 16 constituencies dominated by migrants from Uttar Pradesh (UP) and Bihar, peasant communities dominate 11 constituencies, Punjabis dominate another 16 seats, and all together 27 seats are classified under the category "rest." There are 32 constituencies which are classified as dominated by the lower (income) class, 28 by the middle class, and 10 constituencies are classified as upper-class dominated. Peasant communities are largely concentrated in the periphery, while the Punjabi community and

Table 13.1 Assembly election performance, 1993–2015

Year	Party	Number of contestants	Seats won	Vote share (%)
1993	BJP	70	49	43
	INC	70	14	35
	JD	7	4	13
	Independent	766	3	6
1998	BJP	67	15	34
	INC	70	52	48
	JD	48	1	2
	Independent	353	2	9
2003	BJP	70	20	35
	INC	70	47	48
	NCP	33	1	2
	JD(S)	12	1	1
	Independent	284	1	5
2008	BJP	69	23	37
	BSP	70	2	14
	INC	70	43	40
	LJP	41	1	1
	Independent	358	1	4
2013	BJP	68	31	33
	INC	70	8	25
	AAP	70	28	30
	SAD	2	1	1
	Independent	222	1	3
2015	BJP	69	3	32
	AAP	70	67	54

Source: Author's calculations from the Election Commission of India data (of different years).
Note: SAD stands for Shiromani Akali Dal.

those classified under the category "rest" dominate the constituencies in the city and trans-Yamuna region.

Migrants from UP and Bihar are spread evenly in the three regions and dominate five seats each in the periphery and city regions, and another six in the trans-Yamuna region. A large majority of seats dominated by migrants from UP–Bihar and the peasant community fall under the lower- and middle-class categories, and Punjabis and the "rest" dominate the upper- and middle-class

Table 13.2 Constituency profile

Region	Seats	Community	Seats	Region–wise community distribution	Class	Seats	Class–wise regional distribution	Community–wise class distribution
Periphery	16	UP–Bihar migrants	16	Periphery—5 Trans-Yamuna—6 City—5	Lower	32	Periphery—14 Trans-Yamuna—8 City—10	UP–Bihar dominated—12 Peasant Community—9 Punjabi Dominated—3 Rest-8
City	38	Punjabi dominated	16	City—13 Trans-Yamuna—3	Middle	28	Periphery—2 Trans-Yamuna—7 City—19	UP–Bihar Dominated—4 Peasant Community—2 Punjabi Dominated—9 Rest—12
Trans-Yamuna	16	Peasant community	11	Periphery—11	Upper	10	Trans-Yamuna—1 City—9	Punjabi dominated—4 Rest—6
		Rest	27	City—20 Trans-Yamuna—3				

Source: Lokniti–CSDS Data Unit.

categories. There is not a single seat dominated by migrants from UP and Bihar or the peasant community under the constituencies classified as having an upper-class profile. The constituencies under the periphery category largely have a lower-class profile, while half of those classified under the city category have a middle-class profile. In the trans-Yamuna region, there are eight and seven seats classified as lower and upper classes, respectively.

The 2008 Assembly Verdict

In the 2008 assembly election, the Congress won 43 seats. Its performance was largely the result of outperforming the BJP in most of the seats in trans-Yamuna and city regions, where it won 62 percent and 65 percent of the seats, respectively (Table 13.3). In the periphery region, the Congress did marginally better than the BJP by winning 50 percent of the seats. It won a majority of its seats from the constituencies dominated by the peasant community and those under the category "rest." The Congress also won half the seats dominated by UP–Bihar migrants and Punjabis. Its performance was better in the constituencies dominated by the middle and upper classes; in the constituencies dominated by the lower class, the party won slightly more than half of the seats. The community-wise class distribution of seats further underlines this. It performed well among the more privileged sections across categories.

The victory in 2008 was somewhat perplexing because the party had lost 8 percent vote share from 2003 elections but lost only four seats. The BJP, on the other hand, saw only a marginal increase of 2 percent in its vote share and increased its seat tally by three seats. Though a large section among the lower-class voters did move away from the Congress, they did not gravitate toward the BJP. Instead, a large number of them moved toward the Bahujan Samaj Party (BSP).

The period between 1993 and 2008 witnessed a consistent increase in the BSP vote share in assembly elections, from 2 percent in 1993 to 14 percent in 2008 (though the party's average vote share in national parliamentary elections between 1991 and 2004 remained a marginal 2 percent). There was an 8 percent swing in favor of the BSP compared to the previous assembly election, identical to the 8 percent swing against the Congress (Table 13.4). There were 34 assembly constituencies where the victory margin was less than the BSP candidate votes in 2008, comprising nearly half of the total assembly strength. The Congress won 23 of these seats, BJP 9, and 1 each were won by Lok Janshakti Party (LJP) and an independent candidate.

Table 13.3 Region, community, and class-wise performance of the Congress party, 2008

Region	Seats	Community	Seats	Region-wise community distribution	Class	Seats	Class-wise regional distribution	Community-wise class distribution
Periphery	8	UP–Bihar migrants	8	Periphery—1 Trans-Yamuna—3 City—4	Lower	17	Periphery—6 Trans-Yamuna—4 City—7	UP–Bihar migrants—5 Punjabi dominated—2 Peasant community—6 Rest—4
Trans-Yamuna	10	Punjabi dominated	8	Trans-Yamuna—2 City—6	Middle	18	Periphery—2 Trans-Yamuna—6 City—10	UP–Bihar migrants—3 Punjabi dominated—4 Peasant community—2 Rest—9
City	25	Peasant community	8	Periphery—7 City—1	Upper	8	City—8	Punjabi dominated—2 Rest—6
		Rest	19	Trans-Yamuna—5 City—14				

Source: Lokniti–CSDS Data Unit.

Table 13.4 BSP electoral performance in Delhi, 1993–2015

Assembly elections				Parliamentary elections			
Year	Seats contested	Seats won	Vote share (%)	Year	Seats contested	Seats won	Vote share (%)
1993	55	0	2	1991	7	0	1
1998	58	0	3	1996	–	–	–
2003	40	0	6	1998	6	0	2
2008	70	2	14	1999	3	0	2
2013	69	0	5	2004	7	0	3
2015	70	0	1	2009	7	0	5
				2014	7	0	1

Source: Election Commission of India, Statistical Reports on the General Elections to the Legislative Assembly of Delhi (different years), available at https://eci.gov.in/statistical-report/statistical-reports/, accessed on October 4, 2020.

Therefore, putting the Congress' 2008 performance in perspective, one has to take into account the leadership of incumbent Chief Minister Sheila Dixit, who successfully managed to turn incumbency in her favor by managing factionalism within the party, along with the inroads made by the BSP in Delhi's political landscape. The state unit of the BJP was marred by intense factionalism and absence of any leader of stature to take on Sheila Dixit.[9] Though the Congress vote share did decline, it was compensated by renegotiation of the existing caste and community relations. While a section among the marginalized caste and class supporters of the Congress and the BJP gravitated toward the BSP, the Congress was able to attract some among the BJP's upper-caste and upper-class support base.

The BSP, on the other hand, managed to attract migrants from UP and Bihar to its political fold. These largely low-income migrants had traditionally supported the Congress and now emerged as a support base of the BSP, especially in the 2008 assembly elections.[10] A large percentage of these migrants are from UP and Bihar and are popularly known as Purvanchalis (Table 13.5). While there has been an overall decline in the number of new migrants in recent years, migration from UP and Bihar has increased.[11] Most of these migrants are unskilled, low-paid workers, and reside in the periphery of the NCT or in unauthorized colonies in the city region (see Chapter 3 for details on the distribution and condition of these colonies). This has changed the city's demography and, therefore, its politics.

There were definite signs that Delhi politics was gearing toward a three-cornered contest. The changed social landscape of Delhi contributed

Table 13.5 State-wise migration to Delhi, 2001–2013

State	2001 (%)	2013 (%)
Uttar Pradesh	43	47
Bihar	14	31
Haryana	10	4
Rajasthan	5	3
West Bengal	3	3
Others	24	13

Source: Government of National Capital Territory of Delhi, *Delhi Human Development Report, 2013* (New Delhi: Academic Foundation and Institute for Human Development), available at http://www.ihdindia.org/hdidelhi/pdf/DHDR--2013.pdf, accessed on October 4, 2020.

significantly toward the reworking of caste and class relations in the city. The BSP managed to make inroads into the low-income migrant section of the Congress support base, while the Congress compensated by weaning off the BJP's support base among the upper caste and middle class. Though the upper class did vote for the BJP, the middle- and lower-class voters remained with the Congress.[12] The BSP succeeded in preventing the shift of lower-caste and lower-class Congress support base toward the BJP and marred the BJP's chances, and the Congress was the default beneficiary.[13] Interestingly, the BSP won both its seats from constituencies dominated by migrants, with one each from the periphery and trans-Yamuna with a lower-class profile. It was the large and increasing lower-income migrant population which changed the BSP's political fortunes, paving the way for Delhi politics taking a turn from bipolarity to a three-cornered contest.

It is to be noted here that Delhi assembly elections have generally had a distinct political trajectory than the parliamentary elections. Though the Congress and the BJP have always cornered most of the seats and vote share in all the parliamentary elections, that is not the case when one looks at assembly elections. The effective number of parties by votes was slightly less than three or three in the assembly elections held between 1993 and 2013. In the parliamentary elections too, a similar trend prevailed. However, the two big parties were the beneficiaries of seat–vote disproportionality associated with the first past the post system (Table 13.6).

The Emergence of the Aam Aadmi Party

The emergence of the AAP has to be understood against this background. I am arguing that by 2008, there was a transition toward a three-cornered contest in

Table 13.6   Effective number of parties (by votes and seats) in Delhi

Assembly elections			Parliamentary elections		
Year	Votes	Seats	Year	Votes	Seats
1993	3.138	1.869	1996	2.580	1.690
1998	2.896	1.670	1998	2.271	1.324
2003	2.780	1.876	1999	2.249	1
2008	3.177	2.055	2004	2.144	1.324
2013	3.850	2.704	2009	2.207	1
2015	2.448	1.089	2014	2.883	1

Source: Lokniti–CSDS Data Unit.

Delhi, which is corroborated by a third party garnering 14 percent vote share and managing to secure more votes than the winning margin in half of the assembly seats. The changing demography and social differentiation along class lines created the conditions for a political reconfiguration. Though the BSP succeeded in attracting a significant section of marginalized groups, it failed to attract voters from the more privileged sections of society. The AAP, I will show, succeeded in bridging this gap by drawing from the Congress support base in the 2013 assembly elections and wiping out the BSP's base among the marginalized section.

The AAP was set up in November 2012 for the express purpose of representing "common people." The formation of the party was the outcome of the popular protest movement IAC, which began in 2011 under the leadership of Anna Hazare. Its purpose was to establish some mechanism to curb and eradicate corruption in politics and the bureaucracy.[14] Though Anna Hazare pulled out of the movement in August 2012, an influential section took the decision to launch a political party.[15] The fledgling party succeeded in holding on to the momentum generated by the IAC movement. The AAP sustained the momentum of the IAC movement right up until the assembly elections partly as a result of the insensitive handling of a gang rape (the Nirbhaya case). While the IAC was loosely directed against the entire political class, the Delhi gang rape shifted the focus to the Delhi government and indirectly the central government, and gave the AAP an opportunity to project itself as the successor of the IAC movement.

The IAC movement and the formation of the AAP happened at a time when the ruling Congress party, in both the assembly and the parliament, was on the back foot—fighting anti-incumbency and association with corruption; in Delhi, at least, the main opposition party, the BJP, was faction ridden.[16] The AAP in its early days also benefited from the goodwill Arvind Kejriwal, its leader had garnered among the residents welfare associations (RWAs) through his NGO Parivartan. The RWAs, dominated by the upper and middle classes, provided the much needed support in its initial days. This was further buttressed with the support of sundry slum associations.[17]

Election Results, 2013

The AAP made an impressive debut in the December 2013 assembly election by winning 28 assembly seats. The BJP led the seat tally with 31 seats, while the incumbent Congress party was reduced to the third position with eight seats. This was a phenomenal performance by any yardstick as very few parties in the past had met with such success in their first election. The AAP's vote share was 30 percent. The BJP, INC, and BSP all witnessed a negative swing—of 3 percent, 15 percent, and 9 percent, respectively (Table 13.7). It won 17 seats previously held by the Congress and 11 by the BJP. The BJP, on the other hand, won the two seats won by the BSP in the 2008 election and also the lone seat won by the independent candidate. The AAP ate into the vote share of the BSP and managed to win 13 seats where the victory margin in the previous election was less than BSP's votes.

The AAP performed better than BJP in the city region, where it won 18 of the 25 seats. In the previous election, 10 of these seats had been won by the Congress and 8 by the BJP. The BJP managed to retain only five seats in the city region, which it had won in the previous assembly election. These 18 seats were primarily from the constituencies dominated by upper and middle classes, and the AAP won 7 seats each under each category (Table 13.8). In the constituencies dominated by the upper class, the AAP had an edge over

Table 13.7 Swing in Delhi elections, 2013–2015

2008 Party	Vote share (%)	2013 Party	Vote share (%)	Swing (%)	2014 Party	Vote share (%)	Swing (%)	2015 Party	Vote share (%)	Swing (%)
INC	40	INC	25	−15	INC	15	−10	INC	10	−5
BJP	36	BJP	33	−3	BJP	47	14	BJP	32	−15
BSP	14	BSP	5	−9	BSP	1	−4	BSP	1	0
AAP	–	AAP	30	30	AAP	33	3	AAP	54	21

Source: Election Commission of India: Statistical Reports on the General Elections to the Legislative Assembly of Delhi, and General Election to the Lok Sabha.

Table 13.8 Region, community, and class-wise performance of the AAP, 2013

Region	Seats	Community	Seats	Region-wise community distribution	Class	Seats	Class-wise regional distribution	Community-wise class distribution
Periphery	5	UP-Bihar migrants	5	Periphery—2 Trans-Yamuna—3	Lower	11	Periphery—4 Trans-Yamuna—3 City—4	UP-Bihar migrants—5 Punjabi dominated—2 Peasant community—2 Rest—2
Trans-Yamuna	5	Punjabi dominated	10	City—10	Middle	10	Periphery—1 Trans-Yamuna—2 City—7	Punjabi dominated—4 Peasant community—1 Rest—5
City	18	Peasant community	1	Periphery—1	Upper	7	City—7	Punjabi dominated—4 Rest—3
		Rest	10	Trans-Yamuna—2 City—8				

Source: Author's calculations of election outcome data from the Election Commission of India with the constituency profiles created by Lokniti-CSDS.

Table 13.9 Voting pattern among the migrants from UP, Bihar, and Haryana

	2013			2015		
	Congress	BJP	AAP	Congress	BJP	AAP
Migrants from UP	29	33	24	9	32	55
Migrants from Bihar	22	32	32	4	28	64
Migrants from Haryana	15	45	23	8	43	46

Source: Lokniti–CSDS Data Unit.

the BJP. In these constituencies, while the upper-class support split between the BJP and AAP, the latter secured more seats with the help of lower-caste and lower-class votes (Table 13.9).

The AAP succeeded in making a sizable dent in the two-party competition in the state mainly because, unlike the BSP, it was able to attract supporters across social and economic categories. The constituencies dominated by Purvanchalis and the peasant community were largely won by the BJP.[18] While there was a marginal decline in the BJP's traditional support among the upper caste, it succeeded in retaining much of its core support base and improved across social categories except Muslims. With Dalits and Other Backward Classes (OBCs), the AAP had an edge over the BJP. The AAP managed to eat into the Congress support base, except among Muslims (Tables 13.10, 13.11, and 13.12).

There was a threefold wave against the Congress party in Delhi. There was general anti-incumbency, resentment against the Congress-led United Progressive Alliance (UPA) government at the center (reflected in the groundswell of support garnered by the IAC movement), and the protest against the gang rape in December 2012. Almost half of those who had voted ·for the Congress in 2008 elections were dissatisfied with the performance of the UPA government at the center and voted for the AAP in 2013 election.[19] There was anti-incumbency against the sitting Congress legislative members, a large number of whom had been elected for at least three terms from the same constituency. There were 25 such candidates and constituencies and only 2 candidates were dropped in 2013 election.

Though the BJP emerged as the single largest party, it fell short of the halfway mark to form a government on its own. It decided not to form the government in Delhi and paved the way for the AAP. In Arvind Kejriwal, the AAP had a leader who was the most popular choice among a large section of the electorate in Delhi, the BJP candidate Harsh Vardhan was second, and incumbent Sheila Dixit was a distant third.[20] Kejriwal had led a strong

Table 13.10   Social base of the Congress, BJP, and AAP, 2013–2015

	2013 VS			2014 LS			2015 VS		
	Congress	BJP	AAP	Congress	BJP	AAP	Congress	BJP	AAP
Brahmin	24	46	23	11	65	22	8	47	42
Punjabi Khatri	22	36	39	8	62	15	14	32	52
Rajput	24	37	32	8	56	28	9	42	44
Baniya	18	43	29	12	64	18	8	58	32
Other upper castes	23	33	31	12	62	22	8	37	49
Jat	15	49	24		86	14	5	58	33
Gujjar and Yadav	17	37	35	8	44	44	8	34	54
Other OBCs	18	32	38	13	44	41	10	28	60
Dalit	23	29	36	18	32	42	7	18	69
Muslim	53	12	12	39	2	56	20	2	77
Sikh	23	43	26	10	68	16	8	33	57

Source: Lokniti–CSDS Data Unit.

Table 13.11   Class profile of support base

	2013			2014			2015		
	Congress	BJP	AAP	Congress	BJP	AAP	Congress	BJP	AAP
Upper class	23	37	30	15	45	31	6	43	47
Middle class	24	34	31	15	46	34	13	35	51
Lower class	27	31	29	17	41	38	10	27	60

Source: Lokniti–CSDS Data Unit.

Table 13.12   Voting pattern by rural and urban areas of Delhi, 2008–2015

	2008		2013			2014			2015		
	Congress	BJP	Congress	BJP	AAP	Congress	BJP	AAP	Congress	BJP	AAP
Rural Delhi	37	29	30	35	24	n/a	n/a	n/a	10	31	53
Urban Delhi	42	39	22	34	32	n/a	n/a	n/a	9	33	55

Source: Lokniti–CSDS Data Unit.

campaign against both the BJP and the INC, accusing both of being equally corrupt. However, that did not stop the AAP from forming a minority government with outside support from the Congress.

The government fell due to a standoff between the center and the state government, as well as a fight between the BJP and the AAP on the introduction of the Jan Lokpal Bill. The AAP government fell immediately after it failed to introduce the bill in the assembly as 42 MLAs (members of the legislative assembly)—31 from the BJP, 8 from Congress, and 1 from Janata Dal (United) (JD[U]), and the lone independent—opposed the bill. The AAP had the support of its 28 MLAs in the 70-member assembly.[21] The resignation eventually paved the way for the dissolution of the assembly and president's rule.

The AAP and its leadership in a short span of time had garnered considerable goodwill, to an extent where some observers argued that it had the potential to rock the BJP's parliamentary campaign under Narendra Modi in 2014. However, it failed to sustain the momentum and squandered some goodwill due to political missteps, such as the brazen midnight raid conducted by AAP minister Somnath Bharti, Arvind Kejriwal's protest against his own government, and finally his resignation. These events provided political ammunition to the opposition parties to target the AAP and its holier-than-thou brand of politics. The opposition accused him of being a *bhagoda* (quitter), and the label stuck. The AAP's decision to contest the 2014 parliamentary election in several states was an overambitious miscalculation and led to the party performing poorly, with a majority of its candidates losing their security deposit. The only saving grace was victory in four parliamentary seats in Punjab.

The AAP's poor showing in the parliamentary polls was not surprising because a large number of those who voted for the AAP in 2013 (assembly) desired to see Narendra Modi as the prime minister in 2014 and voted for the BJP in the 2014 parliamentary elections.[22] The AAP read the 2013 mandate incorrectly. Though the party had registered a remarkable performance, the BJP was the single largest party by both seat share and vote share (Table 13.1). Unlike the AAP, the BJP had performed well across regions and across social categories, except for Muslims. Therefore, it was not surprising that in less than six months, the BJP won all seven parliamentary seats in Delhi.

This was followed by a period of in-fighting within the AAP when some of the more prominent figures associated with the party voiced their concerns and were quite critical of Arvind Kejriwal and his style of functioning. There were also some high-profile resignations.[23] Not many gave the AAP a chance when the assembly elections were called; the general expectation was that the 2015 assembly election would be a repeat of 2014 Lok Sabha election and the BJP would register an easy win.

Election Results, 2015

The AAP, however, regrouped and focused on consolidation of its Delhi unit. The party convener, Arvind Kejriwal, tendered an apology for his abrupt resignation.[24] There was an acknowledgment within the party that AAP should consolidate and develop its base in the national capital before it could stake a claim as a credible political alternative in the space increasingly being vacated by the Congress party at the national scale. Therefore, Delhi became its focus once again.

The 2015 assembly election resulted in a landslide victory for the AAP—the most lopsided distribution of seats in any Delhi assembly election. The party won 67 seats of the 70 seats contested, the BJP was reduced to 3 and the Congress failed to win a single seat (Table 13.1). The AAP vote share of 54 percent in 2015 assembly election was a 21 percent swing in favor of the party from the 2014 parliamentary election. The BJP registered a negative swing of 15 percent and the Congress party 5 percent (Table 13.7).

In the 2013 assembly election, the AAP had mostly benefited from the shift of support from the BSP, followed by the Congress, and the BJP. This led to massive erosion in the BSP support base with a large section among them deciding to give the AAP a chance. The INC in 2013, though considerably weakened, was still a force in Delhi politics with 25 percent vote share. In the subsequent elections—parliamentary in 2014 followed by assembly in 2015—a large section of traditional Congress support shifted toward the AAP. It was also able to galvanize support among a substantial number of traditional BJP supporters in 2015 who were dissatisfied with the party's choice of Kiran Bedi as its chief-ministerial candidate.[25] But it was primarily the Congress supporters who drifted toward the AAP in 2015.[26]

The AAP strategy of focusing on the Purvanchali community and Dalits and Sikhs clearly paid off. The social groups among whom the BJP had an edge over the AAP in 2015 were Brahmins, Baniyas, and the peasant communities (Table 13.10), though a substantial number of them did vote for the AAP. This contributed toward the AAP doing well in the periphery and trans-Yamuna region.[27] The AAP attempted to reach out to residents of unauthorized colonies in these regions, comprised largely of migrant and lower-class voters. Its promise of providing better sanitation facilities and housing resonated with them. As in 2015, the AAP continued to be the first choice of the Delhi youth, who were recruited as party volunteers and potential voters.

The AAP registered gains across classes, communities, and regions compared to 2013 (Tables 13.9, 13.10, 13.11, and 13.12). A study of the division of votes on caste and community lines underlines the contours of a new social block carved out by the AAP. The party secured the support of every single caste, class, and religious bloc. While many upper-caste Hindus may still have preferred the BJP, the bulk of the upper-caste vote went to the AAP. The dominant Hindu castes such as Jats, Gujjars, Yadavs, and Tyagis voted for the AAP, breaking rank with the BJP and the Congress. The lower the social category, the higher was its contribution to the AAP's vote share. The AAP strategy of an issue-based campaign with an exclusive focus on Delhi clearly worked for the party.

In Arvind Kejriwal, the party had a chief-ministerial candidate who was more popular than candidates from other parties.[28] A majority of voters felt that Kejriwal was the most suitable candidate to address governance issues. The mistake the BJP committed was to turn the election into a referendum on him. The AAP converted the electoral contest into a David versus Goliath battle. But later the AAP read the favorable local verdict as one against the national Goliath: Narendra Modi.

Though the BJP's vote share in 2015 registered a decline from the peak of the 2014 parliamentary election, it remained relatively stable compared to previous elections and was only 1 percentage point less than its share in 2013. The BJP lost because of the consolidation of anti-BJP and anti-Congress vote for the AAP.

Challenges and Opportunities

Administrative Clashes

After having burnt its fingers in the 2014 Lok Sabha elections, the AAP was wary of venturing out to other states, but it adopted a confrontationist stance with the center from the onset. The center too played along by putting a wrench into the AAP government's initiatives, often through the office of the lieutenant governor and the bureaucracy.[29] The Delhi government under the AAP developed a history of run-ins with two successive lieutenant governors and their bureaucracies after 2015. To some extent, this was due to Delhi's unusual constitutional position, which it shares with Puducherry, whereby the bureaucrats are expected to report to the lieutenant governor appointed by the center. The lieutenant governor is not bound to follow the advice of the Council of Ministers and is answerable only to the center. The situation after the 2010s, where the government at the centre and the union territory were adversaries, was not new. In the recent past, between 1998 and 2004,

Sheila Dixit was heading the Congress government in Delhi when the BJP-led National Democratic Alliance government was at the center. The two did have a working relationship even though they were at loggerheads on many occasions.

The political stalemate in Delhi was the result of a confrontationist stance adopted by both the BJP at the center and the AAP government in Delhi. The union government interpreted the rules pertaining to Delhi's unusual constitutional position narrowly and asserted itself through the office of the lieutenant governor on issues such as appointment of bureaucrats and meddling in the daily working of the state government. This was possible because of the ambiguity surrounding the interpretation of Article 239AA of the Indian Constitution which, when read along with the Government of National Capital Territory of Delhi Act 1992 and the Transaction of Business of the Government of National Capital Territory of Delhi Rules 1993, empowers the lieutenant governor to bypass the elected representatives and seek the opinion of the center. Arvind Kejriwal's confrontations with the lieutenant governor even in his previous government (in 2013) was over the interpretation of Article 239AA. The Delhi High Court upheld the constitutional position and gave the center the upper hand with regard to the affairs of the NCT of Delhi.[30] The AAP with its massive majority was in a position to make a case for bringing about constitutional changes to give Delhi full statehood. However, the AAP government may have squandered this opportunity by indulging in a slugfest with its opponents and making unsubstantiated allegations. The hurry of the AAP to deliver on the promises it had made during the run-up to the elections, to carve out a separate social base for itself in Delhi politics, and the procedural hurdles presented by the center led to several predicaments in the politics of Delhi.

Mainstreaming of the AAP

The AAP's image as the custodian of probity in public life took a hit with the departure of Yogendra Yadav, Shanti Bhushan, and Prashant Bhushan. The trio had been in the forefront of criticizing what they believed was the centralization of power in the hands of Arvind Kejriwal and the coterie surrounding him. This tussle was the reflection of the friction between the "pragmatic" and the "ideological" wings of the party.[31] The pragmatic section of the leadership wanted the party to be more solution oriented; the ideological section believed that the mandate was for welfare along with transformation of the existing system.

The AAP displayed political pragmatism as it attempted to broaden its support base by factoring in the socioreligious profiles of the constituencies. However, this came at a cost and meant making comprises on the issue of probity and accountability in public life. In its attempt to win the assembly elections in 2015, the AAP favored winnability over probity. Of the 38 new faces given a ticket by the AAP, 17 had joined AAP after December 2013. The AAP gave tickets to eight defectors from the BJP, six from the BSP, two from the INC, and one from the LJP. Only 16 of these new candidates won their seats. As many as 21 of the party's candidates had criminal cases pending against them and 28 were *crorepatis*. Ten of the defectors given tickets by the AAP were also part of the list of 12 candidates with tainted profiles released by senior party leader Prashant Bushan before the elections. This made the party vulnerable as it became dependent on those who had joined the party not out of ideological conviction but, as many have argued, political opportunism.

This came in handy for the center to pursue cases against the AAP legislative members. By early 2017, the Delhi Police was investigating cases against 13 of them.[32] Though the party claimed that these cases were politically motivated, they created doubt over the AAP's claim as the custodian of probity in public life. A controversy surrounding "office of profit" cases against 20 AAP legislators added to the doubts. This, along with the AAP's confrontationist stance against the center and Kejriwal's personal antipathy toward a popular prime minister, made the party vulnerable in Delhi. The reversal in AAP's electoral fortune and the BJP's success in the municipal elections of 2017 has to be understood against this backdrop.

Takeaway

The biggest takeaway from the successive elections in Delhi has been the influence exercised by the Purvanchali voters. Up to the 2008 assembly elections, the Purvanchali voters were considered a loyal vote bank of the Congress party. Though the BSP did manage to wean off a substantial number of them in 2008, the Purvanchali voters largely sided with Congress party. By the 2013 assembly election, Purvanchali voters had become a more important voting bloc that started asserting itself by demanding a bigger share in leadership positions and the power structure. The Congress and the BJP failed to accommodate the political aspiration of the newly assertive Purvanchali voters and continued to hold on to the old dynamics of Delhi politics.[33] The newly formed AAP saw an opportunity here and moved in by giving tickets to a large number of Purvanchali candidates in both 2013 and 2015 compared to both the BJP and the INC. Though a majority of the Purvanchali voters opted for the BJP in 2013 (assembly) and 2014 (parliamentary) elections—perhaps, because of a residual ideological alignment with Hindutva imported from their home region—a sizeable number voted for the AAP, perhaps because of the AAP's assurances on public service delivery in unauthorized colonies whereby it succeeded in taking away Purvanchali voters from both the Congress and the BSP.

The gradual increase in the number of Purvanchalis in the NCT has had a corresponding and understandable impact on Delhi's electoral politics. The importance of the Purvanchali voters in Delhi's political landscape can be gauged from the fact that after the debacle in the 2015 assembly elections, the BJP appointed the popular Bhojpuri actor and singer Manoj Tiwari as the BJP president of its Delhi unit just before the municipal elections of 2017.

There were four elections in Delhi between December 2013 and December 2019, and each delivered a remarkably different result from the previous one. The only constant in Delhi politics since 1993 was the stable vote share of the BJP. In fact, the BJP's vote share across social categories remained nearly identical since 2008 (Table 13.13). The rise of the AAP, as explained previously, was mainly due to the decline of the Congress and the BSP. The BJP was able to hold onto its support base and withstand the AAP debut. Though the party was out of power since 1998 (despite being the single largest party in the 2013 assembly election), this ability to hold on to its core support base is what made the BJP a potent political force in Delhi politics. The BJP performance in the 2014 parliamentary election and 2017 Delhi municipal election bore testimony to this. In recent years, it consciously attempted to respond to and acknowledge the influence of newer social groups such as the Purvanchalis and give them more space within the party, a case in point being the appointment of Manoj Tiwari as the party chief. This the party did without deviating from its core ideological agenda of Hindutva.

In contrast, the AAP's fundamental problem remained its inability to negotiate ideological contradictions, reflected in the tussle between the right wing of the party represented by Kumar Vishwas and the left wing perceived to be close to Arvind Kejriwal. The ideological differences were compounded by the struggles of the party to shed its activist and anti-establishment image[34] and move toward more formal politics and the mundane business of governance.

For all its claims about decentralization, the AAP and its Delhi government remained leader centric. Moreover, its confrontationist stance toward a large

Table 13.13   BJP performance, 2008–2015 (in percentage)

	2008	2009	2013	2014	2015
Vote share	37	35	33	47	32
Regions					
Trans-Yamuna	36	34	33	48	36
Periphery	31	36	36	47	31
City	39	36	32	45	33
Class					
Lower	32	34	34	45	31
Middle	39	37	35	47	35
Upper	42	36	31	47	36
Communities					
UP–Bihar migrants	34	36	32	45	30
Punjabi dominated	41	38	35	48	36
Peasant community	32	34	38	48	32
Rest	37	34	32	46	33

Source: Lokniti–CSDS Data Unit.

number of parties meant that it found itself isolated and bereft of allies when attacked. A large section among the middle and lower classes did find the AAP agenda of post-identity politics attractive. However, this prevented the party from taking a clear stand on issues which have the potential to alienate its middle-class supporters who also find the BJP's Hindutva agenda appealing. This ideological ambiguity helped the party keep its diverse social coalition together but it also pulled the party in opposite directions. Herein lay the dilemma about the longevity of the AAP.

Aftermath, 2020

A few weeks before the final manuscript of this book was handed over to the publisher, there was an election for the Delhi Legislative Assembly on February 8, 2020. It was not possible to undertake a detailed analysis of the outcome, but some key findings are discussed here. The AAP won the election handily—getting about 53.5 percent of the vote (roughly the same share as in 2015) and 62 of 70 seats. The BJP increased its vote share to 38.5 percent (from 32.3 percent in 2015) and its seats increased from three to eight. The Congress was wiped out, with 4.3 percent of the vote—a significant drop from the 9.7 percent they had received in 2015—and zero seats.

With so much of the vote share leaving Congress, one natural question was whether previous Congress supporters shifted their votes to the BJP or AAP. Survey data asking voters to recall previous voting behavior is notoriously unreliable in answering such questions, so we looked to constituency-wise results. Figure 13.1 plots the predicted vote share of the AAP and BJP in the 2020 Delhi election as a function of 2015 Congress vote share. Noticeably, the AAP's curve is upward trending while the BJP's is basically flat. This means that two things likely happened. First, the AAP seemed to have disproportionately gained in 2020 where Congress used to be strong. Second, given that the BJP saw a significant increase in vote share across the board (irrespective of the Congress' previous performance), it seemed that the BJP won away some share of the AAP's previous vote base.

The BJP won six of its eight seats in the trans-Yamuna part of east Delhi, an area that has a large Muslim and Purvanchali population (it is on the border with UP). Exit polls suggested that the Purvanchali vote did break for the AAP, but so did the votes of other migrants; there was some suggestive evidence that the BJP was able to wean off some Purvanchali vote share.[35]

The east Delhi region where the BJP did best was precisely the place where, according to reliable accounts, local BJP leaders gave inflammatory speeches that incited several days of religious violence that caused widespread property destruction and 53 deaths (a majority of them Muslims) later in February 2020. These events were widely reported in international media, not least because

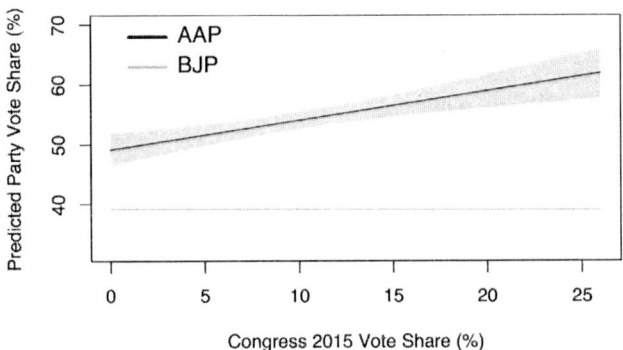

Figure 13.1   The AAP- and BJP-predicted vote share 2020 versus Congress vote share 2015

Source: Author.

Notes: This figure displays the predicted vote shares for the AAP and the BJP from a linear regression controlling for Congress' 2015 vote share. The gray bounds correspond to 95 percent predictive intervals. The AAP has higher predicted vote share where the Congress was strong before. No such relationship is noticeable for the BJP.

US President Trump was on official visit in the city the day the riots began. Our initial analysis suggested that the BJP sought to nationalize the Delhi election using its well-established communal Hindutva strategy, whereas the AAP stayed steadfastly local and focused on their well-established model of governance and performance. This may well turn out to be the template of elections to come in other states for the next few years.

Notes

1. John Harriss, "What are the Prospects for a Social Democratic Alliance in India Today?" (working paper, Simons Papers in Security and Development, 41:5, Simon Fraser University, 2015).
2. Pranab Bardhan, "The Avoidable Tragedy of the Left in India, II," *Economic and Political Weekly* 46, no. 24 (2011): 10–13.
3. Patrick Heller, "BRICS from Below: Counterpower Movements in Brazil, India and South Africa," *Open Democracy*, April 20, 2015, available at https://www.opendemocracy.net/patrick-heller/brics-from-below-counterpower-movements-in-brazil-india-and-south-africa, accessed on August 2, 2020.
4. Delhi Legislative Assembly, "History of Delhi Legislative Assembly," available at http://delhiassembly.nic.in/history_assembly.htm, accessed on November 12, 2017.
5. Delhi Legislative Assembly, "Delhi Metropolitan Council," available at http://delhiassembly.nic.in/metro.htm, accessed on November 12, 2017.
6. Delhi Legislative Assembly, "Present form of Delhi Assembly," available at http://delhiassembly.nic.in/PresentFormAssembly.htm, accessed on November 12, 2017.
7. Christophe Jaffrelot, "The Hindu Nationalist," in *Delhi: Urban Space and Human Destinies*, ed. Veronique Dupont, Emma Tarlo, and Denis Vidal (New Delhi: Manohar, 2000), 193.
8. Ibid., 192–193; V. B. Singh, "Political Profile of Delhi," in *Delhi: Urban Space and Human Destinies*, ed. Veronique Dupont, Emma Tarlo, and Denis Vidal (New Delhi: Manohar, 2000), 223–224.
9. V. Venkatesan, "A Positive Record," *Frontline*, November 8–21, 2003, available at http://www.frontline.in/static/html/fl2023/stories/20031121003203800.htm, accessed on August 2, 2020.
10. Sanjay Kumar, *Changing Electoral Politics in Delhi: From Caste to Class* (New Delhi: Sage Publications, 2013), 73–85.
11. Government of National Capital Territory of Delhi, *Delhi Human Development Report 2013: Improving Lives, Promoting Inclusion* (New Delhi: Government of National Capital Territory of Delhi, 2013).

12. Lokniti–Centre for the Study of Developing Societies (CSDS), *Delhi Assembly Election: Post Poll Survey Findings, 2008* (New Delhi: CSDS, 2008). As per the 2008 post-poll survey conducted by the Lokniti–CSDS, the support for Congress, Bharatiya Janata Party (BJP), and Bahujan Samaj Party (BSP) among lower class was 36 percent, 33 percent, and 20 percent, respectively. Even in the upper-class-dominated constituencies, the BSP was able to wean away some of the Congress party support base, among the poor in the unauthorized colonies, and had a respectable vote share of 14 percent.

13. Lokniti–CSDS, *Delhi 2008*. The BSP had a vote share of 19 percent among the migrants from Uttar Pradesh (UP) and Bihar. The party also did well in the constituencies dominated by peasants where it had a vote share of 18 percent.

14. M. R. Biju, "The Political Significance of Aam Aadmi Party (AAP) and Its Performance in Delhi Poll 2015," *Mainstream Weekly,* February 28, 2015, available at http://mainstreamweekly.net/article5495.html, accessed on July 30, 2020.

15. Gargi Parsai, "Team Kejriwal Is Now Aam Aadmi Party," *Hindu,* November 24, 2012, available at http://www.thehindu.com/news/national/Team-Kejriwal-is-now-quotAam-Aadmi-Partyquot/article15619398.ece, accessed on July 23, 2020.

16. Suhas Palshikar, "Who Is Delhi's Common Man?" *New Left Review* 98 (2016): 8.

17. Ibid., 19.

18. Lokniti–CSDS, *Delhi Assembly Election: Post Poll Survey Findings, 2013* (New Delhi: CSDS, 2013). The BJP won 9 out of 16 seats dominated by the migrants from UP and Bihar.

19. Lokniti–CSDS, *Delhi 2013*. Only 47 percent of those who had voted for the Congress in 2008, and were dissatisfied with the Congress-led United Progressive Alliance (UPA) government at the center, voted for the Aam Aadmi Party (AAP) during the 2013 assembly elections.

20. Ibid. Arvind Kejriwal had an edge over Harsh Vardhan across age groups barring those who were above 55 years of age.

21. Mohammad Ali, Vishal Kant, AMP, and Sowmiya Ashok, "Arvind Kejriwal Quits Over Jan Lokpal," *Hindu,* February 14, 2014, available at http://www.thehindu.com/news/cities/Delhi/arvind-kejriwal-quits-over-jan-lokpal/article5688528.ece, accessed on July 30, 2020; Lokniti–CSDS, *Delhi 2013*.

22. Even in 2013 assembly elections, 48 percent of the AAP voters preferred Narendra Modi as the prime minister and 36 percent of them voted for the BJP in the parliamentary elections in 2014.

23. *Hindu BusinessLine*, "Shazia Ilmi, Capt. Gopinath Quit AAP," May 24, 2014, available at http://www.thehindubusinessline.com/news/shazia-ilmi-capt-gopinath-quit-aap/article6044171.ece, accessed on July 30, 2020.

24. Siddharth Vardarajan, "Kejriwal's Willingness to Say Sorry Has Paid Off," *NDTV*, February 8, 2015, available at https://www.ndtv.com/opinion/kejriwals-willingness-to-say-sorry-has-paid-off-737889, accessed on July 14, 2020.

25. Lokniti–CSDS, *Delhi 2013*; Lokniti–CSDS, *National Election Study: Post-Poll Survey in Delhi, 2014* (New Delhi: CSDS, 2014). Thirty eight percent of the traditional Congress supporters shifted allegiance from the parliamentary elections and voted for the AAP. This was 10 percent more than the shift in 2013 assembly elections. In the 2015 assembly elections, there was massive shift of 67 percent among the Congress supporters toward the AAP; the corresponding figures for the BSP and the BJP were 45 percent and 41 percent, respectively. Almost 40 percent of the BJP's traditional supporters were disappointed with the party's choice of chief-ministerial candidate.

26. Lokniti–CSDS, *Delhi Assembly Election: Post Poll Survey Findings, 2015* (New Delhi: CSDS, 2015). As per the Lokniti–CSDS Survey data.

27. Lokniti–CSDS, *Delhi 2015*. In 2015, the AAP won 15 seats from the trans-Yamuna region and 16 from periphery region. In the previous election in 2013, the AAP's tally was six and five seats from the two regions.

28. Lokniti–CSDS, *Delhi 2015*. Arvind Kejriwal was the preferred choice for chief minister across age groups. His popularity among those between the age groups of 18–45 years was more than double of his nearest rival Kiran Bedi of the BJP. In fact, 44 percent of the traditional BJP voters felt that AAP leader Arvind Kejriwal was capable of running the government, and many rated him better than Kiran Bedi.

29. Akshay Deshmane, "Under Close Watch," *Frontline*, January 20, 2017, available at http://www.frontline.in/cover-story/under-close-watch/article9456570.ece, accessed on June 11, 2020.

30. Maneesh Chibber, "Arvind Kejriwal Needs to Stop Cribbing Now Because He Knew Very Well What He Walked Into," *ThePrint*, February 26, 2018, available at https://theprint.in/politics/kejriwal-needs-stop-whining-now-knew-well-walked/38157/, accessed on May 3, 2020.

31. Srinivasan Ramani, "Managers vs. Ideologues in AAP," *Hindu*, March 21, 2015, available at http://www.thehindu.com/opinion/lead/managers-vs-ideologues-in-aap/article7016170.ece, accessed on 3 May 2020.

32. Prawesh Lama and Heena Kausar, "13 AAP MLA's Booked in Two Years: Delhi Police Face Court Rap over Arrests," *Hindustan Times*, March 5, 2017, available at http://www.hindustantimes.com/delhi-news/police-face-court-rap-over-arrests-of-aap-legislators/story-OcmPB5hzvHl3D4QRC6uixL.html, accessed on May 3, 2020.

33. Vishal Kant, "MCD Election: Purvanchalis Are the New Kingmakers in Delhi Politics," *Hindustan Times*, May 12, 2017, available at https://www.hindustantimes.com/delhi-news/mcd-election-purvanchalis-are-the-new-

kingmakers-in-delhi-politics/story-GtXwZkKZqOQx4cIxwj9FII.html, accessed on June 12, 2020.

34. *Mint*, "Age Old Illness of a Newborn Party," March 12, 2015, available at http://www.livemint.com/Opinion/Z5bI40GV1nQoOZaqMbCEwI/The-ageold-illness-of-a-newborn-party.html, accessed on April 29, 2020.

35. See, for instance, https://www.indiatoday.in/elections/delhi-assembly-polls-2020/story/delhi-election-exit-poll-majority-of-purvanchali-haryanvi-voted-aap-1644707-2020-02-09. See also https://www.outlookindia.com/website/story/news-analysis-delhi-elections-results-2020-how-purvanchali-and-pahadi-vote-blocs-helped-bjp-increase-its-vote-share/347165.

CHAPTER 14

Pollution

Vitiated Air and Thinking about Delhi's Environment

Awadhendra Sharan

The right to health coupled with the right to breathe clean air leaves no manner of doubt that it is important that air pollution deserves to be eliminated and one of the possible methods of reducing it during Diwali is by continuing the suspension of licenses for the sale of fireworks and therefore implicitly, prohibiting the bursting of fireworks.

—Supreme Court judgment[1]

Between the late-nineteenth century and the early twenty-first century, the question of urban air has merited much attention. Curiously though, it is only over the last three decades that academics and policymakers have begun to pay serious attention to it. In part, this may have to do with the fact that vitiated air produces chronic effects, in contrast to the epidemics on account of contaminated water that were of great concern both to the colonial state and to the postcolonial one. Related to this, it is also plausible to suggest that while water purity is seen as a universal public need, issues of air purity have for a long time been seen as the privilege of the rich or those with delicate constitutions. This obviously is no longer so, especially today when Delhi has been declared a gas chamber and smog results in the declaration of public health emergencies. Something qualitatively different has been happening in Delhi over the past three decades as environmental issues, including the issue of air pollution, have come to the fore, demanding our attention to matters of urban planning, those related to issues of science and technology, and finally that having to do with culture and religion. In this chapter, I address each of these issues, while suggesting that it would be useful to locate them in a longer history of colonial and postcolonial urbanism. This would be to mark the continuities with earlier concerns around pollution of air and signal the important ways in which air pollution is differently addressed today.

There is, at an obvious level, the primacy of the visual in concerns around air, far more in the nineteenth century than in the contemporary, but prevalent even today when pollution concerns subside with the onset of the first sunny day, the gases remaining but their presence no longer available to our senses. On the other hand, there is also now a far greater concern with invisible particulate matter and gases than was the case before, perhaps a better appreciation of the correlation between "vitiated air" and bad health and certainly a much better appreciation of needing to define environmental standards against which we can measure progress or decline.

Interventions toward managing atmospheric contaminations were earlier anchored in the quest for greater efficiency and privileged expert knowledge. To an extent, this is the case still, but it is plausible to suggest that contemporary environmentalism is far more focused on sustainability, resilience, and environmental justice. Equally, to imagine discourses of air today as largely a dialogue of experts, of difference in strategy to be resolved through a rough consensus between the same experts, is to miss entirely the social nature of air, the manner in which issues of class, culture, and spatial location are imbricated in the imaginations of clean and healthy cities. In suggesting such continuities and changes, I also suggest that while today Delhi merits the greatest consideration in policies related to air, for much of the colonial period the issue was far more clearly articulated in Bombay and Calcutta. Consequently, there is much to learn from a comparative history of cities in India, even as we focus on Delhi and the National Capital Region (NCR). In lieu of a linear historical account, therefore, what this chapter offers is snapshots from two different moments, the colonial and the contemporary, across three different sites—Bombay, Calcutta, and Delhi—in order to better understand the lineages of our present predicaments.

Colonial Urbanism and the Quest for Pure Air

Modern sanitary science, born in mid-nineteenth century England to deal with the adverse outcomes of urban and industrial revolution, quite expectedly traveled to the colony too. And as with much else related to water and waste, filth and miasma, the difference between spaces of good air and those with vitiated air was articulated with regard to cesspools, dunghills, burial grounds, slaughter houses, marshes, and swamps—the usual sites for the production of gases and vapors. The entirety of the tropics, with its lush vegetation and strong sun, Peter Thorsheim suggests, was imagined as a place entirely different from Europe, with conditions being ripe for the generation and spread of miasmatic diseases and the absence of control over nature considered a suitable condition for imperial control.[2] Air, and its improvement, analogous to water and waste were thus used to mark out the colony as an inferior "Other." Street widening, building regulations, and so on were the usual sanitary responses in Delhi, as elsewhere. "The people in Delhi," Colonel Beadon, president of the New Delhi Municipal Committee, noted in 1912,

> have been huddled into a totally insufficient area so that the streets have been encroached upon, slums have been built and the land has become so valuable that even capitalists cannot build ... the most pressing need of Delhi citizens is room, room to build, room to work, room to play, room to walk, room to drive.[3]

For the most part though, the funds allocated for the same were far less than needed.[4] Further, the relative prioritization of wide streets over slum improvement to ensure air, sunlight, and open space was also a matter of racial division, and residents of the city were not hesitant to take exception to the fact that the rich (and Europeans) were being favored over the poor (and Indians).[5] Street widening was being financially inopportune, observed Sohan Lal, the secretary of the municipal committee, drawing attention instead to the condition of native houses "where tragedies are being enacted every day."[6] An ordinary house, he observed, was a pitiable one, occupied by five or six families, with each family occupying one or two small rooms that served as bedroom, kitchen, dining room, and sitting room all combined. A small courtyard 10 × 10 feet or even less and a narrow lane in front of the house were all the provision for light and air they had. Officials, in turn, shifted the blame on to the cultural habits of natives, the tradition of *purdah*, which confined women to dark and ill-ventilated rooms, a view which found some support among middle-class Indians too.

Not only did air not circulate properly within such congested homes, it was also vitiated on account of smoke from kitchen fires, as also the smoke from factories that drifted into homes of the workers. Attention to this was initially drawn in Bombay and Calcutta where industries had first emerged on a large scale. Workers' homes, the 1901 Census of Bombay noted, were not only blighted by the lack of sewerage but also by the presence of thick black smoke from the coal-powered cotton mills, railway locomotives, and the government mint. Lingering dark clouds, they wrote, brought about "a marked change ... over localities such as Byculla, Parel, Tardeo, Tarwadi and even remote Sewri."[7]

Studies of labor in the postwar period also continued to draw attention to this feature. Among the most influential of these reports was that of Dr. Florence Barnes, submitted to the Bombay Legislative Council in 1922.[8] Housing in Bombay, especially for the working classes, Barnes observed, was extremely unsatisfactory. In one such room, measuring 15 × 12 feet, she found six families living, each with a separate oven for themselves, and without chimneys, such that the atmosphere of the room at night—"filled with the smoke from 6 ovens and other impurities"—grievously harmed both women and children. Conditions were even worse in the basement, where "daylight with difficulty penetrated, sunlight never." The atmosphere of factories could well be laden with fiber, she concluded, but even that was better than the homes of workers, "where every ventilation space was packed to avoid the ingress of fresh air, and where, for fourteen hours of the twenty-four, the family inhaled an atmosphere laden with smoke and other impurities."[9] In Delhi, similarly, the issue was debated at length in the 1930s when a proposal was made for the setting up of an industrial area. The prevailing winds being from west to east, it was feared that gases and fumes, smoke, and obnoxious odors would blow into the neighboring residential districts of Shadipur and Western Extension, causing much nuisance.[10]

Streets and homes apart, the question of vitiated air, more specifically smoke nuisance, was also addressed in relation to quotidian practices of burning the dead and the incineration of refuse. Though sanctioned by long custom and possibly by religious sentiment, the burning of dead in open air, both in itself, and even more, in its consequences, colonial officers argued, was "inconsistent with public decency and detrimental to public health," though there remained some uncertainty about ways to understand it. Was the smoke produced merely a nuisance? Or was it also "noxious to life or health"? Did the fumes and effluvia necessarily give rise to diseases? Were these poisonous in and of themselves or did the extent of harm depend on other factors ranging from the nature of a neighborhood to the direction of wind?[11]

And for these reasons, should burning *ghats* be compulsorily shifted out of cities or merely redesigned? Indians could hardly have been expected to endorse any proposal for relocation, one Ramgopal Ghosh of Calcutta rhetorically asking if the stopping of this practice at Hooghly/Calcutta would be followed by the prevention of the cremation in the holy cities of Benares, Allahabad, and

Haridwar. "Call it custom or usage, or if you prefer, superstitious prejudice," he argued, "I submit you are equally bound to respect it."[12] In other instances, a more nuanced view was offered, disagreement with the official position balanced by a willingness to consider modifications, such as the incorporation of chimneys to draw the smoke away.[13] In courts of law, an attempt was made at arriving at a "balance":

> Although a burning ground may not in itself be a nuisance ... still a Magistrate will have jurisdiction if it is shown that such a *ghat* or ground is in such an offensive state, or that cremation is carried on upon it in such an offensive manner, as to be a source of injury, danger or annoyance to persons living in the vicinity.[14]

Religious sentiments of the people mattered, but so did health and comfort, and all cremation practices, it was ruled, must establish the necessary compromise.

Closely aligned to the question of cremation was the issue of the disposal of rubbish by incineration which began to be debated around the 1860s, when the population of leading Indian cities grew rapidly and municipalities assumed responsibility for managing urban affairs. By the turn of the nineteenth century, David Arnold points out, 883 tonnes of rubbish was being handled in Bombay daily, the corresponding figure for Calcutta being 1,000–1,500 tonnes, a task beyond the capacity of traditional means of handling waste through their consignment in waterbodies (rivers and seas) or in landfill sites. One approach was to make the disposal system more efficient; the alternative was to burn it, though the question remained whether one form of pollution (on the account of waste) was being exchanged for another (smoke and stench).[15] "It will be no gain to the health of the town," the *Statesman* opined, "to poison people living within a certain radius of each incinerator by means of smoke from incinerator chimneys."[16] On the other side of the country, members of the elite European Byculla Club in Bombay complained about the "foul, dense smoke" from waste burned on the nearby Tardeo Flats in the open, while later municipal efforts to erect incinerators floundered on the grounds of financial considerations and possible nuisance.[17]

Smoke apart, there was also the materiality of the refuse to be considered—unlike European and American waste which contained ashes in the form of breeze that kept up the fire in the furnace without needing extra fuel, the waste of Indian cities contained no ashes and, it was feared, would therefore require much additional coal to burn. They also contained much greater moisture content, requiring additional fuel to first dry them before burning, again making incineration a more difficult proposition than in the cities of the West.[18] Not surprisingly, when the question was considered in Delhi in 1911/1912, it was observed that owing to the small proportion of combustible material and the large proportion of vegetable and other damp matter, it would be difficult to burn the refuse of the proposed capital city, not to mention the complaints that the use of a destructor would lead to. Far better, therefore, to dispose the refuse of New Delhi by removing it to the country and using it there for agricultural purposes.[19]

But perhaps most importantly, air pollution in colonial cities was addressed most in relation to fuel use and modern industrial production. Dung, wood, and biomass had been popular fuels for use in native household across India right through the nineteenth and twentieth centuries. In Delhi, as in other cities, licenses had to be obtained for inflammable materials such as depots of hay, straw, thatching grass, wood, or grass, as also for "dangerous or offensive trades"—melting tallow, boiling offal or blood, soap house, oil-boiling house, dyeing house or tannery, brick pottery, lime kiln, or other manufactory "from which offensive or unwholesome smell arise."[20] In time, with the growth of modern industrial enterprises, another fuel, namely coal, came to be increasingly used, and with it came smoke, especially dense black smoke that polluted the air. The reason why this smoke was objectionable was not always evident though. Some argued this on grounds of public health. Others because it constituted an economic waste and yet others because smoke was an uncanny presence in oriental cities, in contrast to its "naturalness" in industrial cities of England.[21] Different measures for abating this smoke were also considered. Laws regarding smoke nuisance were first passed in 1862/1863, in Bombay and Calcutta, respectively, making it mandatory for every furnace in these cities to be so constructed or altered so as to consume or burn the smoke produced *as far as possible.* And when these failed to have much appreciable effect, smoke nuisance commissions were set up for the two cities in 1905 and 1912.

There was also the prospect of industrial relocation, with a suggestion being made to remove jute mills outside Calcutta and to confine the mills in Bombay to the northeastern parts of the city.[22] The possible benefits of such decisions were not entirely lost on the makers of a new capital city of Delhi either:

> The acquisition of land east of the Jumna and its inclusion in the enclave seems to be absolutely necessary. The smoke nuisance in Calcutta would not have been half so bad if the growth and development of Howrah had been controlled as the land east of the Jumna can be controlled if acquired.[23]

Appropriate location, as a strategy of pollution control, however, would have to wait for another two decades to be articulated more fully at the time of the making an industrial area in the 1930s on the outskirts of Delhi, to which many of the existing establishments inside Delhi were expected to migrate.[24] Designed as a measure for ensuring *decongestion*, it was also anticipated that the move would help abate the polluting effect of industries. However, the choice of the location would have to be carefully calibrated, taking into account both the nuisances that were associated with particular industries as also the possible impacts on residential areas in the vicinity of the proposed industrial area. Eventually, an area on either side of the metaled road in Najafgarh in southwest Delhi was chosen as the site for moving industries, though with little real relocation actually taking place. Indeed, if anything, wartime circumstances may have worsened conditions with several colonies getting "infested" with retail shops, service industry, repair shops, small-scale industries, welding and general engineering firms and manufacturing units.

The "City in Decline" and a Renewed Quest for Pure Air

Delhi post Partition was to inherit the legacy of haphazard industrial growth, condensed particularly in the Sabzi Mandi area, leading to the concentration of labor and to the pollution of the atmosphere. In an earlier work, I have examined this legacy at some length to suggest that what was attempted as a response was the adoption of planning and zoning principles, clearly segregating areas of residence from those of industry and commerce.[25] A two-pronged strategy was adopted as far as industry was concerned: first, to attend to those industries that had large requirements of space and water, employed large numbers of people, and created problems of waste disposal, smoke fumes, and water pollution on a large scale; and second, to attend to the many widely dispersed industries that could be both of nuisance and non-nuisance types, but if former, did not pose problems on a large scale. Noise, vibrations, odors, and smoke were the familiar nuisances inquired into and, based on a study of these, recommendations were made regarding where industries may be best located in the city and outside it.

The Plan, however, did not quite succeed—a full decade or so after its notification, arguments continued to be made about the need to shift noxious trades from the lanes of Shahjahanabad, to remove the cattle clusters as also the smoke emitting from *dhobi* kilns.[26] Several of the industries were no more than "industrial shops," small-scale, reliant upon local resources, and with workers living on site or in the immediate vicinity, all of which made it difficult to remove them from the city.

In this context, a second Master Plan for Delhi was notified in 1990, reiterating some of the central propositions made earlier, especially regarding hazardous/noxious/heavy/large industries whose presence was considered undesirable within the city. And yet, as several commentators have suggested, the functional city did not quite materialize. Even more critically, the Master Plan ceased to be a tool of planners alone, and instead became the favored document of the courts through which to shape the city into an ordered space. The plan was legally binding, ruled the Supreme Court of India, at the same time as it pronounced upon clean air and water as aspects of fundamental rights to which all citizens of the country must have access. The argument was echoed in observations of the High Court of Delhi ruling that adherence to planned development was "unexceptionable" and any idea that plans represented only broad guidelines, not fixed and specific provisions, was "clearly misconceived and not based on a correct understanding of the legal position of the Plan."[27]

The context for these arguments were manifold. First, there was the instrumentality of an innovative legal mechanism in the form of public interest litigations (PILs). Initially conceived as enabling a public-minded citizen to appeal to the courts on behalf of a poor and vulnerable person, the mechanism evolved to make space for citizen standing in which an individual could approach the courts not as a representative of others but in her own right, in pursuit of a public good.[28] It is in this capacity that lawyer–activist M. C. Mehta filed several petitions before the Supreme Court of India highlighting various environmental risks that Delhi faced, including smoke and highly toxic gases that were being allowed to pass into the air.[29] In their response, the Court outlined a second context, namely the primacy of Delhi, as a sort of urban lab of PIL courts.

There has as yet been some minor speculation on why Delhi has assumed such importance, though one may imagine that this may have something to do with its status as the national capital. We may also speculate on a possible link between the desire for world-class city which came to be prominently articulated through the 1990s and consequently the desire for slum-free spaces and a pollution-free atmosphere.[30] I wish to suggest something more, however, about the nature of this imagination of world class-ness, taking cue from an oft-repeated remark on the city by judges of the Supreme Court: "Once a beautiful city, Delhi presents a chaotic picture. The city has become a vast and unmanageable conglomeration of commercial, industrial, unauthorised colonies, resettlement colonies and unplanned housing."[31]

Evidently, the contrast is not of the city with the countryside, as had been the more familiar nationalist trope. Instead, the contemporary city is contrasted with its own past, perhaps with the New Delhi established pre-Independence or with the City Functional as imagined by the Master Plans. This rhetorical recourse to an ordered, functionally segregated, beautiful, and pollution-free city, I suggest, following the South African philosopher and architect Hilton Judin's ruminations on Johannesburg, is "nostalgia for what is not really past; it is merely not present, as it has been taken away from us and not just eliminated by time. It is nostalgia for a present denied."[32] It is in this deeper sense of having been denied the ideal urban, I argue, that legal imaginations of urban possibilities came to be anchored. The city that is unruly, messy, and polluted must be made to cohere again, in order that we can rediscover our modern selves.

Framed thus, most interventions have focused on outlining the causes of "failure"—the mushrooming of the city beyond what had been mandated in the plans—and its rectification through spatial relocation. Several orders regarding the shifting of industries that were passed subsequently reflect just such a view. These include the shifting of hazardous units outside the city and putting a stop to stone crushing.[33] Yet again, there were orders to deal firmly with nonconforming industries and those that were polluting. Industries located in residential areas drew the ire of many who feared for those industries' impact on public health. On the other hand, expulsion of industry from the city evoked concerns about its possible implications for livelihood of workers.[34]

This is a story much told, and bears little repetition here, except to highlight that what had been one strain of thought in colonial India, and possibly a minor one, namely relocation of industry to abate smoke, eventually found a logical and coherent formulation in planning laws in the 1960s (and later in the 1990s) whose "implementation" on the urging of the courts have had the effect of shutting down some industries and moving some others out of Delhi on account of the pollution caused by them.[35]

The question of fuel substitution in public transport was another issue that featured prominently in the 1990s and 2000s, following a Supreme Court judgment in July 1998 to ban the use of diesel and make compressed natural gas (CNG) compulsory for public transport. To briefly recapitulate, key issues in this instance included the following:

1. The far greater involvement of civil society actors in framing the issue of pollution, inside courtrooms, and in various media forums;[36]

2. The failure to reach consensus on the merits and demerits of the various fuels which led the Supreme Court to lay emphasis on the Precautionary Principle in arriving at a judgment in instances where the scientific evidence remained disputed;[37] and

3. The imperative to make definitive technical choices as setting standards alone had failed to achieve the desired ends.[38]

The Court's order to substitute the use of diesel in public transport by CNG was subject to much critical review, and at any rate the gains of this move were soon lost as more and more private vehicles using diesel plied on Delhi roads. More recently, there has also been a concerted move to ban the use of certain industrial fuels such as peat coke and furnace oil used by industries in the NCR and substituting them with more environment-friendly fuels such as natural gas.[39] It has also been suggested that commercial establishments shift from the use of coal to electric or gas-based appliances and liquefied petroleum gas be made available to approximately 10 percent of the households that continue to use wood, crop residue, cow dung, and coal for cooking.[40]

In some ways, this mirrors what had been the more dominant strand of thought earlier, namely the use of better quality coal, better furnace design, and latest technology such as scrubbers and mechanical stokers, alongside the greater electrification of households and the far greater use of gas in kitchens. Indeed, as Peter Brimblecombe has argued more generally, at one level the question of air pollution is a question of fuel use, and it is not surprising, therefore, that from time to time efforts are made to introduce changes in this matter.[41] However, as before, the competing pressures of costs and environmental impacts limit what may be possible. Equally, the principle of working through correlations of possible harms rather than through definitive evidence of harm has yet to be accepted across board, with questions continuing to be raised about the extent of harm caused by diesel. However, the onus of proving "no harm" clearly seems to have shifted toward the potential polluter, with the National Green Tribunal reiterating that

> Undisputedly, the applicant [Government of India] had failed to substantiate
> ... that use of diesel vehicles of more than 10 years will not be detrimental to
> the health of people and further failed to negate statistical information that
> the particulate matter level in vehicular emissions consequent to diesel as fuel
> was scientifically proved to be carcinogenic.[42]

Equally importantly, there is now an explicit ambient air quality standard to be achieved, air quality monitoring stations to measure the gases/particles in the air, and an air quality index to examine whether the standards are met (or otherwise) and be easily comprehended. These developments remain limited yet, especially the extent of air data monitoring, but there is little doubt that together this marks a major departure from an earlier moment when the focus was entirely on emission from a specific source and on efficiency measures that could be adopted to minimize emissions.[43]

The Sociability of Air

Evidently, over the past two decades, there has been a proliferation of technical studies on the subject of air pollution in Delhi, beginning with the *White Paper on Pollution in Delhi with an Action Plan* (1997), followed by a study by the Indian Institute of Technology (IIT) Delhi on the effects of diesel operated trucks and so on (2007), another on *Air Quality Monitoring Emission Inventory* (2008) by National Environmental Engineering Research Institute, on *Emissions Inventory of Anthropogenic PM2.5 and PM10* (2011) by System of Air Quality and Weather Forecasting and Research, and most recently, a study on *Air Pollution and Greenhouse Gases in Delhi* (2017) by IIT Kanpur. These have added important new dimensions to our understanding of air in the capital city. However, consensus still remains elusive regarding the specific impacts of varied sources, with different weights being accorded in these studies to industry, vehicular pollution, construction waste and road dust, and so on, some emphasizing road dust as the biggest contributor while others suggesting vehicular emissions as the main source.[44] This in itself poses an interesting question for understanding how air policies may be fashioned in the wake of scientific and technical uncertainty. However, in what follows, I follow a slightly different track, moving away from technical matters to consider the public articulation of the issue of air pollution, its meaning, and significance as perceived by individuals and communities. I do so by way of a brief consideration of two issues—the disposal of rubbish and the bursting of crackers—to illustrate what may be other emerging questions with respect to air, those concerning social movements, cultural beliefs, and the politics of religious claims, issues that curiously return us to some of the debates of the colonial period.

Incineration: The Circularity and Sociability of an Environmental Problem

Incineration, we may recollect, had been briefly flirted with in Calcutta and Bombay in the closing years of the nineteenth century. Notwithstanding, large incinerators had remained quite marginal to municipal arrangements in India. In Delhi too, as mentioned earlier, the adoption of the technology had been briefly debated before being discarded. And so things remained, until the incineration of waste assumed a new lease of life as a possible nonconventional energy source in the 1980s. The initial step in this was in the form of the Timarpur Refuse Incineration-cum-Power Generation Station, commissioned in 1987 on the argument that while quantities of waste were rapidly increasing in Delhi, there was limited space available for landfills.[45] The experiment, however, died a quick death, failing to go beyond a brief 21-day trial phase. The problem that the calorific value of the waste generated in the city was much below the anticipated or required value necessitated additional fuel which made the operations rather costly. Delhi was not alone in this, with similar experiments in Bombay failing for the same reason, namely low calorific value of waste.[46]

Enthusiasm for this project thus seems to have died down for a while, as the *White Paper on Pollution* explicitly rejected it in favor of composting and other technologies of waste disposal. But not for long, with a proposal for another waste-to-energy plant approved in Okhla in south Delhi in 2005, registered under the Clean Development Mechanism for reducing emissions of greenhouse gases such as methane that would otherwise have been emitted from landfill sites. This was followed by another plant at Ghazipur, on the outskirts of the city. Ironically, opposition to the plants soon emerged based on exactly the same logic, namely the potential pollution of air and adverse health impacts of the dioxins emitted by the incinerators. It was argued too that the move entailed significant job loss for traditional waste pickers and recyclers.[47]

Together, these concerns led to the formation of different alliances and different representations of the issues at stake. Residents in Okhla formed the Okhla Anti-Incinerator Committee in 2009, drawing attention to the fact that particulate matter had invaded their bedrooms, implanting itself into their clothes, blankets, and even bodies, and therefore demanding the relocation of the plant.[48] Only secondarily, and with some reluctance, was the issue of the livelihood of workers addressed. By contrast, the Ghazipur Anti-Incinerator Committee evolved as a collaboration between the residents welfare association and the workers' collective of waste pickers demanding, among other things, support for the informal waste recycling sector and the scrapping of all waste-to-energy incinerator projects. Between Okhla and Ghazipur, thus, waste as resource and as environmental hazard actively contested its framing as clean development.

The matter has since reached the courts and has become the subject of political negotiations between the central and the Delhi governments, suggesting that it is not only the data generated by scientists alone that determines how pollution is understood and acted upon but also the perceptions of differently situated communities.[49] The collaboration, moreover, is not only among affected communities alone but also includes civil society organizations, those concerned with ecology, health, or livelihood issues, and who help generate popular knowledge and public movements. Equally, such a politics implies that actors move across different positions, today an activist, tomorrow a policy advisor, to produce a science/policy/activism axis that has been well explored in the context of *contested illnesses*.[50] And finally, such political/environmental understandings, while pitting a known polluter (an industry or stubble-burning agriculturalists) against an identified victim (particular communities or the city at large), must of necessity remain alive to the prospect that the proposed solutions may exact their own environmental costs.[51] What constitutes "clean" matter and what is "dirty" does not inhere in a thing alone, nor is it simply a matter of "fact" deduced in some laboratory setting, but is instead a joint product of research, interpretation, meaning making, articulation of interests, and public action.

Religious Practices, Public Health, and the Environment

If the legal and political articulation of scientific expertise in environmental matters provides one important framing for us to consider anew the quest for pure air, the relationship between religious practices and environmental/health harms provides another vexed dilemma. As I have already suggested, the balancing of air pollution/public health and cultural and religious rights had been attempted with respect to the burning of the dead in colonial cities. In Delhi today, the issue seems to be most discussed with regard to the bursting of firecrackers on Dussehra, Diwali, and other religious/social occasions, posed as a question of Right to Life enshrined in Article 21 of the Constitution of India.

In such cases, the matter is usually raised by way of civil writ petitions. One such petition concerns the Noise Pollution Control and Regulation Rules, enacted by the Government of India in 1999 and subsequently modified in 2002, to empower state governments to permit the use of loudspeaker or public-address system during night hours (between 10 pm and 12 pm) on or during cultural or religious occasions for a limited time period. The matter eventually reached the Supreme Court where some petitioners urged that the use of loudspeakers in religious places such as temples, mosques, churches, gurdwaras, and so on be discontinued or at least regulated and that firecrackers burst during Diwali festival and on other occasions be entirely prohibited.[52] On the other hand, there were petitioners who demanded full exemption in favor of bursting of firecrackers during festivals. It was matter of freedom of expression, the latter argued, a point rebutted by the Supreme Court. Restrictions on the bursting of firecrackers, urged the secretary of the Tamil Nadu Fireworks and Amorces Manufacturers Association, also amounted to the infringement of religious rights under Article 25. Not quite, observed the Court again, opining on what religious texts prescribe, especially in what they mean in India's pluralistic society:

> [T]he festival of Diwali is mainly associated with *pooja* performed on the auspicious day and not with firecrackers. In no religious text book it is written that Diwali has to be celebrated by bursting crackers. Diwali is considered as a festival of lights, not of noise. Shelter in the name of religion cannot be sought for bursting firecrackers and that too at odd hours.... People of this great country belong to different castes and communities, have belief in different religions and customs and celebrate different festivals. We are tolerant for each other. There is unity in diversity. If relaxation is allowed to one there will be no justification for not permitting relaxation to others and if we do so the relaxation will become the rule. It will be difficult to enforce the restriction.[53]

The matter was far from resolved, however, being brought yet again before the Supreme Court a decade later in 2015 on behalf of three children pleading for a ban on the use of fireworks as part of a package of relief sought to ensure "environmental purity."[54] Given high levels of particulate matter and the harmful effects of fireworks on the ambient air and on the lungs, eyes, and ears of people, especially of the ailing and the aged, the Court ruled the best possible remedy was to suspend all licenses that could lead to the sale of fireworks, wholesale and retail, within the territory of the NCR. Arguments were yet to be heard fully, but even as an interim measure, they suggested, the significance and joy of bursting fireworks must yield to health concerns. "A just constitutional balance," they also wrote, "must overwhelmingly prioritize the harmful effects of this hazardous air on present and future generations, irreversible and imperceptible as they are, over the immediate commercial constraints of the manufacturers and suppliers of fireworks." Resort was taken to the precautionary principle to suggest that where there were threats of serious and irreversible damage, lack of scientific certainty should not be used as a reason for postponing measures to prevent environmental degradation.

In response, the respondents for the fireworks industry pointed to just such a lack of certainty. A recent study conducted by IIT Kanpur, they said, listed several sources for high PM2.5 levels but firecrackers was not one of them. Poor wind speed was one of the causes of smog while the burning of crop residues in the neighboring state of Punjab and in Pakistan also caused air pollution in Delhi. The Court would not be moved. Bursting of firecrackers, they reasoned, may be only one among the many causes, but it was certainly an important one, as evident from pollution levels immediately post-Diwali.

The fireworks industry then took recourse to the economic argument stating that the livelihood of workers who were employed in the over 800 units situated in and around Sivakasi that produced and supplied fireworks and sparklers all over the country for festivals such as Diwali, Dusshera, Christmas, Ramzan, and so on would be affected. Commercial gains could not take priority over public health, the Court again reasoned, though given the uncertainty regarding the contribution of various sources of pollution it was willing to modify its order partially, lifting the suspension on those who had permanent licenses. But not for long, as within three weeks it decided yet again to reimpose the ban on sale of fireworks until after Diwali of 2017, leading to much heart burn among traders who had made fresh purchases following the partial lifting of the ban earlier.

Traders were not alone either, with a range of "Hindu" opinion opposing the ruling, and yet other "Hindu" opinion contesting this opposition, both anchoring the debate in considerations regarding the "essential" aspects of Hindu religious observances. Alongside, an entirely different line of critique took exception to the Court's failure to appreciate the importance of customs for which scriptural sanctions could not always be found. In brief, while religious beliefs had been periodically highlighted since colonial times to emphasize the duty to take care of nature, religious practices have continued to pose difficult questions regarding their environmental impacts, in both the colonial city and the contemporary one.

One could cite ever more material on the issue. But the limited point that I wish to make is that environmental issues, especially when these are intertwined with everyday practices of cooking, eating, celebrating festivals or marriages, and birth and death have cultural meanings and associations that are articulated alongside the technical, scientific "facts." The world of scholarship, especially that engaged with policymaking, resource use dynamics, or urban transformation, I suggest, stands to benefit much by bringing this cultural aspect upfront, to provoke a different kind of dialogue about environmental and urban well-being than the more familiar citations from studies by scientific experts and technology groups that inform current decision-making.

Conclusion

This chapter, as I suggest at the outset, is part of an attempt to consider a long history of urban air in India. Over the last century and more, the range of sources that impact our air has considerably multiplied, as has our understanding of how these sources relate to each other. Some aspects of this, especially concerning planning and its failures, have been much discussed and briefly referenced here too. The question of scientific advice, especially in legal settings, has also merited some discussion, though much more still needs to be thought of in regard to "science in context" if we want to move beyond science as data and information. As regards religion and culture, I suggest, however, urbanists have barely begun to fashion a grammar for discussing this, except perhaps when discussing matters of interreligious disputes.

In all this, there is also the special status of Delhi to be considered, as a national capital and as an aspiring world-class city which gives the environmental issues of the city an entirely different symbolic weight than would be the case otherwise. This is not to suggest minimization of the degree of seriousness with which we need to address environmental harms in Delhi and the NCR, but merely to offer the proposition that how we think about our environment is intimately tied to how we produce, consume, or travel and how different aspects of our lives—cultural, religious, and social—are interwoven. Or, to put it differently, the environment we desire to have is fashioned in the shadow of the city that we wish to build.

Notes

1. Supreme Court of India, IA No. 52448/2017 in WP (C) No. 728/2015 on September 12, 2017.
2. Peter Thorsheim, *Inventing Pollution: Coal, Smoke, and Culture in Britain since 1800* (Athens, OH: Ohio University Press, 2006), 10–11.
3. Cited in Bharat Sevak Samaj, *Slums of Old Delhi* (Delhi: Atma Ram and Sons, 1958), 215.
4. Underinvestment by the colonial state in matters of local improvement has, therefore, been a favored explanation among historians to understand the

difference between what was achieved in European cities and what could be possible in the colonies.

5. Delhi State Archives (DSA), File No. 1293, LSG, Local Bodies, CC Office, 1938.

6. DSA, File No. 2 (13), B, Edu, CC Office, 1930.

7. Quoted in Sandip Hazareesingh, *The Colonial City and the Challenge of Modernity: Urban Hegemonies and Civic Contestations in Bombay City, 1900–1925* (New Delhi: Orient Longman, 2007), 238.

8. Dr. Barnes was a distinguished officer of the Women's Medical Service whose services had been lent to the provincial governments in 1921 to investigate the conditions of women's employment, with a special focus on the maternity question.

9. This remark was to be often re-cited, including by the Royal Commission on Labour in 1930, as a true description of conditions in Bombay's *chawls*.

10. DSA, File No. 1330, LSG, Local Bodies, CC Office, 1938.

11. West Bengal State Archives (WBSA), Judl. Progs. 79–82, March 1864.

12. Cited in Ishita Pande, *Medicine, Race and Liberalism in British Bengal: Symptoms of Empire* (London: Routledge, 2010), 131.

13. WBSA, Judl. Progs. 79–82, March 1864.

14. See *Indra Nath Banerjee vs Queen Empress* (1898) ILR 25 Cal 425 concerning a burning ghat on the borders of villages Mohanpur and Naihati in Bengal.

15. David Arnold, "Burning Issues: Cremation and Incineration in Modern India," *NTM* 24, no. 4 (2016) 393–419, doi: 10.1007/s00048-017-0158-7.

16. *Statesman*, "Mr. Harrington's Incinerator," *Statesman*, August 31, 1890.

17. L. W. Michael, *The History of the Municipal Corporation of the City of Bombay* (Bombay: Union Press, 1902), 262.

18. W. J. Simpson, *A Note on the Sanitation of Calcutta and Other Papers: 1893*; Henry Conybeare, Report on the Sanitary State and Sanitary Requirements of Bombay, 1855, available at https://archive.org/details/b21365921.

19. NAI (National Archives of India), Home, Public, A, No. 62–63, July 1913.

20. NAI, Home, Public, A, No. 83–87, September 1883. Among other things, the licensee was expected to make due provision for preventing all noise, smoke, or smell from being a nuisance to neighbors or the public.

21. NAI, Home, Public, A, No. 103, November 1906.

22. The idea was soon dropped; however, the arguments being that prevailing winds would not only bring the soot and the smoke back into the city but that workers who lived in the vicinity of the mills would also continue to suffer at the new locations.

23. NAI, Home, Delhi, A, No. 16, August 1912.

24. A. P. Hume, *Report on the Relief of Congestion in Delhi* (Shimla: Government of India Press, 1936).

25. Awadhendra Sharan, *In the City, Out of Place: Nuisance, Pollution, and Dwelling in Delhi, c. 1860–2000* (New Delhi: Oxford University Press, 2014), esp. ch. 4.

26. Biswajit Banerjee, "Shahjahanabad and the Master Plan for Delhi," *Economic and Political Weekly* 10, no. 46 (November 15, 1975). The article reports upon a seminar on "Redevelopment of Shahjahanabad" organized by the Ministry of Works and Housing.

27. "The Plan in Its Legal Position," Gautam Bhan suggests, serves to simplify a complex process of spatial arrangement to fixed and prescriptive dictates. See Gautam Bhan, *In the Public's Interest* (New Delhi: Orient BlackSwan, 2016), 131–134.

28. Anuj Bhuwania, *Courting the People: Public Litigation in Post Emergency India* (New Delhi: Cambridge University Press, 2017), 30.

29. Sharan, *In the City, Out of Place*, esp. ch. 4.

30. D. Asher Ghertner, *Rule by Aesthetics: World Class City Making in Delhi* (New Delhi: Oxford University Press, 2015).

31. AIR 1996 SC 2231, available at https://www.aironline.in/legal-judgements/1996+%284%29+SCC+750.

32. Hilton Judin, "Unsettling Johannesburg: The Country in the City," in *Other Cities, Other Worlds: Urban Imaginaries in a Globalizing Age*, ed. Andreas Huyssen (Durham, NC: Duke University Press, 2008), 121–146.

33. *M. C. Mehta vs Government of India and Others*, Writ Petition (Civil) 4677, Supreme Court of India, 1985.

34. Delhi Janwadi Adhikar Manch, *How Many Errors Does Time Have Patience For? Report on Industrial Closures and Slum Demolitions in Delhi.* (New Delhi: Delhi Janwadi Adhikar Manch, April 2001); XI Lok Sabha Debates, November 28, 1996. Given Delhi's special status as national capital, several speakers in the parliamentary debate pointed out that decisions in this regard were not simply a matter for Delhi, the NCT, and the Supreme Court but would have implications for other cities as well.

35. This is what would classically be referred to as NIMBY (not in my backyard) proposition, with polluting industries relocated in adjacent towns and cities, possibly causing pollution there instead of in Delhi.

36. On legal cases as media events, see Ravi Sundaram, *Pirate Modernity: Delhi's Media Urbanism* (London: Routledge, 2011).

37. On Precautionary Principle and Indian courts, see Lavanya Rajamani, "The Right to Environmental Protection in India: Many a Slip between the Cup and the Lip?" *Review of European, Comparative and International Environmental Law* 16, no. 3 (2007): 274–286.

38. SCI, WP 13029, order on April 5, 2002.

39. *Times of India*, "Alternatives Available, but Industries Oppose Fuel Ban," November 6, 2017.

40. Indian Institute of Technology (IIT) Kanpur, *Comprehensive Study on Air Pollution and Green House Gases (GHGs) in Delhi*, Final Report: Air Pollution Component (Kanpur: IIT Kanpur, 2016), available at https://cerca.iitd.ac.in/uploads/Reports/1576211826iitk.pdf, accessed on November 24, 2020.

41. Peter Brimblecombe, *The Big Smoke: A History of Air Pollution in London since Medieval Times* (London: Methuen, 1987).

42. On April 7, 2015, the NGT had banned all diesel vehicles over 10 years old from plying in Delhi NCR roads. Later, on July 18 and 20, 2016, it had ordered deregistration of 15 to 10 year old diesel vehicles in the national capital in a phased manner. See *Times of India*, "End of Road for 10-yr-old Diesel Cars in Delhi-NCR: NGT Refuses to Lift Ban," September 14, 2017.

43. On the difference between environmental concerns rooted in ethic of efficiency and that driven by explicitly mandated environmental standards, see Hugh S. Gorman, *Redefining Efficiency: Pollution Concerns, Regulatory Mechanisms, and Technological Change in the U.S. Petroleum Industry* (Akron, OH: University of Akron Press, 2001).

44. *Indian Express*, "What's Fouling Delhi's Air: 4 Studies, 4 Conclusions," October 19, 2017.

45. As initially conceived, the plant was designed to incinerate 300 tonnes of waste every day and generate 3.75 megawatts of power. For more details, see Dharmesh Shah, "The Timarpur-Okhla Waste to Energy Venture," Global Alliance for Incinerator Alternatives, available at http://www.no-burn.org/wp-content/uploads/Timarpur.pdf, accessed on May 3, 2020.

46. This, we may recollect, had been the problem even when the first such plants were experimented with in India in the 1890s.

47. Some scholars have referred to the loss of livelihood because of privatization of waste as accumulation by dispossession. See Seth Schindler, Federico Demaria, and Shashi B. Pandit, "Delhi's Waste Conflict," *Economic and Political Weekly*, 47, no. 42 (October 20, 2012): 18–21.

48. Cited in Federico Demaria and Seth Schindler, "Contesting Urban Metabolism: Struggles over Waste-to-Energy in India," *Antipode* 48, no. 2 (March 2016): 293–313.

49. The issue was first tried in the Delhi High Court and then heard in the National Green Tribunal (NGT). On various occasions, the NGT referred to potential health hazards but in its final ruling allowed the plant to continue its operations. Once again, the issue was one of "balance": "Public interest and public health examined in conjunction with environmental protection, the balance tilts in favour of permitting the plant to continue its operation of processing the municipal solid waste from waste to energy." Sustainable

development, the NGT reasoned, could lead to some inconvenience and cause some impacts on environment. But unless such impact and effect were irretrievable, the tribunal would be inclined to permit such plants to operate. On the other hand, the Precautionary Principles required that all such restrictions and mandates be put upon the project proponent to ensure that it was strictly nonpolluting and compliant. The directions in this instance therefore "would ensure compliance to the Precautionary Principle on the one hand and bring the case within the safe limitations of Sustainable Development." See http://www.indiaenvironmentportal.org.in/files/Sukhdev%20Vihar%20waste%20to%20energy%20plant%20NGT%20Judgement%202017.pdf.

50. Phil Brown et. al., "Clearing the Air and Breathing Freely: The Health Politics of Air Pollution and Asthma," in *Smoke and Mirrors: The Politics and Culture of Air Pollution*, ed. E. Melanie DuPuis (New York: New York University Press, 2004), 261–287. In her own introduction, DuPuis writes that scientists are better understood as part of the social context rather than a neutral source of facts.

51. For a similar argument with respect to car shredding in the USA, see Carl A. Zimring, "The Complex Environmental Legacy of the Automobile Shredder," *Technology and Culture*, 52, no. 3 (2011): 523–547.

52. Supreme Court of India, *Noise Pollution - ... vs Unknown* on July 18, 2005, AIR 2005 SC 3136.

53. In a prior case on the use of firecrackers in Delhi, the Delhi High Court had ruled that while the Right to Freedom of Religion (Article 25) could be restricted on the ground of public health, the nexus between noise and health would have to be judicially established. See Delhi High Court, *Free Legal Aid Cell Shri Sugan ... vs Govt. of NCT of Delhi and Others* on July 23, 2001.

54. The details of this case were drawn upon the Supreme Court of India, *Arjun Gopal vs Union Of India* on September 12, 2017, and October 9, 2017.

Statistical Appendix

The Center for the Advanced Study of India–National Capital Region (CASI–NCR) Survey is a social survey of approximately 5,500 households living in the National Capital Territory (NCT) of Delhi and its surrounding region—together, the NCR. The demand for the survey came from the paucity of data (or insufficiently dense data) on India's urban areas like Delhi to make nuanced social claims. Other high-quality surveys, specifically the Indian Human Development Survey (IHDS) and the National Sample Survey (NSS), have much smaller sample sizes in the urban areas of the NCR as compared to the CASI–NCR Survey.

The CASI–NCR Survey collected data on a breadth of issues in order to provide comprehensive information on the lives of residents in the NCR. The survey includes a roster collecting basic demographic information, other basic household information, and separate modules for education of children in the household, access to services and benefits, gender and marriage, caste/religious practices, and commuting and migration. Results from these modules are reported throughout the book.

Components of the Survey

Upon gaining permission to survey the household, the enumerator (that is, surveyor) coded some basic infrastructural information about the household and surrounding area, in particular the quality of the house (*kuccha/pucca*) and the quality of the approach road to the home. After this, the enumerator moved to the respondent portion of the survey (the method of respondent selection is detailed in the section "Sampling Households").

Household and Education Rosters

The enumerator carried out a household roster exercise. First, basic demographic information was collected about each household member (for example, age, sex, marital status, relation to the head of the household), as well as location of birth and year and reason the person migrated to the NCR if the individual was born out of the region. Information about primary and secondary occupations, as well as educational status and attainment, was recorded for each member (which serves as the basis for Chapter 10). We also asked about forms of identification—driver's license, Aadhaar card, passport—and a formal bank account for each member.

Certain pieces of information were only applicable to some of the household members. For those aged 18 and above, we ascertained whether they were on the local voter list. For female members of the household, we ascertained information on births and children to make basic fertility calculations.

Next, we collected extensive information about school-aged children (those under the age of 15). For those still in school, we asked about the particulars of the school (private/public, language of instruction, fees, as well as donations for admission and political affiliations of the school). For those out of school, we asked about the highest level of education, the particulars of their last school, and reasons for dropping out/never enrolling. We also asked a series of questions more generally about education to the respondent, such as received scholarships for each child, whether the current school(s) were the top choice, how far male and female students would/should study, and whether the respondents knew about the "right to education." This education roster provided a significant amount of detail, but we did not include the information in the volume for concerns of space.

Household Data

We collected a number of basic demographic pieces of information about each household, such as the caste (down to *jati* level) and religion of head of household and spouse, primary language spoken in the home, and assets owned. We also collected core infrastructure information for the dwelling—number of rooms, kitchens, toilets, drainage—as well as ownership/titling status for the dwelling. Finally, we asked about electricity, water, and garbage collection costs, as well as their perception of the Swachh Bharat (Clean India) program. These pieces of information became the basis for chapters on economic well-being and infrastructure (Chapters 2–5) and energy consumption (Chapter 6).

We also asked about access to the state for households in a number of ways: whether the household had a ration card, whether identification cards were obtained recently, and whether they had to pay agents to get them. A short module investigated whether and why households approached local intermediaries—usually for civic services and infrastructure—and whether the issue was resolved (the basis for Chapter 12).

Political and Bureaucratic Engagement

We included a simple module on political and civic engagement. These questions were answered for the respondent, for himself/herself (not the household). First, the respondent was asked about a number of measures of participation from turning out to vote to engaging in elections through donations; putting up posters; active participation such as attending rallies, fundraising, or canvassing for a political party; or participating in a neighborhood society or residents' welfare association (RWA). In addition to participation, party preferences at the center and state levels were ascertained, as well as policy preferences about state versus private provision of schools and hospitals. While this module yielded many interesting insights, we did not include the findings in this volume.

Respondents were also asked if anyone in their household had been the target of a crime in the past five years and whether they approached the police and filed a First Information Report or (FIR). Respondents were asked what other routes they used to deal with the crime if they did not approach police and about their overall satisfaction with whomever they did approach, police or otherwise. Relatedly, respondents were asked about how late they felt safe returning home at night, transportation usage, and the relative safety of the transportation. These questions became the basis for Chapter 7 in the volume.

Marriage

In order to understand the lives of young women in our sample, we fielded a module on marriage beliefs and practices. We began by asking about the age of marriage of the respondent (if applicable) and the age of marriage of his or her parents, as well as the acceptable age of marriage in their household today. We also asked about the relative acceptance in the past and today of marrying outside one's caste, religion, linguistic group, and social class (as well as whether such marriages have taken place in the family). A number of questions were also asked about the process of marriage, usually arranged marriage. We asked who arranges the marriage and how much consent is needed, whether matrimonial sites have been used, and whether a *roka* (engagement period) is undertaken and could be broken. We also asked about certain gendered practices, such as whether daughters-in-law practice veiling/*ghunghat*/*pardah*. These questions served as the basis for Chapter 9.

Outside the Home

We asked a number of questions to get a sense of movement and a family's connections outside the home. We asked the respondent to provide details on their commute to work, and any trips outside of the immediate region. Respondents were also asked about where their outstation parents and children live, whether remittances are involved, and whether they visit or have been visited. The occupations of these parents and children were also ascertained. These were all interesting questions that allow for a more complicated notion of mobility of the household. We decided to sacrifice this material in the volume for more breadth in topics (as mobility is a large subject in and of itself).

Caste and Religious Relations

We discussed a number of issues related to caste and religion in the survey, as these are core to understanding social change and urbanization. We asked about eating practices of households and whether they eat with or invite over individuals from different caste and religious groups (and if not, why). This forms the basis for Chapter 8 in the volume.

We also collected information on a number of other social relations. We asked about the religious and caste identity of emergency contacts, neighbors (discussed in Chapter 2), and the shopkeeper of the local *kirana* (grocery) shop. These data provide insights into the pattern of social relations of our respondents from an identity-based perspective. While these data are not discussed in detail in this volume, they form the basis for serious investigations by other scholars.

The Sample Frame

Because the survey was only intended to study urban populations in the NCR, we had to begin by determining how to sample those regions that could plausibly be described as "urban" in the metropolitan area. We decided to use census definitions of urban areas to conduct our sampling. As discussed in the main text of the book, according to the 2011 Indian Census, the districts included in the NCR had a total population of 50 million of which about 31 million was in urban areas. The current composition of the NCR includes the districts of Karnal and Jind in Haryana and Muzaffarnagar and Shamli in Uttar Pradesh (UP) (the first three of these were notified in 2015 and Shamli in 2017). Because these notifications occurred after our preparations for the survey had already begun, they are not included in the sample.

As we describe in detail in the following paragraphs, the bases for our sampling were the political boundaries—namely, assembly constituencies (ACs) and polling booths in urban areas in the corresponding ACs. There were three major reasons that political boundaries were used for this study: (*a*) the last publicly available census population enumeration was conducted in 2009–2010, which was likely well out of date for a dynamic region like the NCR, (*b*) political data can be linked to voter lists with identifying information such as name, age, and father/spouse of the individual, which tends to yield better response rates in surveying,[1] and (*c*) digitization of the voter list, which is publicly available, permits opportunities for control over sample replacement and monitoring the sampling procedure in real time. The major drawback of using political data and voter lists is that nonvoters may be excluded from the sample.[2] In order to minimize this problem, a "hybrid" strategy was devised and is detailed in the section "Assessing Differences between Voter List and Random Walk."

Based on budget, it was decided that approximately 5,500 households would be sampled across the urban portions of the NCR. This necessitated matching areas delimited as "urban" by the census to polling booths by using the voter list. The first page of the voter list typically gives an urban/rural classification, a census-delimited area in which the polling booth is located, and other key information such as the number of voters in the polling booth. In order to conduct this exercise, we searched every voter list in an AC that was contained in one of the NCR's districts and scanned all relevant information—limiting our sampling frame to those polling booths classified as "urban" using this procedure.

The main phase of surveying took place from October 2016 to April 2017. The surveying was conducted by India Institute led by Baladevan Rangaraju.

Choosing Clusters

Optimally, we desired to maximize the spatial "spread" of the sample, maintaining basic principles of randomization. But, in practice, due to budget constraints, we had to choose clusters within which to do the sampling.

Accordingly, we chose 100 clusters with an aim of sampling an average of 55 voters per cluster—with each cluster corresponding to approximately 5,000 voters within which to do the sampling. The actual size of the cluster was selected to be proportional to the number of voters in a cluster, where the determination of cluster size is detailed in the next two paragraphs.

Because we had collected the number of voters in each polling booth, we were able to stratify the sample further by the states that comprise the NCR. In total, we sampled 61 clusters in Delhi, 23 clusters in UP, 13 clusters in Haryana, and 3 clusters in Rajasthan.

In order to form clusters, we ran a "greedy algorithm" that selected consecutive polling booth numbers within an AC (that is, spatially proximate polling booths) so their sum was as close to 5,000 voters as possible, which typically yielded around five polling booths per cluster. Because ACs are given an "AC number" by the Election Commission of India and because consecutive AC numbers are likely spatially proximate ACs, we used this information to generate spatial spread of our clusters.

To do so, we sorted the AC numbers from lowest to highest and the clusters therein. For example, in Delhi, the first cluster in AC Number 1 would be listed first, then the second cluster in AC Number 1, and so on until the clusters in AC Number 1 were completed. Then we would start with AC Number 2 and continue the pattern until all 70 ACs were completed. The result was a single sequence of clusters all across Delhi, where consecutive clusters were spatially proximate. We then used a modified version of systematic sampling to select the 61 clusters for Delhi to guarantee spatial spread of clusters. Similar procedures were conducted for each of the states.

The result of this process was a set of 100 clusters of approximately 5,000 voters each with significant spatial spread across the NCR, in a manner that was proportional to the number of voters in the population. The total number of polling booths sampled in the NCR was 502—with 314 in Delhi, 116 in UP, 62 in Haryana, and 13 in Rajasthan.

Sampling Households

The number of households selected per polling booth to be sampled was proportionate to its size among other polling booths in the cluster—that is, within the cluster, the sample was further stratified by polling booth. Furthermore, the sample was selected to be proportional to the number of voters in a cluster, as the greedy algorithm does not yield perfectly equally sized clusters in terms of voters. Households were selected in one of two ways, from the voter list or from a "random walk" protocol, with 80 percent from the voter list and 20 percent from the random walk protocol. A random walk was used for a percentage of households to potentially correct for any biases in estimation due to only selecting households from the voter list.

From the Voter List

Once again, the voters were selected to be spatially spread out in the polling booth area using a modified form of systematic sampling. Of course, we were not always able to reach our first targets. Because we were sampling from a known list (the voter list), we were able to directly provide samples for replacement—and guarantee that the replacement was spatially proximate. The selection of spatially proximate replacement has two major benefits (if replacement is to be used). First, people of similar caste, class, and religion tend to live near each other, so demographic biases in the sample can be minimized from replacement. Second, the surveyor does not need to travel far to find his/her replacement, speeding up the time of surveying. In order to generate a spatially proximate replacement, we used the listing number on the voter list.

Because our sample was at the individual voter level, our estimates are broadly representative of the voter population. In principle, the probability a household is selected is inversely proportional to its relative proportion of voting members as compared to others in the same cluster. In practice, this distinction was not meaningful, so we have not used the weights in our analyses—as their use is controversial in the context of regression analyses.

Random Walk

As discussed earlier, one of the major concerns of sampling off of the voter list was that the reachable population of nonvoters had different characteristics than the voter population. In order to sample possibly nonvoter households, we used a random walk methodology. For every four households drawn from the voter list, a fifth household was selected by a random walk using the protocol described in the next two paragraphs.

The strategy employed was a modification of the familiar "right hand rule" that is used in many field studies for use in a complex Indian urban setting. With modern computation, we could meld the principles of a random walk with randomization at the level of each survey to select a random member of the household that is of age 18 or older.

In order to select the respondent, the members of the household were written down from youngest to eldest, and the number of members that were 18 years of age or older were computed (as well as unique serial numbers were assigned for each member of the household regardless of age). Using a "Kish table," one random household member of at least 18 years of age was selected. One replacement respondent was also given from the Kish table. A unique computer-generated Kish table, which associated the number of household members of at least 18 years of age with a selected respondent and replacement, was computed for each random walk.

Sample Characteristics

After this exercise, we reached 5,477 households (24,693 individuals), with 3,352 households (15,173 individuals) in Delhi, 1,251 households (5,474 individuals) in UP, 721 households (3,376 individuals) in Haryana, and 147 households (648 individuals) in Rajasthan. Of the 5,477 households in our sample, 4,431 were drawn from the voter list and 1,046 were drawn by the random walk method.

Assessing Differences between Voter List and Random Walk

After collecting the sample, our first order of business was to assess the differences between the voter list method and the random walk method in the sample. Somewhat surprisingly, there was little to no difference between the samples.

Of particular interest was the extent to which nonvoters were captured in the sample. In order to assess the percentage of eligible voters who were voters in the polling booth (or a nearby polling booth), we made use of a question where we asked whether each household member voted or did not vote in a nearby polling booth. Figure A.1 displays the distributions of eligible voters (that is, those at least 18 years of age in the household) by sample selection type—voter list or random walk. This shows that, at least in terms of eligibility, households selected by the voter list or the random walk method are largely similar.

All told, 87 percent of eligible voters in our sample (those of at least age of 18) voted in a nearby polling booth. More interestingly, almost all nonvoters were found living in households in which there were voters. We only found

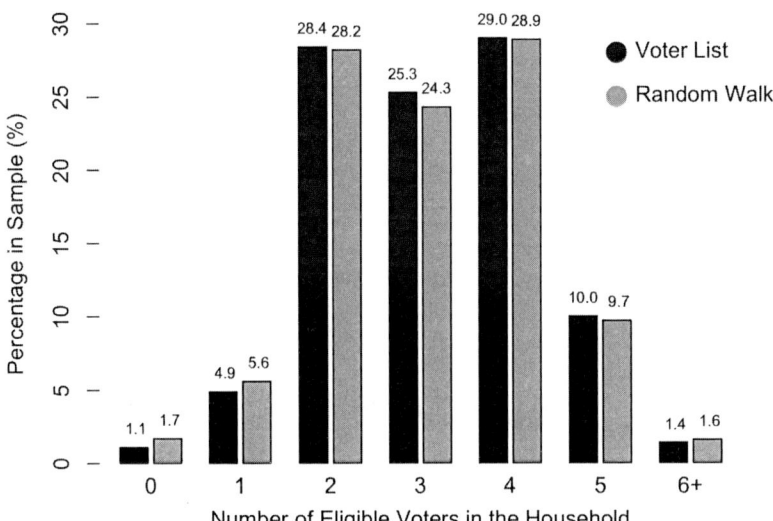

Figure A.1 Distribution of eligible voters by sample selection type

Source: Calculated from the CASI–NCR Survey data.

Notes: This figure shows the distribution of eligible voters (those at least 18 years of age) by selection type—voter list or random walk. The households are not statistically distinguishable in terms of the eligibility criteria by selection type. This suggests certain demographic similarities between the voter list and random walk samples.

68 households (1.2 percent of the sample) with no voters in a nearby polling booth, and 50 of these households were drawn from the voter list, as we allowed voters to tell us they were no longer on the list or voting in the polling booth. However, 34 percent of households in the NCR had at least one eligible voter not voting at a nearby polling booth (that is, not registered to vote near their residence) and 10 percent of households had more than one eligible voter not voting at a nearby polling booth.

Figure A.2 displays the distribution of the number of eligible nonvoters in the samples by sample selection type—voter list or random walk. Once again, there were small differences between the samples in the proportion of nonvoters. One may guess that a much higher proportion of women would be classified as nonvoters given that they are more likely to have migrated to the NCR due to marriage. While we do find a higher proportion of eligible female nonvoters in our sample (13.6 percent, as compared to 12.3 percent for men), these differences are not very large. This suggests little benefit from using the random walk method in detecting "non-voters."

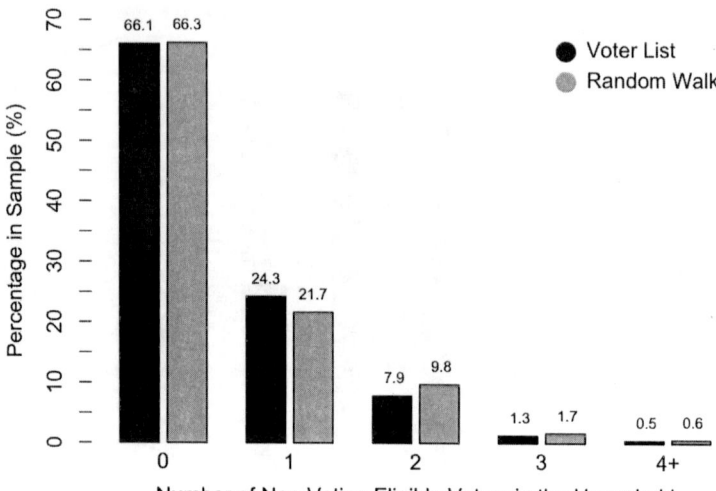

Figure A.2   Distribution of nonvoters by sample selection type

Source: Calculated from the CASI–NCR Survey data.

Notes: The graph shows that a little more than one-third of the households have at least one nonvoting eligible voter (and 10 percent have at least two). However, there is little difference in this distribution whether or not one considers the sample drawn from the voter list or from the random walk method.

Representativeness

We attempted to collect spatial location for each household in the sample, but unfortunately collecting the true global positioning system (GPS) coordinates for a household can be difficult. All told, we collected GPS coordinates for 4,380 (80 percent) of the households. Nonetheless, the spatial spread of the data for which we have GPS coordinates does a good job of tracing out the sample.

Figure A.3 plots the spatial location of households in our sample for those households with usable GPS coordinates. Because we have used voter lists, the distribution follows the population density in urban areas of the NCR. Outside of the big cluster of the sample around Delhi, and surrounding suburbs, there are noticeable separate clusters of data in places like Meerut. Because we have not drawn a rural sample, these clusters correspond to areas delimited as urban across the expanse of the NCR.

Finally, we assess the extent to which our sample is representative of the NCR. Because the NCR is a patchwork of different localities, this cannot be easily compared on the whole. However, we can check whether our sample in

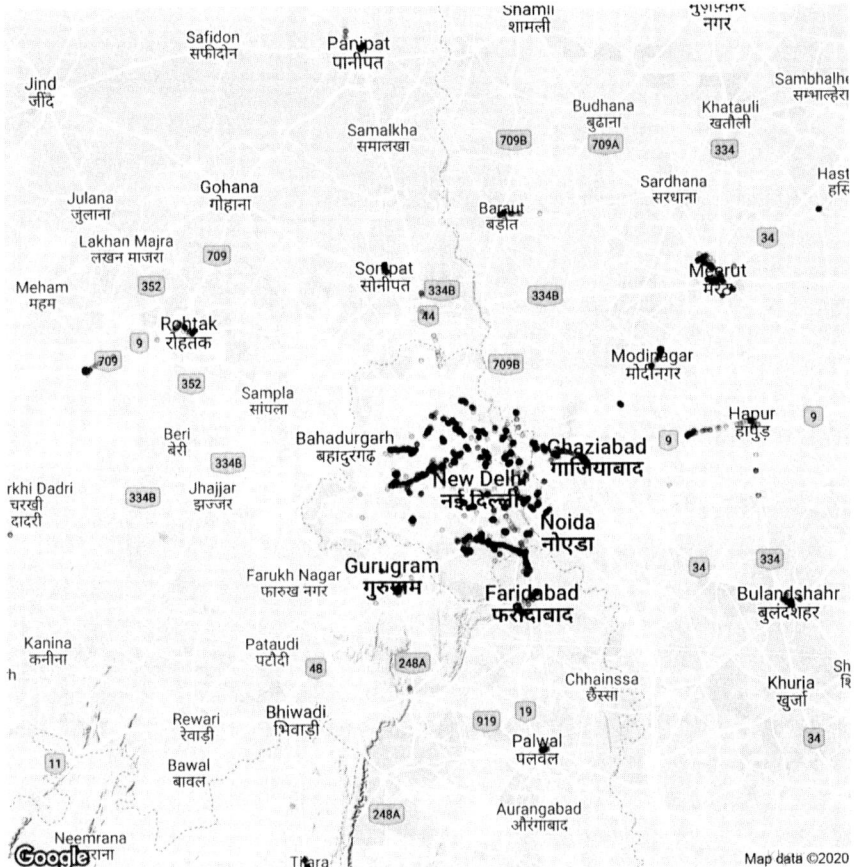

Figure A.3   Spatial distribution of CASI–NCR Survey sample

Source: Authors.

Notes: This map shows the spatial distribution of households in the sample. One should notice how the sampling strategy generates separable clusters in larger urban zones in the NCR. This is due to the fact that the sample is drawn to be proportional to the population and only drawn in urban areas.

Delhi matches estimates from the Indian census and the NSS. We use four major yardsticks, which are also mentioned throughout our text, to assess representativeness, caste, religion, gender, and migration. Table A.1 presents these comparisons. The final comparison (of the percentage of households with at least one migrant) is drawn from the NSS due to ease of comparison. All other estimates are given from the 2011 Indian Census.

The data from the CASI–NCR Survey are presented without weighting. One may naturally wonder about sampling weights. As discussed previously,

Table A.I   Representativeness of the CASI–NCR Survey

	Census 2011/NSS	CASI–NCR Survey
Female (percentage)	46	45
Scheduled Castes (percentage)	17	17
Muslim (percentage)	13	11
Migrant (percentage of households with at least 1 migrant)	60 (NSS)	59

Source: Authors.

Notes: This table demonstrates that the CASI–NCR Survey yields a representative sample in terms of selected indicators of caste, religion, gender, and migration—when compared to the Indian census and the NSS—across Delhi. The percentages from the CASI–NCR Survey sample are provided without weights.

the probability of a household being sampled is proportional to the number of people on the voter list from the household and inversely proportional to the number of households selected in the cluster (which is estimated by the number of sampled households in the cluster divided by the average number of eligible voters per household in the cluster). We found that weighting makes little difference to the marginal estimates. For example, 16.7 percent of our sample was from the Scheduled Caste community unweighted, and 16.3 percent estimated with weights. Given that large increase in variance in estimation, with little benefit in changing point estimates, we chose to ignore sampling weights in the estimation.

The Muslim population in our survey seems to be somewhat under-sampled compared to the Indian census. Similar differences are seen in other major surveys such as the NSS and the IHDS. Some of this may be due to strategic nonresponse, as asking about religion can be sensitive in certain areas. Or perhaps, Muslim populations are simply harder to reach populations. We also note that our age distribution in the data skews a little older than the Indian census, but some of these difficulties are due to the challenges of survey response with regard to age (as many people do not know their age or the ages of their household members).

Finally, it should be noted that there are populations that are largely unreachable in a survey that is not conducted by the government. These include very mobile populations that are less likely to be found, and more likely to refuse to answer a survey, and those in gated colonies and communities where guards can prevent access to homes. Yet, given the overall representativeness of the CASI–NCR Survey, we believe biases to be relatively minor.

This sampling design is also a "proof of concept" that population representative data can be drawn from publicly available voter lists and in a manner that maximizes spatial spread across the sampling frame. Here, the design required a number of field innovations, with the core principle to maintain spatial spread of the sample at all costs. The key idea is that "spatial homophily"—the similarity of demographic (and unobserved) characteristics of those living in the same place—implies that spatial spread will draw a largely representative sample, even if nonresponse and replacing the initial target may generate some biases in the data. By developing a technique to maximize this spatial spread at each stage of sampling (cluster, polling booth, and voter), we guarantee that we reach the demographic breadth of the population. This also suggests that good representative properties can be achieved at smaller sample sizes and at a lower cost than most social surveys. We believe that our methodological innovations should be considered seriously by others seeking to survey Indian cities.

Notes

1. There are broadly two types of surveying that are plausible. The first type is when a household/building is selected at random, identifying information is sought, and then a respondent is selected according to a predetermined survey protocol. The second type is using existing identifiable information in a locality and using the survey protocol to select a respondent at random. The difference in the latter method is that identifying information need not be *a priori* sought by a surveyor, which builds confidence—especially for a survey not conducted by a government entity.

2. These concerns, while legitimate, are likely to be overblown even in a place such as Delhi with high migration. Most people below a certain economic class must enroll in the voter list to receive certain benefits—generating incentives for most people to register on the voter list. In the most 2015 Delhi elections, there were 13.3 million registered voters. The population of the union territory of Delhi was approximately 16.8 million in the 2011 Indian Census. The NGO Janaagraha found many inconsistencies in the Delhi voter list and suggested that as many as one-fifth of the names should be deleted. Doing so leaves about 10.6 million voters on the list. The 2011 Indian Census data found 11.2 million individuals of at least 18 years of age. Allowing for a 2 percent growth rate in this population per year generates an estimate of 11.9 million population of at least 18 years of age in 2014. This projects to about 90 percent coverage on the voter list of the eligible population. Furthermore, many hard-to-reach populations are found on the voter list, whereas many individuals not on the voter list are hard to find using other sampling methods.

Notes on Contributors

Sumitra Badrinathan is a political science PhD student at the University of Pennsylvania. She studies comparative politics with a regional focus on India and uses survey and experimental methods in her research. She holds a master's in political science from the University of Chicago and a bachelor's degree in psychology from St. Xavier's College, Mumbai.

Subhadra Banda trained as a lawyer at the Nalsar University of Law, Hyderabad. She completed her master's in public policy as a Dubin Fellow under the Centre for Public Leadership at Harvard University. Subhadra previously worked at the Centre for Policy Research, New Delhi, where she was a part of the Cities of Delhi project, researching on access to public services in informal settlements in Delhi. She has also previously worked at the Boston Consulting Group and as a judicial clerk at the Supreme Court of India.

Sanjoy Chakravorty is a professor of geography and urban studies and the director of global studies at Temple University and a visiting fellow at the Center for the Advanced Study of India at the University of Pennsylvania. He has written books on information and identity (*The Truth about Us*), land (*The Price of Land* and *Seeking Middle Ground*), the diaspora (*The Other One Percent*), inequality (*Fragments of Inequality*), industrialization (*Made in India*), and fiction (*The Promoter*).

Deepaboli Chatterjee is a research associate based at the Centre for Policy Research, New Delhi. She works on urbanization and the demand side of energy. She holds a master's degree in financial statistics from the London School of Economics and a bachelor's degree in economics from Kirori Mal College, University of Delhi.

Adnan Farooqui is an assistant professor in the Department of Political Science at Jamia Millia Islamia in New Delhi. He studies elections in India. He studied at St. Stephen's College and Jawaharlal Nehru University.

Patrick Heller is a professor of sociology and international and public affairs at Brown University. His main area of research is the comparative study of social inequality and democratic deepening. He is the author of *The Labor of Development: Workers in the Transformation of Capitalism in Kerala, India* and coauthor of *Social Democracy and the Global Periphery* and *Bootstrapping Democracy: Transforming Local Governance and Civil Society in Brazil*. He has published articles on urbanization, comparative democracy, social movements, development policy, civil society, and state transformation.

Devesh Kapur is the Starr Foundation South Asia Studies Professor and the director of Asia Programs at the Paul H. Nitze School of Advanced International Studies (SAIS) at Johns Hopkins University. He is a political scientist whose several recent books include *The Other One Percent: Indians in America*; *Navigating the Labyrinth: Perspectives on India's Higher Education*; *Costs of Democracy: Political Finance in India*; and *Rethinking Public Institutions in India*.

Shrobona Karkun is a doctoral student of geography and urban studies at Temple University. Her dissertation thesis explores the dynamics of land use and land markets, in the context of development of metro rail systems. A trained architect and geospatial analyst, her work focuses on understanding the growth of cities and land use change using spatial technologies and cartography. She has published analytical maps on diverse topics such as urban sprawl, architectural preservation programs, and digital humanities.

Khushdeep Kaur Malhotra is finishing her doctorate in geography and urban studies at Temple University. Her dissertation examines everyday experiences of reconciliation and belonging in a context of increased post-violence militarization, as well as the implications of political violence on migration among Kashmir's Sikh community.

Radhika Khosla is the research director of the Oxford India Centre for Sustainable Development, and a senior researcher at the Smith School of Enterprise and Environment, School of Geography and the Environment, at the University of Oxford. Her work examines the productive tensions between urban transitions, energy services consumption, and climate change, with a focus on developing countries. She leads the Oxford's Future of Cooling Programme and is a contributor to the sixth assessment report of the Intergovernmental Panel on Climate Change. Her other academic affiliations are at the University of Pennsylvania, and the Centre for Policy Research, New Delhi.

Babu Lal is a research associate at the Center for the Advanced Study of India, New Delhi. He is currently researching the supply chain in Indian agriculture and its inefficiencies. He has previously worked at the Centre for Policy Research, New Delhi. He holds an integrated master's degree in economics from Indian Institute of Technology, Kharagpur.

Matthew Lillehaugen is an independent researcher whose work focuses on issues of conflict and governance in South Asia and the Middle East. He coauthored a chapter in this volume while serving as a James C. Gaither Junior Fellow at the Carnegie Endowment for International Peace.

Partha Mukhopadhyay is currently a senior fellow at the Centre for Policy Research in New Delhi. In previous positions, he has been a banker and an academic. He publishes extensively, writes frequently for the national media, and has also been associated with a number of government committees and recently chaired the Working Group on Migration, Government of India. He received his PhD in economics from New York University. His research interests are in infrastructure, the development paths of India and China, and the process of urbanization, especially the growth of non-metropolitan areas.

Shamindra Nath Roy is a senior researcher at the Centre for Policy Research, New Delhi. His primary interest lies in examining inequalities through spatial lens. His areas of research are rural–urban transformations, internal migration in India, and socio-spatial inequalities in human development within the cities. He graduated in geography from the Jawaharlal Nehru University, New Delhi.

Megan N. Reed is a PhD candidate in sociology and demography at the University of Pennsylvania. Her research centers on topics related to gender and family in India. Before joining the PhD program, Megan worked at the Center for the Advanced Study of India at the University of Pennsylvania and was a 2012 Fulbright-Nehru Student Research Fellow in India.

Rimjhim Saxena is a PhD student in economics at the University of Colorado, Boulder. She has previously worked with Center for the Advanced Study of India–University of Pennsylvania and the Centre for Policy Research on a wide range of climate, energy, labor, and migration issues. She holds a master's degree in economics from Boston University and an undergraduate degree in industrial engineering. Her research interests lie in political economy and the interaction of labor markets and climate change.

Awadhendra Sharan is a professor at the Centre for the Study of Developing Societies, New Delhi. Trained as a historian at University of Delhi and the

University of Chicago, Sharan's research interests are in the fields of urban and environmental studies. His publications include *In the City, Out of Place: Nuisance, Pollution and Dwelling in Delhi, c. 1850–2000* and the forthcoming *Dust and Smoke: Air Pollution and Colonial Urbanism, India, c.1860–c.1940.* Sharan's ongoing research is on the history of the river Ganges during the colonial period.

Shahana Sheikh is pursuing her PhD in political science at Yale University. She studies elections, political parties, and voters. Previously, she was a policy researcher focusing on urban governance and public finance in India. During 2013–2015, she worked on the Cities of Delhi project at the Centre for Policy Research, New Delhi. She received her master's in public policy and public administration from National University of Singapore and London School of Economics and Political Science, and her bachelor's degree (Hons) in economics from University of Delhi.

Neelanjan Sircar is an assistant professor of political science at Ashoka University and a senior visiting fellow at the Centre for Policy Research. His research focuses on voting and party behavior in India, urbanization and social change, and gender and the labor market. He holds a PhD from Columbia University in political science and an undergraduate degree from University of California, Berkeley, in applied mathematics and economics.

Sanjay Srivastava is a professor of sociology at the Institute of Economic Growth, New Delhi, and British Academy Global Professor at University College London. His publications include *Constructing Post-Colonial India: National Character and the Doon School*; *Passionate Modernity, Sexuality, Class and Consumption in India*; *Sexuality Studies*; *Entangled Urbanism: Slum, Gated Community and Shopping Mall in Delhi and Gurgaon*; *Critical Theme in Indian Sociology*; and *(Hi)Stories of Desire: Sexualities and Culture in Modern India*. His current research concerns religion and urbanism and ethnographies of satellite mapping in "unauthorised colonies" in Delhi.

Milan Vaishnav is a senior fellow and director of the South Asia Program at the Carnegie Endowment for International Peace. His primary research focus is the political economy of India. He is the author of *When Crime Pays: Money and Muscle in Indian Politics* and coeditor (with Devesh Kapur) of *Costs of Democracy: Political Finance in India* and (with Pratap Bhanu Mehta and Devesh Kapur) of *Rethinking Public Institutions in India*. He also hosts a weekly podcast on Indian politics and policy called "Grand Tamasha."

Index